There's nothing better than a *Taste of Home!*

You'll proudly make these dishes a part of your family's traditions.

39

97

18

Real dishes from real home cooks... that's the hallmark of *Taste of Home* magazine, and it's what makes this cookbook so authentic. Every kitchen-tested recipe—502 in this unique collection—comes from a family cook with a story of his or her own. Now you can share in the narrative and make these dishes your favorites, too, with *Taste of Home Annual Recipes.*

This cookbook features an entire year's worth of fresh and fabulous and recipes from the magazine, plus dozens of bonus recipes never before seen in the publication. It all adds up to hundreds of heartwarming meals for months to come! Consider these chapters:

- **Everyday Fresh**
  Plan a simple, good-for-you meal with a short list of ingredients and fresh, wholesome foods in this new feature. Make it your weeknight go-to!

- **Holiday & Seasonal Celebrations**
  Whether you're planning a summer barbecue or Christmas open house, turn here for the seasonal magic you've come to expect from *Taste of Home.*

- **Classic Comeback**
  Savor more than 30 contemporary twists on all-time favorites such as shrimp cocktail, blackened fish, rumaki and cheese fondue.

Five icons help you easily locate these dishes:

FAST FIX = Finished in 30 minutes or less

EAT SMART = Lower in calories, fat and sodium

SLOW COOKER = Made in a slow cooker

(5) INGREDIENTS = Made with 5 or fewer ingredients (excluding water, salt, pepper and canola/olive oil)

FREEZE IT = Freezing and reheating instructions are included

With *Taste of Home Annual Recipes,* it's simple to find the perfect dish for any occasion. Happy cooking!

BEST-LOVED RECIPES

Simple dinners, hearty snacks and luscious desserts... find them all in *Taste of Home Annual Recipes.* For a five-ingredient slow cooker dish that's big on taste, tote Tex-Mex Shredded Beef Sandwiches (top) to your next gathering. Usher in spring with a good-for-you skillet meal showcasing the season's best with Asparagus Ham Dinner (center). And for a south-of-the-border take on a beloved classic, raise a glass of Bloody Maria (bottom).

44

208

250

263

Taste of Home
Annual Recipes

EDITORIAL

Chief Content Officer **Beth Tomkiw**
Creative Director **Howard Greenberg**
Associate Creative Director **Edwin Robles Jr.**
Vice President, Content Operations **Kerri Balliet**

Managing Editor, Print & Digital Books **Mark Hagen**
Editor **Christine Rukavena**
Art Directors **Maggie Conners, Raeann Thompson**
Graphic Designer **Courtney Lovetere**
Layout Designer **Dalma Vogt**
Copy Chief **Deb Warlaumont Mulvey**
Copy Editors **Dulcie Shoener (senior), Ronald Kovach, Chris McLaughlin, Ellie Piper**
Contributing Copy Editor **Valerie Phillips**
Contributing Layout Designer **Chantell Singleton**
Editorial Services Manager **Kelly Madison-Liebe**
Editorial Production Coordinator **Jill Banks**
Editorial Intern **Stephanie Harte**

Content Director **Julie Blume Benedict**
Food Editors **Rashanda Cobbins; James Schend; Peggy Woodward, RDN**

Culinary Director **Sarah Thompson**
Kitchen Operations Manager **Bethany Van Jacobson**
Recipe Editors **Sue Ryon (lead), Irene Yeh**
Food Stylists **Kathryn Conrad (senior), Lauren Knoelke, Shannon Roum**
Culinary Assistants **Aria C. Thornton, Lynne Belcher**
Food Buyer **Maria Petrella**

Photography Director **Stephanie Marchese**
Photographers **Dan Roberts, Jim Wieland**
Photographer/Set Stylist **Grace Natoli Sheldon**
Set Stylists **Melissa Franco (lead), Stacey Genaw, Dee Dee Schaefer**

Business Architect, Publishing Technologies
Amanda Harmatys
Business Analysts, Publishing Technologies
Dena Ahlers, Kate Unger
Junior Business Analyst, Publishing Technologies
Shannon Stroud

Editorial Business Manager **Kristy Martin**
Editorial Business Associate **Andrea Meiers**
Rights & Permissions Assistant **Jill Godsey**

Executive Editor, *Taste of Home* **Jeanne Ambrose**
Editor, *Taste of Home* **Emily Betz Tyra**
Art Director, *Taste of Home* **Kristin Bowker**

BUSINESS

Publisher, *Taste of Home* **Donna Lindskog**
Strategic Partnerships Manager, Taste of Home Live
Jamie Piette Andrzejewski

TRUSTED MEDIA BRANDS, INC.

President & Chief Executive Officer **Bonnie Kintzer**
Chief Financial Officer **Dean Durbin**
Chief Marketing Officer **C. Alec Casey**
Chief Revenue Officer **Richard Sutton**
Chief Digital Officer **Vince Errico**
Senior Vice President, Global HR & Communications
Phyllis E. Gebhardt, SPHR; SHRM-SCP
General Counsel **Mark Sirota**
Vice President, Product Marketing **Brian Kennedy**
Vice President, Consumer Acquisition **Heather Plant**
Vice President, Operations **Michael Garzone**
Vice President, Consumer Marketing Planning **Jim Woods**
Vice President, Digital Product & Technology **Nick Contardo**
Vice President, Digital Content & Audience Development
Kari Hodes
Vice President, Financial Planning & Analysis
William Houston

COVER PHOTOGRAPHY

Photographer **Dan Roberts**
Food Stylist **Lauren Knoelke**
Set Stylist **Dee Dee Jacq**

© 2018 RDA Enthusiast Brands, LLC
1610 N. 2nd St., Suite 102, Milwaukee WI 53212-3906

International Standard Book Number: 978-1-61765-734-4

International Standard Serial Number: 1094-3463

Component Number: 117400064H

All Rights Reserved.

Taste of Home is a registered trademark of
RDA Enthusiast Brands, LLC.

Printed in USA
1 3 5 7 9 10 8 6 4 2

Contents

PICTURED ON THE COVER
Crown Roast of Pork with Mushroom Dressing (p. 249).

FOR OTHER INCREDIBLE TASTE OF HOME BOOKS AND PRODUCTS, VISIT
ShopTasteofHome.com

**CHARLENE SKJERVEN'S
CRISP CUCUMBER SALSA**
PAGE 12

Appetizers & Beverages

The **best bites** for potlucks, reunions, parties and hanging out with friends are right here. From **sliders, sangria** and nachos to deviled eggs, **dips and wings,** you'll have all the winning recipes you need to get the **party** started!

JULIE RUBLE'S CHILI-LIME ROASTED CHICKPEAS *PAGE 7*

JAMES SCHEND'S ROOT BEER PULLED PORK NACHOS *PAGE 15*

KAREN GRANT'S PARTY CHEESE BREAD *PAGE 21*

EAT SMART Avocado Salsa

I first set out this recipe at a party, and it was an absolute success. People love the garlic, corn and avocado combination.
—**SUSAN VANDERMEER** OGDEN, UT

PREP: 20 MIN. + CHILLING
MAKES: ABOUT 7 CUPS

- 1⅔ cups (about 8¼ ounces) frozen corn, thawed
- 2 cans (2¼ ounces each) sliced ripe olives, drained
- 1 medium sweet red pepper, chopped
- 1 small onion, chopped
- 5 garlic cloves, minced
- ⅓ cup olive oil
- ¼ cup lemon juice
- 3 tablespoons cider vinegar
- 1 teaspoon dried oregano
- ½ teaspoon salt
- ½ teaspoon pepper
- 4 medium ripe avocados, peeled
  Tortilla chips

1. Combine corn, olives, red pepper and onion. In another bowl, mix the next seven ingredients. Pour over corn mixture; toss to coat. Refrigerate, covered, overnight.

2. Just before serving, chop avocados; stir into salsa. Serve with tortilla chips.

Per ¼ cup: 82 cal., 7g fat (1g sat. fat), 0 chol., 85mg sod., 5g carb. (1g sugars, 2g fiber), 1g pro.

Diabetic Exchanges: 1½ fat.

AVOCADO SALSA

COLLARD GREEN & PULLED PORK EGG ROLLS

FREEZE IT Collard Green & Pulled Pork Egg Rolls

It's fun to take remnants of ingredients from my pantry and create a meal. You can make wontons with this same filling for a bite-sized snack, and either bake or deep-fry depending on your preference.
—**MELISSA PELKEY HASS** WALESKA, GA

PREP: 30 MIN. • **BAKE:** 15 MIN.
MAKES: 12 SERVINGS

- 1 pound collard greens
- 1 cup refrigerated fully cooked barbecued shredded pork
- 1 package (8 ounces) cream cheese, softened
- 1 small onion, finely chopped
- ¼ teaspoon salt
- ⅛ teaspoon pepper
- 1 package (16 ounces) egg roll wrappers
- 2 tablespoons butter, melted
  Thai sweet chili sauce

1. Trim collard greens, discarding thick ribs and stems. Coarsely chop leaves. In a large saucepan, bring ½ in. of water to a boil. Add greens; cook, covered, until they begin to wilt, 8-10 minutes. Drain, squeezing out as much water as possible.

2. Preheat oven to 425°. Combine greens, pork, cream cheese, onion and seasonings until well blended. With one corner of an egg roll wrapper facing you, place ¼ cup pork filling just below center of wrapper. (Cover remaining wrappers with a damp paper towel until ready to use.) Fold bottom corner over filling; moisten remaining wrapper edges with water. Fold side corners toward center over filling. Roll the egg roll up tightly, pressing at tip to seal. Repeat until all filling is used.

3. Place egg rolls on a parchment paper-lined baking sheet; brush with melted butter. Bake until golden brown, 15-20 minutes. Serve with sweet chili sauce.

To freeze: Cover and freeze unbaked egg rolls on waxed paper-lined baking sheets until firm. Transfer to resealable plastic freezer bags; return to freezer. To use, bake egg rolls as directed.

Change them up: These can be fried instead. Heat 1 in. oil in an electric skillet or a deep-fat fryer to 375°. Fry rolls, a few at a time, until golden brown, 3-4 minutes, turning occasionally. Drain on paper towels. Serve with sweet chili sauce.

Per 1 egg roll: 227 cal., 10g fat (5g sat. fat), 34mg chol., 472mg sod., 27g carb. (4g sugars, 2g fiber), 8g pro.

(5)INGREDIENTS Chili-Lime Roasted Chickpeas
(PICTURED ON P. 5)

Looking for a lighter snack that'll please a crowd? You've found it! Chili-Lime Roasted Chickpeas will have everyone happily munching.

—JULIE RUBLE CHARLOTTE, NC

PREP: 10 MIN. • **BAKE:** 40 MIN. + COOLING
MAKES: 2 CUPS

- 2 cans (15 ounces each) chickpeas, rinsed, drained and patted dry
- 2 tablespoons extra virgin olive oil
- 1 tablespoon chili powder
- 2 teaspoons ground cumin
- 1 teaspoon grated lime peel
- 1 tablespoon lime juice
- ¾ teaspoon sea salt

1. Preheat oven to 400°. Line a 15x10x1-in. baking sheet with foil. Spread chickpeas in a single layer over foil. Remove any loose skins. Bake until very crunchy, 40-45 minutes, stirring every 15 minutes.

2. Meanwhile, whisk remaining ingredients together. Remove chickpeas from the oven; let cool 5 minutes. Drizzle with oil mixture; shake pan to coat. Cool completely. Store in an airtight container.

Per ⅓ cup: 178 cal., 8g fat (1g sat. fat), 0 chol., 463mg sod., 23g carb. (3g sugars, 6g fiber), 6g pro.

Rosemary-Sea Salt Chickpeas: Prepare chickpeas according to step 1 in the recipe above. Toss with 2 tablespoons extra-virgin olive oil, 1 tablespoon minced fresh rosemary and ½ teaspoon sea salt, then cool completely.

Orange Curry Chickpeas: Prepare chickpeas according to step 1 in recipe above. Whisk 2 tablespoons of extra-virgin olive oil, 1 teaspoon grated orange peel and 1 tablespoon curry powder; toss with chickpeas. Cool completely.

Lemon-Pepper Chickpeas: Prepare chickpeas according to step 1 in the recipe above. Whisk 2 tablespoons extra virgin olive oil, 1 teaspoon grated lemon peel and 2 teaspoons freshly cracked pepper. Toss chickpeas with oil mixture, then cool completely.

FRIED PROSCIUTTO TORTELLINI
Angela Lemoine
Howell, NJ

Fried Prosciutto Tortellini

My take on Italian street food, these fried tortellini are crunchy, gooey good. For the sauce, use the best quality tomatoes you can find.

—ANGELA LEMOINE HOWELL, NJ

PREP: 25 MIN. • **COOK:** 5 MIN./BATCH
MAKES: ABOUT 3½ DOZEN

- 2 large eggs
- 2 tablespoons 2% milk
- ⅔ cup seasoned bread crumbs
- 1 teaspoon garlic powder
- 2 tablespoons grated Pecorino Romano cheese
- 1 tablespoon minced fresh parsley
- ½ teaspoon salt
  Oil for frying
- 1 package (12 ounces) refrigerated prosciutto ricotta tortellini

TOMATO SAUCE
- 1 tablespoon olive oil
- 3 tablespoons finely chopped onion
- 4 garlic cloves, coarsely chopped
- 1 can (15 ounces) tomato puree
- 1 tablespoon minced fresh basil
- ¼ teaspoon salt
- ¼ teaspoon pepper
  Additional minced fresh basil

1. Whisk together eggs and milk. In another bowl, stir together the next five ingredients.

2. In an electric skillet, heat ¼ in. of cooking oil to 375°. Dip tortellini in egg mixture, then in bread crumb mixture to coat. Fry the tortellini in batches, adding oil as necessary, until golden brown, 1½-2 minutes on each side. Drain on paper towels.

3. Meanwhile, in a small saucepan, heat 1 tablespoon olive oil over medium heat. Add onion and garlic; cook until softened. Stir in tomato puree, basil, salt and pepper; bring to a boil. Reduce heat. Simmer, uncovered, for 10 minutes. Sprinkle with minced fresh basil.

4. Serve tortellini with tomato sauce for dipping.

Per 1 appetizer: 48 cal., 2g fat (1g sat. fat), 10mg chol., 98mg sod., 5g carb. (0 sugars, 0 fiber), 1g pro.

Orange-Glazed Chicken & Chorizo Meatballs

These tasty Southwestern meatballs add warmth to any buffet. I add pomegranate seeds, jalapeno pepper jelly and cilantro to make everything pop with color.

—**JEANNE HOLT** MENDOTA HEIGHTS, MN

PREP: 25 MIN. + STANDING • **BAKE:** 15 MIN.
MAKES: ABOUT 3½ DOZEN

- 1 **cup corn bread croutons**
- 1¼ **cups mild picante sauce, divided**
- 5 **tablespoons thawed orange juice concentrate, divided**
- 6 **tablespoons chopped fresh cilantro leaves, divided**
- 1 **large egg, lightly beaten**
- 1 **teaspoon salt**
- 1 **pound ground chicken**
- 6 **ounces fresh chorizo**
- 1¼ **cups orange marmalade**
- ½ **cup jalapeno pepper jelly**
- ⅔ **cup finely chopped peeled mango**
- ⅔ **cup pomegranate seeds, divided, optional**

1. Preheat oven to 375°. Crush croutons into fine crumbs. Add ½ cup picante sauce and 1 tablespoon orange juice concentrate; let stand 10 minutes.
2. Stir in 2 tablespoons cilantro, egg and salt. Crumble chicken and chorizo into crouton mixture; mix well. With wet hands, shape into 1-in. balls. Place on a greased rack in a 15x10-in. baking pan. Bake until a thermometer reads 165°, 15-20 minutes.
3. Meanwhile, in a small saucepan over medium heat, stir marmalade, pepper jelly, and the remaining picante sauce and orange juice concentrate. Bring to a boil. Reduce heat; simmer 5 minutes. Stir in mango, 1 tablespoon cilantro and, if desired, ⅓ cup pomegranate seeds. Pour over meatballs. Serve with remaining cilantro and, if desired, pomegranate.
Per 1 meatball: 71 cal., 2g fat (1g sat. fat), 14mg chol., 169mg sod., 11g carb. (9g sugars, 0 fiber), 3g pro.

ORANGE-GLAZED CHICKEN & CHORIZO MEATBALLS

GRILLED PEACH & PINEAPPLE SANGRIA

Grilled Peach & Pineapple Sangria

Grill up fresh peaches and pineapple slathered in cinnamon butter and use them to make a refreshing summer sangria. I like to add slices of grilled lemon and lime to drop in the glass for a citrusy boost of flavor.

—**HEATHER KING** FROSTBURG, MD

PREP: 25 MIN. + CHILLING • **MAKES:** 8 SERVINGS

- 1 **bottle (750 milliliters) sauvignon blanc or other white wine**
- 2 **cups lemonade**
- ½ **cup orange liqueur**
- 1 **tablespoon butter, melted**
- 1 **tablespoon sugar**
- 1 **teaspoon ground cinnamon**
- 3 **medium peeled peaches, pitted and halved**
- ¼ **fresh pineapple, peeled and cut into 4 slices**

1. Make sangria by combining wine, lemonade and liqueur. Refrigerate. Meanwhile, in a small bowl, combine melted butter, sugar and cinnamon. Mix well.
2. Brush butter mixture over cut side of peaches and all over pineapple slices. Grill fruit, covered, on a greased rack over medium direct heat 4-5 minutes. Turn peaches and pineapple. Grill 4-5 minutes more. Remove from grill.
3. Cut each peach half into five or six slices and each pineapple slice into five or six pieces. Add three-fourths of the fruit to the sangria, reserving remainder. Refrigerate for at least 2 hours.
4. Before serving, thread several pieces of reserved fruit onto appetizer skewers. Pour sangria over ice; serve with fruit skewers.
Per ¾ cup: 206 cal., 2g fat (1g sat. fat), 4mg chol., 20mg sod., 25g carb. (21g sugars, 1g fiber), 1g pro.

Pancetta, Pear & Pecan Puffs

I was recently at a wedding reception where the menu was all small bites. Here's my rendition of the pear pastries they served. They're the perfect combo of savory and sweet.

—**ARLENE ERLBACH** MORTON GROVE, IL

PREP: 25 MIN. • **BAKE:** 10 MIN. + COOLING • **MAKES:** 2 DOZEN

- 1 sheet frozen puff pastry, thawed
- 6 ounces cream cheese, softened
- 2 tablespoons honey
- ⅛ teaspoon salt
- ⅛ teaspoon pepper
- ¼ cup crumbled fresh goat cheese
- 3 tablespoons crumbled crisp pancetta or crumbled cooked bacon
- 3 tablespoons finely chopped peeled ripe pear
- 2 tablespoons finely chopped pecans, toasted

1. Preheat oven to 400°. On a lightly floured surface, unfold pastry dough. Using a 1¾-in. round cookie cutter, cut dough into 24 circles. Transfer to parchment paper-lined baking sheets. Bake until golden brown, 10-12 minutes. Cool completely on a wire rack.

2. Meanwhile, beat cream cheese, honey, salt and pepper until well blended. Fold in the goat cheese, pancetta, pear and pecans.

3. Halve each cooled pastry. Spoon or pipe cream cheese mixture over bottom pastry halves; cover with top halves. Serve at room temperature.

Note: To toast nuts, bake in a shallow pan in a 350° oven 5-10 minutes or cook in a skillet over low heat until lightly browned, stirring occasionally.

Per 1 appetizer: 105 cal., 7g fat (3g sat. fat), 13mg chol., 178mg sod., 8g carb. (2g sugars, 1g fiber), 2g pro.

PICADILLO SLIDERS

Picadillo Sliders

When I'm pressed for time, these beefy sandwiches are my go-to. Any leftover picadillo makes for great nachos or queso dip. It freezes well, too!

—**PATTERSON WATKINS** PHILADELPHIA, PA

PREP: 15 MIN. • **COOK:** 25 MIN. • **MAKES:** 1½ DOZEN

- 1 tablespoon canola oil
- 1 medium yellow onion, diced
- 2 garlic cloves, minced
- 2 pounds ground beef
- ½ cup pimiento-stuffed olives, halved
- 2 cans (14½ ounces each) diced tomatoes, drained
- 1 cup beef broth
- ¼ cup red wine vinegar
- ¼ cup raisins
- 2 tablespoons tomato paste
- 1 tablespoon chili powder
- 2 teaspoons ground cumin
- 1 teaspoon ground cinnamon
- 1½ teaspoons salt
- 18 potato dinner rolls

1. In a large skillet, heat oil over medium heat. Saute the onion until translucent, 6-8 minutes; add garlic, and cook 1 minute more. Add ground beef; cook, crumbling meat, until no longer pink, 6-8 minutes. With a slotted spoon, remove meat; drain excess fat.

2. Return meat to skillet. Add next 10 ingredients. Stir over medium heat until well blended. Reduce heat; simmer until sauce has thickened, 10-15 minutes.

3. Toast rolls. Spoon beef mixture onto each roll (they may be juicy). Serve immediately.

Per 1 slider: 249 cal., 9g fat (2g sat. fat), 31mg chol., 631mg sod., 29g carb. (6g sugars, 2g fiber), 14g pro.

PANCETTA, PEAR & PECAN PUFFS

CHERRY & FONTINA STUFFED PORTOBELLOS

Cherry & Fontina Stuffed Portobellos

I developed this hearty appetizer for my mushroom-lovin' kids. They're grown now with families of their own, but they still lobby for these when they come home.

—WENDY RUSCH CAMERON, WI

PREP: 30 MIN. • **BAKE:** 15 MIN.
MAKES: 12 SERVINGS

- 6 large portobello mushrooms
- ½ cup butter, cubed
- 1 medium onion, chopped
- 1 cup pecan halves, toasted
- 1 package (5 ounces) dried tart cherries, coarsely chopped
- ½ teaspoon poultry seasoning
- ½ teaspoon dried thyme
- 7 ounces (about 4½ cups) seasoned stuffing cubes
- 1½ to 2 cups chicken broth
- 1½ cups shredded fontina cheese, divided

1. Preheat oven to 375°. Wipe mushroom caps clean with a damp paper towel; remove stems and gills and discard. Place caps on a foil-lined 15x10-in. baking pan.
2. In a large skillet, melt butter over medium heat until it begins to brown and smell nutty. Add onion; saute until translucent, stirring occasionally. Stir in pecans, cherries and seasonings; cook and stir 3 minutes. Remove from the heat.
3. Combine onion mixture and stuffing cubes, tossing to coat evenly. Add 1½ cups broth to onion-stuffing mixture, stirring until well mixed. Add the remaining broth as needed. Stir in 1 cup cheese.
4. Fill mushroom caps with stuffing until mounded, about 1 cup each. Sprinkle with remaining cheese. Bake until mushrooms are heated through and cheese is melted, 15-20 minutes.

Note: To toast nuts, bake in a shallow pan in a 350° oven for 5-10 minutes or cook in a skillet over low heat until lightly browned, stirring occasionally.

Per ½ stuffed portobello: 301 cal., 19g fat (8g sat. fat), 37mg chol., 531mg sod., 27g carb. (8g sugars, 6g fiber), 8g pro.

STEAK CROSTINI WITH CARROT-HORSERADISH MARMALADE

Steak Crostini with Carrot-Horseradish Marmalade

I've been making little tweaks to this family favorite for years. Prep everything ahead, then layer up the crostini right before party time.

—GREG FONTENOT THE WOODLANDS, TX

PREP: 1 HOUR • **COOK:** 30 MIN.
MAKES: 3½ DOZEN

- 1 French bread baguette (10½ ounces), cut into ¼-inch slices
- ¼ cup olive oil, divided
- 1 pound medium carrots, grated
- 2 cups water
- 1½ cups sugar
- 1 to 2 tablespoons prepared horseradish
- 1 tablespoon butter
- 1 cup chopped onion
- 2 cups shredded Swiss cheese
- 1 carton (8 ounces) mascarpone cheese
- 2 tablespoons mayonnaise
- 1 tablespoon sour cream
- 1 boneless beef top loin steak (12 to 14 ounces)

1. Preheat oven to 350°. Place the baguette slices on baking sheets; brush with 2 tablespoons olive oil. Bake until toasted, about 10 minutes.
2. Place carrots and water in a large saucepan; bring to a boil over medium-high heat. Cook, uncovered, for 10 minutes. Add sugar; cook on medium heat until thickened, about 15 minutes, stirring occasionally. Remove from heat; stir in desired amount of horseradish. Cool.
3. Meanwhile, in a small saucepan over medium-low heat, melt butter. Add the onion; cook and stir until caramelized, 10-12 minutes. Cool. Stir in cheeses, mayonnaise and sour cream.
4. In a large skillet, heat remaining olive oil over medium-high heat. Add steak; cook 4-6 minutes on each side until meat reaches desired doneness (for medium-rare, a thermometer should read 135°; medium, 140°; medium-well, 145°). Let stand 5 minutes; cut into thin slices.
5. To serve, spread cheese mixture on each baguette slice. Add a piece of steak; top with carrot mixture.

Note: Top loin steak may be labeled as strip steak, Kansas City steak, New York strip steak, ambassador steak or boneless club steak in your region.

Per 1 appetizer: 124 cal., 6g fat (3g sat. fat), 16mg chol., 70mg sod., 13g carb. (8g sugars, 1g fiber), 4g pro.

SPICY BUTTERSCOTCH WINGS

Spicy Butterscotch Wings

We love big-time spicy chicken wings. I do a caramel sauce to balance the heat, but you could also glaze the wings with melted brown sugar.

—AARON SALAZAR WESTMINSTER, CO

PREP: 25 MIN. • **BAKE:** 25 MIN.
MAKES: 10 SERVINGS

- 2 pounds chicken wings
- 2 tablespoons soy sauce
- 2 tablespoons ketchup
- 2 tablespoons Sriracha Asian hot chili sauce
- 1 teaspoon pepper
- 1 teaspoon crushed red pepper flakes
- 1 teaspoon onion powder
- ½ teaspoon salt

BUTTERSCOTCH SAUCE

- ½ cup sugar
- ½ cup 2% milk, warmed
- 2 tablespoons butter

CRUMB TOPPING

- 1 tablespoon butter
- ½ cup panko (Japanese) bread crumbs
- 2 green onions, sliced diagonally, divided
- 1 garlic clove, minced
- ½ teaspoon salt
- ½ teaspoon pepper
- 2 red bird's eye chili peppers, minced, optional

1. Preheat oven to 400°. Using a sharp knife, cut through the two wing joints; discard wing tips. Combine next seven ingredients; add wings and toss to coat.
2. Line a 15x10-in. pan with foil; grease with cooking spray. Bake wings in prepared pan 10 minutes; reduce heat to 350° and bake until juices run clear, 12-15 minutes. Remove from oven; keep warm.
3. Meanwhile, in a small skillet, spread sugar; cook, without stirring, over medium heat until it begins to melt. Gently drag melted sugar to center of pan so it melts evenly. Cook, without stirring, until melted sugar turns amber. Carefully stir in warm milk and butter. Simmer, stirring frequently, until sauce is thickened, 5-7 minutes. Keep warm.
4. In a large skillet over medium heat, melt butter; add bread crumbs, one green onion, garlic, salt and pepper. Cook and stir until bread crumbs are golden brown, about 2 minutes. Set aside.
5. To serve, toss wings in butterscotch sauce. Sprinkle with crumb topping, remaining green onion and, if desired, sliced peppers. Serve hot.
Per 2 pieces : 199 cal., 11g fat (4g sat. fat), 39mg chol., 625mg sod., 15g carb. (12g sugars, 0 fiber), 11g pro.

FAST FIX ## Crisp Cucumber Salsa

(PICTURED ON P. 4)

Here's a fantastic way to use cucumbers. You'll love the creamy and crunchy texture and super fresh flavors.

—CHARLENE SKJERVEN HOOPLE, ND

START TO FINISH: 20 MIN.
MAKES: 2½ CUPS

- 2 cups finely chopped cucumber, peeled and seeded
- ½ cup finely chopped seeded tomato
- ¼ cup chopped red onion
- 2 tablespoons minced fresh parsley
- 1 jalapeno pepper, seeded and chopped
- 4½ teaspoons minced fresh cilantro
- 1 garlic clove, minced
- ¼ cup reduced-fat sour cream
- 1½ teaspoons lemon juice
- 1½ teaspoons lime juice
- ¼ teaspoon ground cumin
- ¼ teaspoon seasoned salt
  Baked tortilla chip scoops

In a small bowl, combine the first seven ingredients. In another bowl, combine the sour cream, lemon juice, lime juice, cumin and seasoned salt. Pour over cucumber mixture and toss gently to coat. Serve immediately with tortilla chips.
Note: Wear disposable gloves when cutting hot peppers; the oils can burn skin. Avoid touching your face.
Per ¼ cup: 16 cal., 1g fat (0 sat. fat), 2mg chol., 44mg sod., 2g carb. (1g sugars, 0 fiber), 1g pro

✳
TEST KITCHEN TIP
Don't skip seeding the cucumber. If you do, you may end up with watery salsa. To make seeding a breeze, halve cucumbers lengthwise and use a spoon to scoop out the pulpy centers. Crisp (but not watery) Cucumber Salsa is a stellar chip dip or topping for simple grilled salmon.

Warm Crab & Spinach Dip

In Maryland, we stayed at a hotel that sent guests home with a crab dip recipe and a spice pouch. Now I've made my own dip that rekindles memories of that trip.
—**KRISTINA WENNER** JAMISON, PA

PREP: 20 MIN. • **COOK:** 15 MIN.
MAKES: 4½ CUPS

- 2 **tablespoons olive oil**
- ⅓ **cup finely chopped sweet onion**
- 2 **garlic cloves, minced**
- 1 **package (8 ounces) softened cream cheese, cubed**
- 1 **package (5.2 ounces) Boursin garlic and fine herbs cheese**
- ¼ **cup 2% milk**
- ¼ **cup half-and-half cream**
- ¼ **cup white wine or chicken broth**
- 1 **tablespoon seafood seasoning**
- 2 **teaspoons Worcestershire sauce**
- 1 **teaspoon Louisiana-style hot sauce**
- ⅛ **teaspoon crushed red pepper flakes, optional**
- 2 **cans (6 ounces each) lump crabmeat, drained and picked over**
- 1 **package (10 ounces) frozen chopped spinach, thawed and squeezed dry**
- 2 **cups shredded cheddar cheese Blue tortilla chips**

1. In a large nonstick skillet, heat oil over medium heat. Add onion and garlic; cook 3 minutes. Stir in cream cheese and Boursin until melted. Add milk, cream and wine, stirring constantly.
2. Add the seafood seasoning, Worcestershire, hot sauce and red pepper flakes. Stir in crab, spinach and cheddar cheese until cheese melts and mixture is bubbly. Serve warm with blue tortilla chips.
Per ¼ cup: 170 cal., 14g fat (8g sat. fat), 55mg chol., 421mg sod., 2g carb. (1g sugars, 1g fiber), 9g pro.

BUFFALO CHICKEN

WARM CRAB & SPINACH DIP

(5)INGREDIENTS SLOW COOKER

Buffalo Chicken

This slow cooker recipe is one of my favorites for game day. Buffalo chicken breast is a nice alternative to traditional pulled pork.
—**KIM CIEPLUCH** KENOSHA, WI

PREP: 5 MIN. • **COOK:** 3 HOURS
MAKES: 6 SERVINGS

- ½ **cup Buffalo wing sauce**
- 2 **tablespoons ranch salad dressing mix**
- 4 **boneless skinless chicken breast halves (6 ounces each) Optional ingredients: celery ribs or crusty sandwich buns, crumbled blue cheese, additional wing sauce and ranch salad dressing**

1. In a 3-qt. slow cooker, mix wing sauce and dressing mix. Add chicken. Cook, covered, on low until meat is tender, 3-4 hours.
2. Shred chicken with two forks. If desired, serve on celery, top with additional wing sauce and cheese, and serve with ranch dressing.
Per ½ cup without optional ingredients: 147 cal., 3g fat (1g sat. fat), 63mg chol., 1288mg sod., 6g carb. (0 sugars, 0 fiber), 23g pro.

Turkey Sliders with Sweet Potato Buns

In this healthier take on sliders, I sandwich a burger between slices of roasted sweet potato. The first time I made these, my wife took one bite and approved the tasty little guys.

—GUY MARTINO CHARLESTON, SC

PREP: 25 MIN. + CHILLING • **COOK:** 45 MIN.
MAKES: 10 SERVINGS

- 4 applewood-smoked bacon strips, finely chopped
- 1 pound ground turkey
- ½ cup panko (Japanese) bread crumbs
- 2 large eggs
- ½ cup grated Parmesan cheese
- 4 tablespoons chopped fresh cilantro
- 1 teaspoon dried basil
- ½ teaspoon ground cumin
- 1 tablespoon soy sauce
- 2 large sweet potatoes
  Shredded Colby-Monterey Jack cheese
  Honey Dijon mustard

1. In a large skillet, cook the bacon over medium heat until crisp; drain on paper towels. Discard all but 2 tablespoons drippings. Set skillet aside. Combine bacon with next eight ingredients until well mixed; cover and refrigerate at least 30 minutes.

2. Preheat oven to 425°. Cut sweet potatoes into 20 rounds about ½-in. thick. Place slices on an ungreased baking sheet; bake until the sweet potatoes are tender but not mushy, 30-35 minutes. Remove slices; cool on a wire rack.

3. Heat skillet with reserved drippings over medium-high heat. Shape turkey mixture into 10 slider-sized patties. Cook sliders in batches, 3-4 minutes on each side, taking care not to crowd the skillet. Add a pinch of shredded cheddar after flipping each slider the first time. Cook until a thermometer reads 165° and juices run clear.

4. To serve, place each burger on a sweet potato slice and dab with honey Dijon mustard. Cover with a second sweet potato slice. Pierce with toothpick.

Per 1 slider: 226 cal., 10g fat (3g sat. fat), 78mg chol., 293mg sod., 20g carb. (7g sugars, 2g fiber), 14g pro.

TURKEY SLIDERS WITH SWEET POTATO BUNS
Guy Martino
Charleston, SC

FAST FIX ## Lemon Lime Almond Tea

I got this delicious tea recipe from a friend and make it about twice a week. It's such a refreshing drink.

—TAMMY GRIFFIN FRANKSTON, TX

START TO FINISH: 10 MIN.
MAKES: 7 SERVINGS

- 6 cups water
- ¾ cup sugar
- ¾ cup thawed limeade concentrate
- 4½ teaspoons unsweetened instant tea
- ½ teaspoon almond extract
- ½ teaspoon vanilla extract
- 1 medium orange, sliced
- 1 medium lemon, sliced
- 1 medium lime, sliced
  Ice cubes

In a 2-quart pitcher, combine the water, sugar, limeade concentrate, instant tea and extracts. Add fruit slices. Serve in glasses over ice.

Per 1 cup: 179 cal., 0 fat (0 sat. fat), 0 chol., 1mg sod., 44g carb. (41g sugars, 0 fiber), 0 pro.

(5) INGREDIENTS FAST FIX
Strawberry Watermelon Slush

We like to relax on the back porch with glasses of my slush after a long hot day. What could be more refreshing on a summer evening?

—PATTY HOWSE GREAT FALLS, MT

START TO FINISH: 10 MIN.
MAKES: 4 SERVINGS

- ⅓ cup lemon juice
- ⅓ cup sugar
- 2 cups cubed seedless watermelon
- 2 cups fresh strawberries, halved
- 2 cups ice cubes

Place first four ingredients in a blender; cover and process until smooth. Add ice; process, covered, until slushy. Serve immediately.

Per 1 cup: 89 cal., 0 fat (0 sat. fat), 0 chol., 3mg sod., 24g carb. (21g sugars, 2g fiber), 1g pro.

CREOLE SHRIMP &
CRAB CHEESECAKE

Root Beer Pulled Pork Nachos

(PICTURED ON P. 5)

I count on my slow cooker to do the honors when I have a house full of summer guests. Teenagers especially love DIY nachos.

—**JAMES SCHEND** PLEASANT PRAIRIE, WI

PREP: 20 MIN. • **COOK:** 8 HOURS
MAKES: 12 SERVINGS

- 1 **boneless pork shoulder butt roast (3 to 4 pounds)**
- 1 **can (12 ounces) root beer or cola**
- 12 **cups tortilla chips**
- 2 **cups shredded cheddar cheese**
- 2 **medium tomatoes, chopped**
   Pico de gallo, chopped green onions and sliced jalapeno peppers, optional

1. In a 4- or 5-qt. slow cooker, combine pork roast and root beer. Cook, covered, on low until meat is tender, 8-9 hours.
2. Remove roast; cool slightly. When cool enough to handle, shred meat with two forks. Return to slow cooker; keep warm.
3. To serve, drain pork. Layer tortilla chips with pork, cheese, tomatoes and, if desired, optional toppings. Serve immediately.
Per serving: 391 cal., 23g fat (8g sat. fat), 86mg chol., 287mg sod., 20g carb. (4g sugars, 1g fiber), 25g pro.

❋
TEST KITCHEN TIP
The cooked, cooled meat can be frozen in freezer containers for up to four months. Just be sure the cooking liquid covers the meat so it doesn't dry out. To use, partially thaw in the refrigerator overnight, then reheat in the microwave or on the stovetop. We tested this recipe with regular root beer, not diet or low-calorie. Don't like root beer? Try cola, ginger ale or lemon-lime soda.

Creole Shrimp & Crab Cheesecake

We live on the beach and love to eat seafood. A stay-at-home mom, I really like to experiment in the kitchen. I came up with this savory cheesecake as a special appetizer.

—**CHRISTY HUGHES** SUNSET BEACH, NC

PREP: 30 MIN. • **BAKE:** 1 HOUR + CHILLING
MAKES: 24 SERVINGS

- ¾ **cup dry bread crumbs**
- ¼ **cup grated Parmesan cheese**
- ½ **teaspoon dill weed**
- 2 **tablespoons butter, melted**

CHEESECAKE

- 2 **tablespoons butter**
- 1 **medium sweet red pepper, finely chopped**
- 1 **small onion, finely chopped**
- 1 **medium carrot, finely chopped**
- ½ **teaspoon dill weed**
- ½ **teaspoon Creole seasoning**
- ¼ **teaspoon salt**
- ¼ **teaspoon pepper**
- 3 **packages (8 ounces each) cream cheese, softened**
- ½ **cup heavy whipping cream**
- 1 **tablespoon sherry or additional cream**
- 4 **large eggs, lightly beaten**
- 1 **pound peeled and deveined cooked shrimp, chopped**
- 2 **cans (6 ounces each) lump crabmeat, drained**
- 1 **cup shredded Gouda cheese**

SAUCE

- 1 **cup mayonnaise**
- 2 **tablespoons Dijon mustard**
- ½ **teaspoon Creole seasoning**
   Assorted crackers

1. Preheat oven to 350°. Mix bread crumbs, Parmesan cheese and dill; stir in butter. Press onto bottom of a greased 9-in. springform pan. Place pan on a baking sheet.
2. For cheesecake, in a large skillet, heat butter over medium-high heat. Add red pepper, onion and carrot; cook and stir until tender. Stir in seasonings. Cool slightly.
3. In a large bowl, beat cream cheese, cream and sherry until smooth. Add eggs; beat on low just until combined. Fold in vegetable mixture, shrimp, crab and Gouda. Pour over crust.
4. Bake 60-65 minutes or until center is almost set. Cool on a wire rack 10 minutes. Loosen sides from pan with a knife. Cool 1 hour longer. Refrigerate overnight, covering cheesecake when completely cooled.
5. In a small bowl, mix mayonnaise, mustard and Creole seasoning. Remove rim from the springform pan. Serve cheesecake with sauce and crackers.
Note: The following spice blend may be substituted for 1 teaspoon Creole seasoning: ¼ teaspoon each salt, garlic powder and paprika, plus a pinch each dried thyme, ground cumin and cayenne pepper.
Per 1 slice without crackers: 283 cal., 24g fat (11g sat. fat), 137mg chol., 411mg sod., 5g carb. (1g sugars, 0 fiber), 12g pro.

HOLIDAY SALSA

Holiday Salsa

When we offer this cream-cheesy salsa of fresh cranberries, cilantro and a little jalapeno kick, guests hover around the serving dish until it's scraped clean.
—**SHELLY PATTISON** LUBBOCK, TX

PREP: 20 MIN. + CHILLING • **MAKES:** 12 SERVINGS

- 1 package (12 ounces) fresh or frozen cranberries
- 1 cup sugar
- 6 green onions, chopped
- ½ cup fresh cilantro leaves, chopped
- 1 jalapeno pepper, seeded and finely chopped
- 1 package (8 ounces) cream cheese, softened
  Assorted crackers or tortilla chips

1. Pulse cranberries and sugar in a food processor until coarsely chopped. Stir together with onions, cilantro and jalapeno. Cover and refrigerate several hours or overnight.
2. To serve, place cream cheese on a serving plate. Drain salsa; spoon over cream cheese. Serve with crackers.
Note: Wear disposable gloves when cutting hot peppers; the oils can burn skin. Avoid touching your face.
Per serving: 146 cal., 7g fat (4g sat. fat), 21mg chol., 71mg sod., 22g carb. (19g sugars, 2g fiber), 1g pro.

EAT SMART Spinach Dip-Stuffed Mushrooms

We make a lighter version of spinach dip to stuff inside mushrooms. Bake or grill them, but use a grill pan so they don't tumble through the grate.
—**ASHLEY PIERCE** BRANTFORD, ON

PREP: 25 MIN. • **BAKE:** 15 MIN. • **MAKES:** 16 APPETIZERS

- 16 large fresh mushrooms (about 1½ pounds)
- 1 tablespoon olive oil
- 2 cups fresh baby spinach, coarsely chopped
- 2 garlic cloves, minced
- ½ cup reduced-fat sour cream
- 3 ounces reduced-fat cream cheese
- ⅓ cup shredded part-skim mozzarella cheese
- 3 tablespoons grated Parmesan cheese
- ¼ teaspoon salt
- ¼ teaspoon cayenne pepper
- ¼ teaspoon pepper

1. Preheat oven to 400°. Remove stems from mushrooms and set caps aside; discard stems or save for another use. In a small skillet, heat olive oil over medium heat. Add spinach; saute until wilted. Add garlic; cook 1 minute longer.
2. Combine spinach mixture with remaining ingredients. Stuff into mushroom caps. Place in a 15x10-in. baking pan coated with cooking spray. Bake, uncovered, until mushrooms are tender, 12-15 minutes. Serve warm.
Per 1 stuffed mushroom: 44 cal., 3g fat (2g sat. fat), 9mg chol., 100mg sod., 1g carb. (1g sugars, 0 fiber), 2g pro.

(5)INGREDIENTS FAST FIX Cerveza Margaritas

One sip of this refreshing drink and you'll picture sand, sea and blue skies that stretch for miles. It's like a vacation in a glass, and you can mix it up in moments. What are you waiting for?
—**CHRISTINA PITTMAN** PARKVILLE, MO

START TO FINISH: 10 MIN. • **MAKES:** 5 SERVINGS

- 1 can (12 ounces) lemon-lime soda, chilled
- 1 bottle (12 ounces) beer
- 1 can (12 ounces) frozen limeade concentrate, thawed
- ¾ cup tequila
  Lime slices and kosher salt, optional
  Crushed ice

In a pitcher, combine liquid ingredients. If desired, moisten rims of five margarita or cocktail glasses with lime slices. Sprinkle salt on a plate; dip rims in salt. Serve margaritas in prepared glasses over crushed ice; if desired, garnish with additional lime slices.
Per 1 cup without salt: 272 cal., 0 fat (0 sat. fat), 0 chol., 14mg sod., 44g carb. (39g sugars, 0 fiber), 0 pro.

SPINACH DIP-STUFFED MUSHROOMS

FAST FIX ▸ Bloody Maria

Tequila, lime and jalapenos give the brunch classic a fresh Mexican twist.

—**TASTE OF HOME** TEST KITCHEN

START TO FINISH: 10 MIN.
MAKES: 6 SERVINGS

- 4 **cups tomato juice, chilled**
- 8 **ounces (1 cup) tequila**
- ½ **cup lime juice**
- 4 **to 8 teaspoons juice from pickled jalapeno slices**
- 1 **tablespoon Worcestershire sauce**
- 2 **to 4 teaspoons hot pepper sauce**
- ¼ **teaspoon celery salt**
- ¼ **teaspoon pepper**
- 2 **teaspoons prepared horseradish, optional**
  Pickled jalapeno slices
  Pepper jack cheese, cubed
  Lime wedges

Mix first eight ingredients in a 2-qt. pitcher; stir in horseradish if desired. Pour over ice; serve with jalapenos, cheese cubes and lime wedges.

Per 1 cup: 122 cal., 1g fat (0 sat. fat), 0 chol., 525mg sod., 8g carb. (5g sugars, 1g fiber), 2g pro.

BLOODY MARIA

RAMEN SLIDERS

⑤ INGREDIENTS Ramen Sliders

I grew up eating ramen and love it to this day. These sliders are a fun spin on my favorite type of noodle soup, which is topped with an egg and kimchi.

—**JULIE TERAMOTO** LOS ANGELES, CA

PREP: 40 MIN. • **BAKE:** 20 MIN.
MAKES: 10 SERVINGS

- 1 **package (3 ounces) beef or pork ramen noodles**
- 1 **pound ground beef**
- 4 **green onions, thinly sliced**
- 2 **hard-boiled large eggs, sliced**
  Sriracha Asian hot chili sauce
  Kimchi, optional

1. Preheat oven to 350°. Grease 20 muffin cups. Cook noodles according to package directions, saving seasoning packet for meat mixture. Drain; divide noodles among prepared muffin cups. Bake until crisp and light golden brown, 20-25 minutes. Remove from pans to wire racks to cool.
2. Meanwhile, combine beef, green onions and reserved seasoning packet, mixing lightly but thoroughly. Shape into ten 2½-in. round patties.
3. In a large nonstick skillet, cook the burgers over medium heat for 4-6 minutes on each side until a thermometer reads 160°. Cut each

egg into five slices. Serve burgers on ramen buns with egg slices, chili sauce and, if desired, kimchi.

Per 1 slider: 137 cal., 8g fat (3g sat. fat), 65mg chol., 185mg sod., 6g carb. (0 sugars, 0 fiber), 10g pro.

⑤ INGREDIENTS FAST FIX ▸ Fluffy Hot Chocolate

This is our daughter's favorite hot chocolate recipe. It may look like ordinary cocoa, but a touch of vanilla sets it apart from the rest. The melted marshmallows give it a frothy body you won't get from a cocoa packet.

—**JO ANN SCHIMCEK** WEIMAR, TX

START TO FINISH: 15 MIN.
MAKES: 4 SERVINGS

- 8 **teaspoons sugar**
- 4 **teaspoons baking cocoa**
- 4 **cups 2% milk**
- 1½ **cups miniature marshmallows**
- 1 **teaspoon vanilla extract**

In a small saucepan, combine the first four ingredients. Cook and stir over medium heat until marshmallows are melted, about 8 minutes. Remove from the heat; stir in vanilla. Ladle into mugs.

Per 1 cup: 249 cal., 8g fat (5g sat. fat), 33mg chol., 128mg sod., 36g carb. (30g sugars, 0 fiber), 9g pro.

Roasted Brussels Sprouts & 3-Cheese Crostini

Brussels sprouts for a snack? Oh, yes. Combine these roasted goodies with cheese for the ultimate toast topper.

—**ATHENA RUSSELL** GREENVILLE, SC

PREP: 20 MIN. • **BAKE:** 20 MIN.
MAKES: ABOUT 2½ DOZEN

- ¾ pound fresh Brussels sprouts, trimmed and thinly sliced
- ¼ cup olive oil, divided
- ¼ teaspoon ground nutmeg
- ¼ teaspoon sea salt
- ¼ teaspoon pepper
- 1 package (4 ounces) crumbled feta cheese
- ⅓ cup whipped cream cheese
- 1 French bread baguette (10½ ounces), cut in ½-inch slices
- 1 cup shredded Gruyere cheese
  Garlic oil, optional

1. Preheat oven to 400°. Toss together Brussels sprouts, 2 tablespoons olive oil, nutmeg, salt and pepper; place on a foil-lined 15x10-in. baking pan. Roast, stirring once, until tender and browned, about 20 minutes.
2. Process feta and cream cheese in food processor until smooth. Place bread slices on a foil-lined baking sheet. Brush with remaining olive oil; broil until just golden, 1-2 minutes. Spread bread slices with feta cheese mixture; top with Brussels sprouts. Sprinkle with Gruyere cheese. Broil 5-6 in. from heat until cheese is melted and starting to brown, 1-2 minutes. If desired, drizzle crostini with garlic oil. Serve immediately.
Per 1 appetizer: 72 cal., 4g fat (2g sat. fat), 9mg chol., 141mg sod., 6g carb. (1g sugars, 1g fiber), 3g pro.

✱
TEST KITCHEN TIP
Salty, crumbly feta cheese is made in Greece with sheep's or goat's milk, but most American brands are made with cow's milk. Not fond of feta? Substitute ricotta salata, which is sharper and not as salty, or queso blanco, which is milky and mild.

FAST FIX
Ham & Cheese Puffs

These marvelous little bites go over well with kids of all ages. They're also good with soups and many of the items you'd expect to find on a buffet table.

—**MARVIN BUFFINGTON** BURLINGTON, IA

START TO FINISH: 30 MIN.
MAKES: 2 DOZEN

- 1 package (2½ ounces) thinly sliced deli ham, chopped
- 1 small onion, chopped
- ½ cup shredded Swiss cheese
- 1 large egg
- 1½ teaspoons Dijon mustard
- ⅛ teaspoon pepper
- 1 tube (8 ounces) refrigerated crescent rolls

1. Preheat oven to 375°. Combine the first six ingredients. Divide crescent dough into 24 portions. Press into greased mini-muffin cups.
2. Spoon 1 tablespoon ham mixture into each cup. Bake until golden brown, 13-15 minutes.
Per 1 appetizer: 110 cal., 6g fat (2g sat. fat), 25mg chol., 263mg sod., 8g carb. (2g sugars, 0 fiber), 4g pro.

EAT SMART ⑤INGREDIENTS FAST FIX
Salsa Dipper Deviled Eggs

Chips and salsa are an all-time favorite on taco night, but add them to fun deviled eggs, and it's an instant fiesta!

—**PEGGY WOODWARD** SHULLSBURG, WI

START TO FINISH: 20 MIN.
MAKES: 1 DOZEN

- 6 hard-boiled large eggs
- ¼ cup salsa
- 2 tablespoons mayonnaise
- 1 green onion, finely chopped
  Dash each salt and pepper
- 12 tortilla chips
  Additional tortilla chips and salsa, optional

1. Cut eggs in half lengthwise. Remove yolks; set whites aside. In a small bowl, mash yolks. Add salsa, mayonnaise, green onion, salt and pepper; mix well. Spoon into egg whites. Or, cut a small hole in the corner of a food-safe plastic bag, transfer egg yolk mixture into bag and pipe into egg whites. Refrigerate.
2. Just before serving, place a tortilla chip in each egg half. If desired, serve with additional chips and salsa.
Per 1 stuffed egg half: 79 cal., 5g fat (1g sat. fat), 93mg chol., 93mg sod., 4g carb. (0 sugars, 0 fiber), 4g pro.

HAM & CHEESE PUFFS

ANTIPASTO KABOBS

Antipasto Kabobs

My husband and I met in a cooking class, and we've loved creating menus and entertaining together ever since. These do-ahead appetizers are always a hit.
—DENISE HAZEN CINCINNATI, OH

PREP: 35 MIN. + MARINATING
MAKES: 40 APPETIZERS

- 1 **package (9 ounces) refrigerated cheese tortellini**
- 40 **pimiento-stuffed olives**
- 40 **large pitted ripe olives**
- ¾ **cup Italian salad dressing**
- 40 **thin slices pepperoni**
- 20 **thin slices hard salami, halved**
  Fresh parsley sprigs, optional

1. Cook tortellini according to package directions; drain and rinse in cold water. In a large resealable plastic bag, combine the tortellini, olives and salad dressing. Seal bag and turn to coat; refrigerate for 4 hours or overnight.
2. Drain and discard marinade. For each appetizer, thread a stuffed olive, folded pepperoni slice, tortellini, folded salami piece, ripe olive and, if desired, a parsley sprig on a toothpick or short skewer.
Per 2 kabobs: 138 cal., 10g fat (3g sat. fat), 18mg chol., 671mg sod., 8g carb. (1g sugars, 1g fiber), 5g pro.
Diabetic Exchanges: 1½ starch, 1 fat.

⑤INGREDIENTS FAST FIX
Raspberry-Lemon Spritzer

For your next summer get-together, go beyond the usual lemonade. This tangy thirst-quencher is so refreshing on warm days. It's not too sweet, and the beautiful pink color makes it even more appealing. Garnish each glass with a lemon slice.
—MARGIE WILLIAMS MOUNT JULIET, TN

START TO FINISH: 15 MIN.
MAKES: 2 SERVINGS

- ½ **cup fresh or frozen raspberries, thawed**
- ⅓ **cup sugar**
- 2½ **cups club soda, chilled**
- ¼ **cup lemon juice**
  Ice cubes
- 2 **lemon slices**

1. Place raspberries and sugar in a food processor; cover and process until pureed. Strain; reserving juice and discarding seeds.
2. In a small pitcher, combine the club soda, lemon juice and raspberry juice. Serve in tall glasses over ice. Garnish with lemon slices.
Per 1½ cups: 148 cal., 0 fat (0 sat. fat), 0 chol., 66mg sod., 39g carb. (36g sugars, 0 fiber), 0 pro.

FAST FIX Chili Shrimp

This spicy shrimp appetizer is a hit at every buffet I host. The fiery sauce clings to the succulent shrimp, which look so pretty arranged on a festive platter. Best of all, you can mix the sauce ingredients and prep the shrimp a day in advance.
—BETH SCHAEFER SHERWOOD, OH

START TO FINISH: 25 MIN.
MAKES: ABOUT 3 DOZEN

- 3 **tablespoons ketchup**
- 1 **tablespoon sugar**
- 1 **tablespoon white wine vinegar**
- 1 **tablespoon soy sauce**
- ⅛ **to ½ teaspoon crushed red pepper flakes**
- 1 **pound uncooked medium shrimp, peeled and deveined**
- 1 **tablespoon canola oil**
- 1 **tablespoon minced fresh gingerroot**
- 3 **garlic cloves, minced**
- 1 **green onion, sliced**
- ½ **teaspoon sesame oil**

1. Combine the first five ingredients; set aside. In a large skillet or wok, stir-fry shrimp in oil for 2 minutes. Add ginger and garlic; stir-fry 2-3 minutes longer or until shrimp turn pink.
2. Add ketchup mixture to the pan and heat through. Stir in onion and sesame oil. Serve warm.
Per 1 shrimp: 19 cal., 1g fat (0 sat. fat), 16mg chol., 58mg sod., 1g carb. (1g sugars, 0 fiber), 2g pro.

CHILI SHRIMP

Party Cheese Bread

(PICTURED ON P. 5)

Cheesy, buttery and finger-licking good, this bread is sinfully tasty. It makes a perfect centerpiece at a party; it's so pretty, guests might be reluctant to dig into it. But once they do, it won't last long!

—**KAREN GRANT** TULARE, CA

PREP: 25 MIN. • **BAKE:** 25 MIN.
MAKES: 8 SERVINGS

- 1 round loaf sourdough bread (1 pound)
- 1 pound Monterey Jack cheese, sliced
- ½ cup butter, melted
- 2 tablespoons lemon juice
- 2 tablespoons Dijon mustard
- 1½ teaspoons garlic powder
- ½ teaspoon onion powder
- ½ teaspoon celery salt
  Minced fresh chives, optional

1. Preheat oven to 350°. Cut bread into 1-in. slices to within ½ in. of bottom of loaf. Repeat cuts in opposite direction. Insert cheese in cuts.
2. Mix all remaining ingredients except chives; drizzle over bread. Wrap in foil; place on a baking sheet.
3. Bake 20 minutes. Unwrap bread and bake until cheese is melted, about 10 minutes. If desired, sprinkle with chives.
Per 1 piece: 491 cal., 30g fat (19g sat. fat), 80mg chol., 1012mg sod., 34g carb. (2g sugars, 1g fiber), 21g pro.

SLOW COOKER
Mulled Dr Pepper

When neighbors or friends visit us on a chilly evening, I'll serve this warm beverage with ham sandwiches and deviled eggs.

—**BERNICE MORRIS** MARSHFIELD, MO

PREP: 10 MIN. • **COOK:** 2 HOURS
MAKES: 10 SERVINGS

- 8 cups Dr Pepper
- ¼ cup packed brown sugar
- ¼ cup lemon juice
- ½ teaspoon ground allspice
- ½ teaspoon whole cloves
- ¼ teaspoon salt
- ¼ teaspoon ground nutmeg
- 3 cinnamon sticks (3 inches)

FRESH LIME MARGARITAS

1. In a 3-qt. slow cooker, combine all ingredients.
2. Cover and cook on low for 2 hours or until heated through. Discard cloves and cinnamon sticks.
Per ¾ cup: 105 cal., 0 fat (0 sat. fat), 0 chol., 69mg sod., 27g carb. (26g sugars, 0 fiber), 0 pro.

FAST FIX ▸ **Fresh Lime Margaritas**

This basic margarita recipe is easy to modify to your tastes. Try it frozen or with strawberries.

—**TASTE OF HOME** TEST KITCHEN

START TO FINISH: 15 MIN.
MAKES: 4 SERVINGS

- ½ cup tequila
- ¼ cup Triple Sec
- ¼ cup lime juice
- ¼ cup lemon juice
- 2 tablespoons superfine sugar
- 4 lime wedges
- 1 tablespoon kosher salt
- 1⅓ cups crushed ice

In a pitcher, combine the first five ingredients; stir until sugar is dissolved. Moisten rims of four margarita or cocktail glasses with lime wedges. Sprinkle salt on a plate; dip rims in salt. Serve margaritas in prepared glasses over crushed ice.
Per ⅓ cup without salt: 149 cal., 0 fat (0 sat. fat), 0 chol., 2mg sod., 15g carb. (13g sugars, 0 fiber), 0 pro.
Frozen Lime Margaritas: Reduce lemon and lime juices to 2 tablespoons each. Increase the superfine sugar to ¼ cup and the crushed ice to 4 cups. Add ¾ cup limeade concentrate. Prepare glasses as directed. In a blender, combine the tequila, Triple Sec, lime juice, lemon juice, limeade concentrate, superfine sugar and crushed ice; cover and process until smooth. Makes 5 cups.
Frozen Strawberry Margaritas: Follow directions for Frozen Lime Margaritas, except reduce crushed ice to 2 cups and add 2 cups frozen unsweetened strawberries. Makes 4 cups.

FAST FIX ► French Quarter Cheese Spread

Topped with toasty pecans, this sweet and savory cheese is simply a hit. Make it ahead of time for convenience, then bring to room temperature and serve.

—HEIDI BLAINE HADBURG SAFETY HARBOR, FL

START TO FINISH: 20 MIN. **• MAKES:** 8 SERVINGS

- 1 package (8 ounces) cream cheese, softened
- 1 tablespoon grated onion
- 1 garlic clove, minced
- ¼ cup butter, cubed
- ¼ cup packed dark brown sugar
- 1 teaspoon Worcestershire sauce
- ½ teaspoon prepared mustard
- 1 cup finely chopped pecans, toasted
  Assorted crackers

1. In a small bowl, combine the cream cheese, onion and garlic. Transfer to a serving plate; shape into a 6-in. disk. Set aside.

2. In a small saucepan, combine the butter, brown sugar, Worcestershire sauce and mustard. Cook and stir over medium heat for 4-5 minutes or until sugar is dissolved. Remove from the heat; stir in pecans.

3. Cool slightly. Spoon over cheese mixture. Serve with assorted crackers.

Per ¼ cup: 280 cal., 26g fat (11g sat. fat), 46mg chol., 138mg sod., 10g carb. (7g sugars, 1g fiber), 4g pro.

FRENCH QUARTER CHEESE SPREAD

Dilly Cheese Ball

The whole family devours this herby cheese spread—even my son, a chef. Serve it with your favorite crackers.

—JANE VINCE LONDON, ON

PREP: 10 MIN. + CHILLING **• MAKES:** 2½ CUPS

- 1 package (8 ounces) cream cheese, softened
- 1 cup dill pickle relish, drained
- ¼ cup finely chopped onion
- 1½ cups shredded cheddar cheese
- 1 tablespoon Worcestershire sauce
- 2 tablespoons mayonnaise
- 2 tablespoons minced fresh parsley
  Assorted crackers

Beat first six ingredients until smooth. Shape into a ball; wrap in plastic. Refrigerate several hours. Sprinkle with parsley; serve with crackers.

Per 2 tablespoons: 100 cal., 8g fat (4g sat. fat), 22mg chol., 244mg sod., 5g carb. (1g sugars, 0 fiber), 3g pro.

FAST FIX ► Sweet & Spicy Jalapeno Poppers

There's no faster way to get a party started than with these bacon-wrapped poppers. Make them ahead and pop them in the oven right when guests arrive.

—DAWN ONUFFER CRESTVIEW, FL

START TO FINISH: 30 MIN. **• MAKES:** 1 DOZEN

- 6 jalapeno peppers
- 4 ounces cream cheese, softened
- 2 tablespoons shredded cheddar cheese
- 6 bacon strips, halved widthwise
- ¼ cup packed brown sugar
- 1 tablespoon chili seasoning mix

1. Cut jalapenos in half lengthwise and remove seeds; set aside. In a small bowl, beat cheeses until blended. Spoon into pepper halves. Wrap a half-strip of bacon around each pepper half.

2. Combine brown sugar and chili seasoning; coat the peppers with sugar mixture. Place in a greased 15x10x1-in. baking pan.

3. Bake at 350° until bacon is firm, 18-20 minutes.

Note: Wear disposable gloves when cutting hot peppers; the oils can burn skin. Avoid touching your face.

Per 1 stuffed pepper half: 66 cal., 5g fat (3g sat. fat), 15mg chol., 115mg sod., 3g carb. (3g sugars, 0 fiber), 2g pro.

Diabetic Exchanges: 1 fat.

TURKEY CROQUETTES WITH CRANBERRY SALSA

Turkey Croquettes with Cranberry Salsa

Instead of serving another round of turkey and sweet potatoes, we make the leftovers into croquettes and pass them around with a tangy apple-cranberry salsa.

—JACQUE CAPURRO ANCHORAGE, AK

PREP: 30 MIN. + CHILLING • **COOK:** 5 MIN./BATCH
MAKES: 16 CROQUETTES (2 CUPS SALSA)

- 2 tablespoons butter
- ⅓ cup chopped onion
- ¼ cup all-purpose flour
- ¼ cup 2% milk
- ¼ cup chicken broth
- 2 cups finely chopped cooked turkey
- ½ cup mashed sweet potato
- ½ teaspoon salt
- ¼ teaspoon pepper
- ⅛ teaspoon cayenne pepper

SALSA
- ¾ cup chopped tart apple
- 1 tablespoon lemon juice
- ½ cup chopped cranberries
- 2 jalapeno peppers, seeded and chopped
- 2 green onions, chopped
- 3 tablespoons golden raisins, chopped
- 1 tablespoon honey

CROQUETTES
- 2 large eggs
- 1 tablespoon water
- ½ cup all-purpose flour
- ½ cup dry bread crumbs
  Oil for deep-fat frying

1. In a large saucepan, heat butter over medium heat. Add onion; cook and stir 3-4 minutes or until tender.

2. Stir in flour until blended. Gradually add milk and broth. Bring to a boil; cook and stir 2 minutes or until thickened. Remove from heat; stir in turkey, sweet potato, salt, pepper and cayenne. Refrigerate, covered, 2 hours or until firm.

3. Meanwhile, in a small bowl, toss apple with lemon juice. Stir in remaining salsa ingredients. Refrigerate, covered, at least 1 hour.

4. For croquettes, in a shallow bowl, beat eggs and water. Place flour and bread crumbs in separate shallow bowls. Shape turkey mixture into 1½-in. balls. Roll in flour; shake off excess. Roll in egg mixture, then in crumbs, patting to help coating adhere.

5. In an electric skillet or deep-fat fryer, heat oil to 375°. Fry croquettes, a few at a time, 1-2 minutes on each side or until golden brown. Drain on paper towels. Serve with salsa.

Note: Wear disposable gloves when cutting hot peppers; the oils can burn skin. Avoid touching your face.

Per 2 appetizers with ¼ cup salsa: 317 cal., 17g fat (4g sat. fat), 90mg chol., 315mg sod., 27g carb. (8g sugars, 2g fiber), 15g pro.

**DEBORAH WILLIAMS'
ARTICHOKE TOMATO SALAD**
PAGE 35

Salads
& Dressings

Make mealtime fresh with veggie, main dish, grain, lettuce and pasta salads. Whether you want a **light, summery dinner** or a **healthy side dish** for the main event, these recipes have you covered. **Homemade dressings** round out the selection.

RADELLE KNAPPENBERGER'S CURRIED CHICKEN & PEACH SALAD
PAGE 30

GINA NISTICO'S STRAWBERRY-BASIL VINEGAR
PAGE 29

MARLA ARBET'S HONEY-PECAN KIWI SALAD
PAGE 32

Fiesta Chopped Salad

We serve this colorful garden feast whenever there's an abundance of vegetables bursting with flavor. It's a flexible recipe, so chop up your own favorites and add to the mix.

—MERWYN GARBINI TUCSON, AZ

START TO FINISH: 30 MIN.
MAKES: 8 SERVINGS

- 1 medium sweet red pepper, chopped
- 1 medium sweet yellow pepper, chopped
- 1 medium tomato, seeded and chopped
- 1 medium cucumber, seeded and chopped
- 1 small zucchini, chopped
- 2 green onions, chopped
- 2 tablespoons minced fresh parsley
- 2 tablespoons olive oil
- 1 tablespoon red wine vinegar
- ½ teaspoon sugar
- ¼ teaspoon salt
- ¼ teaspoon pepper
- 1 large ripe avocado, peeled and chopped
- 1 tablespoon lemon juice

In a large bowl, combine the first seven ingredients. In a small bowl, whisk the oil, vinegar, sugar, salt and pepper. Drizzle over vegetables and toss to coat. Toss avocado with lemon juice; gently fold into salad. Serve with a slotted spoon.

Per ½ cup: 91 cal., 7g fat (1g sat. fat), 0 chol., 81mg sod., 7g carb. (0 sugars, 2g fiber), 1g pro.
Diabetic Exchanges: 1½ fat, 1 vegetable.

FIESTA CHOPPED SALAD

UDON NOODLES WITH PINEAPPLE VINAIGRETTE

Udon Noodles with Pineapple Vinaigrette

Thai food has such wonderfully intense flavors, but the dishes can be heavy and time-consuming. My answer is a Thai-inspired salad with mango, hot pepper, peanuts and the cuisine's signature pop of fresh herbs.

—MELANIE STEVENSON READING, PA

START TO FINISH: 30 MIN.
MAKES: 8 SERVINGS

- 1 package (12.8 ounces) dried Japanese udon noodles
- ½ cup unsweetened pineapple juice
- ¼ cup sesame oil
- 2 tablespoons white wine vinegar
- 2 teaspoons grated fresh gingerroot
- 2 teaspoons minced seeded jalapeno pepper
- 3 cups fresh arugula or baby spinach
- 2 cups chopped peeled mango
- 1 cup salted peanuts
- ½ cup coarsely chopped fresh cilantro leaves
- ¼ cup coarsely chopped fresh mint leaves
- 2 tablespoons black sesame seeds

1. Cook noodles according to package instructions. Rinse with cold water; drain well. Whisk together the next five ingredients. Pour over noodles; toss to coat. Refrigerate until serving.
2. To serve, top noodles with arugula, mango, peanuts, cilantro and mint; toss to combine. Sprinkle with sesame seeds.
Note: Wear disposable gloves when cutting hot peppers; the oils can burn skin. Avoid touching your face.
Per 1⅓ cups: 383 cal., 19g fat (3g sat. fat), 0 chol., 128mg sod., 43g carb. (9g sugars, 5g fiber), 13g pro.

Ranch Dressing & Dip Mix

This versatile recipe converts easily into a creamy dip or smooth dressing. It's delicious served with fresh veggies or drizzled over greens.
—**CAROLYN ZIMMERMAN** FAIRBURY, IL

PREP: 10 MIN. + CHILLING
MAKES: 6 TABLESPOONS MIX (ENOUGH FOR 6 BATCHES)

- 2 tablespoons plus 2 teaspoons dried minced onion
- 1 tablespoon dried parsley flakes
- 2½ teaspoons paprika
- 2 teaspoons sugar
- 2 teaspoons salt
- 2 teaspoons pepper
- 1½ teaspoons garlic powder

ADDITIONAL INGREDIENTS FOR DRESSING
- 1 cup mayonnaise
- 1 cup buttermilk

ADDITIONAL INGREDIENTS FOR DIP
- 1 cup (8 ounces) sour cream

In a small bowl, combine the first seven ingredients. Store in an airtight container in a cool dry place for up to 1 year.

To prepare dressing: In a bowl, combine 1 tablespoon mix with mayonnaise and buttermilk; refrigerate. Makes 2 cups.

Per 2 tablespoons dressing: 107 cal., 11g fat (2g sat. fat), 6mg chol., 140mg sod., 1g carb. (1g sugars, 0 fiber), 1g pro.

To prepare dip: In a bowl, combine 1 tablespoon mix and sour cream; refrigerate for at least 1 hour before serving. Makes 1 cup.

Per 2 tablespoons dip: 252 cal., 26g fat (6g sat. fat), 10mg chol., 306mg sod., 3g carb. (3g sugars, 0 fiber), 2g pro.

✳

DID YOU KNOW?
Ranch dressing was created by Nebraska cowboy-turned-cook Steve Henson more than 60 years ago. While cooking for a work crew in Alaska in the 1940s, Steve perfected his recipe for buttermilk salad dressing. It later became the house dressing at Hidden Valley Ranch, a dude ranch he bought with his wife, Gayle, outside Santa Barbara, California.

PORK & BALSAMIC STRAWBERRY SALAD

EAT SMART
Pork & Balsamic Strawberry Salad

Here's a great way to celebrate spring. If strawberries aren't in season, use thawed frozen instead of fresh.
—**LAURIE LUFKIN** ESSEX, MA

PREP: 20 MIN. + MARINATING
BAKE: 15 MIN. • **MAKES:** 4 SERVINGS

- 1 pork tenderloin (1 pound)
- ½ cup Italian salad dressing
- 1½ cups halved fresh strawberries
- 2 tablespoons balsamic vinegar
- 2 teaspoons sugar
- ¼ teaspoon salt
- ¼ teaspoon pepper
- 2 tablespoons olive oil
- ¼ cup chicken broth
- 1 package (5 ounces) spring mix salad greens
- ½ cup crumbled goat cheese

1. Place pork in a shallow dish. Add salad dressing; turn to coat.

Refrigerate, covered, at least 8 hours. Combine strawberries, vinegar and sugar; cover and refrigerate.

2. Preheat oven to 425°. Drain and wipe off pork, discarding marinade. Sprinkle with salt and pepper. In a large ovenproof skillet, heat oil over medium-high heat. Add pork; brown on all sides.

3. Bake until a thermometer reads 145°, 15-20 minutes. Remove from skillet; let stand 5 minutes. Meanwhile, add broth to skillet; cook over medium heat, stirring to loosen browned bits from pan. Bring to a boil. Reduce heat; add strawberry mixture. Heat through.

4. Place greens on a serving platter; sprinkle with cheese. Slice pork; arrange over greens. Top with strawberry mixture.

Per 2 cups: 291 cal., 16g fat (5g sat. fat), 81mg chol., 444mg sod., 12g carb. (7g sugars, 3g fiber), 26g pro.
Diabetic Exchanges: 3 lean meat, 3 fat, 1 vegetable.

Jambalaya Rice Salad

This cold rice salad has a little hint of spice for that classic jambalaya kick. Shrimp, tomatoes, ham and peppers give it color and crunch.

—**KAREN RAHN** HIXON, TN

PREP: 20 MIN. • **COOK:** 15 MIN. + CHILLING
MAKES: 8 SERVINGS

- 1⅓ cups uncooked long grain rice
- 2 tablespoons olive oil
- 2 cups cubed fully cooked ham
- ⅓ cup chopped onion
- 2 garlic cloves, minced
- 1 teaspoon dried oregano
- 1 teaspoon dried thyme
- ½ to 1 teaspoon salt
- ¼ to ½ teaspoon cayenne pepper
- ¼ teaspoon pepper
- ⅓ cup red wine vinegar
- 1½ pounds peeled and deveined cooked shrimp (31-40 per pound)
- 2 celery ribs, thinly sliced
- 1 small green pepper, julienned
- 1 small sweet red pepper, julienned
- 1 pint cherry tomatoes, halved
- 2 green onions, sliced

1. Prepare rice according to package directions; cool. In a large skillet, heat oil over medium heat. Add ham and onion; cook and stir until onion is tender, about 5 minutes. Add next six ingredients; cook and stir 2 minutes. Remove from heat; stir in vinegar.
2. Combine the rice, ham mixture, shrimp, celery and peppers. Chill, covered, for at least 2 hours. Add tomatoes; toss to combine. Sprinkle with onions.

Per 1¼ cups: 309 cal., 7g fat (1g sat. fat), 150mg chol., 709mg sod., 32g carb. (2g sugars, 2g fiber), 28g pro.
Diabetic Exchanges: 4 lean meat, 2 starch, 1 vegetable, 1 fat.

SPARKLING GELATIN SALAD

Sparkling Gelatin Salad

The fruit really shines through in this refreshing gelatin salad.

—**CASSIE ALEXANDER** MUNCIE, IN

PREP: 15 MIN. + CHILLING
MAKES: 6 SERVINGS

- 2 envelopes unflavored gelatin
- 1½ cups white grape juice, divided
- 1½ cups sweet white wine or additional white grape juice
- ¼ cup sugar
- 1 can (15 ounces) mandarin oranges, drained
- 1 cup green grapes, halved
- ¾ cup fresh raspberries

1. In a small saucepan, sprinkle gelatin over ½ cup juice; let stand for 1 minute. Heat over low heat, stirring until gelatin is completely dissolved. Stir in the wine, sugar and remaining juice. Cook and stir until sugar is dissolved.
2. Pour into a 1½-qt. serving bowl. Refrigerate until set but not firm, about 1 hour. Fold in the oranges, grapes and raspberries. Refrigerate until firm.

Per ¾ cup: 179 cal., 0 fat (0 sat. fat), 0 chol., 15mg sod., 32g carb. (29g sugars, 2g fiber), 3g pro.

JAMBALAYA RICE SALAD

Strawberry-Basil Vinegar

(PICTURED ON P. 25)

The mild, fruity flavor of this vinegar complements any tossed salad.

—GINA NISTICO MILWAUKEE, WI

PREP: 30 MIN. + STANDING
PROCESS: 10 MIN. • **MAKES:** 5 HALF-PINTS

- 4 cups fresh strawberries, hulled
- 4 cups white wine vinegar
- 1 tablespoon grated lemon peel
- 1 cup loosely packed basil leaves

1. Place strawberries in a food processor; cover and process until pureed. Transfer to a large glass bowl; add vinegar and lemon peel. Place ¼ cup basil in a small bowl.

2. With a mortar or a wooden spoon, crush basil until aromas are released. Repeat with remaining basil; stir into strawberry mixture. Cover and let stand in a cool dark place for up to 3 days, stirring once daily.

3. Line a strainer with four layers of cheesecloth or one coffee filter and place over a large saucepan. Strain vinegar into pan (do not press out solids). Discard solids.

4. Heat vinegar to 180° over medium heat. Carefully ladle hot mixture into hot half-pint jars, leaving ¼-in. headspace. Wipe rims and adjust lids. Process for 10 minutes in a boiling-water canner.

Note: The processing time listed is for altitudes of 1,000 feet or less. Add 1 minute to the processing time for each 1,000 feet of additional altitude.

Per 1 tablespoon: 6 cal., 0 fat (0 sat. fat), 0 chol., 0 sod., 1g carb. (0 sugars, 0 fiber), 0 pro.

To make vinaigrette: Combine 1 part vinegar with 1 part oil. Toss with fresh spinach, sliced fresh strawberries and toasted walnuts for a refreshing salad.

GRILLED STONE FRUIT SALAD

Grilled Stone Fruit Salad

Summer is the time we enjoy grilling and adding fresh fruit to our menu, and this smoky-sweet salad is the best of both worlds! I like to marinate the fruits for extra flavor before I grill them.

—NANCY HEISHMAN LAS VEGAS, NV

PREP: 20 MIN. + MARINATING
GRILL: 10 MIN. • **MAKES:** 6 SERVINGS

- 6 tablespoons lemon juice, divided
- 3 tablespoons butter, melted
- 1 tablespoon minced fresh mint
- 2 peeled peaches, pitted and halved
- 3 medium plums, pitted and halved
- 4 apricots, pitted and halved
- ¼ fresh pineapple, cut into 4 slices
- ¼ cup extra virgin olive oil
- 2 tablespoons honey
- ¼ teaspoon kosher salt
- ⅛ teaspoon ground allspice
- 6 ounces fresh baby arugula
- 1 cup crumbled feta cheese

1. In a large shallow bowl, whisk together 3 tablespoons lemon juice, melted butter and mint. Add fruit; marinate 30 minutes, turning once. Drain, reserving marinade.

2. Grill fruit, covered, on a greased grill rack over medium-high direct heat 4-6 minutes. Turn; brush with reserved marinade. Grill, uncovered, brushing again, until fruit is tender but not mushy, 4-6 more minutes. Remove from heat; cool 5-10 minutes. When cool enough to handle, cut fruit into quarters.

3. Whisk together olive oil, honey, kosher salt, allspice and remaining lemon juice. Drizzle half the dressing over arugula, tossing until well coated; place arugula on a large serving platter. Add grilled fruit; drizzle with remaining dressing. Sprinkle with crumbled feta cheese.

Per serving: 268 cal., 18g fat (7g sat. fat), 25mg chol., 315mg sod., 23g carb. (19g sugars, 3g fiber), 5g pro.

Crunchy Broccoli Salad

I never liked broccoli when I was younger, but now I'm hooked on this salad's light, sweet taste. It gives broccoli a whole new look and taste, in my opinion.
—**JESSICA CONREY** CEDAR RAPIDS, IA

START TO FINISH: 25 MIN. • **MAKES:** 10 SERVINGS

- 8 cups fresh broccoli florets (about 1 pound)
- 1 bunch green onions, thinly sliced
- ½ cup dried cranberries
- 3 tablespoons canola oil
- 3 tablespoons seasoned rice vinegar
- 2 tablespoons sugar
- ¼ cup sunflower kernels
- 3 bacon strips, cooked and crumbled

1. In a large bowl, combine the broccoli, green onions and cranberries.

2. Whisk oil, vinegar and sugar until blended; drizzle over broccoli mixture and toss to coat. Refrigerate until serving. Sprinkle with sunflower kernels and bacon before serving.
Per ¾ cup: 121 cal., 7g fat (1g sat. fat), 2mg chol., 233mg sod., 14g carb. (10g sugars, 3g fiber), 3g pro.
Diabetic Exchanges: 1 vegetable, 1 fat, ½ starch.
Creamy Broccoli Salad: Omit oil and vinegar and reduce sugar to 1 tablespoon. Combine 1 cup mayonnaise, 2 tablespoons cider vinegar and sugar. Pour over broccoli mixture and toss to coat.
Crunchy Cauliflower-Broccoli Salad: Substitute 4 cups fresh cauliflowerets for 4 cups of the broccoli florets.

Curried Chicken & Peach Salad

(PICTURED ON P. 25)

This is a healthy and simple salad to make; even my non-cooking husband can whip it together in minutes. We've served this to friends over the years, and they always ask for the recipe.
—**RADELLE KNAPPENBERGER** OVIEDO, FL

START TO FINISH: 10 MIN. • **MAKES:** 4 SERVINGS

- ½ cup fat-free mayonnaise
- 1 teaspoon curry powder
- 2 cups cubed cooked chicken breasts
- ½ cup chopped walnuts
- ¼ cup raisins
- 2 medium peaches, sliced
- 1 package (5 ounces) spring mix salad greens

Mix mayonnaise and curry powder; toss gently with chicken, walnuts and raisins. Serve chicken mixture and peaches over greens.
Per serving: 286 cal., 12g fat (2g sat. fat), 54mg chol., 315mg sod., 23g carb. (14g sugars, 4g fiber), 24g pro.
Diabetic Exchanges: 3 lean meat, 1½ fat, 1 vegetable, 1 fruit.

EMILY'S HONEY LIME COLESLAW

Emily's Honey Lime Coleslaw

Here's a refreshing take on slaw with a honey-lime vinaigrette rather than the traditional mayo. It's a great take-along for all those summer picnics.
—**EMILY TYRA** MILWAUKEE, WI

PREP: 20 MIN. + CHILLING • **MAKES:** 8 SERVINGS

- 1½ teaspoons grated lime peel
- ¼ cup lime juice
- 2 tablespoons honey
- 1 garlic clove, minced
- ½ teaspoon salt
- ¼ teaspoon pepper
- ¼ teaspoon crushed red pepper flakes
- 3 tablespoons canola oil
- 1 small head red cabbage (about ¾ pound), shredded
- 1 cup shredded carrots (about 2 medium carrots)
- 2 green onions, thinly sliced
- ½ cup fresh cilantro leaves

Whisk together the first seven ingredients until smooth. Gradually whisk in oil until blended. Combine cabbage, carrots and green onions; toss with lime mixture to lightly coat. Refrigerate, covered, 2 hours. Sprinkle with cilantro.
Per ½ cup: 86 cal., 5g fat (0 sat. fat), 0 chol., 170mg sod., 10g carb. (7g sugars, 2g fiber), 1g pro.
Diabetic Exchanges: 1 vegetable, 1 fat.

My Favorite Avocado Salad

Tangy lime dressing is the perfect topper for this avocado salad. Toasted walnuts add a great crunch, but go ahead and sprinkle on any kind of nut.

—**ILIA KAKU** NORTH RICHLAND HILLS, TX

START TO FINISH: 25 MIN. • **MAKES:** 9 SERVINGS

- 1 tablespoon lemon juice
- 2 medium avocados, peeled and cubed
- 1 package (5 ounces) spring mix salad greens
- 5 plum tomatoes, chopped
- ½ cup chopped red onion
- ¼ cup chopped walnuts, toasted

LIME DRESSING

- 3 tablespoons olive oil
- 1 tablespoon minced fresh parsley
- 1 tablespoon minced fresh cilantro
- 1 tablespoon sour cream
- 1 tablespoon lime juice
- 1 teaspoon yellow mustard
- ⅛ teaspoon salt
- ⅛ teaspoon pepper
  Dash sugar

Drizzle lemon juice over avocados. In a serving bowl, combine salad greens, tomatoes, onion, walnuts and avocados. Whisk together dressing ingredients; pour over salad. Toss to coat.

Note: To toast nuts, bake in a shallow pan in a 350° oven for 5-10 minutes or cook in a skillet over low heat until lightly browned, stirring occasionally.

Per 1 cup: 130 cal., 12g fat (2g sat. fat), 1mg chol., 57mg sod., 7g carb. (2g sugars, 3g fiber), 2g pro.

Diabetic Exchanges: 2 fat, 1 vegetable.

MY FAVORITE AVOCADO SALAD

Feta Salmon Salad

My son David always ordered the salmon sandwich at a local pub. While trying to replicate it, he came up with this salad. Now our entire family loves it.

—**SUSAN GRIFFITHS** MOUNT PLEASNT, SC

START TO FINISH: 25 MIN. • **MAKES:** 4 SERVINGS

- ¼ teaspoon salt
- ¼ teaspoon garlic powder
- ¼ teaspoon ground ginger
- ¼ teaspoon dried parsley flakes
- ¼ teaspoon pepper
- 4 salmon fillets (6 ounces each)
- 1 package (5 ounces) spring mix salad greens
- 1 large cucumber, chopped
- 1 large tomato, chopped
- ½ cup crumbled feta cheese
- ¼ cup red wine vinaigrette

1. In a small bowl, mix the first five ingredients; sprinkle over salmon.

2. Place salmon on an oiled grill rack, skin side down. Grill, covered, over medium heat or broil 4 in. from heat 10-12 minutes or until fish just begins to flake easily with a fork.

3. In a large bowl, toss salad greens with cucumber, tomato and cheese; divide among four plates. Top with salmon; drizzle with vinaigrette.

Per serving: 416 cal., 25g fat (6g sat. fat), 108mg chol., 636mg sod., 7g carb. (4g sugars, 2g fiber), 38g pro.

Diabetic Exchanges: 5 lean meat, 3 fat, 2 vegetable.

Dandelion Salad

This is one of my favorite salads, and it is so healthy for you! Guests will be surprised how wonderful it tastes.

—**FRANCES SHERIDAN GOULART** WESTON, CT

START TO FINISH: 10 MIN. • **MAKES:** 2 SERVINGS

- 1 tablespoon canola oil
- 1 teaspoon lemon juice
- 2 cups torn dandelion greens or arugula
- 2 green onions or 1 medium leek (white portion only), thinly sliced
- 2 hard-boiled large eggs, sliced
- ½ cup grapefruit or tangerine sections

1. In a small bowl, whisk oil and lemon juice. In a large bowl, combine dandelion greens and onions. Drizzle with dressing; toss to coat.

2. Arrange sliced eggs and grapefruit sections over greens.

Note: Verify that dandelion greens haven't been treated with lawn-care chemicals.

Per serving: 166 cal., 12g fat (3g sat. fat), 212mg chol., 67mg sod., 8g carb. (5g sugars, 1g fiber), 7g pro.

Diabetic Exchanges: 1½ fat, 1 medium-fat meat, 1 vegetable.

⑤INGREDIENTS
CB's Creamy Coleslaw

My classic slaw is great with spare ribs or pork roast and always hits the spot after a day of fishing.
—**EMILY TYRA** MILWAUKEE, WI

PREP: 15 MIN. + CHILLING
MAKES: 8 SERVINGS

- 1 cup mayonnaise
- ⅓ cup sugar
- ⅓ cup white vinegar
- ¼ teaspoon salt
- ¼ teaspoon pepper
- ¼ teaspoon paprika
- 1 pound cabbage, cored, cubed and chopped

Whisk together first six ingredients until smooth. Toss cabbage with mayonnaise mixture. Refrigerate, covered, for 2 hours.
Per ¾ cup: 227 cal., 20g fat (3g sat. fat), 2mg chol., 224mg sod., 12g carb. (10g sugars, 1g fiber), 1g pro.

EAT SMART FAST FIX
Honey-Pecan Kiwi Salad
(PICTURED ON P. 25)

This dish won second place in a summer salad recipe feature published in our local newspaper.
—**MARLA ARBET** KENOSHA, WI

START TO FINISH: 10 MIN.
MAKES: 6 SERVINGS

- 5 cups torn Boston lettuce
- 3 medium kiwifruit, peeled and sliced
- ¼ cup chopped pecans, toasted
- 2 tablespoons vanilla yogurt
- 2 tablespoons lemon juice
- 1 tablespoon olive oil
- 1 tablespoon honey

Combine lettuce, kiwi and pecans. In a separate bowl, mix yogurt, lemon juice, oil and honey until smooth. Pour over salad and toss; serve immediately.
Note: To toast nuts, bake in a shallow pan in a 350° oven for 5-10 minutes or cook in a skillet over low heat until lightly browned, stirring occasionally.
Per ¾ cup: 94 cal., 6g fat (1g sat. fat), 0 chol., 7mg sod., 11g carb. (7g sugars, 2g fiber), 2g pro.
Diabetic Exchanges: 1 vegetable, 1 fat, ½ starch.

KALE SLAW SPRING SALAD

EAT SMART FAST FIX
Kale Slaw Spring Salad

My parents and in-laws are retired and like to spend winters in Florida. This tangy spring salad brings the snowbirds back for our Easter celebration!
—**JENNIFER GILBERT** BRIGHTON, MI

START TO FINISH: 25 MIN.
MAKES: 10 SERVINGS

- 5 cups chopped fresh kale
- 3 cups torn romaine
- 1 package (14 ounces) coleslaw mix
- 1 medium fennel bulb, thinly sliced
- 1 cup chopped fresh broccoli
- ½ cup shredded red cabbage
- 1 cup crumbled feta cheese
- ¼ cup sesame seeds, toasted
- ⅓ cup extra virgin olive oil
- 3 tablespoons sesame oil
- 2 tablespoons honey
- 2 tablespoons cider vinegar
- 2 tablespoons lemon juice
- ⅓ cup pureed strawberries
  Sliced fresh strawberries

1. Combine kale and romaine. Add coleslaw mix, fennel, broccoli and red cabbage; sprinkle with feta cheese and sesame seeds. Toss to combine.
2. Stir together olive oil and sesame oil. Whisk in honey, vinegar and lemon juice. Add pureed strawberries. Whisk until combined. Dress salad just before serving; top with sliced strawberries.
Per 1⅓ cups: 192 cal., 15g fat (3g sat. fat), 6mg chol., 140mg sod., 12g carb. (7g sugars, 3g fiber), 4g pro.
Diabetic Exchanges: 3 fat, 1 starch.

Fresh Heirloom Tomato Salad

Our tomato salad is a summertime must. The standout dressing takes these tasty ingredients to a brand-new level.
—*TASTE OF HOME* TEST KITCHEN

START TO FINISH: 20 MIN.
MAKES: 12 SERVINGS

- 1 package (5 ounces) spring mix salad greens
- 3 tablespoons olive oil
- 2 tablespoons balsamic vinegar
- 1 teaspoon Dijon mustard
- 1 garlic clove, minced
- ½ teaspoon sugar
- ¼ teaspoon dried oregano
- 3 large heirloom tomatoes, sliced
- ½ cup fresh basil leaves
- ⅓ cup pine nuts, toasted
- 3 tablespoons chopped red onion
- 2 ounces fresh goat cheese, crumbled

Place salad greens in a large bowl. In a small bowl, whisk oil, vinegar, mustard, garlic, sugar and oregano until blended. Pour over salad greens; toss to coat. Transfer to a large platter. Arrange tomato slices over greens. Top with basil, pine nuts, onion and cheese. Serve immediately.

Note: To toast nuts, bake in a shallow pan in a 350° oven for 5-10 minutes or cook in a skillet over low heat until lightly browned, stirring occasionally.

Per serving: 74 cal., 6g fat (1g sat. fat), 3mg chol., 35mg sod., 4g carb. (2g sugars, 1g fiber), 2g pro.

Diabetic Exchanges: 1 vegetable, 1 fat.

FRESH HEIRLOOM
TOMATO SALAD

BRUSSELS SPROUTS
& QUINOA SALAD
Cameron Stell
Los Angeles, CA

Brussels Sprouts & Quinoa Salad

With Brussels sprouts for the green and cranberries for the red, I make a cheery Christmastime salad. Refreshing and versatile, it works with any kind of nut or dried fruit.
—**CAMERON STELL** LOS ANGELES, CA

PREP: 15 MIN.
COOK: 20 MIN. + CHILLING
MAKES: 6 SERVINGS

- 3 tablespoons olive oil, divided
- 3 shallots, minced
- 3 garlic cloves, minced
- 2 cups plus 2 tablespoons water, divided
- 1 cup quinoa, rinsed
- 1 cup fresh Brussels sprouts
- ½ cup dried cranberries
- ½ cup chopped walnuts, toasted
- 2 tablespoons chopped fresh parsley
- ¼ cup lemon juice
- ½ teaspoon salt
- ⅛ teaspoon pepper

1. In a small saucepan, heat 1 tablespoon olive oil over medium heat. Add shallots; cook and stir 3 minutes. Add garlic; cook 1 minute longer. Remove.

2. In same saucepan, bring 2 cups water to a boil. Add quinoa. Reduce heat; simmer, covered, until liquid is absorbed, 12-15 minutes. Remove from heat; fluff with a fork. Cool.

3. Meanwhile, microwave Brussels sprouts with remaining water, covered, on high until tender, 6-8 minutes, stirring every 2 minutes. Drain. When cool enough to handle, remove leaves from sprouts. Discard cores.

4. Combine cooled quinoa, Brussels sprouts leaves, cranberries, walnuts and parsley. Whisk together lemon juice, salt, pepper and remaining olive oil. Stir in shallots and garlic. Toss with quinoa mixture. Refrigerate, covered, 20 minutes.

Per ⅔ cup: 286 cal., 15g fat (2g sat. fat), 0 chol., 206mg sod., 34g carb. (8g sugars, 4g fiber), 7g pro.

Diabetic Exchanges: 2 starch, 2 fat.

SESAME BEEF & ASPARAGUS SALAD

Turkey Taco Salad

I discovered this dish while I was on a health kick. My husband and I love it now. When I served it at a family birthday party, everyone eagerly asked for the recipe.

—**ANGELA MATSON** KENNEWICK, WA

START TO FINISH: 30 MIN.
MAKES: 4 SERVINGS

- 12 ounces ground turkey
- 1 medium sweet red pepper, chopped
- 1 small sweet yellow pepper, chopped
- ⅓ cup chopped onion
- 3 garlic cloves, minced
- 1½ cups salsa
- ½ cup canned kidney beans, rinsed and drained
- 2 teaspoons chili powder
- 1 teaspoon ground cumin
- 8 cups torn romaine
- 2 tablespoons fresh cilantro leaves
  Optional toppings: chopped tomatoes, shredded cheddar cheese and crushed tortilla chips

1. In a large skillet, cook turkey, peppers, onion and garlic over medium heat 6-8 minutes or until turkey is no longer pink and vegetables are tender, breaking up turkey into crumbles; drain.

2. Stir in salsa, beans, chili powder and cumin; heat through. Divide romaine among four plates. Top with turkey mixture; sprinkle with cilantro and toppings of your choice.

Per 1 cup turkey mixture with 2 cups romaine without optional toppings: 275 cal., 13g fat (4g sat. fat), 58mg chol., 525mg sod., 21g carb. (7g sugars, 6g fiber), 18g pro.
Diabetic Exchanges: 2 medium-fat meat, 1½ starch.

TURKEY TACO SALAD

Sesame Beef & Asparagus Salad

Cooking is one of my favorite hobbies— especially when I get to experiment with fresh ingredients. This salad is wonderful at the start of asparagus season.

—**TAMARA STEEB** ISSAQUAH, WA

START TO FINISH: 30 MIN.
MAKES: 6 SERVINGS

- 1 beef top round steak (1 pound)
- 4 cups sliced fresh asparagus (cut in 2-inch pieces)
- 3 tablespoons reduced-sodium soy sauce
- 2 tablespoons sesame oil
- 1 tablespoon rice vinegar
- ½ teaspoon grated gingerroot
  Sesame seeds
  Lettuce leaves, shredded carrots, sliced radishes, fresh cilantro leaves and lime wedges, optional

1. Preheat broiler. Broil meat 3-4 in. from heat on each side to desired degree of doneness (medium-rare, 135°; medium, 140°; medium-well, 145°), 6-7 minutes per side. Cool the steak; cut into thin diagonal strips.

2. In a large saucepan, bring ½ in. water to a boil. Add asparagus; cook, uncovered, just until crisp-tender, 3-5 minutes. Drain and cool.

3. Combine beef and asparagus. Stir together the soy sauce, sesame oil, vinegar and ginger; pour over the beef and asparagus. Sprinkle with sesame seeds; toss lightly. If desired, serve mixture on lettuce leaves with shredded carrots, sliced radishes, cilantro and lime wedges.

Per 1 cup without optional ingredients: 160 cal., 7g fat (1g sat. fat), 42mg chol., 350mg sod., 5g carb. (2g sugars, 2g fiber), 19g pro.
Diabetic Exchanges: 2 lean meat, 1 vegetable, 1 fat.

Apricot Orange Vinaigrette

This sweet and tangy citrus dressing perks up any salad, lending appeal to even a simple blend of mixed greens.

—**DIANA RIOS** LYTLE, TX

START TO FINISH: 5 MIN.
MAKES: ABOUT ¾ CUP

- ¼ cup apricot preserves
- 2 tablespoons orange juice
- 2 tablespoons rice vinegar
- 2 tablespoons canola oil
- 1 tablespoon water
- ⅛ teaspoon salt
  Dash pepper

Place all ingredients in a jar with a tight-fitting lid; shake well. Cover and refrigerate until serving.
Per 2 tablespoons: 78 cal., 5g fat (0 sat. fat), 0 chol., 55mg sod., 10g carb. (6g sugars, 0 fiber), 0 pro.
Diabetic Exchanges: 1 fat, ½ starch.

Artichoke Tomato Salad

(PICTURED ON P. 24)

For a little zip, crumble feta over the top of this salad. Or add shredded rotisserie chicken for a beautiful main dish.

—**DEBORAH WILLIAMS** PEORIA, AZ

START TO FINISH: 20 MIN.
MAKES: 8 SERVINGS

- 5 large tomatoes (about 2 pounds), cut into wedges
- ¼ teaspoon salt
- ¼ teaspoon pepper
- 1 jar (7½ ounces) marinated quartered artichoke hearts, drained
- 1 can (2¼ ounces) sliced ripe olives, drained
- 2 tablespoons minced fresh parsley
- 2 tablespoons white wine vinegar
- 2 garlic cloves, minced

Arrange tomato wedges on a large platter; sprinkle with salt and pepper. In a small bowl, toss remaining ingredients; spoon over tomatoes.
Per ¾ cup: 74 cal., 5g fat (1g sat. fat), 0 chol., 241mg sod., 7g carb. (3g sugars, 2g fiber), 1g pro.
Diabetic Exchanges: 1 vegetable, 1 fat.

POTLUCK GERMAN POTATO SALAD

Potluck German Potato Salad

This is a big hit at church potlucks. One man says he shows up just so he can eat my potato salad!

—**KATHLEEN RABE** KIEL, WI

PREP: 20 MIN. • **COOK:** 25 MIN.
MAKES: 12 SERVINGS

- 3 pounds small Yukon Gold potatoes, unpeeled (about 10)
- 2 celery ribs, chopped
- 1 small onion, chopped
- 1 cup water
- ½ cup white vinegar
- ¾ cup sugar
- 1 tablespoon cornstarch
- ¼ teaspoon salt
- ¼ teaspoon pepper
- ½ pound bacon strips, cooked and crumbled

1. Place potatoes in a large saucepan; add water to cover. Bring to a boil. Reduce heat; simmer, uncovered, just until tender, 12-15 minutes. Add celery and onion; continue cooking until vegetables are tender, about 5 minutes longer. Drain; set aside.
2. Meanwhile, in a small saucepan, whisk together next six ingredients. Bring to a boil; cook until thickened, about 2 minutes.
3. When cool enough to handle, slice potatoes; return to large saucepan with celery and onions. Add vinegar mixture, tossing to combine. Add bacon. Simmer mixture until heated through, 10-12 minutes. Serve warm.
Per ⅔ cup: 194 cal., 3g fat (1g sat. fat), 7mg chol., 181mg sod., 39g carb. (15g sugars, 2g fiber), 5g pro.

**KELLIE FOGLIO'S
MARKET BASKET SOUP**
PAGE 46

Soups & Sandwiches

It's a classic combo: **piping hot soup** and a piled-high **sandwich ready for dunking.** With the satisfying, nutritious, season-spanning recipes in this chapter, **lunchtime** just got a whole lot better.

**LISA'S ALL-DAY
SUGAR & SALT PORK ROAST
FROM LISA ALLEN**
PAGE 41

**CINDY BEBERMAN'S
HAZELNUT ASPARAGUS SOUP**
PAGE 38

**THE ULTIMATE
GRILLED CHEESE
FROM KATHY NORRIS**
PAGE 49

Steak & Vegetable Soup

This weeknight steak soup packs rich flavor into a light broth. My family loves the blend of southwestern flavors.

—REBECCA RIDPATH CEDAR PARK, TX

PREP: 10 MIN. • **COOK:** 30 MIN.
MAKES: 8 SERVINGS

- 1 tablespoon canola oil
- 1 beef top sirloin steak (about 1 pound), cut into 1-inch pieces
- 1 teaspoon dried basil
- ½ teaspoon salt
- ¼ teaspoon pepper
- 2 garlic cloves, minced
- 1 package (16 ounces) frozen vegetables for stew, thawed
- 1 jar (16 ounces) picante sauce
- 2 cans (14½ ounces each) beef broth
- 1 can (15½ ounces) great northern beans, rinsed and drained
- 1 cup fresh baby spinach

1. In a Dutch oven, heat oil over medium-high heat. Add steak, basil, salt and pepper. Stir-fry until meat is no longer pink, 4-5 minutes; drain. Add garlic; cook 1 minute more.
2. Stir in vegetables and picante sauce. Add broth; bring to a boil. Reduce heat; simmer, uncovered, until vegetables are tender, 15-20 minutes. Stir in beans and heat through. Add the spinach; cook until just starting to wilt, 1-2 minutes.

Per 1¼ cups: 191 cal., 5g fat (1g sat. fat), 23mg chol., 1144mg sod., 19g carb. (3g sugars, 3g fiber), 17g pro.

STEAK & VEGETABLE SOUP

Hazelnut Asparagus Soup
(PICTURED ON P. 37)

My heart is happy when bundles of tender local asparagus start to appear at my grocery store in spring. No one would ever guess this restaurant-quality vegetarian soup can be prepared in around 30 minutes.

—CINDY BEBERMAN ORLAND PARK, IL

PREP: 20 MIN. • **COOK:** 15 MIN.
MAKES: 4 SERVINGS (3 CUPS)

- 1 tablespoon olive oil
- ½ cup chopped sweet onion
- 3 garlic cloves, sliced
  Dash crushed red pepper flakes
- 2½ cups cut fresh asparagus (about 1½ pounds), trimmed
- 2 cups vegetable broth
- ⅓ cup whole hazelnuts, toasted
- 2 tablespoons chopped fresh basil
- 2 tablespoons lemon juice
- ½ cup unsweetened almond milk
- 2 teaspoons gluten-free reduced-sodium tamari soy sauce
- ¼ teaspoon salt
  Shaved asparagus, optional

1. In a large saucepan, heat oil over medium heat. Add onion, garlic and pepper flakes; cook and stir until the onion is softened, 4-5 minutes. Add asparagus and broth; bring to a boil. Reduce heat; simmer, covered, until asparagus is tender, 6-8 minutes. Remove from heat; cool slightly.
2. Place nuts, basil and lemon juice in a blender. Add asparagus mixture. Process until smooth and creamy. Return to saucepan. Stir in almond milk, tamari soy sauce and salt. Heat through, taking care not to boil soup. If desired, top with shaved asparagus.

Notes: To toast nuts, bake in a shallow pan in a 350° oven for 5-10 minutes or cook in a skillet over low heat until lightly browned, stirring occasionally. Reduced-sodium soy sauce may be used in place of the tamari soy sauce.

Per ¾ cup: 164 cal., 13g fat (1g sat. fat), 0 chol., 623mg sod., 11g carb. (4g sugars, 4g fiber), 5g pro.
Diabetic Exchanges: 2½ fat, ½ starch.

Stuffed Pepper Soup

Some of us cooks at the restaurant where I work were talking about stuffed peppers. We decided to stir up similar ingredients for a soup. Customer response was overwhelming!

—KRISTA MUDDIMAN MEADVILLE, PA

PREP: 15 MIN. • **COOK:** 45 MIN.
MAKES: 8 SERVINGS (2 QUARTS)

- 2 pounds ground beef
- 6 cups water
- 1 can (28 ounces) tomato sauce
- 1 can (28 ounces) diced tomatoes, undrained
- 2 cups chopped green peppers
- ¼ cup packed brown sugar
- 2 teaspoons salt
- 2 teaspoons beef bouillon granules
- 1 teaspoon pepper
- 2 cups cooked long grain rice
  Chopped fresh parsley, optional

1. In a Dutch oven over medium heat, cook and stir beef until no longer pink; drain. Stir in next eight ingredients; bring to a boil. Reduce heat; simmer, uncovered, until peppers are tender, about 30 minutes.
2. Add cooked rice and simmer, uncovered, 10 minutes longer. If desired, sprinkle with chopped fresh parsley.
Per 1 cup: 337 cal., 14g fat (5g sat. fat), 70mg chol., 1466mg sod., 30g carb. (13g sugars, 4g fiber), 24g pro.

STUFFED PEPPER SOUP

TEX-MEX SHREDDED BEEF SANDWICHES

Tex-Mex Shredded Beef Sandwiches

You only need a few ingredients to make my delicious shredded beef. While the meat simmers to tender perfection, you will have time to do other things.

—KATHY WHITE HENDERSON, NV

PREP: 5 MIN. • **COOK:** 8 HOURS
MAKES: 8 SERVINGS

- 1 boneless beef chuck roast (3 pounds)
- 1 envelope chili seasoning
- ½ cup barbecue sauce
- 8 onion rolls, split
- 8 slices cheddar cheese

1. Cut beef roast in half; place in a 3-qt. slow cooker. Sprinkle with chili seasoning and pour barbecue sauce over the top. Cover and cook on low for 8-10 hours or until the meat is tender.
2. Remove roast; cool slightly. Shred meat with two forks. Skim fat from cooking juices. Return meat to slow cooker; heat through.
3. Using a slotted spoon, place ½ cup of meat mixture on each roll bottom; top sandwiches with cheese. Replace bun tops.
Per 1 sandwich: 573 cal., 29g fat (13g sat. fat), 140mg chol., 955mg sod., 29g carb. (6g sugars, 2g fiber), 47g pro.

Taco Avocado Wraps

I came up with this sandwich one summer evening when we wanted a light supper and didn't want to turn on the oven. You can serve it for lunch, as a snack or paired with refried beans for dinner.

—RENEE RUTHERFORD ANDOVER, MN

START TO FINISH: 30 MIN.
MAKES: 4 SERVINGS

- 1 package (8 ounces) cream cheese, softened
- ½ cup sour cream
- 1 can (4 ounces) chopped green chilies, drained
- 1 tablespoon taco seasoning
- 4 flour tortillas (10 inches), room temperature
- 2 medium ripe avocados, peeled and sliced
- 2 plum tomatoes, thinly sliced
- 5 green onions, sliced
- 1 can (4 ounces) sliced ripe olives, drained

In a small bowl, combine the cream cheese, sour cream, chilies and taco seasoning. Spread about ½ cup over each tortilla. Top with the avocados, tomatoes, onions and olives; roll up.
Per 1 wrap: 683 cal., 47g fat (20g sat. fat), 82mg chol., 1158mg sod., 47g carb. (5g sugars, 12g fiber), 14g pro.

CREAMY CARROT &
TOMATO SOUP

Creamy Carrot & Tomato Soup

I often double this recipe and freeze half, so we can enjoy a taste of summer during the cold winter months. If I do freeze it, I omit the yogurt and stir it in after the soup's reheated.
—SUE GRONHOLZ BEAVER DAM, WI

PREP: 15 MIN. • **COOK:** 25 MIN. • **MAKES:** 4 SERVINGS

- 1 tablespoon olive oil
- 1 medium onion, chopped
- 3 garlic cloves, minced
- 3 cups peeled and shredded carrots (4 to 5 medium carrots)
- 2 cups reduced-sodium chicken broth
- ⅓ cup minced fresh basil
- 3 tablespoons minced fresh parsley
- 3 cups reduced-sodium tomato juice
- 2 tablespoons butter
- 2 tablespoons all-purpose flour
- ¼ teaspoon salt
- ¼ teaspoon pepper
- ½ cup plain Greek yogurt
  Additional plain Greek yogurt, optional
  Additional torn fresh basil, optional

1. In a large saucepan, heat oil over medium heat. Add onion; cook and stir until tender. Add garlic; cook 1 minute longer. Stir in carrots, chicken broth, basil and parsley. Bring to a boil. Reduce heat; simmer, covered, until carrots are tender, 10-12 minutes. Stir in tomato juice. Pulse mixture in a blender until smooth.

2. In another large saucepan, melt butter over medium heat. Stir in flour until smooth; gradually whisk in tomato mixture, salt and pepper.

3. Bring to a boil, stirring constantly; cook and stir until slightly thickened, 5-7 minutes. Remove from heat; stir in yogurt until blended. If desired, top with additional yogurt and basil.

To freeze: Before stirring in yogurt, cool soup; freeze in freezer containers. To use, partially thaw in refrigerator overnight. Heat through in a large saucepan over medium-low heat, stirring occasionally and adding a little broth or water if necessary. Stir in ½ cup Greek yogurt and, if desired, add toppings before serving.

Per 1¼ cups: 225 cal., 12g fat (6g sat. fat), 23mg chol., 683mg sod., 25g carb. (14g sugars, 5g fiber), 5g pro.

✳

TEST KITCHEN TIP
By using reduced-sodium broth and tomato juice in this soup, you save a whopping 677 milligrams of sodium per serving—cutting the salt content nearly in half.

LISA'S ALL-DAY
SUGAR & SALT
PORK ROAST

Lisa's All-Day Sugar & Salt Pork Roast

My family loves this tender, juicy roast, so we eat it a lot. The salty crust is so delicious mixed into the pulled pork.
—LISA ALLEN JOPPA, AL

PREP: 15 MIN. + MARINATING • **BAKE:** 6¼ HOURS
MAKES: 12 SERVINGS

- 1 cup plus 1 tablespoon sea salt, divided
- 1 cup granulated sugar
- 1 bone-in pork shoulder butt roast (6 to 8 pounds)
- ¼ cup barbecue seasoning
- ½ teaspoon pepper
- ½ cup packed brown sugar
- 12 hamburger buns or kaiser rolls, split

1. Combine 1 cup sea salt and granulated sugar; rub onto all sides of roast. Place in a shallow dish; refrigerate, covered, overnight.

2. Preheat oven to 300°. Using a kitchen knife, scrape salt and sugar coating from roast; discard any accumulated juices. Transfer pork to a large shallow roasting pan. Rub with barbecue seasoning; sprinkle with pepper. Roast until tender, 6-8 hours.

3. Increase oven temperature to 500°. Combine brown sugar and 1 Tbsp. sea salt; sprinkle over cooked pork. Return pork to the oven until a crisp crust forms, 10-15 minutes. Remove; when cool enough to handle, shred meat with two forks. Serve warm on buns or rolls.

Per 1 sandwich: 534 cal., 24g fat (9g sat. fat), 135mg chol., 2240mg sod., 33g carb. (14g sugars, 1g fiber), 43g pro.

Chicken Wild Rice Soup

I'm originally from Minnesota, where wild rice is popular in recipes. This soup has been part of our Christmas Eve menu for years. To save time, I cook the chicken and rice and cut up the veggies the day before.

—**VIRGINIA MONTMARQUET** RIVERSIDE, CA

PREP: 10 MIN. • **COOK:** 40 MIN.
MAKES: 14 SERVINGS (3½ QUARTS)

- 2 quarts chicken broth
- ½ pound fresh mushrooms, chopped
- 1 cup finely chopped celery
- 1 cup shredded carrots
- ½ cup finely chopped onion
- 1 teaspoon chicken bouillon granules
- 1 teaspoon dried parsley flakes
- ¼ teaspoon garlic powder
- ¼ teaspoon dried thyme
- ¼ cup butter, cubed
- ¼ cup all-purpose flour
- 1 can (10¾ ounces) condensed cream of mushroom soup, undiluted
- ½ cup dry white wine or additional chicken broth
- 3 cups cooked wild rice
- 2 cups cubed cooked chicken

1. In a large saucepan, bring the first nine ingredients to a boil. Reduce heat; cover and simmer for 30 minutes.
2. In a Dutch oven, melt butter; stir in flour until smooth. Gradually whisk in broth mixture. Bring to a boil; cook and stir 2 minutes or until thickened. Whisk in soup and wine. Add rice and chicken; heat through.
Per 1 cup: 154 cal., 6g fat (3g sat. fat), 27mg chol., 807mg sod., 14g carb. (2g sugars, 2g fiber), 10g pro.

CHICKEN WILD RICE SOUP

HEALTHY CHICKEN DUMPLING SOUP

Healthy Chicken Dumpling Soup

My husband was fooled by this low-fat recipe and I'm sure your family will be, too! A savory broth, hearty chunks of chicken and rich dumplings provide plenty of comforting flavor.

—**BRENDA WHITE** MORRISON, IL

PREP: 15 MIN. • **COOK:** 50 MIN.
MAKES: 4 SERVINGS

- 1 pound boneless skinless chicken breasts, cut into 1½-inch cubes
- 3 cans (14½ ounces each) reduced-sodium chicken broth
- 3 cups water
- 4 medium carrots, chopped
- 1 medium onion, chopped
- 1 celery rib, chopped
- 1 teaspoon minced fresh parsley
- ½ teaspoon salt
- ¼ teaspoon garlic powder
- ¼ teaspoon poultry seasoning
- ¼ teaspoon pepper

DUMPLINGS
- 3 large egg whites
- ½ cup 1% cottage cheese
- 2 tablespoons water
- ¼ teaspoon salt
- 1 cup all-purpose flour

1. In a large nonstick skillet coated with cooking spray, cook chicken until no longer pink. Add the broth, water, vegetables and seasonings. Bring to a boil. Reduce heat; simmer, uncovered, for 30 minutes or until vegetables are tender.
2. Meanwhile, for dumplings, in a large bowl, beat the egg whites and cottage cheese until blended. Add water and salt. Stir in the flour and mix well.
3. Bring soup to a boil. Drop the dumplings by tablespoonfuls into the boiling soup. Reduce heat; cover and simmer for 15 minutes or until a toothpick inserted in dumplings comes out clean (do not lift cover while simmering).
Per 1½ cups: 363 cal., 4g fat (2g sat. fat), 73mg chol., 900mg sod., 39g carb. (0 sugars, 4g fiber), 42g pro.

Sweet Potato & Black Bean Chili

My whole family enjoys this vegetarian chili, but my daughter especially loves it. I like to make it because it's so easy and very flavorful.

—**JOY PENDLEY** ORTONVILLE, MI

PREP: 25 MIN. • **COOK:** 35 MIN.
MAKES: 8 SERVINGS (2 QUARTS)

- 3 large sweet potatoes, peeled and cut into ½-inch cubes
- 1 large onion, chopped
- 1 tablespoon olive oil
- 2 tablespoons chili powder
- 3 garlic cloves, minced
- 1 teaspoon ground cumin
- ¼ teaspoon cayenne pepper
- 2 cans (15 ounces each) black beans, rinsed and drained
- 1 can (28 ounces) diced tomatoes, undrained
- ¼ cup brewed coffee
- 2 tablespoons honey
- ½ teaspoon salt
- ¼ teaspoon pepper
- ½ cup shredded reduced-fat Monterey Jack cheese or reduced-fat Mexican cheese blend

1. In a nonstick Dutch oven coated with cooking spray, saute sweet potatoes and onion in oil until crisp-tender. Add the chili powder, garlic, cumin and cayenne; cook 1 minute longer. Stir in the beans, tomatoes, coffee, honey, salt and pepper.

2. Bring chili to a boil. Reduce heat; cover and simmer for 30-35 minutes or until sweet potatoes are tender. Sprinkle with cheese.

Per 1 cup: 252 cal., 4g fat (1g sat. fat), 5mg chol., 554mg sod., 47g carb. (17g sugars, 9g fiber), 10g pro.
Diabetic Exchanges: 3 starch, ½ fat.

✳
TEST KITCHEN TIP
It's important to drain and rinse canned beans because the thick, cloudy liquid inside often contains excess sodium and starch. Draining and rinsing can improve the flavor, texture and nutritional content of a dish.

GRILLED HAM BURGERS
Susan Bickta
Kutztown, PA

Grilled Ham Burgers

My family loves my ham loaf, so I decided to make the ham loaf mixture into patties and grill them—and it was an instant hit. Adding the arugula gives these burgers a peppery bite, and honey mustard dressing adds just the right sweet and sour flavor.

—**SUSAN BICKTA** KUTZTOWN, PA

PREP: 20 MIN. + CHILLING • **GRILL:** 10 MIN.
MAKES: 8 SERVINGS

- 1½ pounds fully cooked boneless ham
- ¾ pound ground pork
- 2 large eggs
- ⅔ cup graham cracker crumbs
- ⅓ cup packed brown sugar
- ⅓ cup unsweetened crushed pineapple plus 3 tablespoons juice
- 1 tablespoon spicy brown mustard
- ¼ teaspoon ground cloves
- 8 slices Swiss cheese (1 ounce each)
- 8 kaiser rolls, split
- 2 large tomatoes, cut in sixteen ¼-inch slices
- ½ cup honey mustard salad dressing
- 1½ cups fresh baby arugula, packed
  Additional honey mustard salad dressing, optional

1. Pulse ham in food processor until finely ground. Combine with pork, eggs, cracker crumbs, brown sugar, pineapple and juice, mustard and cloves. Mix lightly but thoroughly. Shape into eight patties. Using fingertips, make a shallow indentation in center of each patty so it remains flat while grilling. Refrigerate 1 hour.

2. Grill burgers, covered, on a greased rack over medium-high direct heat for 5-6 minutes; turn and grill 3-4 minutes longer. Add a slice of cheese to each burger; grill, covered, until cheese melts, 1-2 minutes more. Remove from heat when a thermometer reads 160°.

3. Place a burger on bottom half of each roll; add two tomato slices. Drizzle with 1 tablespoon honey mustard dressing. Divide arugula evenly among rolls; top each burger with a few sprigs. Replace top half of roll. If desired, serve with additional honey mustard dressing.

Per 1 burger: 632 cal., 28g fat (9g sat. fat), 149mg chol., 1430mg sod., 55g carb. (18g sugars, 2g fiber), 40g pro.

SOUPS & SANDWICHES

Homemade Chicken Tortilla Soup

This colorful soup is as good as (if not better than) any I've had in a restaurant. It also freezes well; just save the chips and cheese until ready to serve.

—**LAURA BLACK JOHNSON** LARGO, FL

START TO FINISH: 30 MIN.
MAKES: 8 SERVINGS

- 2 tablespoons olive oil
- 1 large onion, chopped
- 1 can (4 ounces) chopped green chilies
- 2 garlic cloves, minced
- 1 jalapeno pepper, seeded and chopped
- 1 teaspoon ground cumin
- 1 can (15 ounces) tomato sauce
- 1 can (14½ ounces) diced tomatoes with garlic and onion, undrained
- 5 cups reduced-sodium chicken broth
- 1 rotisserie chicken, shredded, skin removed
- ¼ cup minced fresh cilantro
- 2 teaspoons lime juice
- ¼ teaspoon salt
- ¼ teaspoon pepper

Crushed tortilla chips
Shredded Monterey Jack or cheddar cheese

1. In a Dutch oven, heat oil over medium heat; saute onion until tender, about 5 minutes. Add chilies, garlic, jalapeno and cumin; cook 1 minute. Stir in tomato sauce, tomatoes and broth. Bring to a boil; reduce heat. Stir in chicken.
2. Simmer, uncovered, 10 minutes. Add cilantro, lime juice, salt and pepper. Top each serving with chips and cheese.
To freeze: Before adding chips and cheese, cool soup; freeze in freezer containers. To use, partially thaw in refrigerator overnight. Heat through in a large saucepan over medium-low heat, stirring occasionally and adding a little broth or water if necessary. Add chips and cheese before serving.
Note: Wear disposable gloves when cutting hot peppers; the oils can burn skin. Avoid touching your face.
Per 1¼ cups: 200 cal., 8g fat (2g sat. fat), 55mg chol., 941mg sod., 9g carb. (4g sugars, 2g fiber), 22g pro.

CUCUMBER-EGG SALAD SANDWICHES

Cucumber-Egg Salad Sandwiches

Cool, crisp cucumber adds a refreshing crunch to these tasty egg sandwiches. I sometimes substitute rye bread for sourdough and add chopped celery to the salad mixture.

—**KELLY McCUNE** WESTERVILLE, OH

START TO FINISH: 15 MIN.
MAKES: 6 SERVINGS

- ½ cup chopped red onion
- ½ cup mayonnaise
- ¼ cup sour cream
- 2 tablespoons Dijon mustard
- ½ teaspoon pepper
- ¼ teaspoon salt
- 8 hard-boiled large eggs, chopped
- 1 large cucumber, sliced
- 1 tablespoon dill weed
- 12 slices sourdough bread, toasted

1. In a small bowl, combine the first six ingredients. Add eggs; stir gently to combine.
2. In another bowl, toss cucumber and dill. Spread egg salad over six slices of toast; top with cucumbers and the remaining toast.
Per 1 sandwich: 458 cal., 25g fat (6g sat. fat), 296mg chol., 823mg sod., 41g carb. (4g sugars, 2g fiber), 17g pro.

HOMEMADE CHICKEN TORTILLA SOUP

Rich French Onion Soup

When entertaining guests, I bring out this savory soup while we're waiting for the main course. It's simple to make—just saute the onions early in the day and let the soup simmer until dinnertime. In winter, big bowls of it make a warming supper with a salad and biscuits.

—**LINDA ADOLPH** EDMONTON, AB

PREP: 20 MIN. • **COOK:** 5 HOURS
MAKES: 10 SERVINGS

- 6 large onions, chopped
- ½ cup butter
- 6 cans (10½ ounces each) condensed beef broth, undiluted
- 1½ teaspoons Worcestershire sauce
- 3 bay leaves
- 10 slices French bread, toasted
  Shredded Parmesan and shredded part-skim mozzarella cheese, optional

1. In a large skillet, saute onions in butter until crisp-tender. Transfer to a 5-qt. slow cooker. Add the broth, Worcestershire sauce and bay leaves.
2. Cover and cook on low for 5-7 hours or until the onions are tender. Discard bay leaves.
3. Ladle soup into ovenproof bowls. Top each with a slice of toast; sprinkle with desired amount of cheese, if using. Place bowls on a baking sheet. Broil soup for 2-3 minutes or until cheese is lightly golden brown.
Per serving without cheese: 296 cal., 11g fat (6g sat. fat), 25mg chol., 722mg sod., 41g carb. (6g sugars, 4g fiber), 8g pro.

✳️
TEST KITCHEN TIP
Soups can be brightened up before serving by adding a little citrus juice or vinegar. A teaspoon or two of cider vinegar tastes great in this onion soup.

BROCCOLI BEER
CHEESE SOUP

FREEZE IT
Broccoli Beer Cheese Soup

This recipe tastes just as wonderful without the beer, making a great broccoli cheese soup. I always prepare extras and pop individual servings into the freezer for quick cozy meals.

—**LORI LEE** BROOKSVILLE, FL

PREP: 20 MIN. • **COOK:** 30 MIN.
MAKES: 10 SERVINGS (2½ QUARTS)

- 3 tablespoons butter
- 5 celery ribs, finely chopped
- 3 medium carrots, finely chopped
- 1 small onion, finely chopped
- 4 cups fresh broccoli florets, chopped
- ¼ cup chopped sweet red pepper
- 4 cans (14½ ounces each) chicken broth
- ½ teaspoon pepper
- ½ cup all-purpose flour
- ½ cup water
- 3 cups shredded cheddar cheese
- 1 package (8 ounces) cream cheese, cubed
- 1 bottle (12 ounces) beer or nonalcoholic beer

Optional toppings: crumbled cooked bacon, chopped green onions, sour cream, salad croutons and additional shredded cheddar cheese

1. In a Dutch oven, melt butter over medium-high heat. Add celery, carrots and onion; saute until crisp-tender. Add broccoli, red pepper, broth and pepper. Combine flour and water until smooth; gradually stir into pan. Bring to a boil. Reduce the heat and simmer, uncovered, until soup is thickened and vegetables are tender, 25-30 minutes.
2. Stir in cheeses and beer until cheeses are melted (do not boil). Serve with toppings as desired.
To freeze: Before adding toppings, cool soup; transfer to freezer containers. Freeze for up to 3 months. To use, partially thaw in refrigerator overnight; heat through in a large saucepan over medium-low heat, stirring occasionally (do not boil). Add toppings as desired.
Per 1 cup: 316 cal., 23g fat (13g sat. fat), 69mg chol., 1068mg sod., 13g carb. (5g sugars, 2g fiber), 12g pro.

RED LENTIL SOUP MIX

Red Lentil Soup Mix

Give your friends the gift of good health. Red lentils are a protein powerhouse and are loaded with folate, iron and fiber. Oh, and this soup tastes amazing, too.
—**TASTE OF HOME** TEST KITCHEN

PREP: 25 MIN. • **COOK:** 25 MIN. • **MAKES:** 4 CUPS PER BATCH

- ¼ cup dried minced onion
- 2 tablespoons dried parsley flakes
- 2 teaspoons ground allspice
- 2 teaspoons ground cumin
- 2 teaspoons ground turmeric
- 1½ teaspoons salt
- 1 teaspoon garlic powder
- 1 teaspoon ground cardamom
- 1 teaspoon ground cinnamon
- 1 teaspoon pepper
- ½ teaspoon ground cloves
- 2 packages (1 pound each) dried red lentils

ADDITIONAL INGREDIENTS (FOR EACH BATCH)
- 1 medium carrot, finely chopped
- 1 celery rib, finely chopped
- 1 tablespoon olive oil
- 2 cans (14½ ounces each) vegetable broth

Combine the first 11 ingredients. Place 1⅓ cups lentils in each of four 12-oz. jelly jars. Evenly divide onion mixture among four small cellophane bags; place sealed bags inside of jars, on top of lentils. Store in a cool, dry place for up to 6 months. Makes 4 batches.

To prepare one batch: Rinse lentils and drain. In a large saucepan, saute carrot and celery in oil until tender. Add lentils, onion mixture and broth. Bring to a boil. Reduce heat; simmer, covered, until lentils are tender, 10-15 minutes.

Per 1 cup: 257 cal., 4g fat (1g sat. fat), 0 chol., 1067mg sod., 42g carb. (4g sugars, 7g fiber), 14g pro.

EAT SMART

Market Basket Soup

(PICTURED ON P. 36)

I use kohlrabi in this soothing veggie soup. It's got a mellow broccoli-cabbage flavor and can be served raw, but I like it in a warm bowl of wholesome soup.
—**KELLIE FOGLIO** SALEM, WI

PREP: 25 MIN. • **COOK:** 40 MIN. • **MAKES:** 11 SERVINGS (2¾ QUARTS)

- 1 tablespoon olive oil
- 1 large kohlrabi bulb, peeled and chopped
- 4 celery ribs, chopped
- 2 medium onions, chopped
- 2 medium carrots, chopped
- 3 garlic cloves, minced
- 1 teaspoon salt
- 1 teaspoon coarsely ground pepper
- 6 cups vegetable stock or water
- 2 cans (15½ ounces each) great northern beans, rinsed and drained
- 2 bay leaves
- 2 medium tomatoes, chopped
- 2 tablespoons minced fresh parsley
- 2 tablespoons minced fresh tarragon
- 2 tablespoons minced fresh thyme

1. In a stockpot, heat oil over medium-high heat. Stir in kohlrabi, celery, onions and carrots; cook 5 minutes or until onions are softened. Add garlic, salt and pepper; cook and stir 5 minutes.

2. Stir in stock, beans and bay leaves. Bring to a boil over medium-high heat. Reduce heat; simmer, covered, until vegetables are tender, 20-25 minutes. Add remaining ingredients; simmer 5 minutes more. Discard bay leaves.

Per 1 cup: 110 cal., 2g fat (0 sat. fat), 0 chol., 664mg sod., 19g carb. (3g sugars, 6g fiber), 5g pro.

Diabetic Exchanges: 1 starch, 1 vegetable.

☆ ☆ ☆ ☆ ☆ **READER REVIEW**

"This was very filling and fresh-tasting. My grocery store didn't have kohlrabi so I used a turnip. I also made a half batch and still had leftovers since this makes a very large batch to start with."
CURLYLIS85 TASTEOFHOME.COM

Creamy Cauliflower Pakora Soup

My husband and I often crave pakoras, deep-fried fritters from India. I wanted to get the same flavors but use a healthier cooking technique, so I made soup using all the classic spices and our favorite veggie, cauliflower!

—MELODY JOHNSON PULASKI, WI

PREP: 20 MIN. • **COOK:** 20 MIN. • **MAKES:** 8 SERVINGS (3 QUARTS)

- 1 large head cauliflower, cut into small florets
- 5 medium potatoes, peeled and diced
- 1 large onion, diced
- 4 medium carrots, peeled and diced
- 2 celery ribs, diced
- 1 carton (32 ounces) vegetable stock
- 1 teaspoon garam masala
- 1 teaspoon garlic powder
- 1 teaspoon ground coriander
- 1 teaspoon ground turmeric
- 1 teaspoon ground cumin
- 1 teaspoon pepper
- 1 teaspoon salt
- ½ teaspoon crushed red pepper flakes
  Water or additional vegetable stock
  Fresh cilantro leaves
  Lime wedges, optional

In a Dutch oven over medium-high heat, bring the first 14 ingredients to a boil. Cook and stir until vegetables are tender, about 20 minutes. Remove from heat; cool slightly. Process in batches in a blender or food processor until smooth. Adjust consistency as desired with water (or additional stock). Sprinkle with fresh cilantro. If desired, serve with lime wedges.

To freeze: Before adding cilantro, freeze cooled soup in freezer containers. To use, partially thaw in refrigerator overnight. Heat through in a saucepan, stirring occasionally and adding a little water or stock if necessary. Sprinkle with cilantro. If desired, serve with lime wedges.

Note: Look for garam masala in the spice aisle.

Per 1½ cups: 135 cal., 1g fat (0 sat. fat), 0 chol., 645mg sod., 30g carb. (6g sugars, 5g fiber), 4g pro.

Diabetic Exchanges: 1½ starch, 1 vegetable.

FAST FIX
Ground Beef Gyros

If your family likes gyros as much as mine, they'll love this easy version that's made with ground beef instead of lamb. A cucumber yogurt sauce adds an authentic finishing touch.

—RUTH STAHL SHEPHERD, MT

START TO FINISH: 30 MIN. • **MAKES:** 4 SERVINGS

- 1 cup (8 ounces) plain yogurt
- ⅓ cup chopped seeded cucumber
- 2 tablespoons finely chopped onion
- 1 garlic clove, minced
- 1 teaspoon sugar

GYROS

- 1½ teaspoons dried oregano
- 1 teaspoon garlic powder
- 1 teaspoon onion powder
- 1 teaspoon salt, optional
- ¾ teaspoon pepper
- 1 pound ground beef
- 4 pita pocket halves
- 3 cups shredded lettuce
- 1 large tomato, chopped
- 1 small onion, sliced

1. In a small bowl, combine the first five ingredients. Chill. In a large bowl, combine seasonings (including salt, if desired); crumble beef over mixture and mix well. Shape into four patties.

2. Grill, covered, over medium heat or broil 4 in. from heat for 6-7 minutes on each side or until a thermometer reads 160°. Cut patties into thin slices; stuff into pita halves. Add lettuce, tomato and onion. Serve with the yogurt sauce.

Per 1 gyro without salt: 357 cal., 16g fat (6g sat. fat), 78mg chol., 257mg sod., 27g carb. (7g sugars, 3g fiber), 26g pro.

CREAMY CAULIFLOWER PAKORA SOUP

**GRILLED WATERMELON
GAZPACHO**
George Levinthal
Goleta, CA

Grilled Watermelon Gazpacho

Here's the perfect starter for a summer dinner. It's cool and tangy with a whole lot of great grilled flavor. If you like a bit more heat, simply add more jalapenos.

—**GEORGE LEVINTHAL** GOLETA, CA

PREP: 10 MIN. + CHILLING
GRILL: 10 MIN. + COOLING
MAKES: 4 SERVINGS

- 2 tablespoons olive oil, divided
- ¼ seedless watermelon, cut into three 1½-in.-thick slices
- 1 large beefsteak tomato, halved
- ½ English cucumber, peeled and halved lengthwise
- 1 jalapeno pepper, seeded and halved lengthwise
- ¼ cup plus 2 tablespoons diced red onion, divided
- 2 tablespoons sherry vinegar
- 1 tablespoon lime juice
- ½ teaspoon kosher or sea salt
- ¼ teaspoon pepper
- 1 small ripe avocado, peeled, pitted and diced

1. Brush 1 tablespoon olive oil over watermelon slices, tomato, cucumber and jalapeno; grill, covered, on a greased grill rack over medium-high direct heat until seared, 5-6 minutes on each side. Remove from heat, reserving one watermelon slice.

2. When cool enough to handle, remove rind from the remaining watermelon slices; cut flesh into chunks. Remove skin and seeds from tomato and jalapeno; chop. Coarsely chop cucumber. Combine grilled vegetables; add ¼ cup onion, vinegar, lime juice and seasonings. Process in batches in a blender until smooth, adding remaining olive oil during final minute. If desired, strain through a fine-mesh strainer; adjust seasonings as needed. Refrigerate soup, covered, until chilled.

3. To serve, pour gazpacho into bowls or glasses. Top with diced avocado and remaining onion. Cut the reserved watermelon slice into wedges and serve with soup. Or, cut slits in narrow end of wedges; slip wedges over rims of bowls or glasses.

Per 1 cup: 181 cal., 12g fat (2g sat. fat), 0 chol., 248mg sod., 19g carb. (13g sugars, 4g fiber), 2g pro.
Diabetic Exchanges: 2 fat, 1 vegetable, 1 fruit.

Cranberry Chicken Wraps

Loaded with cranberries, chicken, apples and spinach, these nutritious wraps are fast and flavorful.

—**SARAH WHITE** SALT LAKE CITY, UT

START TO FINISH: 20 MIN.
MAKES: 2 SERVINGS

- 1 cup shredded cooked chicken breast
- 1 cup chopped apple
- ¼ cup plus 2 teaspoons fat-free Miracle Whip, divided
- ¼ cup dried cranberries
- 3 tablespoons crumbled feta cheese
- ¼ teaspoon minced fresh rosemary or ⅛ teaspoon dried rosemary, crushed
- ⅛ teaspoon pepper
- 2 whole wheat tortillas (8 inches), room temperature
- ½ cup fresh baby spinach

In a small bowl, combine the chicken, chopped apple, ¼ cup Miracle Whip, cranberries, feta cheese, rosemary and pepper. Spread remaining Miracle Whip over tortillas. Top with chicken mixture and spinach. Serve open-faced or rolled up and secured with toothpicks.

Per 1 wrap: 387 cal., 7g fat (2g sat. fat), 60mg chol., 614mg sod., 49g carb. (22g sugars, 5g fiber), 27g pro.

CRANBERRY CHICKEN WRAPS

THE ULTIMATE
GRILLED CHEESE

FAST FIX >

The Ultimate Grilled Cheese

These gooey grilled cheese sandwiches, subtly seasoned with garlic, taste amazing for lunch with sliced apples. They're also really fast to whip up. To save a little time, I usually soften the cream cheese in the microwave, then blend it with the rest of the ingredients in the same bowl. This makes cleanup a breeze.

—**KATHY NORRIS** STREATOR, IL

START TO FINISH: 15 MIN.
MAKES: 5 SERVINGS

- 3 ounces cream cheese, softened
- ¾ cup mayonnaise
- 1 cup shredded part-skim mozzarella cheese
- 1 cup shredded cheddar cheese
- ½ teaspoon garlic powder
- ⅛ teaspoon seasoned salt
- 10 slices Italian bread (½ inch thick)
- 2 tablespoons butter, softened

1. In a large bowl, beat the cream cheese and mayonnaise until smooth. Stir in cheeses, garlic powder and seasoned salt. Spread five slices of Italian bread with the cheese mixture, about ⅓ cup on each. Top with the remaining bread.
2. Butter the outsides of sandwiches. In a skillet over medium heat, toast sandwiches for 4-5 minutes on each side or until bread is lightly browned and cheese is melted.
Per 1 sandwich: 646 cal., 50g fat (18g sat. fat), 84mg chol., 885mg sod., 32g carb. (3g sugars, 2g fiber), 16g pro.

EAT SMART

Turkey White Chili

Growing up in a Pennsylvania Dutch area, I was surrounded by excellent cooks and wonderful foods. I enjoy experimenting with new recipes, like this change-of-pace white chili.

—**KAYE WHITEMAN** CHARLESTON, WV

PREP: 15 MIN. • **COOK:** 70 MIN.
MAKES: 6 SERVINGS (6 CUPS)

- 2 tablespoons canola oil
- ½ cup chopped onion
- 3 garlic cloves, minced
- 2½ teaspoons ground cumin
- 1 pound boneless skinless turkey breast, cut into 1-inch cubes
- ½ pound ground turkey
- 3 cups chicken broth
- 1 can (15 ounces) garbanzo beans or chickpeas, rinsed and drained
- 1 tablespoon minced jalapeno pepper
- ½ teaspoon dried marjoram
- ¼ teaspoon dried savory
- 2 teaspoons cornstarch
- 1 tablespoon water
  Shredded Monterey Jack cheese and sliced red onion, optional

1. In a large saucepan or Dutch oven, heat canola oil over medium heat. Add the onion; saute until tender, about 5 minutes. Add the garlic and cook 1 minute more. Stir in cumin; cook for 5 minutes. Add turkey; cook, crumbling ground turkey, until no longer pink. Add broth, beans, jalapeno, marjoram and savory. Bring chili to a boil. Reduce heat; simmer, covered, for 45 minutes, stirring occasionally.
2. Uncover; cook 15 minutes more. Dissolve cornstarch in water; stir into chili. Bring to a boil. Cook and stir for 2 minutes. If desired, serve chili with cheese and sliced red onion.
Note: Wear disposable gloves when cutting hot peppers; the oils can burn skin. Avoid touching your face.
Per 1 cup: 288 cal., 12g fat (2g sat. fat), 73mg chol., 635mg sod., 15g carb. (3g sugars, 3g fiber), 29g pro.
Diabetic Exchanges: 3 lean meat, 1 starch, 1 fat.

FAST FIX >

Open-Fac... Cheeseste...

You might need a... this big sandwich... pepper jack chees... roast beef and veg...

—**MICHAEL KLOTZ...**

START TO FINISH: ...MIN.
MAKES: 2 SERVINGS

- 1 French roll, split
- 2 teaspoons butter
- ¼ teaspoon garlic powder
- ½ cup julienned green pepper
- ¼ cup sliced onion
- ¼ teaspoon salt
- ¼ teaspoon pepper
- 2 tablespoons canola oil, divided
- ⅓ pound sliced deli roast beef
- ½ teaspoon hot pepper sauce
- 4 slices pepper jack cheese

1. Spread roll halves with butter; sprinkle with garlic powder. Set aside.
2. In a small skillet, saute the green pepper, onion, salt and pepper in 1 tablespoon oil until tender. Remove and keep warm. In same pan, saute beef and hot sauce in remaining oil until heated through. Spoon onto buns; top with the pepper mixture and cheese.
3. Place on a baking sheet. Broil 2-3 in. from the heat for 2-4 minutes or until cheese is melted.
Per 1 sandwich: 485 cal., 33g fat (11g sat. fat), 92mg chol., 1165mg sod., 20g carb. (2g sugars, 1g fiber), 29g pro.

OPEN-FACED
CHEESESTEAK
SANDWICHES

**STACIA SLAGLE'S
APPLE CHICKEN QUESADILLAS**
PAGE 57

Quick Fixes

Get dinner on the table in **record time** with these entrees **ready in 30 minutes** or less. Bowl your family over with the comfort food **everybody craves:** tacos, pizza, chicken tenders and meat loaf.

**SHERI WHITE'S
SWEET & SPICY CHICKEN**
PAGE 54

**KAYLA CAPPER'S
SWEET POTATOES WITH
CILANTRO BLACK BEANS**
PAGE 63

**VICKY PRIESTLEY'S
STIR-FRIED STEAK
& VEGGIES** *PAGE 54*

EAT SMART (5) INGREDIENTS FAST FIX

Caesar Salmon with Roasted Tomatoes & Artichokes

This is my go-to recipe for quick dinners. The entree is colorful, healthy, easy to prepare and absolutely delicious. Hard to believe it has so few ingredients!

—**MARY HAWKES** PRESCOTT, AZ

START TO FINISH: 25 MIN. • **MAKES:** 4 SERVINGS

- 4 salmon fillets (5 ounces each)
- 5 tablespoons reduced-fat Caesar vinaigrette, divided
- ¼ teaspoon pepper, divided
- 2 cups grape tomatoes
- 1 can (14 ounces) water-packed artichoke hearts, drained and quartered
- 1 medium sweet orange or yellow pepper, cut into 1-inch pieces

1. Preheat oven to 425°. Place salmon on one half of a 15x10x1-in. baking pan coated with cooking spray. Brush with 2 tablespoons vinaigrette and sprinkle with ⅛ teaspoon pepper.

2. In a large bowl, combine tomatoes, artichoke hearts and sweet pepper. Add the remaining vinaigrette and pepper; toss to coat. Place tomato mixture on remaining half of pan. Roast 12-15 minutes or until fish just begins to flake easily with a fork and vegetables are tender.

Per 1 fillet with ¾ cup tomato mixture: 318 cal., 16g fat (3g sat. fat), 73mg chol., 674mg sod., 12g carb. (4g sugars, 2g fiber), 28g pro.

Diabetic Exchanges: 4 lean meat, 1 vegetable, 1 fat.

MEDITERRANEAN CHICKPEAS

EAT SMART FAST FIX

Mediterranean Chickpeas

Add this to your meatless Monday lineup. It's great with feta cheese crumbled over the top.

—**ELAINE OBER** BROOKLINE, MA

START TO FINISH: 25 MIN. • **MAKES:** 4 SERVINGS

- 1 cup water
- ¾ cup uncooked whole wheat couscous
- 1 tablespoon olive oil
- 1 medium onion, chopped
- 2 garlic cloves, minced
- 1 can (15 ounces) garbanzo beans or chickpeas, rinsed and drained
- 1 can (14½ ounces) no-salt-added stewed tomatoes, cut up
- 1 can (14 ounces) water-packed artichoke hearts, rinsed, drained and chopped
- ½ cup pitted Greek olives, coarsely chopped
- 1 tablespoon lemon juice
- ½ teaspoon dried oregano
   Dash each pepper and cayenne pepper

1. In a small saucepan, bring water to a boil. Stir in couscous. Remove from heat; let stand, covered, for 5-10 minutes or until water is absorbed. Fluff with a fork.

2. Meanwhile, in a large nonstick skillet, heat oil over medium-high heat. Add onion; cook and stir until tender. Add garlic; cook 1 minute longer. Sir in the remaining ingredients; heat through, stirring occasionally. Serve with couscous.

Per 1 cup chickpea mixture with ⅔ cup couscous: 340 cal., 10g fat (1g sat. fat), 0 chol., 677mg sod., 51g carb. (9g sugars, 9g fiber), 11g pro.

CAESAR SALMON WITH
ROASTED TOMATOES & ARTICHOKES

Cinnamon-Apple Pork Chops

When I found this recipe online years ago, it quickly became a favorite. The ingredients are usually on hand in my kitchen, and the one-pan cleanup is a bonus.

—**CHRISTINA PRICE** PITTSBURGH, PA

START TO FINISH: 25 MIN. • **MAKES:** 4 SERVINGS

- 2 tablespoons reduced-fat butter, divided
- 4 boneless pork loin chops (4 ounces each)
- 3 tablespoons brown sugar
- 1 teaspoon ground cinnamon
- ½ teaspoon ground nutmeg
- ¼ teaspoon salt
- 4 medium tart apples, thinly sliced
- 2 tablespoons chopped pecans

1. In a large skillet, heat 1 tablespoon butter over medium heat. Add pork chops; cook 4-5 minutes on each side or until a thermometer reads 145°. Meanwhile, in a small bowl, mix brown sugar, cinnamon, nutmeg and salt.

2. Remove chops; keep warm. Add apples, pecans, brown sugar mixture and remaining butter to pan; cook and stir until apples are tender. Serve with chops.

Note: This recipe was tested with Land O'Lakes light stick butter.

Per 1 pork chop with ⅔ cup apple mixture: 316 cal., 12g fat (4g sat. fat), 62mg chol., 232mg sod., 31g carb. (25g sugars, 4g fiber), 22g pro.

Diabetic Exchanges: 3 lean meat, 1 starch, 1 fruit, 1 fat.

GREEK SAUSAGE PITA PIZZAS

CINNAMON-APPLE PORK CHOPS

Greek Sausage Pita Pizzas

I turned my favorite sandwich into a pizza. It's great for lunch or dinner, but don't forget it when you're having a bunch of people over, because it makes a great appetizer, too.

—**MARION McNEILL** MAYFIELD HEIGHTS, OH

START TO FINISH: 30 MIN. • **MAKES:** 4 SERVINGS

- 1 package (19 ounces) Italian sausage links, casings removed
- 2 garlic cloves, minced
- 4 whole pita breads
- 2 plum tomatoes, seeded and chopped
- 1 medium ripe avocado, peeled and cubed
- ½ cup crumbled feta cheese
- 1 small cucumber, sliced
- ½ cup refrigerated tzatziki sauce

1. Preheat oven to 350°. In a large skillet, cook sausage and garlic over medium heat 6-8 minutes or until no longer pink, breaking up sausage into large crumbles; drain.

2. Meanwhile, place pita breads on ungreased baking sheets. Bake 3-4 minutes on each side or until browned and almost crisp.

3. Top pita breads with sausage mixture, tomatoes, avocado and feta cheese. Bake 3-4 minutes longer or until heated through. Top with cucumber; drizzle with tzatziki sauce.

Per 1 pizza: 632 cal., 40g fat (12g sat. fat), 85mg chol., 1336mg sod., 43g carb. (3g sugars, 5g fiber), 25g pro.

EAT SMART FAST FIX
Stir-Fried Steak & Veggies
(PICTURED ON P. 51)

Here's a stir-fry that's even faster than dialing for Chinese takeout.
—**VICKY PRIESTLEY** ALUM CREEK, WV

START TO FINISH: 25 MIN.
MAKES: 6 SERVINGS

- 1½ cups uncooked instant brown rice
- 1 tablespoon cornstarch
- ½ cup cold water
- ¼ cup reduced-sodium soy sauce
- 1 tablespoon brown sugar
- ¾ teaspoon ground ginger
- ½ teaspoon chili powder
- ¼ teaspoon garlic powder
- ¼ teaspoon pepper
- 2 tablespoons canola oil, divided
- 1 pound beef top sirloin steak, cut into ½-inch cubes
- 1 package (16 ounces) frozen stir-fry vegetable blend, thawed

1. Cook rice according to package directions. Meanwhile, mix the cornstarch, water, soy sauce, brown sugar and seasonings until smooth.
2. In a large nonstick skillet coated with cooking spray, heat 1 tablespoon oil over medium-high heat. Add beef; stir-fry until no longer pink. Remove from pan. Stir-fry vegetables in remaining oil until crisp-tender.
3. Stir cornstarch mixture and add to pan. Bring to a boil; cook and stir for 1-2 minutes or until sauce is thickened. Return beef to pan; heat through. Serve with rice.
Per ¾ cup stir-fry with ½ cup rice: 304 cal., 8g fat (2g sat. fat), 42mg chol., 470mg sod., 37g carb. (3g sugars, 3g fiber), 19g pro.
Diabetic Exchanges: 2 lean meat, 2 vegetable, 1½ starch, 1 fat.

★ ★ ★ ★ ★ **READER REVIEW**
"My family loved this recipe. I will make it often. The only thing I'll do differently next time is add another pack of vegetables."
ANGEL182009
TASTEOFHOME.COM

BROILED COD
Kim Russell
North Wales, PA

EAT SMART FAST FIX
Broiled Cod

This is the easiest and tastiest fish you'll serve. Even finicky eaters will love the beautiful and flaky results.
—**KIM RUSSELL** NORTH WALES, PA

START TO FINISH: 30 MIN.
MAKES: 2 SERVINGS

- ¼ cup fat-free Italian salad dressing
- ½ teaspoon sugar
- ⅛ teaspoon salt
- ⅛ teaspoon garlic powder
- ⅛ teaspoon curry powder
- ⅛ teaspoon paprika
- ⅛ teaspoon pepper
- 2 cod fillets (6 ounces each)
- 2 teaspoons butter

1. Preheat broiler. In a shallow bowl, mix the first seven ingredients; add cod, turning to coat. Let stand for 10-15 minutes.
2. Place fillets on a greased rack of a broiler pan; discard remaining marinade. Broil 3-4 in. from heat until fish just begins to flake easily with a fork, 10-12 minutes. Top with butter.
Per 1 fillet: 168 cal., 5g fat (3g sat. fat), 75mg chol., 365mg sod., 2g carb. (2g sugars, 0 fiber), 27g pro.
Diabetic Exchanges: 4 lean meat, 1 fat.

⑤ INGREDIENTS FAST FIX
Sweet & Spicy Chicken
(PICTURED ON P. 51)

My husband and children love this tender chicken and spicy sauce. Peach preserves add just a touch of sweetness, while taco seasoning and salsa give this dish some extra kick.
—**SHERI WHITE** HIGLEY, AZ

START TO FINISH: 20 MIN.
MAKES: 4 SERVINGS

- 3 tablespoons taco seasoning
- 1 pound boneless skinless chicken breasts, cut into ½-inch cubes
- 1 to 2 tablespoons canola oil
- 1⅓ cups chunky salsa
- ½ cup peach preserves
  Hot cooked rice

1. Place taco seasoning in a large resealable plastic bag; add chicken and toss to coat.
2. In a large skillet, brown chicken in oil until no longer pink. Combine salsa and preserves; stir into skillet. Bring to a boil. Reduce heat; cover and simmer for 2-3 minutes or until sauce is heated through. Serve with rice.
Per 1 cup: 301 cal., 6g fat (1g sat. fat), 63mg chol., 985mg sod., 37g carb. (27g sugars, 0 fiber), 23g pro.

Loaded Mexican Pizza

My husband is a picky eater, but this healthy pizza has lots of flavor, and he actually looks forward to it. Leftovers are no problem, because this meal tastes better the next day.

—**MARY BARKER** KNOXVILLE, TN

START TO FINISH: 30 MIN.
MAKES: 6 SLICES

- 1 can (15 ounces) black beans, rinsed and drained
- 1 medium red onion, chopped
- 1 small sweet yellow pepper, chopped
- 3 teaspoons chili powder
- ¾ teaspoon ground cumin
- 3 medium tomatoes, chopped
- 1 jalapeno pepper, seeded and finely chopped
- 1 garlic clove, minced
- 1 prebaked 12-inch thin pizza crust
- 2 cups chopped fresh spinach
- 2 tablespoons minced fresh cilantro
  Hot pepper sauce to taste
- ½ cup shredded reduced-fat cheddar cheese
- ½ cup shredded pepper jack cheese

1. In a small bowl, mash black beans. Stir in the onion, yellow pepper, chili powder and cumin. In another bowl, combine the tomatoes, jalapeno and minced garlic.

2. Place crust on an ungreased 12-in. pizza pan; spread with bean mixture. Top with tomato mixture and spinach. Sprinkle with cilantro, pepper sauce and cheeses.

3. Bake at 400° for 12-15 minutes or until cheese is melted.

Note: Wear disposable gloves when cutting hot peppers; the oils can burn skin. Avoid touching your face.

Per 1 slice: 297 cal., 9g fat (4g sat. fat), 17mg chol., 566mg sod., 41g carb. (5g sugars, 6g fiber), 15g pro.

Diabetic Exchanges: 2½ starch, 1 lean meat, 1 vegetable.

CHICKEN & GARLIC WITH FRESH HERBS

Chicken & Garlic with Fresh Herbs

The key to this savory chicken is the combination of garlic, rosemary and thyme. Served with homemade bread or a side of mashed potatoes, it's a wonderful 30-minute dish.

—**JAN VALDEZ** LOMBARD, IL

START TO FINISH: 30 MIN.
MAKES: 6 SERVINGS

- 6 boneless skinless chicken thighs (about 1½ pounds)
- ½ teaspoon salt
- ¼ teaspoon pepper
- 1 tablespoon olive oil
- 10 garlic cloves, peeled and halved
- 2 tablespoons brandy or chicken stock
- 1 cup chicken stock
- 1 teaspoon minced fresh rosemary or ¼ teaspoon dried rosemary, crushed
- ½ teaspoon minced fresh thyme or ⅛ teaspoon dried thyme
- 1 tablespoon minced fresh chives

1. Sprinkle chicken with salt and pepper. In a large skillet, heat oil over medium-high heat. Brown chicken on both sides. Remove from pan.

2. Remove skillet from heat; add halved garlic cloves and brandy. Return to heat; cook and stir over medium heat 1-2 minutes or until liquid is almost evaporated.

3. Stir in stock, rosemary and thyme; return chicken to pan. Bring to a boil. Reduce heat; simmer, uncovered, 6-8 minutes or until a thermometer reads 170°. Sprinkle with chives.

Per 1 chicken thigh with 2 tablespoons cooking juices: 203 cal., 11g fat (3g sat. fat), 76mg chol., 346mg sod., 2g carb. (0 sugars, 0 fiber), 22g pro.

Diabetic Exchanges: 3 lean meat, ½ fat.

GRILLED
TILAPIA PICCATA

Soupy Chicken Noodle Supper

At least once a week, my six-year-old son, also known as Dr. John, hands me a prescription for chicken noodle soup. I'm always happy to fill it.

—**HEIDI HALL** NORTH SAINT PAUL, MN

START TO FINISH: 30 MIN. • **MAKES:** 4 SERVINGS

- 1 tablespoon butter
- 1 medium carrot, sliced
- 1 celery rib, sliced
- 1 small onion, chopped
- 4 cups water
- 4 teaspoons chicken bouillon granules
- 1½ teaspoons dried parsley flakes
- ¼ teaspoon Italian seasoning
- ⅛ teaspoon celery seed
- ⅛ teaspoon pepper
- 3 cups uncooked wide egg noodles
- 1½ cups cubed rotisserie chicken
- 1 can (10¾ ounces) condensed cream of chicken soup, undiluted
- ½ cup sour cream
  Hot cooked stuffing, optional

1. In a large saucepan, heat butter over medium-high heat. Add carrot, celery and onion; cook and stir 6-8 minutes or until tender.
2. Stir in water, bouillon and seasonings; bring to a boil. Add noodles; cook, uncovered, 5-7 minutes or until tender. Stir in chicken, soup and sour cream; heat through. If desired, serve with stuffing.
Per 1⅔ cups without stuffing: 392 cal., 19g fat (8g sat. fat), 92mg chol., 1497mg sod., 32g carb. (4g sugars, 3g fiber), 22g pro.

SOUPY CHICKEN NOODLE SUPPER

Grilled Tilapia Piccata

We aren't big fish eaters, but when a friend made this for us, we couldn't believe how wonderful it was! Now we eat it regularly. I love preparing it for guests because it is simple, looks lovely and tastes restaurant-worthy.

—**BETH COOPER** COLUMBUS, OH

START TO FINISH: 25 MIN. • **MAKES:** 4 SERVINGS

- ½ teaspoon grated lemon peel
- 3 tablespoons lemon juice
- 2 tablespoons olive oil
- 2 garlic cloves, minced
- 2 teaspoons capers, drained
- 3 tablespoons minced fresh basil, divided
- 4 tilapia fillets (6 ounces each)
- ½ teaspoon salt
- ¼ teaspoon pepper

1. In a small bowl, whisk lemon peel, lemon juice, oil and garlic until blended; stir in capers and 2 tablespoons basil. Reserve 2 tablespoons mixture for drizzling on cooked fish. Brush remaining mixture onto both sides of tilapia; sprinkle with salt and pepper.
2. On a lightly oiled grill rack, grill tilapia, covered, over medium heat or broil 4 in. from heat 3-4 minutes on each side or until fish just begins to flake easily with a fork. Drizzle with reserved lemon mixture; sprinkle with remaining basil.
Per 1 fillet: 206 cal., 8g fat (2g sat. fat), 83mg chol., 398mg sod., 2g carb. (0 sugars, 0 fiber), 32g pro.
Diabetic Exchanges: 5 lean meat, 1½ fat.

Turkey a la King with Rice

Whenever I have leftover turkey, I go right to this quick and versatile recipe. It's a nice change from casseroles and so simple to make. Serve it over rice, noodles, biscuits or toast.

—**PAT LEMKE** BRANDON, WI

START TO FINISH: 30 MIN. • **MAKES:** 4 SERVINGS

- 2 tablespoons butter
- 1¾ cups sliced fresh mushrooms
- 1 celery rib, chopped
- ¼ cup chopped onion
- ¼ cup chopped green pepper
- ¼ cup all-purpose flour
- 1 cup reduced-sodium chicken broth
- 1 cup fat-free milk
- 2 cups cubed cooked turkey breast
- 1 cup frozen peas
- ½ teaspoon salt
- 2 cups hot cooked rice

1. In a large nonstick skillet, heat butter over medium-high heat. Add mushrooms, celery, onion and pepper; cook and stir until tender.

2. In a small bowl, mix flour and broth until smooth; stir into vegetable mixture. Stir in milk. Bring to a boil; cook and stir 1-2 minutes or until thickened. Add turkey, peas and salt; heat through. Serve with rice.

Per 1¼ cups turkey mixture with ½ cup rice: 350 cal., 7g fat (4g sat. fat), 76mg chol., 594mg sod., 40g carb. (7g sugars, 3g fiber), 30g pro.

Diabetic Exchanges: 3 lean meat, 2 starch, 1½ fat, 1 vegetable.

APPLE CHICKEN QUESADILLAS

Apple Chicken Quesadillas

My sister came up with this easy recipe that can be served as a main course or an appetizer. People are surprised by the combination of chicken, apples, tomatoes and corn inside the crispy tortillas, but they love it.

—**STACIA SLAGLE** MAYSVILLE, MO

START TO FINISH: 25 MIN. • **MAKES:** 6 SERVINGS

- 2 medium tart apples, sliced
- 1 cup diced cooked chicken breast
- ½ cup shredded cheddar cheese
- ½ cup shredded part-skim mozzarella cheese
- ½ cup fresh or frozen corn, thawed
- ½ cup chopped fresh tomatoes
- ½ cup chopped onion
- ¼ teaspoon salt
- 6 flour tortillas (8 inches), warmed
  Optional toppings: shredded lettuce, salsa and sour cream

1. Preheat oven to 400°. Toss together first eight ingredients. Place ¾ cup mixture on one half of each tortilla. Fold tortillas to close; secure with toothpicks.

2. Place on a baking sheet coated with cooking spray. Bake until golden brown, 13-18 minutes, turning halfway through baking. Discard toothpicks. Serve with toppings as desired.

Per 1 quesadilla: 300 cal., 10g fat (4g sat. fat), 33mg chol., 475mg sod., 38g carb. (6g sugars, 3g fiber), 16g pro.

Diabetic Exchanges: 2½ starch, 2 medium-fat meat.

TURKEY A LA KING WITH RICE

TAKEOUT BEEF FRIED RICE

EAT SMART **FAST FIX**

Takeout Beef Fried Rice

Transform leftover beef into tonight's dinner for six. Hoisin-flavored chuck roast works wonders in this recipe, but you can use flank steak or roast beef instead.

—*TASTE OF HOME* TEST KITCHEN

START TO FINISH: 30 MIN.
MAKES: 6 SERVINGS

- 1 tablespoon plus 1 teaspoon canola oil, divided
- 3 large eggs
- 1 can (11 ounces) mandarin oranges
- 2 medium sweet red peppers, chopped
- 1 cup fresh sugar snap peas, trimmed
- 1 small onion, thinly sliced
- 3 garlic cloves, minced
- ½ teaspoon crushed red pepper flakes
- 4 cups cold cooked rice
- 2 cups cooked beef, sliced across grain into bite-sized pieces
- 1 cup beef broth
- ¼ cup reduced-sodium soy sauce
- ½ teaspoon salt
- ¼ teaspoon ground ginger

1. In a large skillet, heat 1 tablespoon oil over medium-high heat. Whisk eggs until blended; pour into skillet. Mixture should set immediately at edge. As eggs set, push cooked portions toward center, letting uncooked portions flow underneath. When eggs are thickened and no liquid egg remains, remove to a cutting board and chop. Meanwhile, drain oranges, reserving 2 tablespoons juice.

2. In same skillet, heat remaining oil over medium-high heat. Add peppers, sugar snap peas and onion; cook and stir until crisp-tender, 1-2 minutes. Add garlic and pepper flakes; cook 1 minute longer. Add remaining ingredients and reserved juice; heat through. Gently stir in eggs and drained oranges.

Note: This recipe was tested with Slow-Cooked Hoisin Pot Roast, page 81.

Per 1⅓ cups: 367 cal., 9g fat (2g sat. fat), 136mg chol., 793mg sod., 45g carb. (11g sugars, 3g fiber), 26g pro.

Diabetic Exchanges: 3 starch, 3 lean meat, 1 fat.

EAT SMART **FAST FIX**

Fantastic Fish Tacos

Searching for a lighter substitute to traditional fried fish tacos, I came up with this entree. It's been a real hit with friends and family. The fillets are so mild that even those who don't typically like fish are pleasantly surprised.

—JENNIFER PALMER

RANCHO CUCAMONGA, CA

START TO FINISH: 30 MIN.
MAKES: 4 SERVINGS

- ½ cup fat-free mayonnaise
- 1 tablespoon lime juice
- 2 teaspoons fat-free milk
- 1 large egg
- 1 teaspoon water
- ⅓ cup dry bread crumbs
- 2 tablespoons salt-free lemon-pepper seasoning
- 1 pound mahi mahi or cod fillets, cut into 1-inch strips
- 4 corn tortillas (6 inches), warmed

TOPPINGS

- 1 cup coleslaw mix
- 2 medium tomatoes, chopped
- 1 cup shredded reduced-fat Mexican cheese blend
- 1 tablespoon minced fresh cilantro

1. For sauce, in a small bowl, mix mayonnaise, lime juice and milk; refrigerate until serving.

2. In a shallow bowl, whisk together egg and water. In another bowl, toss bread crumbs with lemon pepper. Dip fish in the egg mixture, then in crumb mixture, patting to help the coating adhere.

3. Place a large nonstick skillet coated with cooking spray over medium-high heat. Add fish; cook 2-4 minutes per side or until golden brown and fish just begins to flake easily with a fork. Serve in tortillas with toppings and sauce.

Per 1 taco: 321 cal., 10g fat (5g sat. fat), 148mg chol., 632mg sod., 29g carb. (5g sugars, 4g fiber), 34g pro.

Diabetic Exchanges: 4 lean meat, 2 starch.

FANTASTIC
FISH TACOS

CHIP IN!

WHETHER THEY CRAVE BBQ, CORN, NACHO CHEESE OR PLAIN, OUR FACEBOOK FANS CRUSH IT WITH CREATIVE WAYS TO USE CHIPS.

1 My kids love **macaroni salad** with shoestring potatoes stirred in.
—*Pat Carney, Lincoln, NE*

2 BBQ potato chips **on a bagel with cream cheese.** It was a HUGE sell in the cafeteria of my high school.
—*Connie Ignieri Lane, Oklahoma City, OK*

3 I make a **Tex-Mex meat loaf,** adding crushed Doritos instead of bread crumbs.
—*Tina Evans, Killeen, TX*

4 **Crunchy baked BBQ chicken:** Brush chicken pieces with barbecue sauce, roll in finely crushed BBQ chips and bake.
—*Latitia Hedrick, Marquez, TX*

5 Favorite thing ever: Crumble potato chips **into fresh buttered popcorn** (not microwaved). So good!
—*Linda Coleman, Dearborn Heights, MI*

6 I love broken-up maple bacon kettle chips **on my peanut butter and jelly sandwich.** Sweet, salty, smoky and crunchy!
—*Lisa Bartel, Pittsburgh, PA*

7 Crush organic white corn chips into a **bowl of Mexican bean soup** with sour cream and diced avocado.
—*Deena JeNiro, West Palm Beach, FL*

8 **Potato chip cookies:** Butter cookies made with crushed potato chips and chopped pecans. Dust with powdered sugar.
—*Aina Blake, Universal City, TX*

9 Sprinkle smashed potato chips and shredded Parmesan **on tuna tetrazzini** and broil until golden brown. Absolutely delicious!
—*Terri Marsh, Frederick, CO*

10 **Vanilla ice cream** with crunched-up potato chips and chocolate syrup on top. Can't beat that sweet and salty combination.
—*Sharon Phillips, Lafayette, IN*

Crispy BBQ Chip Tenders

These crunchy chicken tenders are a little sweet, a little tangy and a whole lot of fun. In half an hour, your family's new favorite dish is ready to eat. When I have extra time, I roast garlic and add it to the sauce.

—ANDREANN GEISE MYRTLE BEACH, SC

START TO FINISH: 30 MIN.
MAKES: 6 SERVINGS (1 CUP SAUCE)

- 1 cup (8 ounces) sour cream
- ¼ cup minced fresh chives
- 2 garlic cloves, minced
- ½ teaspoon salt

CHICKEN

- ¼ cup all-purpose flour
- 2 tablespoons light brown sugar
- 1 teaspoon ground mustard
- ¾ teaspoon pepper
- ½ teaspoon salt
- ¼ teaspoon cayenne pepper
- 2 large eggs, lightly beaten
- 2½ cups coarsely crushed barbecue potato chips
- 1½ pounds chicken tenderloins
  Cooking spray

1. Preheat the oven to 400°.
2. In a small bowl, mix sour cream, chives, garlic and salt. Refrigerate until serving. In a shallow bowl, mix flour, brown sugar and seasonings. Place eggs and potato chips in separate shallow bowls. Dip chicken into flour mixture to coat both sides; shake off excess. Dip into eggs, then potato chips, patting to help coating adhere.
3. Place on a rack in a 15x10x1-in. baking pan; spritz with cooking spray.
4. Bake 12-15 minutes or until coating is golden brown and chicken is no longer pink. Serve with sauce.

Per 4 ounces cooked chicken with 2 tablespoons sauce: 338 cal., 18g fat (6g sat. fat), 109mg chol., 494mg sod., 15g carb. (4g sugars, 1g fiber), 31g pro.

✱
TEST KITCHEN TIP
Thinly sliced green onions are an economical substitute for fresh chives.

REFRIED BEAN TOSTADAS

Refried Bean Tostadas

Your family won't miss the meat in tasty tostadas topped with refried beans, corn, zucchini and salsa.

—*TASTE OF HOME* TEST KITCHEN

START TO FINISH: 30 MIN.
MAKES: 6 SERVINGS

- 6 flour tortillas (8 inches)
- ½ pound sliced fresh mushrooms
- 1 cup diced zucchini
- 2 tablespoons canola oil
- 1 jar (16 ounces) chunky salsa
- 1 can (7 ounces) white or shoepeg corn, drained
- 1 can (16 ounces) vegetarian refried beans, warmed
- 1½ cups shredded lettuce
- 1½ cups shredded cheddar cheese
- 2 medium ripe avocados, peeled and sliced
- 1½ cups chopped tomatoes
- 6 tablespoons sour cream

1. In a large ungreased skillet, cook tortillas for 1-2 minutes on each side or until lightly browned. Remove and set aside.
2. In the same skillet, saute the mushrooms and zucchini in oil until crisp-tender. Add salsa and corn; cook for 2-3 minutes or until mixture is heated through.
3. Spread the warmed refried beans over each tortilla; top with lettuce, salsa mixture, cheese, avocados, tomatoes and sour cream.

Per 1 tostada: 588 cal., 31g fat (10g sat. fat), 40mg chol., 1250mg sod., 60g carb. (9g sugars, 12g fiber), 19g pro.

FAST FIX ▶
Bacon & Rosemary Chicken

Simple ingredients add up to simply fantastic flavor in this fast recipe that everyone will rave about. It's likely to become a new family favorite at your house.

—**YVONNE STARLIN** WESTMORELAND, TN

START TO FINISH: 30 MIN.
MAKES: 4 SERVINGS

- 4 boneless skinless chicken breast halves (5 ounces each)
- ½ teaspoon salt
- ¼ teaspoon pepper
- ¼ cup all-purpose flour
- 5 bacon strips, chopped
- 1 tablespoon butter
- 4 garlic cloves, thinly sliced
- 1 tablespoon minced fresh rosemary or 1 teaspoon dried rosemary, crushed
- ⅛ teaspoon crushed red pepper flakes
- 1 cup reduced-sodium chicken broth
- 2 tablespoons lemon juice

1. Pound chicken breasts slightly with a meat mallet to uniform thickness; sprinkle with salt and pepper. Place flour in a shallow bowl. Dip the chicken in flour to coat both sides; shake off excess.
2. In a large skillet, cook bacon over medium heat until crisp, stirring occasionally. Remove with a slotted spoon; drain on paper towels. Discard drippings, reserving 2 tablespoons in pan. Cook chicken in butter and reserved drippings 4-6 minutes on each side or until a thermometer reads 165°. Remove and keep warm.
3. Add garlic, rosemary and pepper flakes to skillet; cook and stir 1 minute. Add broth and lemon juice; bring to a boil. Cook until liquid is reduced by half. Return chicken and bacon to skillet; heat through.
Per serving: 304 cal., 16g fat (6g sat. fat), 101mg chol., 719mg sod., 5g carb. (1g sugars, 0 fiber), 33g pro.

SIMPLE GRILLED STEAK FAJITAS
Shannen Mahoney
Odessa, MO

EAT SMART FAST FIX ▶
Simple Grilled Steak Fajitas

Moving to a new state with two toddlers in tow, I needed some time-saving recipes. I came up with effortless fajitas—an easy weeknight meal made on the grill or in a cast-iron skillet.

—**SHANNEN MAHONEY** ODESSA, MO

START TO FINISH: 30 MIN.
MAKES: 4 SERVINGS

- 1 beef top sirloin steak (¾ inch thick and 1 pound)
- 2 tablespoons fajita seasoning mix
- 1 large sweet onion, cut crosswise into ½-inch slices
- 1 medium sweet red pepper, halved
- 1 medium green pepper, halved
- 1 tablespoon olive oil
- 4 whole wheat tortillas (8 inches), warmed
  Sliced avocado, optional
  Minced fresh cilantro, optional
  Lime wedges, optional

1. Rub steak with seasoning mix. Brush onion and peppers with oil.
2. Grill steak and vegetables, covered, on a greased rack over medium direct heat 4-6 minutes on each side, until meat reaches desired doneness (for medium-rare, a thermometer should read 135°; medium, 140°; and medium well, 145°) and vegetables are tender. Remove from grill. Let steak stand, covered, 5 minutes before slicing.
3. Cut vegetables and steak into strips; serve in tortillas. If desired, top with avocado and cilantro and serve with lime wedges.
Per serving: 363 cal., 13g fat (4g sat. fat), 54mg chol., 686mg sod., 34g carb. (6g sugars, 5g fiber), 27g pro.
Diabetic Exchanges: 3 lean meat, 2 starch, 1 vegetable, ½ fat.

Sweet Potatoes with Cilantro Black Beans

(PICTURED ON P. 51)

As a vegan, I'm always looking for impressive, satisfying dishes that all my friends can enjoy. Sweet potatoes with black beans and a touch of peanut butter is one of my standout recipes.
—**KAYLA CAPPER** OJAI, CA

START TO FINISH: 20 MIN.
MAKES: 4 SERVINGS

- 4 medium sweet potatoes (about 8 ounces each)
- 1 tablespoon olive oil
- 1 small sweet red pepper, chopped
- 2 green onions, chopped
- 1 can (15 ounces) black beans, rinsed and drained
- ½ cup salsa
- ¼ cup frozen corn
- 2 tablespoons lime juice
- 1 tablespoon creamy peanut butter
- 1 teaspoon ground cumin
- ¼ teaspoon garlic salt
- ¼ cup minced fresh cilantro
  Additional minced fresh cilantro, optional

1. Scrub sweet potatoes; pierce several times with a fork. Place on a microwave-safe plate. Microwave, uncovered, on high 6-8 minutes or until tender, turning once.
2. Meanwhile, in a large skillet, heat oil over medium-high heat. Add red pepper and green onions; cook and stir for 3-4 minutes or until tender. Stir in beans, salsa, corn, lime juice, peanut butter, cumin and garlic salt; heat through. Stir in cilantro.
3. With a sharp knife, cut an "X" in each sweet potato. Fluff pulp with a fork. Spoon bean mixture over potatoes. If desired, sprinkle with additional cilantro.
Per 1 potato with ½ cup black bean mixture: 400 cal., 6g fat (1g sat. fat), 0 chol., 426mg sod., 77g carb. (26g sugars, 12g fiber), 11g pro.

MEAT LOAF MUFFINS

Meat Loaf Muffins

Serve these tangy meat loaf muffins for dinner or slice them up for a sandwich lunch. They're just as tasty after freezing.
—**CHERYL NORWOOD** CANTON, GA

START TO FINISH: 30 MIN.
MAKES: 6 SERVINGS

- 1 large egg, lightly beaten
- ½ cup dry bread crumbs
- ½ cup finely chopped onion
- ½ cup finely chopped green pepper
- ¼ cup barbecue sauce
- 1½ pounds lean ground beef (90% lean)
- 3 tablespoons ketchup
  Additional ketchup, optional

1. Preheat oven to 375°. Mix first five ingredients. Add beef; mix lightly but thoroughly. Press about ⅓ cupfuls into each of 12 ungreased muffin cups.
2. Bake 15 minutes. Brush tops with 3 tablespoons ketchup; bake until a thermometer reads 160°, 5-7 minutes more. If desired, serve loaves with additional ketchup.
To freeze: Bake meat loaves without ketchup; freeze on a plastic wrap-lined baking sheet until firm. Transfer to a resealable plastic freezer bag; return to freezer. To use, partially thaw overnight in refrigerator. Place meat loaves in a greased shallow baking pan. Spread with ketchup. Bake at 350° until heated through.
Per 2 mini meat loaves: 260 cal., 11g fat (4g sat. fat), 102mg chol., 350mg sod., 15g carb. (7g sugars, 1g fiber), 24g pro.

Tortellini & Ham

Here's a terrific quick meal. It's sure to become a staple when you need a great last-minute weeknight supper.
—*TASTE OF HOME* TEST KITCHEN

START TO FINISH: 25 MIN.
MAKES: 4 SERVINGS

- 1 package (19 ounces) frozen cheese tortellini
- 1 cup frozen pepper strips, thawed
- 3 tablespoons butter
- 1¼ cups cubed fully cooked ham
- 1 teaspoon minced garlic
- 1½ teaspoons cornstarch
- ½ cup chicken broth
- 1 teaspoon dried basil
- ½ teaspoon dried parsley flakes
- ¼ teaspoon pepper
- 4 tablespoons grated Parmesan cheese, divided

1. Cook tortellini according to the package directions. Meanwhile, in a large skillet, saute pepper strips in butter until crisp-tender. Add ham and garlic; saute 1 minute longer.
2. Combine the cornstarch, broth, basil, parsley and pepper; stir into ham mixture. Bring to a boil; cook and stir 2 minutes or until thickened.
3. Add 2 tablespoons cheese. Drain tortellini; toss with ham mixture. Sprinkle with remaining cheese.
Per 1½ cups: 453 cal., 22g fat (11g sat. fat), 72mg chol., 1168mg sod., 40g carb. (3g sugars, 2g fiber), 23g pro.

EAT SMART FAST FIX
Crunchy Oven-Baked Tilapia

This baked tilapia is perfectly crunchy. The fresh lime mayo sends it over the top.
—**LESLIE PALMER** SWAMPSCOTT, MA

START TO FINISH: 25 MIN.
MAKES: 4 SERVINGS

- 4 tilapia fillets (6 ounces each)
- 1 tablespoon reduced-fat mayonnaise
- 1 tablespoon lime juice
- ¼ teaspoon grated lime peel
- ½ teaspoon salt
- ¼ teaspoon onion powder
- ¼ teaspoon pepper
- ½ cup panko (Japanese) bread crumbs
  Cooking spray
- 2 tablespoons minced fresh cilantro or parsley

1. Preheat the oven to 425°. Place fillets on a baking sheet coated with cooking spray. In a small bowl, mix the mayonnaise, lime juice and peel, salt, onion powder and pepper. Spread mayonnaise mixture over fish. Sprinkle with bread crumbs; spritz with cooking spray.
2. Bake 15-20 minutes or until fish just begins to flake easily with a fork. Sprinkle with cilantro.
Per 1 fillet: 186 cal., 3g fat (1g sat. fat), 84mg chol., 401mg sod., 6g carb. (0 sugars, 0 fiber), 33g pro.
Diabetic Exchanges: 5 lean meat, ½ starch.

CHICKEN VERDE QUESADILLAS
Julie Merriman
Seattle, WA

CRUNCHY OVEN-BAKED TILAPIA

FAST FIX Chicken Verde Quesadillas

I used the corn, peppers and zucchini in my fridge to create these quick quesadillas. Dollop with sour cream and you're good to go!
—**JULIE MERRIMAN** SEATTLE, WA

START TO FINISH: 30 MIN.
MAKES: 4 SERVINGS

- 2 tablespoons olive oil, divided
- 1 large sweet onion, halved and thinly sliced
- 1½ cups (about 7½ ounces) frozen corn
- 1 small zucchini, chopped
- 1 poblano pepper, thinly sliced
- 2 cups frozen grilled chicken breast strips, thawed and chopped
- ¾ cup green enchilada sauce
- ¼ cup minced fresh cilantro
- ¼ teaspoon salt
- ⅛ teaspoon pepper
- 8 flour tortillas (10 inches)
- 4 cups shredded Monterey Jack cheese
  Pico de gallo, optional
  Sour cream, optional

1. Preheat oven to 400°. In a large skillet, heat 1 tablespoon oil over medium-high heat. Add onion, corn, zucchini and poblano pepper; cook and stir 8-10 minutes or until tender. Add chicken, enchilada sauce, cilantro, salt and pepper; heat through.
2. Brush remaining oil over one side of each tortilla. Place half of the tortillas on two baking sheets, oiled side down. Sprinkle each with ½ cup cheese and top with 1 cup chicken mixture, remaining cheese and remaining tortillas, oiled side up. Bake until golden brown and cheese is melted, 7-9 minutes. If desired, serve with pico de gallo and sour cream.
Per 1 quesadilla without pico de gallo and sour cream: 1083 cal., 55g fat (27g sat. fat), 132mg chol., 2449mg sod., 94g carb. (13g sugars, 8g fiber), 56g pro.

Turkey Scallopini

Quick-cooking turkey breast slices make it easy to prepare a satisfying meal in minutes. I've also flattened boneless skinless chicken breast halves to use in place of the turkey.

—**KAREN ADAMS** CLEVELAND, TN

START TO FINISH: 20 MIN.
MAKES: 4 SERVINGS

- 1 package (17.6 ounces) turkey breast cutlets
- ¼ cup all-purpose flour
- ⅛ teaspoon salt
- ⅛ teaspoon pepper
- 1 large egg
- 2 tablespoons water
- 1 cup soft bread crumbs
- ½ cup grated Parmesan cheese
- ¼ cup butter, cubed
  Minced fresh parsley

1. Flatten turkey to ¼-in. thickness. In a shallow bowl, combine the flour, salt and pepper. In another bowl, beat egg and water. In a third shallow bowl, combine bread crumbs and cheese.
2. Dredge turkey in flour mixture, then dip in egg mixture and coat with crumbs. Let stand for 5 minutes.
3. Melt butter in a large skillet over medium-high heat; cook turkey for 2-3 minutes on each side or until meat is no longer pink and coating is golden brown. Sprinkle with parsley.
Per 4¼ ounces cooked turkey:
358 cal., 17g fat (10g sat. fat), 169mg chol., 463mg sod., 12g carb. (1g sugars, 0 fiber), 38g pro.
Chicken Scallopini: Substitute 4 boneless skinless chicken breast halves for the turkey; flatten to ¼-in. thickness and proceed as directed.

✳

TEST KITCHEN TIP
Tear several slices of fresh white, French or whole wheat bread into 1-in. pieces. Place in a food processor or blender; cover and push pulse button several times to make coarse crumbs. One slice of bread yields about 1/2 cup of crumbs.

CHILI-STUFFED
POBLANO PEPPERS

Chili-Stuffed Poblano Peppers

After tasting chiles rellenos, I wanted to try them at home. My husband and I teamed up to create this new favorite recipe.

—**LORRIE GRABCZYNSKI**
COMMERCE TOWNSHIP, MI

START TO FINISH: 30 MIN.
MAKES: 4 SERVINGS

- 1 pound lean ground turkey
- 1 can (15 ounces) chili without beans
- ¼ teaspoon salt
- 1½ cups shredded Mexican cheese blend, divided
- 1 medium tomato, finely chopped
- 4 green onions, chopped
- 4 large poblano peppers
- 1 tablespoon olive oil

1. Preheat broiler. In a large skillet over medium heat, cook turkey, crumbling meat, until no longer pink, 5-7 minutes; drain. Add chili and salt; heat through. Stir in ½ cup cheese, tomato and green onions.
2. Meanwhile, cut peppers lengthwise in half; remove the seeds. Place on a foil-lined 15x10x1-in. baking pan, cut side down; brush with oil. Broil 4 in. from heat until skins blister, about 5 minutes.
3. With tongs, turn peppers. Fill with turkey mixture and sprinkle with the remaining cheese. Broil until cheese is melted, 1-2 minutes longer.
Note: Wear disposable gloves when cutting hot peppers; the oils can burn skin. Avoid touching your face.
Per 2 stuffed pepper halves: 496 cal., 30g fat (11g sat. fat), 134mg chol., 913mg sod., 17g carb. (5g sugars, 4g fiber), 40g pro.

DEANNA ZEWEN'S
BACON CHEESEBURGER
TATER TOT BAKE PAGE 68

Main Dishes

Three cheers for **roasted** chicken, **bubbling** casseroles and **barbecued** ribs! Make mealtime extra special with these **Sunday dinner-worthy entrees** from family cooks like you. Gather around the table where **delicious, hearty fare** is served.

TRISHA KRUSE'S GERMAN BRAT SEAFOOD BOIL
PAGE 88

TATIANA KIREEVA'S BARLEY RISOTTO & BEEF STROGANOFF *PAGE 74*

LYNN BERNSTETTER'S ZUCCHINI PIZZA CASSEROLE
PAGE 90

Bacon Cheeseburger Tater Tot Bake

(PICTURED ON P. 66)

Household chores get completed quickly when my kids know this casserole with all the flavors they love is on the menu!

—**DEANNA ZEWEN** UNION GROVE, WI

PREP: 25 MIN. • **BAKE:** 35 MIN.
MAKES: 12 SERVINGS

- 2 pounds ground beef
- 1 large onion, chopped, divided
- 1 can (15 ounces) tomato sauce
- 1 package (8 ounces) process cheese (Velveeta)
- 1 tablespoon ground mustard
- 1 tablespoon Worcestershire sauce
- 2 cups shredded cheddar cheese
- 12 bacon strips, cooked and crumbled
- 1 package (32 ounces) frozen Tater Tots
- 1 cup grape tomatoes, chopped
- ⅓ cup sliced dill pickles

1. Preheat oven to 400°. In a large skillet over medium heat, cook beef and 1 cup onion, crumbling the meat, until beef is no longer pink and onion is tender, 6-8 minutes. Drain. Stir in tomato sauce, process cheese, mustard and Worcestershire sauce until cheese is melted, 4-6 minutes.

2. Transfer to a greased 13x9-in. or 3½-qt. baking dish. Sprinkle with cheddar cheese and bacon. Top with Tater Tots. Bake, uncovered, for 35-40 minutes or until bubbly. Top casserole with tomatoes, pickles and remaining onion.

Per 1 cup: 479 cal., 31g fat (12g sat. fat), 92mg chol., 1144mg sod., 24g carb. (4g sugars, 3g fiber), 27g pro.

✳

DID YOU KNOW?
Worcestershire sauce was originally considered a mistake. In 1835, an English lord commissioned two chemists to duplicate a sauce he had tried in India. The pungent batch was disappointing and wound up in the cellar. When the pair stumbled upon the aged concoction 2 years later, they were pleasantly surprised by its taste.

THE ULTIMATE FISH TACOS

EAT SMART

The Ultimate Fish Tacos

This recipe is my favorite meal to prepare. I added my own touch to the marinade to make these fish tacos pop with flavor. Warm corn tortillas on the grill, and add salsa, cilantro, purple cabbage and fresh squeezed lime.

—**YVONNE MOLINA** MORENO VALLEY, CA

PREP: 20 MIN. + MARINATING
GRILL: 10 MIN. • **MAKES:** 6 SERVINGS

- ¼ cup olive oil
- 1 teaspoon ground cardamom
- 1 teaspoon paprika
- 1 teaspoon salt
- 1 teaspoon pepper
- 6 mahi mahi fillets (6 ounces each)
- 12 corn tortillas (6 inches)
- 2 cups chopped red cabbage
- 1 cup chopped fresh cilantro
  Salsa verde, optional
- 2 medium limes, cut into wedges
  Hot pepper sauce (Tapatio preferred)

1. In a 13x9-in. baking dish, whisk the first five ingredients. Add fish fillets; turn to coat. Refrigerate, covered, for 30 minutes.

2. Drain fish and discard marinade. On an oiled grill rack, grill mahi mahi, covered, over medium-high heat (or broil 4 in. from heat) until it flakes easily with a fork, 4-5 minutes per side. Remove fish. Place tortillas on grill rack; heat through, 30-45 seconds. Keep warm.

3. To assemble, divide fish among the tortillas; layer with red cabbage, cilantro and salsa verde if desired. Squeeze a little lime juice and hot pepper sauce over taco contents; fold sides of tortilla over mixture. Serve with lime wedges and additional pepper sauce.

Per 2 tacos: 284 cal., 5g fat (1g sat. fat), 124mg chol., 278mg sod., 26g carb. (2g sugars, 4g fiber), 35g pro.
Diabetic Exchanges: 5 lean meat, 1½ starch, ½ fat.

Chorizo & Chipotle Stuffed Cabbage Cups

FREEZE IT

Our family and friends enjoy Polish recipes, and my hubby loves Mexican ones, too. These delicious cabbage rolls highlight the flavors of both nations.
—**BRENDA WATTS** GAFFNEY, SC

PREP: 45 MIN. • **BAKE:** 15 MIN.
MAKES: 6 SERVINGS

- 8 ounces pepper jack cheese, divided
- 2 finely chopped chipotle peppers in adobo sauce, divided, plus 1 tablespoon sauce
- 1 can (15 ounces) crushed tomatoes
- ½ cup chili sauce
- 1 medium head cabbage
- 2 tablespoons olive oil
- 8 ounces bulk pork sausage
- 8 ounces fresh chorizo
- ⅔ cup chopped onion
- 1 jalapeno pepper, seeded and finely chopped
- 2 garlic cloves, minced
- ½ cup dry bread crumbs

CHORIZO & CHIPOTLE
STUFFED CABBAGE CUPS

1. Preheat oven to 350°. Grease 12 muffin cups. Shred a fourth of the cheese; cut remaining cheese into 12 cubes. Set aside.

2. In a small saucepan, bring one chipotle, the adobo sauce, crushed tomatoes and chili sauce to a boil over medium heat. Reduce heat; simmer, uncovered, for 5 minutes. Reserve ½ cup; cover remaining sauce and keep warm.

3. Meanwhile, core cabbage head. In a Dutch oven, cook cabbage, stem side down, in boiling water to cover just until outer leaves begin to separate from head, about 2 minutes. Carefully remove outer leaves and repeat until there are 12 leaves. (Refrigerate the remaining cabbage for another use.) Pat leaves dry. Trim the thick vein from the bottom of each leaf, making a V-shaped cut. Set aside.

4. In a large nonstick skillet, heat oil over medium-high heat. Add sausage and chorizo; cook and stir, crumbling meat, 3 to 4 minutes. Stir in onion, jalapeno and remaining chipotle; cook until meat is no longer pink and the vegetables are tender. Add garlic; cook 1 minute more. Stir in bread crumbs and reserved sauce.

5. To assemble each cabbage roll, spoon 2 teaspoons sauce onto a cabbage leaf; add about 3 tablespoons sausage mixture. Top with a cheese cube. Pull together cabbage edges to overlap; fold over filling. Place roll folded side down in prepared muffin cup. Repeat with remaining cabbage leaves. Top with the remaining sauce. Bake until heated through, 15-20 minutes. Sprinkle cabbage cups with shredded cheese.

To freeze: Cover and freeze baked cabbage cups on waxed paper-lined baking sheets until firm. Transfer to resealable plastic freezer bags; return to freezer. To use, bake cabbage cups as directed, increasing time as necessary to heat through. Top with cheese.

Per 2 cabbage cups: 521 cal., 37g fat (14g sat. fat), 94mg chol., 1483mg sod., 24g carb. (10g sugars, 3g fiber), 26g pro.

TUNA TERIYAKI
KABOBS

Tuna Teriyaki Kabobs

I love to barbecue but don't always want a heavy dinner. These kabobs are perfect because you'll still have room for dessert!

—HOLLY BATTISTE BARRINGTON, NJ

PREP: 25 MIN. + MARINATING
GRILL: 15 MIN. • **MAKES:** 8 KABOBS

- 1½ pounds tuna steaks, cut into 1½-in. chunks
- 2 medium sweet red peppers, cut into 1-in. pieces
- 1 large sweet onion, cut into 1-in. pieces

MARINADE/DRESSING
- ¼ cup minced fresh cilantro
- ¼ cup sesame oil
- 3 tablespoons lime juice
- 2 tablespoons soy sauce
- 2 tablespoons extra virgin olive oil
- 1 tablespoon minced fresh gingerroot
- 2 garlic cloves, minced

SALAD
- 1 package (5 ounces) fresh baby spinach
- 1 medium sweet yellow pepper, cut into 1-in. pieces
- 8 cherry tomatoes, halved

1. Thread tuna onto four metal or soaked wooden skewers; thread pepper and onion onto four more skewers. Place the skewers in a 13x9-in. dish.
2. Whisk marinade ingredients. Reserve half of mixture for salad dressing. Pour remaining marinade over skewers; chill 30 minutes.
3. Grill the kabobs, covered, on a greased grill rack over medium heat, turning occasionally, until tuna is slightly pink in center for medium-rare (2-3 minutes per side) and the vegetables are crisp-tender (10-12 minutes). Remove the tuna kabobs from direct heat and keep warm while vegetables finish grilling.
4. Toss salad ingredients with reserved dressing. For each portion, serve a tuna kabob and vegetable kabob over salad.
Per 2 kabobs: 389 cal., 16g fat (2g sat. fat), 66mg chol., 444mg sod., 15g carb. (9g sugars, 4g fiber), 45g pro.
Diabetic Exchanges: 5 lean meat, 2 vegetable, 2 fat.

CHICKEN CURRY LASAGNA
Elisabeth Larsen
Pleasant Grove, UT

Chicken Curry Lasagna

My family loves Indian food, and I thought the creamy tomato-based sauce in our favorite curry would be tasty as part of a lasagna. This makes a yummy and exciting comfort food variation!

—ELISABETH LARSEN PLEASANT GROVE, UT

PREP: 30 MIN. • **BAKE:** 40 MIN. + STANDING
MAKES: 12 SERVINGS

- 1 tablespoon canola oil
- 1 medium onion, chopped
- 4 teaspoons curry powder
- 3 garlic cloves, minced
- 1 can (6 ounces) tomato paste
- 2 cans (13.66 ounces each) coconut milk
- 1 pound (about 4 cups) shredded rotisserie chicken, skin removed
- 12 lasagna noodles, uncooked
- 2 cups part-skim ricotta cheese
- 2 large eggs
- ½ cup chopped fresh cilantro, divided
- 1 package (10 ounces) frozen chopped spinach, thawed and squeezed dry
- ½ teaspoon salt
- ¼ teaspoon pepper
- 2 cups shredded part-skim mozzarella cheese
  Lime wedges

1. Preheat oven to 350°. In a large skillet, heat oil over medium-high heat. Add onion; cook and stir until softened, about 5 minutes. Add curry powder and garlic; cook 1 minute more. Stir in tomato paste; pour coconut milk into skillet. Bring to a boil. Reduce heat and simmer for 5 minutes. Stir in cooked chicken.
2. Meanwhile, cook lasagna noodles according to package directions. Drain. Combine ricotta, eggs, ¼ cup cilantro, spinach and seasonings.
3. Spread one-fourth of chicken mixture into a 13x9-in. baking dish coated with cooking spray. Layer with four noodles, half of ricotta mixture, one-fourth of chicken mixture and ½ cup mozzarella. Repeat layers. Top with remaining noodles, remaining chicken mixture and the remaining mozzarella cheese.
4. Bake, uncovered, until bubbly, 40-45 minutes. Let stand 10 minutes before cutting. Top with remaining cilantro; serve with lime wedges.
Per 1 serving: 343 cal., 17g fat (11g sat. fat), 68mg chol., 322mg sod., 28g carb. (3g sugars, 2g fiber), 20g pro.

Crunchy Baked Chicken

I've fixed this dish many times for company, and I've never had anyone fail to ask for the recipe. The leftovers—if there are any—are very good heated up in the microwave.

—ELVA JEAN CRISWELL CHARLESTON, MS

PREP: 10 MIN. • **BAKE:** 50 MIN.
MAKES: 6 SERVINGS

- 1 large egg
- 1 tablespoon milk
- 1 can (2.8 ounces) french-fried onions, crushed
- ¾ cup grated Parmesan cheese
- ¼ cup dry bread crumbs
- 1 teaspoon paprika
- ½ teaspoon salt
  Dash pepper
- 1 broiler/fryer chicken (3 to 4 pounds), cut up
- ¼ cup butter, melted

1. In a shallow bowl, whisk egg and milk. In another shallow bowl, combine the onions, cheese, bread crumbs, paprika, salt and pepper. Dip chicken in egg mixture, then roll in onion mixture.

2. Place in a greased 13x9-in. baking dish. Drizzle pieces with butter. Bake, uncovered, at 350° for 50-60 minutes or until juices run clear.

Per 1 serving: 418 cal., 28g fat (11g sat. fat), 148mg chol., 423mg sod., 8g carb. (1g sugars, 0 fiber), 32g pro.

CRUNCHY BAKED CHICKEN

JIM'S SECRET FAMILY RECIPE RIBS

Jim's Secret Family Recipe Ribs

For more than 30 years, my brother-in-law Jim kept his famous rib recipe a secret, much to the chagrin of my husband, Dennis. When he finally came around to sharing it, we loved it so much we just had to pass it along. This one's for you, Jim!

—VICKI AND DENNIS YOUNG BRIGHTON, CO

PREP: 20 MIN. + CHILLING
COOK: 3 HOURS 10 MIN.
MAKES: 8 SERVINGS

- 2 racks pork baby back ribs (about 5 pounds)
- ¼ cup soy sauce
- ¼ cup dried oregano
- 2 tablespoons onion powder
- 2 teaspoons garlic powder
- 1 liter lemon-lime soda
- ½ cup unsweetened pineapple or orange juice, optional

BARBECUE SAUCE

- ½ cup granulated or packed brown sugar
- ½ cup hot water
- 1 cup ketchup
- ¼ cup honey mustard
- ¼ cup barbecue sauce of choice
- 3 tablespoons lemon juice
- 1½ teaspoons white vinegar

1. Brush ribs with soy sauce. Combine oregano, onion powder and garlic powder; rub over both sides of ribs. Transfer to a large shallow roasting pan; refrigerate, covered, overnight.

2. Preheat oven to 225°. Add soda and juice, if desired, to roasting pan (do not pour over ribs). Bake, covered, until tender, about 3 hours.

3. Meanwhile, for sauce, dissolve sugar in hot water; combine with remaining ingredients, thinning with additional lemon-lime soda or juice if necessary. Reserve 1 cup for serving.

4. Remove ribs from oven; discard juices. Brush both sides with barbecue sauce. Grill ribs, covered, on a greased grill rack over low direct heat, turning and brushing occasionally with the remaining sauce, until heated through, about 10 minutes. Cut into serving-size pieces; serve with reserved sauce.

Per 1 serving: 483 cal., 27g fat (10g sat. fat), 102mg chol., 1107mg sod., 31g carb. (26g sugars, 1g fiber), 30g pro.

Individual Shepherd's Pies

These little pies make a fun St. Patrick's Day surprise for the family. Extras are easy to freeze and eat later on busy weeknights.

—**ELLEN OSBORNE** CLARKSVILLE, TN

PREP: 30 MIN. • **BAKE:** 20 MIN.
MAKES: 5 SERVINGS (2 MINI PIES)

- 1 pound ground beef
- 3 tablespoons chopped onion
- ½ teaspoon minced garlic
- ⅓ cup chili sauce or ketchup
- 1 tablespoon cider vinegar
- 2 cups hot mashed potatoes (with added milk and butter)
- 3 ounces cream cheese, softened
- 1 tube (12 ounces) refrigerated buttermilk biscuits
- ½ cup crushed potato chips
  Paprika, optional

1. Preheat oven to 375°. In a large skillet, cook beef and onion over medium heat 5-7 minutes or until beef is no longer pink, breaking up beef into crumbles. Add garlic; cook 1 minute or until tender. Drain. Stir in chili sauce and vinegar.

2. In a small bowl, mix the mashed potatoes and cream cheese until blended. Press one biscuit dough onto the bottom and up the sides of each of 10 greased muffin cups. Fill with beef mixture. Spread potato mixture over tops. Sprinkle with the potato chips, pressing down lightly.

3. Bake pies for 20-25 minutes or until golden brown. If desired, sprinkle with paprika.

Per 2 mini pies: 567 cal., 30g fat (12g sat. fat), 84mg chol., 1378mg sod., 51g carb. (9g sugars, 2g fiber), 23g pro.

INDIVIDUAL SHEPHERD'S PIES

OVEN SWISS STEAK

Oven Swiss Steak

I was really glad to find this recipe since it's a great way to use round steak and it picks up fabulous flavor from one of my favorite herbs—tarragon. I am a homemaker with three children and enjoy cooking tasty dinners like this one for my family.

—**LORNA DICKAU** VANDERHOOF, BC

PREP: 30 MIN. • **BAKE:** 1¼ HOURS
MAKES: 6 SERVINGS

- 8 bacon strips
- 2 pounds beef top round steak (¾ inch thick)
- 2 cups sliced fresh mushrooms
- 1 can (14½ ounces) diced tomatoes, undrained
- ½ cup chopped onion
- 1 to 2 teaspoons dried tarragon
- 2 tablespoons cornstarch
- 2 tablespoons water
- 1 cup heavy whipping cream
  Minced fresh parsley, optional

1. In a large ovenproof skillet, cook bacon over medium heat until crisp. Remove to paper towels to drain, reserving ¼ cup drippings. Crumble bacon and set aside.

2. Trim beef; cut into serving-size pieces. Brown on both sides in bacon drippings. Top meat with mushrooms, tomatoes and onion. Sprinkle with tarragon and bacon. Cover and bake at 325° for 1¼-1¾ hours or until meat is tender, basting twice.

3. Remove meat to a serving platter; keep warm. Combine cornstarch and water until smooth; add to skillet. Bring to a boil; cook and stir 2 minutes or until thickened. Reduce heat; stir in cream and heat through. Return meat to the skillet and turn to coat with sauce. If desired, sprinkle parsley over the top.

Per 1 serving: 385 cal., 26g fat (12g sat. fat), 116mg chol., 308mg sod., 7g carb. (4g sugars, 1g fiber), 31g pro.

Barley Risotto & Beef Stroganoff

(PICTURED ON P. 67)

I miss my Russian grandma's barley porridge and her beef Stroganoff, so I combined the two dishes. My secret? Cook the barley using the risotto method to keep the grains whole and irresistibly chewy.

—**TATIANA KIREEVA** NEW YORK, NY

PREP: 25 MIN. + MARINATING • **COOK:** 45 MIN.
MAKES: 4 SERVINGS

- 1 pound beef top sirloin steak, cut into 1-inch cubes
- 3 tablespoons Cognac or brandy
- 3 tablespoons butter, divided
- 1 tablespoon all-purpose flour
- 2 cups chicken stock
- 1 teaspoon Dijon mustard
- 1 medium Beefsteak tomato
- 1 teaspoon coarsely ground pepper
- ¼ teaspoon salt
- 2 tablespoons sour cream
- 1 medium onion, sliced

BARLEY RISOTTO

- 5 cups water
- 1 medium onion, finely chopped
- ½ teaspoon salt
- 1 tablespoon white wine, optional
- 1 cup medium pearl barley
- 2 tablespoons minced fresh parsley

1. In a shallow dish, toss beef with Cognac. Refrigerate, covered, 2 hours. In a small saucepan, melt 1 tablespoon butter over medium heat. Stir in flour until smooth; gradually whisk in chicken stock and mustard. Bring to a boil, stirring constantly; cook and stir until thickened, 3-5 minutes. Reduce heat; simmer, uncovered, 5 minutes.
2. Meanwhile, cut tomato into thick strips. In a large skillet over medium-low heat, cook tomato until softened, 3-5 minutes. Stir tomato into mustard sauce; add pepper and salt. Stir in the sour cream.
3. In same skillet, melt 1 tablespoon butter over medium-high heat. Drain beef; pat dry. Add sliced onion and beef to pan; cook and stir until onions are softened, 6-8 minutes. Add mustard sauce; reduce heat to low and simmer, uncovered, about 15 minutes, until thickened. Keep warm.
4. For risotto, bring water to a boil in a large saucepan. Reduce heat to maintain simmer. In another large saucepan, melt remaining butter over medium heat. Add chopped onion, salt and, if desired, white wine. Cook and stir until liquid evaporates. Add barley; toast in pan.
5. Stir hot water into barley 1 cup at a time, waiting until liquid is almost absorbed before adding more. Cook until barley is softened but still slightly chewy, 15-20 minutes; stir in parsley. Serve immediately with beef.
Per 4 ounces cooked steak with 1 cup barley: 463 cal., 15g fat (8g sat. fat), 74mg chol., 859mg sod., 48g carb. (4g sugars, 9g fiber), 33g pro.

GRILLED RIBEYE
WITH GARLIC BLUE CHEESE
MUSTARD SAUCE

⑤ INGREDIENTS Grilled Ribeye with Garlic Blue Cheese Mustard Sauce

This simple steak gets a big flavor boost from two of my favorites: mustard and blue cheese. My husband and I make this recipe to celebrate our anniversary each year!

—**ASHLEY LECKER** GREEN BAY, WI

PREP: 20 MIN. • **GRILL:** 10 MIN. + STANDING
MAKES: 4 SERVINGS

- 1 cup half-and-half cream
- ½ cup Dijon mustard
- ¼ cup plus 2 teaspoons crumbled blue cheese, divided
- 1 garlic clove, minced
- 2 beef ribeye steaks (1½ inches thick and 12 ounces each)
- 1 tablespoon olive oil
- ¼ teaspoon salt
- ¼ teaspoon pepper

1. In a small saucepan over medium heat, whisk together cream, mustard, ¼ cup blue cheese and garlic. Bring to a simmer. Reduce heat to low; whisk occasionally.
2. Meanwhile, rub meat with oil; sprinkle with salt and pepper. Grill steaks, covered, on a greased rack over high direct heat 4-6 minutes on each side until meat reaches desired doneness (for medium-rare, a thermometer should read 135°; medium, 140°; medium-well, 145°). Remove from the grill; let stand 10 minutes while sauce finishes cooking. When sauce is reduced by half, pour over steaks; top with remaining blue cheese.
Per ½ steak with 3 tablespoons sauce: 547 cal., 39g fat (17g sat. fat), 138mg chol., 1088mg sod., 3g carb. (2g sugars, 0 fiber), 34g pro.

Chicken Piccata Pockets

My husband loves chicken piccata. I tried it in puff pastry with a bit of cream cheese; it tasted sensational. When he took leftovers to work, everyone asked about it because it smelled so good.
—ARLENE ERLBACH MORTON GROVE, IL

PREP: 15 MIN. • **COOK:** 20 MIN. • **MAKES:** 4 SERVINGS

- 1 package (8 ounces) cream cheese, softened
- 2 tablespoons lemon juice
- ¼ teaspoon salt
- ¼ teaspoon pepper
- 2 tablespoons capers, drained
- 1 large shallot, finely chopped
- 1 sheet frozen puff pastry, thawed
- 4 chicken tenderloins, cubed
- 1 large egg, well beaten
- 1 tablespoon water
- 4 thin lemon slices
- 2 tablespoons chopped fresh parsley

1. Preheat oven to 425°. Beat cream cheese, lemon juice, salt and pepper until blended. Fold in capers and shallot.
2. Unfold puff pastry; roll into a 12-in. square. Cut into four smaller squares. Spread with cream cheese mixture to within ¼ in. of edges; top with chicken.
3. Fold one corner of each square over chicken, forming a triangle. Seal edges with a fork. Whisk egg and water; brush over pastry pockets, including edges. Pierce each pocket twice with a fork to vent.
4. Bake on a parchment paper-lined baking sheet until golden brown, 18 to 25 minutes. Remove from oven; cool 5 minutes. Serve with lemon and parsley.
To freeze: Cover and freeze unbaked pockets on a waxed paper-lined baking sheet until firm. Transfer to a resealable plastic freezer bag; return to freezer. To use, bake as directed, increasing time by about 5 minutes.
Per 1 chicken pocket: 559 cal., 38g fat (15g sat. fat), 126mg chol., 698mg sod., 40g carb. (3g sugars, 5g fiber), 18g pro.

CHICKEN PICCATA POCKETS

QUICK & EASY STROMBOLI
Catherine Cassidy
Milwaukee, WI

Quick & Easy Stromboli

Sandwich fixin's like roast turkey, pickled peppers and mustard get rolled into a shortcut dinner favorite, thanks to refrigerated pizza dough.
—CATHERINE CASSIDY MILWAUKEE, WI

START TO FINISH: 30 MIN. • **MAKES:** 8 SERVINGS

- 1 tube (13.80 ounces) refrigerated pizza crust
- ½ pound thinly sliced deli turkey
- ½ pound thinly sliced Muenster cheese
- ¼ cup pickled pepper rings
- 2 teaspoons yellow mustard
- 2 teaspoons minced fresh herbs or ½ teaspoon dried herbs
- 1 large egg, beaten
- 1 tablespoon water

1. Preheat oven to 350°. Unroll pizza dough onto a greased baking sheet. Layer with sliced turkey breast, Muenster cheese and pickled peppers or other deli meats, cheeses and vegetables of your choice. Spread with yellow mustard; sprinkle with fresh or dried herbs.
2. Reroll dough. Whisk egg with water; brush over dough. Bake until crust is lightly browned, 20-25 minutes. Slice.
Per 1 slice: 271 cal., 11g fat (6g sat. fat), 42mg chol., 965mg sod., 25g carb. (3g sugars, 1g fiber), 19g pro.

HEARTY CHICKPEA POTPIE

Hearty Chickpea Potpie

You won't miss the meat in this savory veggie potpie! The spring veggies, easy prep and impressive presentation make this a perfect addition to Easter or other family dinners.

—**DEANNA MCDONALD** GRAND RAPIDS, MI

PREP: 35 MIN. • **COOK:** 25 MIN.
MAKES: 6 SERVINGS

 1 package (14.1 ounces) refrigerated pie pastry
 3 tablespoons butter
 1 cup each diced onions, celery and carrots
 1 cup diced potatoes
 1 cup (4 ounces) frozen peas, thawed
 ¼ cup all-purpose flour
 1 teaspoon poultry seasoning
 ½ teaspoon ground turmeric
 ¼ teaspoon salt
 ¼ teaspoon pepper
 2 cups vegetable broth
 1 can (15 ounces) chickpeas or garbanzo beans, rinsed and drained

1. Preheat oven to 400°. Unroll one pastry sheet into a 9-in. pie plate; trim even with rim. Line unpricked pastry with parchment paper. Fill with pie weights or dried beans. Bake on a lower oven rack until edges are light golden brown, 15-20 minutes. Remove parchment and weights; bake until crust is golden brown, 3-6 minutes longer. Cool on a wire rack.

2. Meanwhile, in a large skillet, melt butter over medium heat. Add the onions, celery and carrots; cook and stir until onions are translucent, about 5 minutes. Stir in potatoes and peas, cooking until vegetables are tender, 5-7 minutes. Whisk in the next five ingredients. Increase heat to medium-high; gradually whisk in broth. Bring to a boil; cook, stirring constantly, until thickened, 4-6 minutes. Stir in chickpeas. Remove from heat.

3. Spoon filling into crust. Unroll remaining pastry; place over filling. Trim; cut slits in top. Bake until top crust is golden, about 15 minutes. Cool potpie for 5 minutes before serving.
Per 1 serving: 496 cal., 25g fat (11g sat. fat), 28mg chol., 760mg sod., 61g carb. (8g sugars, 6g fiber), 8g pro.

Roasted Butternut Squash Tacos

Spicy butternut squash makes a great base for these vegetarian tacos. I'm always looking for quick and nutritious weeknight dinners for my family, and these fun tacos are delicious, too!

—**ELISABETH LARSEN** PLEASANT GROVE, UT

PREP: 10 MIN. • **BAKE:** 30 MIN.
MAKES: 6 SERVINGS

 2 tablespoons canola oil
 1 tablespoon chili powder
 ½ teaspoon ground cumin
 ½ teaspoon ground coriander
 ½ teaspoon salt
 ¼ teaspoon cayenne pepper
 1 medium butternut squash (3 to 4 pounds), peeled and cut into ½-inch pieces
 12 corn tortillas (6 inches), warmed
 1 cup crumbled queso fresco or feta cheese
 1 medium ripe avocado, peeled and sliced thin
 ¼ cup diced red onion
 Pico de gallo, optional

1. Preheat oven to 425°. Combine the first six ingredients. Add squash cubes; toss to coat. Transfer to a foil-lined 15x10x1-in. baking pan. Bake, stirring occasionally, until tender, about 30-35 minutes.

2. Divide squash among tortillas. Top with queso fresco, avocado, onion and, if desired, pico de gallo.
Per 2 tacos: 353 cal., 13g fat (3g sat. fat), 13mg chol., 322mg sod., 54g carb. (7g sugars, 13g fiber), 11g pro.

ROASTED BUTTERNUT SQUASH TACOS

Simple Creamy Chicken Enchiladas

This is one of the first recipes I created and cooked for my husband right after we got married. He was so impressed! Now we fix these enchiladas regularly for friends.

—MELISSA ROGERS TUSCALOOSA, AL

PREP: 30 MIN. • **BAKE:** 30 MIN.
MAKES: 2 CASSEROLES (5 SERVINGS EACH)

- 1 rotisserie chicken
- 2 cans (14½ ounces each) diced tomatoes with mild green chilies, undrained
- 2 cans (10¾ ounces each) condensed cream of chicken soup, undiluted
- 1 can (10¾ ounces) condensed cheddar cheese soup, undiluted
- ¼ cup 2% milk
- 1 tablespoon ground cumin
- 1 tablespoon chili powder
- 2 teaspoons garlic powder
- 2 teaspoons dried oregano
- 1 package (8 ounces) cream cheese, cubed
- 20 flour tortillas (8 inches), warmed
- 4 cups shredded Mexican cheese blend

1. Preheat oven to 350°. Remove meat from bones; discard bones. Shred chicken with two forks and set aside. In a large bowl, combine the tomatoes, soups, milk and seasonings. Transfer 3½ cups to another bowl; add chicken and cream cheese.

2. Spread ¼ cup soup mixture into each of two greased 13x9-in. baking dishes. Place ⅓ cup chicken mixture down the center of each tortilla. Roll up and place seam side down in baking dishes. Pour remaining soup mixture over tops; sprinkle with cheese.

3. Bake, uncovered, 30-35 minutes or until heated through and the cheese is melted.

To freeze: Cover and freeze unbaked casseroles up to 3 months. To use, partially thaw in refrigerator overnight. Remove from refrigerator 30 minutes before baking. Preheat oven to 350°. Cover casserole with foil; bake 45 minutes or until casserole is heated through and a thermometer inserted in center reads 165°. Uncover; bake 5-10 minutes longer or until cheese is melted.

Per 2 enchiladas: 789 cal., 38g fat (18g sat. fat), 129mg chol., 1930mg sod., 69g carb. (6g sugars, 3g fiber), 42g pro.

SIMPLE CREAMY
CHICKEN ENCHILADAS

Greek Salad Ravioli

Turn the fresh flavors of a Greek salad into a warm dish for cold winter nights. I like to make a large batch, freeze them, then simply drop into simmering water to have dinner in five minutes!

—CARLA MENDRES WINNIPEG, MB

PREP: 45 MIN. • **COOK:** 5 MIN./BATCH
MAKES: 4 DOZEN

- 10 ounces (about 12 cups) fresh baby spinach
- ½ cup finely chopped roasted sweet red peppers
- ½ cup pitted and finely chopped ripe olives
- ½ cup crumbled feta cheese
- 3 tablespoons snipped fresh dill
- 2 to 3 teaspoons dried oregano
- 2 tablespoons butter
- 3 tablespoons all-purpose flour
- 2 cups whole milk
- 96 pot sticker or gyoza wrappers
  Snipped fresh dill and sauce of choice, optional

1. In a large skillet over medium heat, cook and stir spinach in batches until wilted, 3-4 minutes. Drain on paper towels. Combine with the next five ingredients.

2. In a small saucepan, melt butter over medium heat. Stir in flour until smooth; gradually whisk in milk. Bring to a boil, stirring constantly, until sauce thickens and coats a spoon, 2-3 minutes. Stir into spinach mixture.

3. Place 1 tablespoon spinach mixture in center of a pot sticker wrapper. (Cover remaining wrappers with a damp paper towel until ready to use.) Moisten wrapper edges with water, and place another wrapper on top. Press edges to seal. Repeat with remaining wrappers.

4. Fill a Dutch oven two-thirds full with water; bring to a boil. Reduce heat; drop ravioli in batches into simmering water until cooked through, 3-4 minutes. If desired, sprinkle with additional dill and serve with sauce of choice.

Note: Wonton wrappers may be substituted for pot sticker or gyoza wrappers. Stack two or three wonton wrappers on a work surface; cut into circles with a 3½-in. biscuit or round cookie cutter. Fill and wrap as directed.

To freeze: Cover and freeze uncooked ravioli on waxed paper-lined baking sheets until firm. Transfer to resealable plastic freezer bags; return to freezer. To use, cook as directed, increasing time to 6 minutes.

Per 1 ravioli: 47 cal., 1g fat (1g sat. fat), 4mg chol., 74mg sod., 7g carb. (1g sugars, 0 fiber), 2g pro.

LEMON-BASIL CHICKEN

Lemon-Basil Chicken

No matter when I eat it, this tangy slow-cooked chicken reminds me of summer meals with friends and family.

—DEBORAH POSEY VIRGINIA BEACH, VA

PREP: 5 MIN. • **COOK:** 3 HOURS
MAKES: 4 SERVINGS

- 4 boneless skinless chicken breast halves (6 ounces each)
- 2 medium lemons
- 1 bunch fresh basil leaves (¾ ounce)
- 2 cups chicken stock
  Additional grated lemon peel and chopped basil, optional

1. Place chicken breasts in a 3-qt. slow cooker. Finely grate enough peel from lemons to measure 4 teaspoons. Cut lemons in half; squeeze juice. Add peel and juice to slow cooker.

2. Tear basil leaves directly into slow cooker. Add chicken stock. Cook, covered, on low until meat is tender, 3-4 hours. When cool enough to handle, shred meat with two forks. If desired, stir in additional lemon peel and chopped basil.

Per 1 chicken breast half: 200 cal., 4g fat (1g sat. fat), 94mg chol., 337mg sod., 3g carb. (1g sugars, 0 fiber), 37g pro.
Diabetic Exchanges: 5 lean meat.

GREEK SALAD RAVIOLI

Chicken with Sugar Pumpkins & Apricots

When we have family gatherings, we give the slow cooker kitchen duty. Chicken with pumpkin and apricots has the warm flavors and colors of Morocco.

—**NANCY HEISHMAN** LAS VEGAS, NV

PREP: 20 MIN. • **COOK:** 4 HOURS.
MAKES: 8 SERVINGS

- 3 peeled, cubed fresh Sugar Baby pumpkins (5 to 6 cups each)
- 1 tablespoon canola oil
- 8 boneless skinless chicken thighs (4 ounces each)
- 1 medium red onion, chopped
- 2 garlic cloves, minced
- ¾ cup dried Turkish apricots, diced
- ½ cup apricot nectar
- ⅓ cup apricot preserves
- 2 tablespoons lemon juice
- 1 teaspoon ground ginger
- 1 teaspoon ground cinnamon
- 1 teaspoon salt
- ½ teaspoon pepper
- 3 tablespoons minced fresh parsley
  Hot cooked rice
- ½ cup pomegranate seeds, optional

1. Place pumpkin in a 5-qt. slow cooker coated with cooking spray.
2. In a large nonstick skillet, heat oil over medium-high heat; brown the chicken thighs on all sides. Transfer chicken to slow cooker. In same skillet, saute onions and garlic 1-2 minutes; transfer to slow cooker.
3. Add next eight ingredients to slow cooker. Cook, covered, on low until meat is tender, 4-5 hours. Top with parsley. If desired, serve with rice and sprinkle with pomegranate seeds.
Note: If Sugar Baby pumpkins are unavailable, you may substitute one large (5-6 pound) butternut squash, peeled and cut into 1-in. cubes. You should have 15-18 cups of cubed squash.
Per 1 chicken thigh with 1 cup pumpkin: 318 cal., 10g fat (3g sat. fat), 76mg chol., 376mg sod., 36g carb. (20g sugars, 3g fiber), 24g pro.
Diabetic Exchanges: 2 starch, 3 lean meat, ½ fat.

VEGGIE CALZONES

FREEZE IT

Veggie Calzones

Bread dough makes assembling these savory meatless calzones a breeze. They freeze well, and once frozen, they can be heated in half an hour. If you have a favorite pizza dough you'd like to try instead, use that.

—**LEE ANN LOWE** GRAY, ME

PREP: 25 MIN. + RISING • **BAKE:** 35 MIN.
MAKES: 8 SERVINGS

- ½ pound fresh mushrooms, chopped
- 1 medium onion, chopped
- 1 medium green pepper, chopped
- 2 tablespoons canola oil
- 3 plum tomatoes, seeded and chopped
- 1 can (6 ounces) tomato paste
- 1 cup shredded Monterey Jack cheese
- 1 cup shredded part-skim mozzarella cheese
- ½ cup grated Parmesan cheese
- 2 loaves (1 pound each) frozen bread dough, thawed
- 1 large egg
- 1 tablespoon water.

1. In a large skillet, saute mushrooms, onion and green pepper in oil until tender. Add tomatoes; cook and stir 3 minutes. Stir in tomato paste; set aside. Combine cheeses and set aside.
2. On a lightly floured surface, divide dough into eight pieces. Roll each piece into a 7-in. circle. Spoon a scant ½ cup of vegetable mixture and ¼ cup of cheese mixture over one side of each circle. Brush edges of the dough with water; fold dough over filling and press the edges with a fork to seal. Place the calzones 3 in. apart on greased baking sheets. Cover and let rise in a warm place for 20 minutes.
3. Preheat oven to 375°. Whisk egg and water; brush over calzones. Bake 33-37 minutes or until golden brown.
To freeze: Bake calzones 15 minutes and cool completely. Place in resealable freezer bags; seal and freeze up to 3 months. To use, preheat oven to 350°. Place frozen calzones 2 in. apart on a greased baking sheet. Bake 30-35 minutes or until golden brown.
Per 1 calzone: 503 cal., 15g fat (4g sat. fat), 45mg chol., 953mg sod., 67g carb. (9g sugars, 6g fiber), 23g pro.

SLOW COOKER
Slow Cooker Char Siu Pork

I based this juicy pork dish on the Asian influence in Hawaiin cuisine. It's tasty as is, in a bun or over rice. Use the leftovers in fried rice, ramen and salads.

—KAREN NAIHE KAMUELA, HI

PREP: 25 MIN. + MARINATING
COOK: 5 HOURS • **MAKES:** 8 SERVINGS

- ½ cup honey
- ½ cup hoisin sauce
- ¼ cup soy sauce
- ¼ cup ketchup
- 4 garlic cloves, minced
- 4 teaspoons minced fresh gingerroot
- 1 teaspoon Chinese five-spice powder
- 1 boneless pork shoulder butt roast (3 to 4 pounds)
- ½ cup chicken broth
  Fresh cilantro leaves

1. Combine first seven ingredients; pour into a large resealable plastic bag. Add the pork and turn to coat. Refrigerate overnight.
2. Transfer pork and marinade to a 4-qt. slow cooker. Cook, covered, for 5-6 hours on low or until tender. Remove; when cool enough to handle, shred meat using two forks. Skim fat from cooking juices; stir in chicken broth. Return pork to slow cooker and heat through. Top with fresh cilantro.
Per 4 ounces cooked pork: 392 cal., 18g fat (6g sat. fat), 102mg chol., 981mg sod., 27g carb. (24g sugars, 1g fiber), 31g pro.

SLOW COOKER CHAR SIU PORK

RAGIN' CAJUN EGGPLANT & SHRIMP SKILLET

Ragin' Cajun Eggplant & Shrimp Skillet

We always have a large summer garden where lots of produce lingers into fall. That's when we harvest our onion, bell pepper, tomatoes and eggplant, the main ingredient of this dish. This recipe turns Cajun with the Holy Trinity (onion, celery and bell pepper) plus red pepper flakes.

—BARBARA HAHN PARK HILLS, MO

PREP: 30 MIN. • **BAKE:** 35 MIN.
MAKES: 4 SERVINGS

- 1 medium eggplant, peeled and cut into ½-inch cubes
- 3 tablespoons olive oil
- 2 celery ribs, diced
- 1 medium onion, diced
- 1 small green pepper, seeded and diced
- 3 plum tomatoes, diced
- 1 teaspoon crushed red pepper flakes
- ½ teaspoon pepper
- 12 ounces uncooked shell-on shrimp (31-40 per pound), peeled and deveined
- ½ cup seasoned bread crumbs
- 1½ cups shredded part-skim mozzarella cheese

1. Place eggplant in a large saucepan; add water to cover. Bring to a boil. Reduce heat; simmer, covered, until tender, 3-4 minutes. Drain.
2. Preheat the oven to 350°. In an ovenproof skillet, heat the oil over medium-high heat. Add celery, onion and green pepper; saute until tender, for about 5 minutes. Reduce heat to medium; stir in the tomatoes and eggplant. Saute for 5 minutes. Stir in seasonings. Add shrimp and bread crumbs; saute 5 minutes longer, stirring well.
3. Bake 30 minutes. Remove skillet from oven; top with cheese. Bake 5 minutes more.
Per 1 serving: 399 cal., 21g fat (7g sat. fat), 131mg chol., 641mg sod., 26g carb. (9g sugars, 5g fiber), 28g pro.

Slow-Cooked Hoisin Pot Roast

One day my husband commented that he loves plums and meat. The next time I put a roast in the slow cooker, I added some plums. He was onto something!

—**JACKIE COLE** DUNNELLON, FL

PREP: 20 MIN. • **COOK:** 8 HOURS
MAKES: 10 SERVINGS

- 1 medium onion, cut into 1-inch pieces
- 1 boneless beef chuck roast (4 to 5 pounds)
- 1 tablespoon canola oil
- 1 cup water
- 1 cup hoisin sauce
- 3 medium plums or 6 pitted dried plums, halved

Place onion in a 5-qt. slow cooker. Cut roast in half. In a large skillet, heat oil over medium-high heat; brown meat. Transfer the meat to a slow cooker. Combine water and hoisin sauce; pour over meat. Top with plums. Cook, covered, on low until meat is tender, 8-10 hours. If desired, skim fat.

Per 7 ounces cooked meat with ¼ cup sauce: 389 cal., 20g fat (7g sat. fat), 119mg chol., 488mg sod., 15g carb. (9g sugars, 1g fiber), 37g pro.

Honey-Brined Turkey Breast

This recipe will give you a beautifully sweet and spicy, lightly salted turkey breast that makes tasty sandwiches, salads and soups. I prefer to use cider or apple juice instead of water for my brine.

—**DEIRDRE COX** KANSAS CITY, MO

PREP: 50 MIN. + CHILLING
BAKE: 1¾ HOURS • **MAKES:** 12 SERVINGS

- ½ cup kosher salt
- ⅓ cup honey
- 2 tablespoons Dijon mustard
- 1½ teaspoons crushed red pepper flakes
- 2 quarts apple cider or juice, divided
- 1 fresh rosemary sprig
- 2 large oven roasting bags
- 1 bone-in turkey breast (4 to 5 pounds)
- 1 tablespoon olive oil

1. For the brine, place the first four ingredients and 4 cups cider in a Dutch oven; bring to a boil. Cook and stir until salt is dissolved. Add rosemary; remove from heat. Stir in remaining cider; cool to room temperature.
2. Place one roasting bag inside the other. Place turkey breast inside both bags; add brine. Seal bags, pressing out as much air as possible; turn to coat turkey. Place in a baking pan. Refrigerate 6-24 hours, turning occasionally.
3. Preheat oven to 325°. Line bottom of a roasting pan with foil. Drain turkey, discarding brine. Place on a rack in prepared pan; pat dry.
4. Roast turkey 30 minutes. Brush with oil; roast until a thermometer reads 170°, 1¼-1¾ hours. (Cover loosely with foil if turkey browns too quickly.) Remove from the oven; tent with foil. Let turkey stand 15 minutes before carving.

Note: This recipe was tested with Morton brand kosher salt. It is best not to use a prebasted turkey breast for this recipe. However, if you do, omit the salt in the recipe.

Per 4 ounces cooked turkey (skin removed): 138 cal., 2g fat (0 sat. fat), 78mg chol., 88mg sod., 0 carb. (0 sugars, 0 fiber), 28g pro.

Diabetic Exchanges: 4 lean meat.

Spicy Lime Chicken

I've been turning this spicy lime chicken into tacos for years, but it was my son Austin who put it on cooked rice with all his favorite taco toppings. A family favorite was created out of leftovers!

—**CHRISTINE HAIR** ODESSA, FL

PREP: 10 MIN. • **COOK:** 3 HOURS
MAKES: 6 SERVINGS

- 1½ pounds boneless skinless chicken breast halves (about 4)
- 2 cups chicken broth
- 3 tablespoons lime juice
- 1 tablespoon chili powder
- 1 teaspoon grated lime peel

1. Place chicken in a 3-qt. slow cooker. Combine broth, lime juice and chili powder; pour over chicken. Cook, covered, on low until chicken is tender, about 3 hours.
2. Remove chicken. When cool enough to handle, shred meat with two forks; return to slow cooker. Stir in lime peel.

Per 1 serving: 132 cal., 3g fat (1g sat. fat), 64mg chol., 420mg sod., 2g carb. (1g sugars, 1g fiber), 23g pro.

Diabetic Exchanges: 3 lean meat.

SLOW-COOKED
HOISIN POT ROAST

Almond Turkey Casserole

One of my cousins shared the recipe for this comforting casserole. The almonds and water chestnuts give it a fun crunch.

—JILL BLACK TROY, ON

PREP: 15 MIN. • **BAKE:** 35 MIN. • **MAKES:** 8 SERVINGS

- 2 cans (10¾ ounces each) condensed cream of mushroom soup, undiluted
- ½ cup mayonnaise
- ½ cup sour cream
- 2 tablespoons chopped onion
- 2 tablespoons lemon juice
- 1 teaspoon salt
- ½ teaspoon white pepper
- 5 cups cubed cooked turkey
- 3 cups cooked rice
- 4 celery ribs, chopped
- 1 can (8 ounces) sliced water chestnuts, drained
- 1 cup sliced almonds

TOPPING

- 1½ cups crushed Ritz crackers (about 40 crackers)
- ⅓ cup butter, melted
- ¼ cup sliced almonds

1. In a large bowl, combine the soup, mayonnaise, sour cream, onion, lemon juice, salt and pepper. Stir in the turkey, rice, celery, water chestnuts and almonds.
2. Transfer to a greased 13x9-in. baking dish. Bake, uncovered, at 350° for 25 minutes. Combine topping ingredients; sprinkle over turkey mixture. Return to oven; bake until bubbly and golden brown, another 10-15 minutes.
Per 1 cup: 678 cal., 41g fat (12g sat. fat), 105mg chol., 1211mg sod., 43g carb. (5g sugars, 4g fiber), 34g pro.

ALMOND TURKEY CASSEROLE

VEGGIE PIZZA WITH ZUCCHINI CRUST

EAT SMART

Veggie Pizza with Zucchini Crust

My mother-in-law shared the recipe for this unique pizza with me. Its nutritious zucchini crust makes it just right for brunch, lunch or a light supper.

—RUTH DENOMME ENGLEHART, ON

PREP: 20 MIN. • **BAKE:** 25 MIN. • **MAKES:** 6 SLICES

- 2 cups shredded zucchini (1 to 1½ medium), squeezed dry
- ½ cup egg substitute or 2 large eggs, lightly beaten
- ¼ cup all-purpose flour
- ¼ teaspoon salt
- 2 cups shredded part-skim mozzarella cheese, divided
- ½ cup grated Parmesan cheese, divided
- 2 small tomatoes, halved, seeded and sliced
- ½ cup chopped onion
- ½ cup julienned green pepper
- 1 teaspoon dried oregano
- ½ teaspoon dried basil

1. Preheat oven to 450°. In a large bowl, combine first four ingredients; stir in ½ cup mozzarella cheese and ¼ cup Parmesan cheese. Transfer to a 12-in. pizza pan coated generously with cooking spray; spread to an 11-in. circle.
2. Bake until golden brown, 13-16 minutes. Reduce oven setting to 400°. Sprinkle with remaining mozzarella cheese; top with tomatoes, onion, pepper, herbs and remaining Parmesan cheese. Bake until edges are golden brown and cheese is melted, 10-15 minutes.
Per 1 slice: 188 cal., 10g fat (5g sat. fat), 30mg chol., 514mg sod., 12g carb. (4g sugars, 1g fiber), 14g pro.
Diabetic Exchanges: 2 lean meat, 2 vegetable, ½ fat.

Apple-Butter Barbecued Chicken

I love cooking so much I sometimes think of recipes in my sleep and wake up to write them down! This dream-inspired dish is my family's most-requested chicken recipe.

—HOLLY KILBEL AKRON, OH

PREP: 15 MIN. • **GRILL:** 1½ HOURS + STANDING
MAKES: 8 SERVINGS

- 1 teaspoon salt
- ¾ teaspoon garlic powder
- ¼ teaspoon pepper
- ⅛ teaspoon cayenne pepper
- 1 roasting chicken (6 to 7 pounds)
- 1 can (11½ ounces) unsweetened apple juice
- ½ cup apple butter
- ¼ cup barbecue sauce

1. Combine the salt, garlic powder, pepper and cayenne; sprinkle over chicken.
2. Prepare grill for indirect heat, using a drip pan. Pour half of the apple juice into another container and save for another use. With a can opener, poke additional holes in the top of the can. Holding the chicken with legs pointed down, lower chicken over the can so it fills the body cavity. Place chicken on grill rack over drip pan.
3. Grill, covered, over indirect medium heat for 1½-2 hours or until a thermometer reads 180°. Combine apple butter and barbecue sauce; baste chicken occasionally during the last 30 minutes. Remove chicken from grill; cover and let stand for 10 minutes. Remove chicken from can before carving.

Per 6 ounces: 441 cal., 24g fat (7g sat. fat), 134mg chol., 489mg sod., 11g carb. (10g sugars, 0 fiber), 43g pro.

APPLE-BUTTER
BARBECUED CHICKEN

SWEET-AND-SOUR
MEAT LOAF

FREEZE IT Sweet-and-Sour Meat Loaf

My husband and I like basic, hearty meat-and-potatoes meals. The sweet-and-sour flavor combo adds a deliciously different twist to a longtime standby. I hardly ever make plain meat loaf anymore. You may not, either, once you've taste this one.

—DEBBIE HANEKE STAFFORD, KS

PREP: 15 MIN. • **BAKE:** 1 HOUR • **MAKES:** 6 SERVINGS

- 1 cup dry bread crumbs
- 1 teaspoon salt
- ¼ teaspoon pepper
- 2 large eggs, lightly beaten
- 1½ pounds ground beef
- 1 teaspoon dried minced onion
- 1 can (15 ounces) tomato sauce, divided
- ½ cup sugar
- 2 tablespoons brown sugar
- 2 tablespoons cider vinegar
- 2 teaspoons prepared mustard

1. In a large bowl, combine the bread crumbs, salt, pepper and eggs; crumble beef over top and mix well. Add onion and half of the tomato sauce. Press into a 9x5-in. loaf pan.
2. Bake at 350° for 50 minutes. In a saucepan, combine the sugars, vinegar, mustard and remaining tomato sauce; bring to a boil. Pour over meat loaf; bake 10 minutes longer or until no pink remains and a thermometer reads 160°.
To freeze: Securely wrap cooled meat loaf in plastic wrap and foil and freeze. To use, partially thaw in refrigerator overnight. Unwrap meat loaf; reheat on a greased 15x10x1-in. baking pan in a preheated 350° oven until heated through and a thermometer inserted in center reads 165°.

Per 1 serving: 419 cal., 17g fat (6g sat. fat), 146mg chol., 969mg sod., 38g carb. (23g sugars, 1g fiber), 28g pro.

BUTTERNUT SQUASH & SAUSAGE STUFFED SHELLS

Butternut Squash & Sausage Stuffed Shells

I rarely invite friends over for dinner without someone requesting this easy pasta casserole. The sweet squash complements the spicy sausage, and the creamy goat cheese makes it all just melt in your mouth! You can substitute manicotti or even rolled lasagna noodles for the shells.

—**TAYLOR HALE** SONOMA, CA

PREP: 55 MIN. • **BAKE:** 30 MIN. + STANDING
MAKES: 10 SERVINGS

- 5 cups peeled butternut squash, cut into 1-inch cubes
- 3 tablespoons extra virgin olive oil, divided
- 32 uncooked jumbo pasta shells
- ¾ pound bulk hot Italian sausage
- 2 cups finely chopped sweet onion, divided
- 1 package (5 ounces) baby kale salad blend, chopped
- 8 ounces crumbled goat cheese, divided
- 4 garlic cloves, minced
- 1 carton (26.46 ounces) chopped tomatoes, undrained
- 2 tablespoons fresh sage
- 1 tablespoon sugar
- ½ cup fat-free half-and-half

1. Preheat oven to 400°. On a foil-lined baking sheet, toss squash with 1 tablespoon olive oil. Roast squash, stirring halfway through, until tender and starting to caramelize, 40 minutes. Transfer to a large bowl; roughly mash. Reduce heat to 350°.

2. Cook pasta according to package directions. Drain. In a large nonstick skillet over medium-high heat, cook sausage and 1 cup onion, crumbling meat, until no longer pink. Add kale; cook until kale is tender, 3-5 minutes. Mix with the squash. Stir in 4 ounces goat cheese.

3. In same skillet, heat remaining olive oil. Add remaining onion; cook until softened, 3-5 minutes. Add garlic; cook, stirring, for 1 minute more. Add tomatoes, sage and sugar; bring to a boil. Reduce heat; simmer, stirring occasionally, until sauce is thickened, about 15 minutes. Cool for about 5 minutes. Pulse in a blender until combined. Add half-and-half; pulse until smooth. Pour about half of sauce in a greased 13x9-in. baking dish.

4. Stuff each pasta shell with about 2 tablespoons squash mixture; place in baking dish. Pour remaining sauce over shells; top with remaining goat cheese. Bake, covered, until beginning to bubble, 20 minutes. Uncover; bake another 10 minutes. Let stand for 10 minutes before serving.

Per 1 serving: 379 cal., 18g fat (7g sat. fat), 47mg chol., 344mg sod., 43g carb. (9g sugars, 6g fiber), 15g pro.

Deep-Dish Beef & Bean Taco Pizza

My whole family enjoys this dish that tastes like a taco and eats like a pizza. The thick crust can handle lots of toppings, so load it up for a bright, fun meal.

—**NANCY CIRCLE** PERKINS, OK

PREP: 15 MIN. + RESTING • **BAKE:** 15 MIN.
MAKES: 8 SERVINGS

- 3 cups all-purpose flour
- ½ cup cornmeal
- 1 teaspoon salt
- 1 package (¼ ounce) quick-rise yeast
- 2 cups warm water (120° to 130°), divided
- 1 tablespoon honey
- 1 pound ground beef
- 1 envelope taco seasoning
- 1 cup refried beans
- ⅓ cup taco sauce
- 2 cups shredded Colby-Monterey Jack cheese

OPTIONAL TOPPINGS

Shredded lettuce
Chopped tomatoes
Crushed tortilla chips
Sliced ripe olives, drained
Diced avocado
Sour cream
Salsa

1. Preheat oven to 400°. Combine 2½ cups flour, cornmeal, salt and yeast. In another bowl, combine 1¼ cups warm water and honey. Gradually add dry ingredients; beat just until moistened. Stir in enough remaining flour to form a soft dough. Do not knead. Cover; let rest 20 minutes.

2. Meanwhile, in a small skillet over medium heat, cook and stir beef, crumbling meat, until no longer pink; drain. Add the taco seasoning and remaining water. Cook and stir until thickened, about 2 minutes.

3. Press dough to fit a greased 13x9-in. baking pan. Combine beans and taco sauce; spread over dough. Top with beef mixture and cheese. Bake on a lower oven rack until crust is golden and cheese is melted, 15-18 minutes. Let stand 5 minutes. If desired, serve with optional toppings.

Per 1 piece: 469 cal., 16g fat (9g sat. fat), 60mg chol., 1050mg sod., 55g carb. (3g sugars, 3g fiber), 23g pro.

DEEP-DISH BEEF & BEAN
TACO PIZZA

FREEZE IT
Italian Stuffed Shells

A dear friend first brought me this casserole. Now I take it to other friends' homes and to potlucks, because it's always a big hit!
—**BEVERLY AUSTIN** FULTON, MO

PREP: 50 MIN. • **BAKE:** 35 MIN. • **MAKES:** 8 SERVINGS

- 1 pound ground beef
- 1 cup chopped onion
- 1 garlic clove, minced
- 2 cups hot water
- 1 can (12 ounces) tomato paste
- 1 tablespoon beef bouillon granules
- 1½ teaspoons dried oregano
- 1 large egg, lightly beaten
- 2 cups (16 ounces) 4% cottage cheese
- 2 cups shredded part-skim mozzarella cheese, divided
- ½ cup grated Parmesan cheese
- 24 jumbo pasta shells, cooked and drained

1. In a large skillet, cook beef, onion and garlic over medium heat, crumbling beef, until meat is no longer pink; drain. Stir in water, tomato paste, bouillon and oregano. Reduce heat; simmer, uncovered, for 30 minutes.

2. Meanwhile, combine egg, cottage cheese, 1 cup mozzarella and Parmesan cheese. Stuff shells with the cheese mixture.

3. Preheat oven to 350°. Place shells in a greased 13x9-in. or 3-qt. baking dish. Pour meat sauce over shells. Cover; bake 30 minutes. Uncover; sprinkle with remaining mozzarella. Bake until cheese is melted, about 5 minutes longer.

To freeze: After assembling, cover and freeze. To use, partially thaw in refrigerator overnight. Remove 30 minutes before baking. Preheat oven to 350°. Bake as directed, adding remaining 1 cup mozzarella after 30-40 minutes and increasing time as necessary for a thermometer inserted in center to read 165°.

Per 4 stuffed shells and sauce: 430 cal., 17g fat (8g sat. fat), 94mg chol., 866mg sod., 37g carb. (9g sugars, 3g fiber), 32g pro.

ITALIAN STUFFED SHELLS

BUTTERNUT SQUASH, CAULIFLOWER & BEEF SHEPHERD'S PIE

Butternut Squash, Cauliflower & Beef Shepherd's Pie

I love to get creative with classic dishes, such as this colorful version of shepherd's pie. Adding squash and cauliflower boosts the nutritional value and cuts the calories.
—**JENN TIDWELL** FAIR OAKS, CA

PREP: 50 MIN. • **BAKE:** 35 MIN. + STANDING • **MAKES:** 6 SERVINGS

- 4 tablespoons butter, melted and divided
- 2 tablespoons maple syrup
  Dash pepper
- 1 medium butternut squash (about 2½ pounds), peeled and cubed
- 1 tablespoon minced fresh thyme or 1 teaspoon dried thyme
- 1¼ pounds ground beef
- 1 envelope onion soup mix
- 1 cup water
- 1 medium head cauliflower, broken into small florets
- 4 garlic cloves, minced
- 1 cup freshly grated Parmesan cheese

1. Preheat oven to 350°. Combine 2 tablespoons melted butter, syrup and pepper; toss with squash to coat. Roast squash in a greased 15x10x1-in. baking pan until tender, 40-45 minutes. Transfer to a large bowl; mash until smooth, stirring in thyme.

2. In a large skillet over medium heat, cook and stir beef, crumbling meat, until no longer pink, 6-8 minutes; drain. Stir in soup mix and water; bring to a boil. Reduce heat; simmer, uncovered, until slightly thickened, 4-6 minutes. Transfer to a greased 13x9-in. baking dish.

3. Top with cauliflower. Sprinkle with garlic; drizzle with remaining butter. Spread squash mixture over top. Bake, uncovered, until cauliflower is tender, 35-40 minutes. Sprinkle with cheese. Let stand 10 minutes before serving.

Per 1½ cups: 438 cal., 23g fat (11g sat. fat), 90mg chol., 798mg sod., 37g carb. (11g sugars, 9g fiber), 25g pro.

Honey BBQ Chicken

I grill everything—veggies, oxtail, tofu. This saucy chicken is our favorite. I keep a ready supply of sauce and rub, so the prep couldn't be easier.
—**JERRY T.H. ROSIEK** EUGENE, OR

PREP: 15 MIN. + CHILLING • **GRILL:** 40 MIN. • **MAKES:** 6 SERVINGS

- 6 chicken leg quarters

RUB
- ¼ cup packed brown sugar
- 1 tablespoon kosher salt
- ½ teaspoon garlic powder
- ⅛ teaspoon ground cinnamon

SAUCE
- 2 tablespoons butter
- ⅔ cup ketchup
- ½ cup honey
- 3 tablespoons balsamic vinegar
- 2 tablespoons yellow mustard
- 2 teaspoons reduced-sodium soy sauce
  Dash cayenne pepper, optional

1. Pat chicken dry. Combine rub ingredients. Rub over chicken pieces; refrigerate, covered, in a shallow dish 2 hours.
2. Meanwhile, in a small saucepan over medium heat, combine the sauce ingredients, adding cayenne if desired. Bring to a boil, stirring constantly; reduce heat and simmer, uncovered, to allow flavors to blend, 8-10 minutes.
3. On an oiled grill rack, grill chicken, covered, over indirect medium heat, turning frequently, until a thermometer reads 165°, 35-45 minutes.
4. Reduce heat to medium-low. Brush chicken with sauce, reserving ½ cup. Cook, covered, until a thermometer reads 170°, 4-6 minutes. Serve with reserved sauce.

Per 1 chicken leg quarter: 466 cal., 20g fat (7g sat. fat), 114mg chol., 1542mg sod., 42g carb. (41g sugars, 0 fiber), 30g pro.

HONEY BBQ CHICKEN

BURRITO BAKE

Burrito Bake

When I was in college, my roommate often made this shortcut southwestern casserole. One slice fills you right up.
—**CINDEE NESS** HORACE, ND

PREP: 25 MIN. • **BAKE:** 30 MIN. • **MAKES:** 6 SERVINGS

- 1 pound ground beef
- 1 can (16 ounces) refried beans
- ¼ cup chopped onion
- 1 envelope taco seasoning
- 1 tube (8 ounces) refrigerated crescent rolls
- 1 to 2 cups shredded cheddar cheese
- 1 to 2 cups shredded part-skim mozzarella cheese
  Optional toppings: chopped green pepper, shredded lettuce, chopped tomatoes and sliced ripe olives

1. Preheat oven to 350°. In a large skillet, cook and crumble beef over medium heat until no longer pink; drain. Add beans, onion and taco seasoning.
2. Unroll the crescent roll dough. Press onto bottom and up the sides of a greased 13x9-in. baking dish; seal seams and perforations.
3. Spread beef mixture over crust; sprinkle with cheeses. Bake, uncovered, until golden brown, about 30 minutes. If desired, sprinkle with toppings.

Per 1 serving: 509 cal., 29g fat (12g sat. fat), 78mg chol., 1403mg sod., 32g carb. (4g sugars, 3g fiber), 29g pro.

Florentine Spaghetti Bake

This plate-filling sausage dish appeals to most every appetite. My daughter, a Montana wheat rancher's wife, serves it often to satisfy her hardworking family.
—**LORRAINE MARTIN** LINCOLN, CA

PREP: 30 MIN. • **BAKE:** 1 HOUR + STANDING
MAKES: 9 SERVINGS

- 8 ounces uncooked spaghetti
- 1 pound bulk Italian sausage
- 1 large onion, chopped
- 1 garlic clove, minced
- 1 jar (24 ounces) pasta sauce
- 1 can (4 ounces) mushroom stems and pieces, drained
- 1 large egg, lightly beaten
- 2 cups (16 ounces) 4% cottage cheese
- 1 package (10 ounces) frozen chopped spinach, thawed and squeezed dry
- ¼ cup grated Parmesan cheese
- ½ teaspoon seasoned salt
- ¼ teaspoon pepper
- 2 cups shredded part-skim mozzarella cheese

1. Preheat oven to 375°. Cook pasta according to package directions. Meanwhile, in a large skillet over medium heat, cook sausage and onion, crumbling meat, until sausage is no longer pink. Add garlic; cook 1 minute longer. Drain. Stir in pasta sauce and mushrooms. Bring to a boil. Reduce heat; cover and cook until heated through, about 15 minutes.

2. Drain pasta. Combine the egg with the next five ingredients. Spread 1 cup sausage mixture in a greased 13x9-in. baking dish. Top with spaghetti and remaining sausage mixture. Layer with egg mixture; sprinkle with mozzarella cheese.

3. Cover and bake 45 minutes. Uncover; bake until lightly browned and heated through, about 15 minutes longer. Let casserole stand 15 minutes before cutting.

Per 1 serving: 449 cal., 23g fat (9g sat. fat), 83mg chol., 1218mg sod., 35g carb. (10g sugars, 4g fiber), 25g pro.

German Brat Seafood Boil
(PICTURED ON P. 67)

The grilled bratwurst and onion add a smoky flavor to corn, potatoes and fish for a hearty meal that's always a hit with my family.
—**TRISHA KRUSE** EAGLE, ID

PREP: 25 MIN. • **COOK:** 30 MIN.
MAKES: 6 SERVINGS

- 1 package (19 ounces) uncooked bratwurst links
- 1 medium onion, quartered
- 2 quarts water
- 2 bottles (12 ounces each) beer or 3 cups reduced-sodium chicken broth
- ½ cup seafood seasoning
- 5 medium ears sweet corn, cut into 2-inch pieces
- 2 pounds small red potatoes
- 1 medium lemon, halved
- 1 pound cod fillet, cut into 1-inch pieces
  Coarsely ground pepper

1. Grill bratwurst, covered, over medium heat, turning frequently, until meat is no longer pink, 15-20 minutes. Grill onion, covered, until lightly browned, 3-4 minutes on each side. Cut bratwurst into 2-in. pieces.

2. In a stockpot, combine water, beer and seafood seasoning; add corn, potatoes, lemon, bratwurst and onion. Bring to a boil. Reduce heat; simmer, uncovered, until potatoes are tender, 15-20 minutes.

3. Stir in cod; cook until fish flakes easily with a fork, 4-6 minutes. Drain; transfer to a large serving bowl. Sprinkle with pepper.

Per 1 serving: 553 cal., 28g fat (9g sat. fat), 95mg chol., 1620mg sod., 46g carb. (8g sugars, 5g fiber), 30g pro.

FLORENTINE SPAGHETTI BAKE

HOT BROWN
TURKEY CASSEROLE
Diane Halferty,
Corpus Christi, TX

Garlic Lover's Chicken

This is a great recipe for all you garlic fans! The easy crumb coating makes for crisp, ultra-flavorful chicken. I've shared the recipe with several friends who say their families went wild over it.

—**JANICE STEINMETZ** SOMERS, CT

PREP: 15 MIN. • **BAKE:** 25 MIN.
MAKES: 6 SERVINGS

- ½ cup dry bread crumbs
- ⅓ cup grated Parmesan cheese
- 2 tablespoons minced fresh parsley
- ½ teaspoon salt, optional
- ⅛ teaspoon pepper
- ¼ cup milk
- 6 boneless skinless chicken breast halves (1½ pounds)
- 1 to 2 garlic cloves, minced
- ¼ cup butter, melted
- 2 tablespoons lemon juice
  Paprika

1. In a large resealable plastic bag, combine the bread crumbs, cheese, parsley, salt if desired and pepper. Place milk in a shallow bowl. Dip chicken in milk, then shake in the crumb mixture.
2. Place chicken in a greased 13x9-in. baking dish. Combine the butter, garlic and lemon juice; drizzle over the chicken. Sprinkle with paprika.
3. Bake the chicken, uncovered, at 350° for 25-30 minutes or until a thermometer reads 170°.
Per 1 chicken breast half: 234 cal., 8g fat (0 sat. fat), 75mg chol., 331mg sod., 8g carb. (0 sugars, 0 fiber), 30g pro.
Diabetic Exchanges: 3 lean meat, 1 fat, ½ starch.

Hot Brown Turkey Casserole

If you've ever enjoyed the famous Hot Brown Sandwich at the Brown Hotel in Louisville, Kentucky, you'll love this home-cooked version. It can be made ahead and refrigerated; just adjust the baking time accordingly if it's cold.

—**DIANE HALFERTY** CORPUS CHRISTI, TX

PREP: 40 MIN. • **BAKE:** 20 MIN.
MAKES: 12 SERVINGS

- ¼ cup butter
- ¼ cup all-purpose flour
- 4 cups 2% milk
- 1 large egg
- ⅔ cup grated Parmesan cheese, divided
- ¼ teaspoon salt
- ¼ teaspoon pepper
- 12 slices bread, toasted and divided
- 2 pounds thinly sliced cooked turkey or chicken
- ¼ teaspoon paprika
- 6 bacon strips, cooked and crumbled
- 1 cup tomatoes, chopped and seeded
- 1 teaspoon minced fresh parsley

1. Preheat oven to 350°. In a large saucepan, melt butter over medium heat. Stir in flour until smooth; gradually whisk in milk. Bring to a boil, stirring constantly; cook until slightly thickened, 6-8 minutes. Remove sauce from heat.
2. In a small bowl, lightly beat egg. Gradually whisk in ½ cup sauce. Slowly return all to the pan, whisking constantly. Add ½ cup Parmesan cheese, salt and pepper. Cook and stir until thickened. (Do not allow to boil.)
3. In a greased 13x9-in. baking dish, layer 6 toast slices and turkey; pour sauce over top. Sprinkle the casserole with paprika, bacon and remaining Parmesan cheese.
4. Bake until heated through, about 20-25 minutes. Top with tomatoes and parsley. Cut remaining toast slices in half diagonally; serve on the side.
Per 1 serving: 316 cal., 13g fat (6g sat. fat), 117mg chol., 472mg sod., 19g carb. (6g sugars, 1g fiber), 30g pro.

GARLIC LOVER'S
CHICKEN

Zucchini Pizza Casserole

(PICTURED ON P. 67)

My husband has a hearty appetite. Our two kids never tire of pizza. And I grow lots of zucchini. So this tasty, tomatoey casserole is absolutely tops with us throughout the entire year. Once you've tried the recipe, you may even decide to grow more zucchini in your own garden!

—**LYNN BERNSTETTER** WHITE BEAR LAKE, MN

PREP: 20 MIN. • **BAKE:** 40 MIN.
MAKES: 8 SERVINGS

- 4 cups shredded unpeeled zucchini
- ½ teaspoon salt
- 2 large eggs
- ½ cup grated Parmesan cheese
- 2 cups shredded part-skim mozzarella cheese, divided
- 1 cup shredded cheddar cheese, divided
- 1 pound ground beef
- ½ cup chopped onion
- 1 can (15 ounces) Italian tomato sauce
- 1 medium green or sweet red pepper, chopped

1. Preheat oven to 400°. Place zucchini in colander; sprinkle with salt. Let stand 10 minutes, then squeeze out moisture.

2. Combine zucchini with eggs, Parmesan and half of mozzarella and cheddar cheeses. Press into a greased 13x9-in. or 3-qt. baking dish. Bake for 20 minutes.

3. Meanwhile, in a large saucepan, cook beef and onion over medium heat, crumbling beef, until meat is no longer pink; drain. Add tomato sauce; spoon over zucchini mixture. Sprinkle with remaining cheeses; add red pepper. Bake until heated through, about 20 minutes longer.

To freeze: Cool baked casserole; cover and freeze. To use, partially thaw in refrigerator overnight. Remove from refrigerator 30 minutes before baking. Preheat oven to 350°. Unwrap casserole; reheat on a lower oven rack until heated through and a thermometer inserted in center reads 165°.

Per 1 cup: 315 cal., 20g fat (10g sat. fat), 119mg chol., 855mg sod., 10g carb. (4g sugars, 2g fiber), 25g pro.

SOUTHWESTERN
CASSEROLE

Southwestern Casserole

I've made this family-pleasing casserole for years. It's bold and budget-friendly—and you get a second casserole to freeze and keep for up to three months.

—**JOAN HALLFORD** NORTH RICHLAND HILLS, TX

PREP: 15 MIN. • **BAKE:** 40 MIN.
MAKES: 2 CASSEROLES (6 SERVINGS EACH)

- 2 cups (8 ounces) uncooked elbow macaroni
- 2 pounds ground beef
- 1 large onion, chopped
- 2 garlic cloves, minced
- 2 cans (14½ ounces each) diced tomatoes, undrained
- 1 can (16 ounces) kidney beans, rinsed and drained
- 1 can (6 ounces) tomato paste
- 1 can (4 ounces) chopped green chilies, drained
- 1½ teaspoons salt
- 1 teaspoon chili powder
- ½ teaspoon ground cumin
- ½ teaspoon pepper
- 2 cups shredded Monterey Jack cheese
- 2 jalapeno peppers, seeded and chopped

1. Cook macaroni according to package directions. Meanwhile, in a large saucepan, cook beef and onion over medium heat, crumbling beef, until meat is no longer pink. Add garlic; cook 1 minute longer. Drain. Stir in next eight ingredients. Bring to a boil. Reduce heat; simmer, uncovered, for 10 minutes. Drain macaroni; stir into beef mixture.

2. Preheat oven to 375°. Transfer macaroni mixture to two greased 2-qt. baking dishes. Top with cheese and jalapenos. Cover and bake at 375° for 30 minutes. Uncover; bake until bubbly and heated through, about 10 minutes longer. Serve one casserole. Cool the second; cover and freeze up to 3 months.

To use frozen casserole: Thaw in refrigerator 8 hours. Preheat oven to 375°. Remove from refrigerator 30 minutes before baking. Cover and bake, increasing time as necessary to heat through and for a thermometer inserted in center to read 165°, 20-25 minutes.

Note: Wear disposable gloves when cutting hot peppers; the oils can burn skin. Avoid touching your face.

Per 1 cup: 321 cal., 15g fat (7g sat. fat), 64mg chol., 673mg sod., 23g carb. (5g sugars, 4g fiber), 24g pro.

Carrie's Cincinnati Chili

Every time we had a gathering or company, folks would request this. My husband convinced me to enter it in a local chili contest, where it won third place! It's quick and easy to prepare. Use minced garlic in a jar if you don't have fresh.

—**CARRIE BIRDSALL** DALLAS, GA

PREP: 20 MIN. • **COOK:** 6 HOURS
MAKES: 6 SERVINGS

- 1½ pounds ground beef
- 1 small onion, chopped
- 1 can (29 ounces) tomato puree
- 1 can (14½ ounces) whole tomatoes, crushed
- 2 tablespoons brown sugar
- 4 teaspoons chili powder
- 1 tablespoon white vinegar
- 1 teaspoon salt
- ¾ teaspoon ground cinnamon
- ½ teaspoon ground allspice
- ½ teaspoon pepper
- 1 garlic clove, crushed
- 3 bay leaves
  Hot cooked spaghetti
  Shredded cheddar cheese, optional
  Additional chopped onion, optional

1. In a large skillet over medium heat, cook beef and onion, crumbling meat, until beef is no longer pink and onion is tender, 6-8 minutes; drain. Transfer to a 3- or 4-qt. slow cooker. Add next 11 ingredients.
2. Cook, covered, on low 6-8 hours. Discard garlic clove and bay leaves. Serve on hot cooked spaghetti; if desired, top with shredded cheddar cheese and additional chopped onion.
To freeze: Before adding toppings, cool chili. Freeze chili in freezer containers. To use, partially chili thaw in refrigerator overnight. Heat through in a saucepan, stirring occasionally, adding a little water or broth if necessary. Serve as directed.
Per 1 cup: 315 cal., 14g fat (5g sat. fat), 70mg chol., 644mg sod., 19g carb. (9g sugars, 4g fiber), 23g pro.

CITRUS SALMON
EN PAPILLOTE

Citrus Salmon en Papillote

This salmon dish is so simple, nutritious and easy to make—yet it's so delicious, elegant and impressive.

—**DAHLIA ABRAMS** DETROIT, MI

PREP: 20 MIN. • **BAKE:** 15 MIN.
MAKES: 6 SERVINGS

- 6 orange slices
- 6 lime slices
- 6 salmon fillets (4 ounces each)
- 1 pound fresh asparagus, trimmed and halved
  Olive oil-flavored cooking spray
- ½ teaspoon salt
- ¼ teaspoon pepper
- 2 tablespoons minced fresh parsley
- 3 tablespoons lemon juice

1. Preheat the oven to 425°. Cut parchment paper or heavy-duty foil into six 15x10-in. sheets; fold in half. Arrange citrus slices on one side of each sheet. Top with fish and asparagus. Spritz with cooking spray. Sprinkle with salt, pepper and parsley. Drizzle with lemon juice.
2. Fold parchment paper over fish; draw edges together and crimp with fingers to form tightly sealed packets. Place on baking sheets.
3. Bake 12-15 minutes, until fish flakes easily with a fork. Open packets carefully to allow steam to escape.
Per 1 packet: 224 cal., 13g fat (2g sat. fat), 57mg chol., 261mg sod., 6g carb. (3g sugars, 1g fiber), 20g pro.
Diabetic Exchanges: 3 lean meat, 1 vegetable.

CARRIE'S
CINCINNATI CHILI

**JANET BOULGER'S
PEPPER RICOTTA PRIMAVERA**
PAGE 100

Everyday Fresh

This chapter is packed with **quick-prep, good-for-you meals** made from **real ingredients**—perfect for your everyday dinners. Here you will find dozens of fresh **supper ideas,** plus 13 easy accompaniments perfect for serving alongside.

KELLY FERGUSON'S HONEY-ROASTED CHICKEN & ROOT VEGETABLES
PAGE 94

DARLENE KENNEDY'S TURKEY ASPARAGUS STIR-FRY
PAGE 99

TIFFANY IHLE'S GINGER VEGGIE BROWN RICE PASTA
PAGE 101

EAT SMART Honey-Roasted Chicken & Root Vegetables
(PICTURED ON P. 93)

When my whole family comes over for dinner, I make a big platter of roast chicken with sweet potatoes, carrots and fennel. My dad leads the fan club.

—KELLY FERGUSON CONSHOHOCKEN, PA

PREP: 25 MIN. • **COOK:** 40 MIN.
MAKES: 6 SERVINGS

- 1 teaspoon salt
- 1 teaspoon pepper
- 1 teaspoon minced fresh rosemary
- 1 teaspoon minced fresh thyme
- 2 tablespoons olive oil, divided
- 1 tablespoon butter
- 6 boneless skinless chicken breast halves (6 ounces each)
- ½ cup white wine
- 3 tablespoons honey, divided
- 3 medium sweet potatoes, peeled and chopped
- 4 medium carrots, chopped
- 2 medium fennel bulbs, chopped
- 2 cups chicken stock
- 3 bay leaves

1. Preheat oven to 375°. Combine salt, pepper, rosemary and thyme. In a large skillet, heat 1 tablespoon oil and butter over medium-high heat. Sprinkle half the seasoning mixture over chicken breasts. Add to skillet; cook until golden brown, 2-3 minutes per side. Remove. Add the wine and 2 tablespoons honey to pan; cook for 2-3 minutes, stirring to loosen browned bits.

2. Combine sweet potatoes, carrots and fennel in a microwave-safe bowl. Add remaining olive oil, seasonings and honey to vegetables; stir to combine. Microwave, covered, until potatoes are just tender, 10 minutes.

3. Transfer vegetables to a foil-lined 15x10-in. baking pan. Add stock, wine mixture and bay leaves; top with chicken. Roast until a thermometer inserted in chicken reads 165°, 25-30 minutes. Discard bay leaves. Serve chicken with vegetables and sauce.

Per serving: 432 cal., 11g fat (3g sat. fat), 99mg chol., 543mg sod., 42g carb. (23g sugars, 6g fiber), 39g pro.

Diabetic Exchanges: 5 lean meat, 3 starch, 1½ fat.

APPLE CIDER PORK CHOPS

EAT SMART FAST FIX
Apple Cider Pork Chops

With cider gravy, these pork chops are a must for fall family dinners. I serve them with buttered egg noodles to soak up more of that delicious sauce. This recipe is easy to double when company pops in.

—DEBIANA CASTERLINE
EGG HARBOR TOWNSHIP, NJ

START TO FINISH: 25 MIN.
MAKES: 6 SERVINGS

- 2 tablespoons olive oil
- 6 boneless pork loin chops (6 to 8 ounces each), about ¾ inch thick
- 1 garlic clove, minced
- 1 tablespoon Dijon mustard
- 1 teaspoon honey
- ½ teaspoon apple pie spice
- ½ teaspoon coarsely ground pepper
- ¼ teaspoon dried thyme
- ¼ teaspoon salt
- 1 cup apple cider
- 1 tablespoon plus 1 teaspoon cornstarch
- 2 tablespoons water
  Minced fresh parsley

1. In a large skillet, heat olive oil over medium heat. Brown pork chops on both sides.

2. Meanwhile, in a small bowl, combine next seven ingredients; stir in apple cider. Pour over pork chops. Reduce heat to medium-low; cook, covered, until a thermometer inserted into chops reads 145°, about 4-5 minutes. Remove chops from skillet; let stand for 5 minutes.

3. In a small bowl, mix cornstarch and water until smooth; stir into cider mixture in skillet. Return to a boil, stirring constantly; cook and stir until thickened, 1-2 minutes. Pour over chops; sprinkle with fresh parsley.

Per 1 pork chop: 301 cal., 14g fat (4g sat. fat), 82mg chol., 210mg sod., 8g carb. (5g sugars, 0 fiber), 33g pro.

Diabetic Exchanges: 4 lean meat, 1 fat, ½ starch.

Grilled Kiwi-Chicken Kabobs with Honey-Chipotle Glaze

When guests bite into these juicy kabobs, their eyes always widen with satisfaction. Our four kids go crazy for the spicy sauce.

—**JONI HILTON** ROCKLIN, CA

PREP: 20 MIN. + MARINATING
GRILL: 10 MIN. • **MAKES:** 8 KABOBS

- 6 **garlic cloves, minced**
- 2 **tablespoons lime juice**
- 1 **tablespoon olive oil**
- 1 **teaspoon salt**
- 1 **pound boneless skinless chicken breasts, cut into 1-inch cubes**
- 8 **medium kiwifruit, peeled and halved**
- 3 **tablespoons honey**
- 1 **tablespoon minced chipotle peppers in adobo sauce**

1. Combine garlic, lime juice, oil and salt. Add chicken and kiwi; turn to coat. Refrigerate, covered, up to 30 minutes.

2. Mix honey and chipotle peppers. Drain chicken and kiwi, discarding marinade. On eight metal or soaked wooden skewers, alternately thread chicken and kiwi.

3. Grill, covered, on an oiled rack over medium heat, turning occasionally, until juices run clear, 10-12 minutes. During last 4 minutes, baste kabobs frequently with honey mixture.

Per 2 kabobs: 284 cal., 5g fat (1g sat. fat), 63mg chol., 380mg sod., 37g carb. (27g sugars, 5g fiber), 25g pro.

GRILLED KIWI-CHICKEN KABOBS WITH HONEY-CHIPOTLE GLAZE

THE SOUTH IN A POT SOUP

The South in a Pot Soup

With black-eyed peas, sweet potatoes, ground beef and spices, this soup has every wonderful memory from my childhood simmered together in one pot.

—**STEPHANIE RABBITT-SCHAPP** CINCINNATI, OH

PREP: 15 MIN. • **COOK:** 45 MIN.
MAKES: 8 SERVINGS (2½ QUARTS)

- 1 **tablespoon canola oil**
- 1½ **pounds lean ground beef (90% lean)**
- 1 **large sweet potato, peeled and diced**
- 1 **large sweet onion, diced**
- 1 **medium sweet pepper (any color), diced**
- 1 **can (15½ ounces) black-eyed peas, rinsed and drained**
- 1 **tablespoon ground cumin**
- 1 **tablespoon curry powder**
- ¾ **teaspoon salt**
- ½ **teaspoon coarsely ground pepper**
- 2 **cans (14½ ounces each) reduced-sodium beef broth**
- 4 **cups chopped collard greens**

1. In a Dutch oven, heat oil over medium heat. Cook and stir ground beef, crumbling meat, until no longer pink, 8 to 10 minutes. Add sweet potato, onion and pepper; saute until onion and pepper are slightly softened, 4-5 minutes.

2. Add black-eyed peas, cumin, curry, salt and pepper; stir in broth and bring to a boil. Reduce the heat; simmer until sweet potato is almost tender, 15-18 minutes.

3. Add collard greens; cook until tender, 15-18 minutes. If desired, add more cumin and curry.

Per 1¼ cups: 267 cal., 9g fat (3g sat. fat), 55mg chol., 544mg sod., 23g carb. (8g sugars, 5g fiber), 22g pro. **Diabetic Exchanges:** 2 lean meat, 1 starch, 1 vegetable, ½ fat.

TANGY APPLE
SLAW BURGERS

**BAKED
SWEET POTATO FRIES**
Amber Massey
Argyle, TX

Tangy Apple Slaw Burgers

I'm always looking for fresh new ways to make burgers. We love to grill and have several varieties of apple trees, so this recipe was a natural! Extra apple slaw makes an instant side dish.

—TRISHA KRUSE EAGLE, ID

PREP: 20 MIN. • **GRILL:** 15 MIN.
MAKES: 4 SERVINGS

- ½ **medium head cabbage, finely shredded**
- 2 **crisp unpeeled medium apples, shredded**
- 1 **medium carrot, peeled and grated**
- 3 **tablespoons finely chopped onion**
- 1 **garlic clove, finely minced**
- ¼ **cup fat-free mayonnaise**
- ½ **teaspoon grated lime peel**
- 1 **teaspoon lime juice**
- ½ **teaspoon pepper**
- ¼ **teaspoon salt**

BURGERS
- 1½ **pounds lean ground beef (90% lean)**
- ½ **teaspoon salt**
- ¼ **teaspoon pepper**
- 4 **hamburger buns, split**

1. Combine first five ingredients; remove ¼ cup cabbage mixture and reserve. Add the mayonnaise, lime peel, lime juice, pepper and salt to remaining cabbage mixture, tossing well to coat. Refrigerate, covered, until burgers are grilled.

2. For burgers, gently combine beef and reserved cabbage mixture. Mix lightly but thoroughly; shape into four patties. Season with salt and pepper.

3. Grill burgers, covered, on a greased grill rack over medium-high direct heat 5-7 minutes on each side until a thermometer reads 160°. Grill buns just until toasted, about 1 minute. To serve, place a burger and ¼ cup apple slaw on each bun bottom; replace tops. Serve with remaining slaw.

Per 1 burger with ½ cup additional slaw: 479 cal., 16g fat (6g sat. fat), 106mg chol., 902mg sod., 44g carb. (17g sugars, 6g fiber), 39g pro.

GOES GREAT WITH

Baked Sweet Potato Fries

2 large sweet potatoes, cut into thin strips • 2 Tbsp. canola oil • 1 tsp. garlic powder • 1 tsp. paprika • 1 tsp. kosher salt • ¼ tsp. cayenne pepper • Preheat oven to 425°. In a large bowl, combine all ingredients; toss well to coat. Spread fries in a single layer on two baking sheets. Bake until crispy and speckled brown, 35-40 minutes. Serve immediately. **Makes 4 servings.** —Amber Massey, Argyle, TX

✳

TEST KITCHEN TIP
Give your fries the gourmet treatment with a honey barbecue ketchup for dipping. Mix ¼ cup each of ketchup and honey, 2 tablespoons barbecue sauce and 1½ teaspoons each cider vinegar and molasses.

Asparagus Ham Dinner

I've been making this light meal for my family for years now, and it's always well received. With asparagus, tomato, pasta and chunks of ham, it's a tempting blend of tastes and textures.

—**RHONDA ZAVODNY** DAVID CITY, NE

START TO FINISH: 25 MIN.
MAKES: 6 SERVINGS

- 2 **cups uncooked corkscrew or spiral pasta**
- ¾ **pound fresh asparagus, cut into 1-inch pieces**
- 1 **medium sweet yellow pepper, julienned**
- 1 **tablespoon olive oil**
- 6 **medium tomatoes, diced**
- 6 **ounces boneless fully cooked ham, cubed**
- ¼ **cup minced fresh parsley**
- ½ **teaspoon salt**
- ½ **teaspoon dried oregano**
- ½ **teaspoon dried basil**
- ⅛ **to ¼ teaspoon cayenne pepper**
- ¼ **cup shredded Parmesan cheese**

Cook pasta according to package directions. Meanwhile, in a large nonstick skillet, saute asparagus and yellow pepper in oil until crisp-tender. Add tomatoes and ham; heat through. Drain pasta; add to vegetable mixture. Stir in parsley and seasonings. Sprinkle with cheese.

Per 1⅓ cups: 204 cal., 5g fat (1g sat. fat), 17mg chol., 561mg sod., 29g carb. (5g sugars, 3g fiber), 12g pro. **Diabetic Exchanges:** 1½ starch, 1 lean meat, 1 vegetable, ½ fat.

GOES **GREAT** WITH

Cinnamon-Strawberry Sundaes

1 Tbsp. butter • 2 Tbsp. brown sugar • 1 Tbsp. lime juice • ¼ tsp. ground cinnamon • 2 cups sliced fresh or frozen strawberries, thawed • 2 cups vanilla ice cream • 1 tsp. grated lime peel • In a small saucepan, melt butter over medium heat. Stir in brown sugar, lime juice and cinnamon. Cook and stir until sugar is dissolved. Add strawberries; cook until tender, about 2 minutes longer. Serve with ice cream; sprinkle with lime peel. **Makes 4 servings.**
—*Cory Roberts, Riverton, UT*

ASPARAGUS
HAM DINNER

CINNAMON-STRAWBERRY
SUNDAES

EAT SMART **FAST FIX** ▶

Asian-Style Salmon Packets

My husband and I love salmon, so I'm always looking for fun ways to change it up. We both love the blend of heat and citrus, plus the foil packet makes for easy cooking and cleanup!

—ROXANNE CHAN ALBANY, CA

START TO FINISH: 25 MIN.
MAKES: 4 SERVINGS

- 4 slices sweet onion
- 4 salmon fillets (6 ounces each)
- 3 tablespoons chili sauce
- 1 tablespoon lime juice
- 1 tablespoon sesame oil
- 1 garlic clove, minced
- 1 teaspoon mustard seed
- 1 teaspoon minced fresh gingerroot
- ½ teaspoon black sesame seeds
  Chopped fresh mint
  Grated lime peel

1. Preheat oven to 400°. Place each onion slice on a double thickness of heavy-duty foil (about 12 in. square). Top with salmon. Combine next seven ingredients; spoon over fillets. Fold foil around mixture; crimp edges to seal.
2. Place on a baking sheet. Bake until fish flakes easily with a fork, 15-20 minutes. Be careful of escaping steam when opening packets. Serve with mint and lime peel.

Per 1 salmon fillet with 1 tablespoon sauce: 319 cal., 19g fat (4g sat. fat), 85mg chol., 259mg sod., 5g carb. (3g sugars, 0 fiber), 29g pro.
Diabetic Exchanges: 4 lean meat, 1 fat.

GOES GREAT WITH

Cilantro-Lime Rice

1 cup uncooked jasmine rice • 2 cups reduced-sodium chicken broth • 2 Tbsp. fresh lime juice • 2 Tbsp. minced fresh cilantro • ⅛ tsp. ground nutmeg • In a small saucepan, combine rice and broth; bring to a boil. Reduce heat; simmer, covered, for 12-15 minutes or until liquid is absorbed and rice is tender. Add lime juice, cilantro and nutmeg; fluff with a fork.
Makes 3 cups.
—Robin Baskette, Lexington, KY

ASIAN-STYLE
SALMON PACKETS

CILANTRO-LIME RICE

Turkey Asparagus Stir-Fry

(PICTURED ON P. 93)

Twenty minutes is all you'll need to make this quick stir-fry. Lean turkey, asparagus and mushrooms make it super nutritious and satisfying, too.

—**DARLENE KENNEDY** GALION, OH

START TO FINISH: 20 MIN.
MAKES: 5 SERVINGS

- 1 tablespoon olive oil
- 1 pound boneless skinless turkey breast halves, cut into strips
- 1 pound fresh asparagus, cut into 1-inch pieces
- 4 ounces fresh mushrooms, sliced
- 2 medium carrots, quartered lengthwise and cut into 1-inch pieces
- 4 green onions, cut into 1-inch pieces
- 2 garlic cloves, minced
- ½ teaspoon ground ginger
- ⅔ cup cold water
- 2 tablespoons reduced-sodium soy sauce
- 4 teaspoons cornstarch
- 1 can (8 ounces) sliced water chestnuts, drained
- 3½ cups hot cooked white or brown rice
- 1 medium tomato, cut into wedges

1. In a large skillet or wok, heat oil over medium-high heat. Add turkey; stir-fry until no longer pink, about 5 minutes. Remove and keep warm.
2. Add next six ingredients to pan; stir-fry until vegetables are crisp-tender, about 5 minutes. Combine water, soy sauce and cornstarch; add to skillet with water chestnuts. Bring to a boil; cook and stir 1-2 minutes or until sauce is thickened. Return turkey to skillet and heat through. Serve with rice and tomato wedges.

Per 1 cup with ¾ cup rice: 343 cal., 5g fat (1g sat. fat), 52mg chol., 363mg sod., 47g carb. (4g sugars, 4g fiber), 28g pro.
Diabetic Exchanges: 3 starch, 3 lean meat, 1 vegetable, ½ fat.

WEEKNIGHT APPLE CRISP

PORK TENDERLOIN WITH CRANBERRY-ORANGE RELISH

Pork Tenderloin with Cranberry-Orange Relish

I like how grilled pork and fruit bring out the best in each other. If you have leftover relish, break out the tortilla chips!

—**CINDY ESPOSITO** BLOOMFIELD, NJ

PREP: 15 MIN. • **COOK:** 15 MIN. + STANDING
MAKES: 4 SERVINGS

- 1½ cups fresh cranberries
- 2 green onions, minced
- 1 seeded jalapeno pepper, minced
- ⅓ cup sugar
- 3 tablespoons minced fresh mint
- 2 tablespoons lime juice
- 1 tablespoon orange juice
- ¼ teaspoon ground ginger
- 2 pork tenderloins (¾ pound each)
- 1 tablespoon olive oil
- ½ teaspoon salt
- ½ teaspoon pepper

1. To make relish, pulse cranberries in food processor until finely chopped. Combine with next seven ingredients. Reserve ½ cup relish for grilling; cover and refrigerate the rest.
2. Brush tenderloins with olive oil; sprinkle with salt and pepper. Grill, covered, over direct heat 12-15 minutes, turning occasionally and spooning with reserved relish, until thermometer reads 145°. Let stand 10-15 minutes. Discard used relish. Slice meat; serve with refrigerated relish.

Per serving: 319 cal., 9g fat (2g sat. fat), 95mg chol., 366mg sod., 24g carb. (19g sugars, 2g fiber), 34g pro.

GOES GREAT WITH

Weeknight Apple Crisp

¼ cup granulated sugar • 1½ tsp. cinnamon, divided • 5 large apples, peeled and sliced • ¾ cup old-fashioned oats • ¾ cup packed brown sugar • ½ cup all-purpose flour • 6 Tbsp. cold butter, cubed • Preheat oven to 350°. Stir together granulated sugar and ½ tsp. cinnamon; toss with apples. In a greased microwave-safe 11x7-in. baking dish, microwave apples until slightly softened, about 4 minutes. Meanwhile, using a fork, combine oats, brown sugar, flour and remaining cinnamon. Cut in butter until crumbly; sprinkle over apples. Bake until apples are soft and topping is golden brown, 30-40 minutes. Serve warm. **Makes 6 servings.**
—*Sally Treonze, Hillsborough, NJ*

EAT SMART FAST FIX ▶ Oven-Fried Green Tomato BLT

I have used this frying method on eggplant slices for years and decided to try it on my green tomatoes. It worked! Now my family loves them in BLTs.

—JOLENE MARTINELLI FREMONT, NH

START TO FINISH: 25 MIN.
MAKES: 4 SERVINGS

- 1 large green tomato (about 8 ounces)
- 1 large egg, beaten
- 1 cup panko (Japanese) bread crumbs
- ¼ teaspoon salt
- ¼ cup reduced-fat mayonnaise
- 2 green onions, thinly sliced
- 1 teaspoon snipped fresh dill or ¼ teaspoon dill weed
- 8 slices whole wheat bread, toasted
- 8 cooked center-cut bacon strips
- 4 Bibb or Boston lettuce leaves

1. Preheat broiler. Cut tomato into eight slices, each about ¼ in. thick. Place egg and bread crumbs in separate shallow bowls; mix salt into bread crumbs. Dip tomato slices in egg, then in bread crumb mixture, patting to help adhere.

2. Place tomato slices on a wire rack set in a 15x10x1-in. baking pan; broil 4-5 in. from heat until golden brown, about 30-45 seconds per side.

3. Mix mayonnaise, green onions and dill. Layer each of four slices of bread with two bacon strips, one lettuce leaf and two tomato slices. Spread mayonnaise mixture over remaining bread; place over top.

Per 1 sandwich: 313 cal., 12g fat (2g sat. fat), 55mg chol., 744mg sod., 36g carb. (5g sugars, 4g fiber), 16g pro.
Diabetic Exchanges: 2 starch, 2 high-fat meat, 1 fat.

GOES GREAT WITH

Simple Waldorf Salad

2 large Gala or Honeycrisp apples, chopped (about 3 cups) • 2 cups chopped celery • ¼ cup raisins • ¼ cup chopped walnuts, toasted • ⅓ cup reduced-fat mayonnaise • ⅓ cup plain yogurt

Combine apples, celery, raisins and walnuts. Add mayonnaise and yogurt; toss to coat. Refrigerate until serving. **Makes 6 servings.**

—*Wendy Masters, East Garafraxa, ON*

EAT SMART FAST FIX ▶

Pepper Ricotta Primavera

(PICTURED ON P. 92)

Garlic, peppers and herbs meet creamy ricotta cheese in this meatless skillet meal you can make in just 20 minutes.

—JANET BOULGER BOTWOOD, NL

START TO FINISH: 20 MIN.
MAKES: 6 SERVINGS

- 1 cup part-skim ricotta cheese
- ½ cup fat-free milk
- 4 teaspoons olive oil
- 1 garlic clove, minced
- ½ teaspoon crushed red pepper flakes
- 1 medium green pepper, julienned
- 1 medium sweet red pepper, julienned
- 1 medium sweet yellow pepper, julienned
- 1 medium zucchini, sliced
- 1 cup frozen peas, thawed
- ¼ teaspoon dried oregano
- ¼ teaspoon dried basil
- 6 ounces fettuccine, cooked and drained

Whisk together ricotta cheese and milk; set aside. In a large skillet, heat oil over medium heat. Add garlic and pepper flakes; saute 1 minute. Add next seven ingredients. Cook and stir over medium heat until vegetables are crisp-tender, about 5 minutes. Add the cheese mixture to fettuccine; top with vegetables. Toss to coat. Serve immediately.

Per 1 cup: 229 cal., 7g fat (3g sat. fat), 13mg chol., 88mg sod., 31g carb. (6g sugars, 4g fiber), 11g pro.
Diabetic Exchanges: 2 starch, 1 medium-fat meat, ½ fat.

SIMPLE WALDORF SALAD

OVEN-FRIED GREEN TOMATO BLT

Ginger Veggie Brown Rice Pasta

(PICTURED ON P. 93)

Once I discovered brown rice pasta, I never looked back. Tossed with ginger, bright veggies and rotisserie chicken, it tastes like a deconstructed egg roll!

—**TIFFANY IHLE** BRONX, NY

START TO FINISH: 30 MIN.
MAKES: 8 SERVINGS

- 2 cups uncooked brown rice elbow pasta
- 1 tablespoon coconut oil
- ½ small red onion, sliced
- 2 teaspoons ginger paste
- 2 teaspoons garlic paste
- 1½ cups chopped fresh Brussels sprouts
- ½ cup chopped red cabbage
- ½ cup shredded carrots
- ½ medium sweet red pepper, chopped
- ½ teaspoon salt
- ¼ teaspoon ground ancho chili pepper
- ¼ teaspoon coarsely ground pepper
- 1 shredded rotisserie chicken, skin removed
- 2 green onions, chopped

1. In a Dutch oven, cook pasta according to package directions.
2. Meanwhile, in a large skillet, heat coconut oil over medium heat. Add red onion, ginger paste and garlic paste; saute 2 minutes. Stir in next seven ingredients; cook until vegetables are crisp-tender, 4-6 minutes. Add chicken; heat through.
3. Drain pasta, reserving 1 cup pasta water. Return pasta to Dutch oven. Add vegetable mixture; toss to coat, adding enough reserved pasta water to moisten pasta. Sprinkle with green onions before serving.

Per 1 cup: 270 cal., 7g fat (3g sat. fat), 55mg chol., 257mg sod., 29g carb. (2g sugars, 2g fiber), 21g pro.
Diabetic Exchanges: 3 lean meat, 2 starch, 1 fat.
Notes: You may substitute an equal volume of minced fresh garlic and ginger for the pastes. Canola or olive oil may be substituted for coconut oil.

GLAZED PORK
ON SWEET POTATO BEDS

Glazed Pork on Sweet Potato Beds

When solving the what's-for-dinner puzzle, this maple-glazed pork tenderloin is often our top choice. Add sweet potatoes for a comfy side.

—**JESSIE GREARSON-SAPAT** FALMOUTH, ME

PREP: 20 MIN. • **COOK:** 30 MIN.
MAKES: 6 SERVINGS

- 1½ pounds sweet potatoes, peeled and cubed
- 1 medium apple, peeled and cut into 8 pieces
- 2 tablespoons butter
- 1 tablespoon lemon juice
- 2 teaspoons minced fresh gingerroot
- ½ teaspoon salt
- ½ teaspoon pepper

PORK

- 1 teaspoon water
- ½ teaspoon cornstarch
- 3 tablespoons maple syrup
- 2 teaspoons wasabi mustard
- 2 teaspoons soy sauce
- ½ teaspoon pepper
- 1½ pounds pork tenderloin, cut into 1-inch slices
- 1 tablespoon olive oil
- 2 garlic cloves, minced

1. Place sweet potatoes and apple in a large saucepan with water to cover. Bring to a boil over high heat. Reduce heat to medium; cover and cook just until tender, 10-12 minutes. Drain. Mash potatoes and apple. Add the next five ingredients; keep warm.
2. Stir water into cornstarch until smooth; add syrup, mustard, soy sauce and pepper. Add pork; stir to coat.
3. In a large skillet, heat oil over medium heat. Brown pork. Add garlic; cook until meat is no longer pink, 3-5 minutes longer. Serve with sweet potatoes and pan juices.

Per 3 ounces pork with ½ cup sweet potato mixture: 327 cal., 10g fat (4g sat. fat), 74mg chol., 473mg sod., 33g carb. (13g sugars, 4g fiber), 25g pro.
Diabetic Exchanges: 3 lean meat, 2 starch, 1 fat.

SONORAN SUNSET
WATERMELON ICE

PORK BANH MI WRAPS
Nicole Hood
Leesville, LA

FAST FIX

Pork Banh Mi Wraps

Crunchy veggies and Asian flavors make this a great wrap for summer. You can substitute a baguette for the wrap, or switch up the meat for five-spice chicken or spicy beef. Even lemongrass shrimp would be delicious!

—**NICOLE HOOD** LEESVILLE, LA

START TO FINISH: 30 MIN.
MAKES: 4 SERVINGS

- 4 **boneless pork loin chops (4 ounces each)**
- ¼ **teaspoon pepper**
- 1 **tablespoon olive oil**
- ½ **cup sweet chili sauce, divided**
- 2 **tablespoons reduced-sodium soy sauce**
- 1¼ **cups shredded lettuce**
- 1 **medium carrot, peeled and shredded**
- 2 **tablespoons rice vinegar**
- 4 **bread wraps (9 inches)**
- ¼ **cup reduced-fat mayonnaise**
- 1 **small cucumber, peeled and sliced into 3-inch strips**
- ¼ **cup chopped fresh cilantro**
- 2 **green onions, chopped**
- ½ **jalapeno pepper, seeded and thinly sliced**
  Sriracha Asian hot chili sauce

1. Sprinkle pork chops with pepper. In a large skillet, heat oil over medium heat. Add chops; cook 2-3 minutes on each side until a thermometer reads 145°. Combine ¼ cup sweet chili sauce with soy sauce; pour over pork chops. Reduce heat to medium-low; cook and stir until sauce is slightly thickened, 2-3 minutes. Remove from heat.

2. Combine lettuce and carrot with rice vinegar; set aside. When the pork is cool enough to handle, slice into 2-in.-long strips; return to skillet to coat with sauce. Toast bread wraps lightly, then spread with mayonnaise.

3. Spoon pork evenly over wraps. Cover with lettuce mixture, cucumber, cilantro, green onions and jalapeno. Top with remaining sweet chili sauce. Fold wraps over filling and serve immediately with Sriracha sauce.

Per 1 filled wrap: 471 cal., 18g fat (4g sat. fat), 60mg chol., 1344mg sod., 54g carb. (21g sugars, 7g fiber), 26g pro.

GOES GREAT WITH

Sonoran Sunset Watermelon Ice

½ cup sugar • ¼ cup water • 4 cups cubed seedless watermelon • 3 Tbsp. lime juice • 2 Tbsp. pomegranate juice • 1 Tbsp. minced fresh cilantro • Dash salt • In a saucepan, bring sugar and water to a boil; cook and stir until sugar is dissolved. Cool. Puree watermelon. Transfer to a bowl; stir in the sugar syrup and remaining ingredients. Refrigerate until cold. Pour into ice cream maker; freeze according to manufacturer's directions. Transfer to freezer containers, allowing some headspace for expansion. Freeze 4 hours. **Makes 6 servings.**

—*Jeanne Holt, Mendota Heights, MN*

Sauteed Pork Chops with Garlic Spinach

My family enjoys cooking up easy and delicious meals. This pork chop recipe is also inexpensive, which makes cooking easier for everyone.

—**JOE VALERIO** WHITINSVILLE, MA

START TO FINISH: 20 MIN.
MAKES: 4 SERVINGS

- 1 **tablespoon olive oil**
- 4 **bone-in pork loin chops (8 ounces each)**
- ¼ **teaspoon salt**
- ¼ **teaspoon pepper**
- 1 **medium lemon**

GARLIC SPINACH

- 1 **tablespoon olive oil**
- 3 **garlic cloves, thinly sliced**
- 2 **packages (5 ounces each) fresh spinach, stems removed**
- ½ **teaspoon salt**
- ¼ **teaspoon coarsely ground pepper**
- 1 **teaspoon lemon juice**

1. In a large skillet, heat oil over medium-high heat. Sprinkle pork chops with salt and pepper; add to skillet. Saute until a thermometer reads 145°, about 5 minutes per side. Remove to a serving platter; squeeze juice from lemon over chops. Tent with foil; let stand at least 5 minutes before serving.
2. For garlic spinach, heat oil over medium-high heat in same skillet. Add garlic; cook until it just begins to brown, about 45 seconds. Add the spinach; cook and stir just until wilted, 2-3 minutes. Sprinkle with salt and pepper. Remove from heat; add lemon juice. Transfer to serving platter. Remove foil from pork; serve spinach with chops.
Per 1 pork chop with ½ cup spinach: 396 cal., 25g fat (8g sat. fat), 111mg chol., 612mg sod., 4g carb. (1g sugars, 1g fiber), 37g pro.

Lemon & Garlic New Potatoes

1 lb. small red potatoes • 2 Tbsp. olive oil • 2 garlic cloves, minced • ¼ cup shredded Parmesan cheese • 2 Tbsp. lemon juice • ¼ tsp. salt • ¼ tsp. pepper • Cut potatoes in wedges and place in large saucepan; add water to cover. Bring to a boil. Cook, covered, until potatoes are tender, 10-15 minutes; drain. In the same pan, heat oil over medium-high heat. Add the potatoes; cook until browned, 4-6 minutes. Add garlic; cook 1 minute. Remove from heat. Stir in remaining ingredients. **Makes 4 servings.**
—*Katie Bartle, Parkville, MO*

Curried Squash & Sausage

This stovetop supper is simple to make, and it charms my whole family of curry lovers. My kids even like it cold and ask to have it packed that way in their school lunches.

—**COLETTE LOWER** YORK, PA

PREP: 15 MIN. • **COOK:** 20 MIN.
MAKES: 8 SERVINGS

- 1 **pound mild bulk Italian sausage**
- 1 **tablespoon olive oil**
- 1 **medium onion, chopped**
- 1 **medium green pepper, chopped**
- 1 **large acorn squash or 6 cups butternut squash, seeded, peeled and cubed (½ in.)**
- 1 **large unpeeled apple, cubed (½ in.)**
- 2 **to 3 teaspoons curry powder**
- 1 **teaspoon salt**
- 3 **cups cooked small pasta shells**
- ¼ **cup water**

1. In a stockpot, cook and crumble sausage over medium heat until no longer pink, 5-6 minutes; remove.
2. In same pan, heat oil; cook and stir onion and pepper 3 minutes. Add squash; cook 5 minutes. Stir in apple, curry powder and salt until vegetables are crisp-tender, 3-4 minutes.
3. Return sausage to pan; add pasta and water. Heat through.
Per 1⅓ cups: 385 cal., 18g fat (5g sat. fat), 38mg chol., 735mg sod., 44g carb. (7g sugars, 4g fiber), 14g pro.

LEMON & GARLIC
NEW POTATOES

SAUTEED PORK CHOPS
WITH GARLIC SPINACH

PORK CHOPS WITH
HONEY-GARLIC SAUCE

CRANBERRY-PECAN
WHEAT BERRY SALAD

ROASTED BEET WEDGES

CHICKEN PESTO ROLL-UPS

Cranberry-Pecan Wheat Berry Salad

I love to experiment with different grains and wanted to give wheat berries a try. My whole family goes nuts for this salad, especially my mom.
—**KRISTEN HEIGL** STATEN ISLAND, NY

PREP: 20 MIN. • **COOK:** 70 MIN. + COOLING
MAKES: 8 SERVINGS

- 1 cup uncooked wheat berries, rinsed
- 2 celery ribs, finely chopped
- 1 medium tart apple, diced
- 4 green onions, sliced
- 1 cup dried cranberries
- 1 cup chopped pecans

DRESSING
- 3 tablespoons walnut oil
- 2 tablespoons cider vinegar
- 1 tablespoon minced fresh sage or 1 teaspoon rubbed sage
- 2 teaspoons minced fresh thyme or ¾ teaspoon dried thyme
- 2 teaspoons Worcestershire sauce
- 1 teaspoon Dijon mustard
- ¾ teaspoon salt
- ½ teaspoon pepper

Cook wheat berries according to package directions; drain and cool. Meanwhile, combine next five ingredients; add wheat berries. Whisk together dressing ingredients. Pour over salad; toss to coat. Serve at room temperature or chilled.

Per ¾ cup: 298 cal., 15g fat (1g sat. fat), 0 chol., 261mg sod., 39g carb. (17g sugars, 6g fiber), 5g pro.

GOES GREAT WITH

Pork Chops with Honey-Garlic Sauce

4 bone-in pork loin chops (6 oz. each) • ¼ cup lemon juice • ¼ cup honey • 2 Tbsp. reduced-sodium soy sauce • 1 garlic clove, minced • In a large nonstick skillet coated with cooking spray, cook pork chops over medium heat until a thermometer reads 145°, 5-6 minutes on each side. Remove; let stand 5 minutes. Combine remaining ingredients; add to pan. Cook over medium heat 3-4 minutes, stirring occasionally. Serve with chops. **Makes 4 servings.**
—*Michelle Smith, Eldersburg, MD*

Chicken Pesto Roll-Ups

One night I looked in the refrigerator and thought, "What can I make with chicken, cheese, mushrooms and pesto?" This pretty dish was the result. Add Italian bread and fruit salad and you have a meal!
—**MELISSA NORDMANN** MOBILE, AL

PREP: 15 MIN. • **BAKE:** 30 MIN.
MAKES: 4 SERVINGS

- 4 boneless skinless chicken breast halves (6 ounces each)
- ½ cup prepared pesto, divided
- 1 pound medium fresh mushrooms, sliced
- 4 slices reduced-fat provolone cheese, halved

1. Preheat oven to 350°. Pound chicken breasts with a meat mallet to ¼-in. thickness. Spread ¼ cup pesto over chicken breasts.
2. Coarsely chop half of the sliced mushrooms; scatter remaining sliced mushrooms in a 15x10x1-in. baking pan coated with cooking spray. Top each chicken breast with a fourth of the chopped mushrooms and a halved cheese slice. Roll up chicken from a short side; secure with toothpicks. Place seam side down on top of the sliced mushrooms.
3. Bake, covered, until chicken is no longer pink, 25-30 minutes. Preheat broiler; top chicken with remaining pesto and remaining cheese. Broil until cheese is melted and browned, 3-5 minutes longer. Discard toothpicks.

Per 1 stuffed chicken breast half: 374 cal., 17g fat (5g sat. fat), 104mg chol., 582mg sod., 7g carb. (1g sugars, 1g fiber), 44g pro.
Diabetic Exchanges: 5 lean meat, 2 fat.

GOES GREAT WITH

Roasted Beet Wedges

1 lb. medium fresh beets, peeled • 4 tsp. olive oil • ½ tsp. kosher salt • 3 to 5 fresh rosemary sprigs • Preheat oven to 400°. Cut each beet into six wedges. Toss with oil and salt. Place a 12-in.-long piece of foil in a 15x10x1-in. baking pan. Top with beets and rosemary. Fold foil around beets and seal. Bake until tender, 1¼-1½ hours. Open foil carefully to allow steam to escape. Serve warm or cold. **Makes 4 servings.**
—*Wendy Stenman, Germantown, WI*

JICAMA CITRUS SALAD
Crystal Bruns
Illiff, CO

BUTTERNUT GOULASH

Butternut Goulash

We make this treasured family goulash recipe using squash from our backyard. The chili powder and cayenne really warm you up!

—ALLISON WILMARTH FOREST CITY, PA

PREP: 25 MIN.
COOK: 45 MIN.
MAKES: 8 SERVINGS (2½ QUARTS)

- 2 tablespoons butter
- 1 pound lean ground beef (90% lean)
- 1 large red pepper, chopped
- 1 cup chopped onion
- 1 can (28 ounces) no-salt-added crushed tomatoes
- 1½ cups peeled butternut squash, cut into ½-inch cubes
- 1 can (8 ounces) no-salt-added tomato sauce
- 1 cup reduced-sodium beef broth
- 1 teaspoon salt
- ½ to ¾ teaspoon chili powder
- ⅛ to ¼ teaspoon cayenne pepper
- ⅛ teaspoon dried oregano
- 2 cups chopped zucchini
  Shredded cheddar cheese, optional

1. In a Dutch oven, heat butter over medium-high heat. Add beef, red pepper and onion; cook, crumbling beef, until meat is no longer pink and vegetables are tender, 6-8 minutes; drain.
2. Add the next eight ingredients. Bring to a boil; reduce heat to low. Simmer, covered, about 20 minutes; add zucchini. Continue simmering until vegetables are tender, another 20-25 minutes. Just before serving, sprinkle with cheese if desired.

Per 1¼ cups: 196 cal., 8g fat (4g sat. fat), 44mg chol., 450mg sod., 17g carb. (7g sugars, 5g fiber), 14g pro.
Diabetic Exchanges: 2 lean meat, 1 starch, 1 fat.

GOES **GREAT** WITH

Jicama Citrus Salad

8 tangerines, peeled, quartered and sliced • 1 lb. medium jicama, peeled and cubed • 2 shallots, thinly sliced • 2 Tbsp. lemon or lime juice • ¼ cup chopped fresh cilantro • ½ tsp. salt • ½ tsp. pepper

Combine all ingredients; refrigerate until serving. **Makes 10 servings.**

—*Crystal Bruns, Illiff, CO*

FAST FIX ▶ Shrimp Po'Boys with Pineapple Slaw

This great twist on the traditional po'boy sandwich adds flavor and grains while reducing fat and calories. For a smoked flavor, grill the shrimp. For a low-carb option, serve the po'boy open-faced on a baguette half.

—MELISSA PELKEY HASS WALESKA, GA

START TO FINISH: 30 MIN.
MAKES: 6 SERVINGS

- ⅓ cup egg substitute
- ½ cup panko (Japanese) bread crumbs
- 2 tablespoons reduced-sodium Creole seasoning (Tony Chachere)
- 1 pound uncooked shrimp (16-20 per pound), peeled and deveined
- 2 cups broccoli coleslaw mix
- 1 cup unsweetened pineapple tidbits, drained, 3 tablespoons liquid reserved
- 2 green onions, chopped
- ½ cup reduced-fat mayonnaise
- 6 hoagie buns, split and toasted
- 4 tablespoons reduced-fat or fat-free tartar sauce
- 3 medium tomatoes, sliced

1. Preheat oven to 400°. Pour egg substitute into a shallow bowl. In a separate shallow bowl, mix bread crumbs and Creole seasoning. Dip shrimp in egg substitute, then in crumb mixture, patting to help coating adhere. Bake in a greased 15x10x1-in. pan until shrimp turns pink, 7-9 minutes. Keep warm.
2. Meanwhile, combine broccoli slaw, pineapple and green onions. In a small bowl, whisk mayonnaise and the reserved pineapple liquid until smooth. Add to broccoli mixture; toss to coat.
3. To serve, spread hoagie buns with tartar sauce. Divide the tomato slices and shrimp among buns. Top with pineapple broccoli slaw.
Per 1 sandwich: 420 cal., 13g fat (2g sat. fat), 99mg chol., 1430mg sod., 54g carb. (15g sugars, 3g fiber), 23g pro.

SPICY PLUM SALMON

SHRIMP PO'BOYS WITH PINEAPPLE SLAW

EAT SMART ⑤INGREDIENTS
Spicy Plum Salmon

I created this sweet and spicy salmon for a healthy recipe challenge. The fresh plum sauce really complements the smoky grilled fish.

—CHERYL HOCHSTETTLER RICHMOND, TX

PREP: 25 MIN. • **GRILL:** 10 MIN.
MAKES: 6 SERVINGS

- 5 medium plums, divided
- ½ cup water
- 2 tablespoons ketchup
- 1 chipotle pepper in adobo sauce, finely chopped
- 1 tablespoon sugar
- 1 tablespoon olive oil
- 6 salmon fillets (6 ounces each)
- ¾ teaspoon salt

1. Coarsely chop two plums; place in a small saucepan. Add water; bring to a boil. Reduce heat; simmer, uncovered, 10-15 minutes or until plums are softened and the liquid is almost evaporated. Cool slightly. Transfer to a food processor; add ketchup, chipotle, sugar and oil. Process until pureed. Reserve ¾ cup sauce for serving.
2. Sprinkle salmon with salt; place on a greased grill rack, skin side up. Grill, covered, over medium heat until fish just begins to flake easily with a fork, about 10 minutes. Brush with the remaining sauce during last 3 minutes. Slice remaining plums. Serve salmon with plum slices and reserved sauce.
Per 1 salmon fillet with ½ plum and 2 tablespoons sauce: 325 cal., 18g fat (3g sat. fat), 85mg chol., 460mg sod., 10g carb. (9g sugars, 1g fiber), 29g pro.
Diabetic Exchanges: 5 lean meat, 1 fruit, ½ fat.

Balsamic Roasted Vegetable Primavera

Roasting makes these end-of-summer veggies irresistible. Toss them with balsamic vinegar and pasta for a light but satisfying dinner.

—**CARLY CURTIN** ELLICOTT CITY, MD

PREP: 15 MIN. • **BAKE:** 20 MIN.
MAKES: 4 SERVINGS

- 4 **medium carrots, sliced**
- 2 **medium zucchini, coarsely chopped (about 3 cups)**
- 1⅔ **cups cherry tomatoes**
- ¼ **cup olive oil**
- 3 **tablespoons balsamic vinegar**
- 1 **tablespoon minced fresh thyme or 1 teaspoon dried thyme**
- 2 **teaspoons minced fresh rosemary or ½ teaspoon dried rosemary, crushed**
- 1 **teaspoon salt**
- ½ **teaspoon garlic powder**
- 8 **ounces uncooked rigatoni or whole wheat rigatoni**
- ¼ **cup shredded Parmesan cheese**

1. Preheat oven to 400°. Combine carrots, zucchini and tomatoes in a greased 15x10x1-in. baking pan. Whisk together next six ingredients; reserve half. Drizzle remaining balsamic mixture over vegetables; toss to coat. Bake until carrots are crisp-tender, 20-25 minutes.

2. Meanwhile, cook the rigatoni according to package directions; drain. Toss rigatoni with roasted vegetables, pan juices and reserved balsamic mixture. Sprinkle with cheese.

Per 1½ cups: 410 cal., 17g fat (3g sat. fat), 4mg chol., 731mg sod., 56g carb. (12g sugars, 5g fiber), 12g pro.
Diabetic Exchanges: 2 starch, 1 medium-fat meat, ½ fat.

✳
TEST KITCHEN TIP
If your garden is overflowing with large tomatoes, swap two in place of the cherry tomatoes. Don't be afraid to sprinkle additional fresh herbs just before serving, too. You'll be amazed at how they can perk up a dish.

PEPPER STEAK WITH SQUASH

Pepper Steak with Squash

My family loves it when I fix this colorful stir-fry with savory strips of flank steak and plenty of veggies. Served over rice, it's a satisfying supper that's on the table in just half an hour.

—**GAYLE LEWIS** YUCAIPA, CA

START TO FINISH: 30 MIN.
MAKES: 6 SERVINGS

- 1 **can (14½ ounces) reduced-sodium beef broth**
- 2 **tablespoons reduced-sodium soy sauce**
- 3 **tablespoons cornstarch**
- 2 **tablespoons canola oil, divided**
- 1 **beef flank steak (1 pound), cut into thin strips**
- 1 **medium green pepper, cut into thin strips**
- 1 **medium sweet red pepper, cut into thin strips**
- 2 **medium zucchini, cut into thin strips**
- 1 **small onion, cut into thin strips**
- 3 **garlic cloves, minced**
- 1 **cup fresh snow peas**
- 1 **cup sliced fresh mushrooms**
- 1 **can (8 ounces) sliced water chestnuts, drained**
  Hot cooked rice

1. Mix broth and soy sauce with cornstarch until smooth. Set aside.

2. In a large skillet, heat 1 tablespoon oil over medium-high heat. Add the beef; stir-fry until no longer pink, 2-3 minutes. Remove from pan.

3. In same skillet, heat remaining oil. Stir-fry peppers about 2 minutes. Add zucchini, onion and garlic; cook and stir 2 minutes longer. Add snow peas, mushrooms and water chestnuts. Stir-fry until crisp-tender, about 2 minutes more.

4. Stir cornstarch mixture and add to pan. Bring to a boil; cook and stir until sauce is thickened, 1-2 minutes. Return beef to skillet; heat through. Serve with hot cooked rice.

Per 1½ cups stir-fry without rice: 229 cal., 11g fat (3g sat. fat), 37mg chol., 381mg sod., 16g carb. (5g sugars, 3g fiber), 18g pro.
Diabetic Exchanges: 2 lean meat, 1 vegetable, ½ starch.

Apple Sausage Salad with Cinnamon Vinaigrette

Making croutons with cinnamon raisin bread is sweet genius. Toss together the rest of the salad while they toast.

—KIM VAN DUNK CALDWELL, NJ

PREP: 25 MIN. • **BAKE:** 10 MIN.
MAKES: 6 SERVINGS

- 4 **slices cinnamon-raisin bread**
- ⅓ **cup olive oil**
- 3 **tablespoons cider vinegar**
- 2 **teaspoons honey**
- ½ **teaspoon ground cinnamon**
- ⅛ **teaspoon sea salt**
  Dash pepper
- 1 **package (12 ounces) fully cooked apple chicken sausage links, cut diagonally in ½-inch-thick slices**
- 2 **packages (5 ounces each) spring mix salad greens**
- 2 **cups sliced fresh Bartlett pears**
- ½ **cup chopped walnuts, toasted**
- ½ **cup dried sweet cherries**

1. Preheat oven to 375°. Cut each slice of bread into 12 cubes; scatter over a 15x10-in. pan. Bake until toasted, 8-10 minutes, stirring halfway. Cool 5 minutes.

2. Meanwhile, combine next six ingredients in a jar with a tight-fitting lid. Shake until blended. In a large nonstick skillet, cook sausage over medium heat until browned and heated through, 2-3 minutes per side.

3. Divide salad greens among four dinner-size plates; add sausage to each plate. Top with pear slices, walnuts, cherries and croutons. Shake dressing again; spoon over salad and serve immediately.

Note: To toast walnuts, bake in a shallow pan in a 350° oven for 5-10 minutes or cook in a skillet over low heat until lightly browned, stirring occasionally.

Per serving: 404 cal., 23g fat (4g sat. fat), 40mg chol., 441mg sod., 39g carb. (23g sugars, 5g fiber), 14g pro.

COCONUT CURRY
CAULIFLOWER SOUP

APPLE SAUSAGE SALAD WITH
CINNAMON VINAIGRETTE

GOES GREAT WITH

Coconut Curry Cauliflower Soup

2 Tbsp. olive oil • 1 medium onion, finely chopped • 3 Tbsp. yellow curry paste • 2 medium heads cauliflower, broken into florets • 1 carton (32 oz.) vegetable broth • 1 cup coconut milk • In a large saucepan, heat oil over medium heat. Add onion; cook and stir until softened, 2-3 minutes. Add curry paste; cook until fragrant, 1-2 minutes. Add cauliflower and broth. Increase heat to high; bring to a boil. Reduce heat to medium-low; cook, covered, about 20 minutes. Stir in coconut milk; cook an additional minute. Remove from heat; cool slightly. Puree in batches in a blender or food processor. **Makes 10 servings (1 cup each).** —*Elizabeth DeHart, West Jordan, UT*

Thai Scallop Saute

Just open a bottle of Thai peanut sauce to give this seafood stir-fry some serious authenticity.

—*TASTE OF HOME* TEST KITCHEN

PREP: 15 MIN. • **COOK:** 20 MIN.
MAKES: 4 SERVINGS

- 3 teaspoons olive oil, divided
- 1½ pounds sea scallops
- 2 cups fresh broccoli florets
- 2 medium onions, halved and sliced
- 1 medium zucchini, sliced
- 4 small carrots, sliced
- ¼ cup Thai peanut sauce
- ¼ teaspoon salt
  Hot cooked rice
  Lime wedges, optional

1. In a large skillet, heat 1 teaspoon oil over medium-high heat. Add half of scallops; stir-fry until firm and opaque. Remove from pan. Repeat with an additional 1 teaspoon oil and remaining scallops.

2. In same skillet, heat remaining oil over medium-high heat. Add vegetables; stir-fry until crisp-tender, 7-9 minutes. Stir in peanut sauce and salt. Return scallops to pan; heat through. Serve with rice and, if desired, lime wedges.

Per 1½ cups without rice: 268 cal., 8g fat (1g sat. fat), 41mg chol., 1000mg sod., 24g carb. (10g sugars, 4g fiber), 25g pro.

THAI SCALLOP SAUTE

CONFETTI QUINOA

BALSAMIC CHICKEN & PEARS

EAT SMART | **FAST FIX** ▶

Balsamic Chicken & Pears

Pears and dried cherries go amazingly well with chicken and balsamic vinegar. It's easy enough to make for a weeknight meal, but you can also dress it up for company.

—**MARCIA WHITNEY** GAINESVILLE, FL

START TO FINISH: 30 MIN.
MAKES: 4 SERVINGS

- 4 boneless skinless chicken breast halves (6 ounces each)
- ¾ teaspoon salt
- ½ teaspoon pepper
- 1 tablespoon canola oil
- 1 cup reduced-sodium chicken broth
- 3 tablespoons white balsamic vinegar
- ½ teaspoon minced fresh rosemary
- 2 teaspoons cornstarch
- 1½ teaspoons sugar
- 2 medium unpeeled pears, each cut into 8 wedges
- ⅓ cup dried cherries or dried cranberries

1. Sprinkle chicken breasts with salt and pepper. In a large nonstick skillet, heat oil over medium-high heat. Add chicken; cook until a thermometer reads 165°, 8-10 minutes. Remove.

2. Meanwhile, stir together next five ingredients until blended. Pour into skillet; add pears and dried cherries. Bring to a boil over medium-high heat; reduce heat and simmer, covered, until pears are tender, about 5 minutes. Return chicken to skillet; simmer, uncovered, until heated through, 3-5 minutes. If desired, sprinkle with additional minced rosemary.

Per 1 chicken breast half with ⅓ cup sauce and 4 pear wedges: 335 cal., 8g fat (1g sat. fat), 94mg chol., 670mg sod., 30g carb. (22g sugars, 3g fiber), 36g pro. **Diabetic Exchanges:** 3 lean meat, 1½ starch, ½ fruit.

GOES GREAT WITH

Confetti Quinoa

2 cups water • 1 cup quinoa, rinsed • ½ cup chopped fresh broccoli • ½ cup coarsely chopped zucchini • ¼ cup shredded carrots • ½ tsp. salt • 1 Tbsp. lemon juice • 1 Tbsp. olive oil • In a large saucepan, bring water to a boil. Add the next five ingredients. Reduce the heat; simmer, covered, until liquid is absorbed, 12-15 minutes. Stir in lemon juice and oil; heat through. Remove from heat; fluff with a fork. **Makes 4 servings.**

—*Kim Ciepluch, Kenosha, WI*

Grecian Chicken

The caper, tomato and olive flavors whisk you away to the Greek isles in this easy skillet dish that's perfect for hectic weeknights.

—**JAN MARLER** MURCHISON, TX

START TO FINISH: 30 MIN.
MAKES: 4 SERVINGS

- **3 teaspoons olive oil, divided**
- **1 pound chicken tenderloins**
- **2 medium tomatoes, sliced**
- **1 cup sliced fresh mushrooms**
- **½ cup chopped onion**
- **1 tablespoon capers, drained**
- **1 tablespoon lemon-pepper seasoning**
- **1 tablespoon salt-free Greek seasoning**
- **1 medium garlic clove, minced**
- **½ cup water**
- **2 tablespoons chopped ripe olives**
  Hot cooked orzo pasta, optional

1. In a large skillet, heat 2 teaspoons olive oil over medium heat. Add chicken; saute until no longer pink, 7-9 minutes. Remove and keep warm.

2. In same skillet, heat remaining oil; add next six ingredients. Cook and stir until the onion is translucent, about 2-3 minutes. Stir in garlic; cook 1 minute more. Add water; bring to a boil. Reduce the heat; simmer, uncovered, until vegetables are tender, 3-4 minutes. Return chicken to skillet; add olives. Simmer, uncovered, until heated through, 2-3 minutes. If desired, serve with orzo.

Per serving without orzo: 172 cal., 5g fat (1g sat. fat), 56mg chol., 393mg sod., 6g carb. (3g sugars, 2g fiber), 28g pro. **Diabetic Exchanges:** 3 lean meat, 1 vegetable, 1 fat.

GOES GREAT WITH

Pesto Tomato-Cucumber Salad

½ cup Italian salad dressing
• **¼ cup prepared pesto** • **¼ tsp. salt**
• **¼ tsp. pepper** • **3 large tomatoes, quartered and sliced ½ in. thick**
• **2 medium peeled seeded cucumbers, halved lengthwise and sliced ¼ in. thick**
• **1 small red onion, halved and thinly sliced** • Whisk salad dressing, pesto, salt and pepper. Toss with tomatoes, cucumbers and onion. Refrigerate, covered, 30 minutes before serving. **Makes 8 servings.**

—*Jennifer Freier, Algonquin, IL*

PESTO TOMATO-CUCUMBER SALAD

GRECIAN CHICKEN

Grilled Asian Chicken Pasta Salad

This cool noodle salad makes a great casual one-bowl dinner or a perfect dish for a potluck or buffet.

—**SHARON TIPTON** CASSELBERRY, FL

PREP: 25 MIN. + MARINATING
GRILL: 10 MIN.
MAKES: 6 SERVINGS

- ¾ cup lime juice
- 3 tablespoons olive oil
- 3 tablespoons sesame oil
- 3 tablespoons reduced-sodium soy sauce
- 2 tablespoons minced fresh gingerroot
- 3 garlic cloves, minced
- 1 tablespoon sugar
- 1½ pounds boneless skinless chicken breasts
- 12 ounces uncooked angel hair pasta, broken
- 1 large sweet yellow pepper, chopped
- 1 large sweet red pepper, chopped
- 1 medium cucumber, peeled and chopped
- ¼ cup minced fresh parsley
- 2 green onions, sliced
- ¼ teaspoon crushed red pepper flakes

1. Combine first seven ingredients. Pour ¼ cup of marinade into a shallow dish, reserving the remainder. Add chicken and turn to coat. Refrigerate 30 minutes.

2. Drain chicken; discard marinade. Grill chicken, covered, on an oiled grill rack over medium heat (or broil 4 in. from heat) 5-7 minutes on each side, until a thermometer reads 165°.

3. Meanwhile, cook pasta according to package directions; drain and rinse in cold water. Combine remaining ingredients with reserved marinade. Cut chicken into 1-in. slices. Add pasta and chicken to vegetable mixture; toss to coat. Refrigerate until serving.

Per 1⅓ cups: 478 cal., 16g fat (3g sat. fat), 63mg chol., 321mg sod., 51g carb. (6g sugars, 3g fiber), 32g pro

Ginger Halibut with Brussels Sprouts

I moved to the United States from Russia and love cooking Russian food for family and friends. Halibut with soy sauce, ginger and pepper is a favorite.

—**MARGARITA PARKER** NEW BERN, NC

START TO FINISH: 25 MIN.
MAKES: SERVINGS

- 4 teaspoons lemon juice
- 4 halibut fillets (4 to 6 ounces each)
- 1 teaspoon minced fresh gingerroot
- ¼ to ¾ teaspoon salt, divided
- ¼ teaspoon pepper
- ½ cup water
- 10 ounces (about 2½ cups) fresh Brussels sprouts, halved
  Crushed red pepper flakes
- 1 tablespoon canola oil
- 5 garlic cloves, sliced lengthwise
- 2 tablespoons sesame oil
- 2 tablespoons soy sauce
  Lemon slices, optional

1. Brush lemon juice over halibut fillets. Sprinkle with minced ginger, ¼ teaspoon salt and pepper.

2. Place fish on an oiled grill rack, skin side down. Grill, covered, over medium heat (or broil 6 in. from heat) until fish just begins to flake easily with a fork, 6-8 minutes.

3. In a large skillet, bring water to a boil over medium-high heat. Add Brussels sprouts, pepper flakes and, if desired, remaining salt. Cook, covered, until tender, 5-7 minutes. Meanwhile, in a small skillet, heat oil over medium heat. Add garlic; cook until golden brown. Drain on paper towels.

4. Drizzle sesame oil and soy sauce over halibut. Serve with Brussels sprouts; sprinkle with fried garlic. If desired, serve with lemon slices.

Per 1 fillet with Brussels sprouts: 234 cal., 12g fat (2g sat. fat), 56mg chol., 701mg sod., 7g carb. (2g sugars, 3g fiber), 24g pro.
Diabetic Exchanges: 3 lean meat, 2 fat, 1 vegetable.

GRILLED ASIAN CHICKEN PASTA SALAD

GINGER HALIBUT WITH
BRUSSELS SPROUTS

**TERI RASEY'S
GREEK-STYLE STUFFED ACORN SQUASH**
PAGE 120

Side Dishes & Condiments

Enhance any meal with a side dish that's just as **special** as the entree. The **grain, veggie, bean, potato and pasta dishes** you'll find here make it easy. Give lip-smacking **barbecue sauce** and **homemade jam** a go, too!

KALLEE KRONG-MCCREERY'S SPICED CRAN-APPLE & GRAPE CONSERVE
PAGE 126

NANCY HEISHMAN'S CHINESE CHARD WITH ALMONDS
PAGE 130

KENDRA DOSS' GARDEN RISOTTO
PAGE 117

(5) INGREDIENTS
Raspberry Peach Jam

While my jam won a first-place ribbon at our county fair, that may not be the highest compliment it's received. Two girlfriends I share it with tell me that if they don't hide the jam from their husbands and children, they'll devour an entire jarful in just one sitting!

—PATRICIA LARSEN LESLIEVILLE, AB

PREP: 35 MIN. • **PROCESS:** 15 MIN.
MAKES: 3 HALF-PINTS

- 2⅔ cups finely chopped peeled peaches
- 1½ cups crushed raspberries
- 3 cups sugar
- 1½ teaspoons lemon juice

1. In a Dutch oven, combine all ingredients. Cook over low heat, stirring occasionally, until sugar has dissolved and mixture is bubbly, about 10 minutes. Bring to a full rolling boil; boil for 15 minutes, stirring constantly. Remove from the heat; skim off foam.
2. Carefully ladle the hot mixture into hot half-pint jars, leaving ¼-in. headspace. Remove the air bubbles, wipe rims and adjust lids. Process for 15 minutes in a boiling-water canner. **Note:** The processing time listed applies to altitudes of 1,000 feet or less. Add 1 minute to the processing time for each 1,000 feet of additional altitude.

Per 2 tablespoons: 33 cal., 0 fat (0 sat. fat), 0 chol., 0 sod., 8g carb. (8g sugars, 0 fiber), 0 pro.

RASPBERRY
PEACH JAM

PEAS PLEASE
ASIAN NOODLES

FAST FIX
Peas Please Asian Noodles

My Asian-inspired pasta doubles up on the peas for some serious crunch and springtime sweetness.

—CATHERINE CASSIDY MILWAUKEE, WI

START TO FINISH: 20 MIN.
MAKES: 8 SERVINGS

- 12 ounces uncooked Japanese soba noodles or whole wheat spaghetti
- ¼ cup water
- 1 cup fresh snow peas or sugar snap peas, trimmed
- 3 cups ice water
- ¾ cup frozen green peas, thawed
- 1 small cucumber, chopped
- 3 green onions, finely chopped

SAUCE
- ¼ cup creamy peanut butter
- 3 tablespoons orange juice
- 3 tablespoons white or rice vinegar
- 3 tablespoons soy sauce
- 4 teaspoons sesame oil or tahini
- 4 teaspoons canola oil
- 1 tablespoon garlic powder
- 2 to 3 teaspoons hot pepper sauce
- 2¼ teaspoons sugar

TOPPINGS
- ½ cup chopped fresh cilantro
  Sesame seeds, toasted

1. Cook noodles according to package directions. Meanwhile, in a small saucepan, bring ¼ cup water to a boil over medium-high heat. Add snow peas; cook, uncovered, just until crisp-tender, 1-2 minutes. Drain; immediately drop snow peas into ice water. Remove and pat dry.
2. Drain noodles; rinse with cold water and drain again. Combine noodles with snow peas, green peas, cucumber and green onions.
3. In another bowl, whisk together sauce ingredients until blended; pour over noodles and vegetables. Toss to coat. To serve, sprinkle with cilantro and sesame seeds.

Per 1 cup: 264 cal., 9g fat (1g sat. fat), 0 chol., 740mg sod., 39g carb. (4g sugars, 2g fiber), 10g pro.

Garden Risotto

(PICTURED ON P. 115)

Celebrate spring with a trio of the season's best—peas, asparagus and spinach—tucked inside a creamy white wine risotto. It's perfect paired with pork loin.

—**KENDRA DOSS** COLORADO SPRINGS, CO

PREP: 20 MIN. • **COOK:** 25 MIN.
MAKES: 8 SERVINGS

- ½ pound fresh asparagus, trimmed and cut into ¾-inch pieces
- 4½ cups reduced-sodium chicken broth
- 1 medium onion, chopped
- 2 teaspoons olive oil
- 1½ cups uncooked arborio rice
- ½ cup dry white wine or additional reduced-sodium chicken broth
- ½ teaspoon salt
- ¼ teaspoon pepper
- 3 cups fresh baby spinach
- 1 cup frozen peas
- ¼ cup grated Parmesan cheese

1. Place asparagus in a steamer basket; place in a small saucepan over 1 in. of water. Bring to a boil; cover and steam for 2-3 minutes or until crisp-tender. Set aside.

2. Meanwhile, in a small saucepan, heat broth and keep warm. In a large nonstick skillet coated with cooking spray, saute onion in oil until tender. Add rice; cook and stir for 2-3 minutes. Reduce heat; stir in the wine, salt and pepper. Cook and stir until all of the liquid is absorbed.

3. Add heated broth, ½ cup at a time, stirring constantly. Allow the liquid to absorb between additions. Cook just until risotto is creamy and rice is almost tender. (Cooking time is about 20 minutes.)

4. Add the spinach, peas, cheese and reserved asparagus; cook and stir until heated through. Serve immediately.

Per ¾ cup: 203 cal., 2g fat (1g sat. fat), 2mg chol., 539mg sod., 36g carb. (3g sugars, 2g fiber), 7g pro.

BRUSSELS SPROUTS & GRAPES AU GRATIN

FAST FIX ▶ Brussels Sprouts & Grapes au Gratin

Red grapes add pops of sweetness to this bubbly, cheesy veggie side. I make mine with Swiss, but if you're feeling fancy, try Gruyere. And if you have one on hand, toss in a sliced apple.

—**LORIE DURRANT** NASHVILLE, TN

START TO FINISH: 30 MIN.
MAKES: 6 SERVINGS

- 1 pound fresh Brussels sprouts, halved
- ½ cup seedless red grapes, halved
- 1 tablespoon butter
- 2 tablespoons arrowroot flour
- ¾ cup 2% milk
- ¼ teaspoon salt
- ¼ teaspoon pepper
- 1 cup shredded Swiss cheese
  Grated Parmesan cheese

1. Preheat oven to 400°. In a large saucepan, bring ½ in. water to a boil. Add Brussels sprouts; cook, covered, until crisp-tender, about 5 minutes. Drain and transfer to a greased 8-in. square baking dish. Add grapes.

2. Meanwhile, in a small saucepan, melt butter over medium heat. Stir in the arrowroot flour until smooth; gradually whisk in milk. Bring to a boil, stirring constantly; cook and stir until thickened, 5 minutes. Add salt and pepper. Pour over Brussels sprouts and grapes.

3. Top with shredded Swiss cheese. Sprinkle with grated Parmesan. Bake until bubbly, about 20 minutes.

Per ⅔ cup: 152 cal., 8g fat (5g sat. fat), 24mg chol., 180mg sod., 13g carb. (5g sugars, 3g fiber), 8g pro.

Curried Carrots with Crunchy Peanut Topping

My homegrown carrots are sweet and tender. When I have a bumper crop, I use this recipe to make the most of them. Warm curry spice and crunchy, peanutty topping make this a no-leftovers dish. If you want to add a burst of green, use half carrots and half broccoli florets.

—TRISHA KRUSE EAGLE, ID

PREP: 20 MIN. • **BAKE:** 20 MIN. • **MAKES:** 6 SERVINGS

- 2 pounds fresh carrots, cut into ½-inch slices
- 2 medium onions, halved and sliced ¼-in. thick
- ¾ cup mayonnaise
- ⅓ cup half-and-half cream
- 1 to 2 tablespoons curry powder
- 1 teaspoon salt
- ¼ teaspoon pepper
- 20 Ritz crackers, crushed (about 1 cup)
- ½ cup chopped salted peanuts
- 2 tablespoons butter, melted

1. Preheat oven to 350°. In a large saucepan, bring 2 in. of water to a boil. Add carrots; return to a boil. Reduce heat; simmer 4 minutes. Add onions; return to a boil. Reduce heat; simmer until carrots are tender, 4-5 minutes. Drain vegetables; return to pan.
2. Whisk together mayonnaise, cream, curry powder, salt and pepper. Pour over vegetables; toss to coat. Transfer to a greased 11x7-in. or 8-in. square baking dish. Combine crushed crackers and peanuts; sprinkle over carrots. Drizzle melted butter over top. Bake, uncovered, until bubbly, 20-25 minutes.
Per ⅔ cup: 438 cal., 35g fat (8g sat. fat), 19mg chol., 820mg sod., 28g carb. (10g sugars, 6g fiber), 6g pro.

STUFFING FROM
THE SLOW COOKER

EAT SMART **SLOW COOKER**
Stuffing from the Slow Cooker

If you're hosting a big Thanksgiving dinner this year, add this simple slow-cooked stuffing to your menu to ease entertaining. The recipe comes in handy when you run out of oven space at large family gatherings. I use it often.

—DONALD SEILER MACON, MS

PREP: 30 MIN. • **COOK:** 3 HOURS • **MAKES:** 10 SERVINGS

- 1 cup chopped onion
- 1 cup chopped celery
- ¼ cup butter
- 6 cups cubed day-old white bread
- 6 cups cubed day-old whole wheat bread
- 1 teaspoon salt
- 1 teaspoon poultry seasoning
- 1 teaspoon rubbed sage
- ½ teaspoon pepper
- 1 can (14½ ounces) reduced-sodium chicken broth or vegetable broth
- 2 large eggs, beaten

1. In a small nonstick skillet over medium heat, cook onion and celery in butter until tender.
2. In a large bowl, combine the bread cubes, salt, poultry seasoning, sage and pepper. Stir in onion mixture. Combine the broth and eggs; add to bread mixture and toss to coat.
3. Transfer to a 3-qt. slow cooker coated with cooking spray. Cover and cook on low for 3-4 hours or until a thermometer reads 160°.
Per ¾ cup: 178 cal., 7g fat (4g sat. fat), 49mg chol., 635mg sod., 23g carb. (3g sugars, 3g fiber), 6g pro.
Diabetic Exchanges: 1½ starch, 1 fat.

★ ★ ★ ★ ★ **READER REVIEW**

"How great it is with freeing up oven space! I have added ½ pound chopped and cooked bacon to the stuffing for additional flavor during the holidays."

ILUVWISC TASTEOFHOME.COM

CURRIED CARROTS WITH
CRUNCHY PEANUT TOPPING

Red Eye Barbecue Sauce

I made this recipe for an assignment in culinary school—my first time making barbecue sauce. I have to say, it was the best barbecue sauce I had in a long time! The hint of coffee livens up the sweet barbecue sauce perfectly.

—**EVAN HAUT** CANTON, OH

PREP: 15 MIN. • **COOK:** 1 HOUR • **MAKES:** 4 CUPS

- ¼ cup butter
- 4 garlic cloves, minced
- 1 shallot, finely chopped
- 1½ cups packed brown sugar
- 12 plum tomatoes, peeled, chopped and drained
- ½ cup cider vinegar
- 3 tablespoons instant coffee granules
- 1 tablespoon salt
- 1 teaspoon pepper
- 1 teaspoon adobo seasoning
- 1 teaspoon harissa chili paste
- 1 teaspoon cayenne pepper

1. In a Dutch oven, heat butter over medium heat. Add garlic and shallot; cook and stir until softened, 5-7 minutes. Add brown sugar. Reduce heat to medium-low; cook, stirring occasionally, until deep golden brown, about 15-17 minutes.

2. Add remaining ingredients; simmer 10 minutes. Remove from heat. Puree sauce using an immersion blender, or cool slightly and puree in batches in a blender. Strain through a fine-mesh strainer. Return to pan; cook and stir until liquid is reduced by a third, 30-40 minutes.

3. Refrigerate, covered, until serving. Serve sauce with grilled meats.

Per 2 tablespoons: 60 cal., 2g fat (1g sat. fat), 4mg chol., 281mg sod., 12g carb. (11g sugars, 0 fiber), 0 pro.

RED EYE BARBECUE SAUCE

CHEESY GRITS

(5) INGREDIENTS FAST FIX

Cheesy Grits

As a comfy side dish, grits have great potential but sometimes need a flavor boost. For add-ins, try red pepper flakes, fresh rosemary or crushed garlic.

—**JAMES SCHEND** PLEASANT PRAIRIE, WI

START TO FINISH: 25 MIN. • **MAKES:** 8 SERVINGS

- 2 cups 2% milk
- 1 cup chicken or vegetable broth
- 1 cup water
- 1 teaspoon salt
- 1 cup uncooked old-fashioned grits
- 2 to 3 cups shredded sharp cheddar or Monterey Jack cheese
  Salt and pepper to taste

1. Combine milk, broth and water in a large saucepan; bring to a boil. Add salt.

2. Whisk in grits; reduce heat to low. Cook, stirring frequently, until creamy, 15-20 minutes.

3. Stir in cheese until melted. Season with pepper and additional salt to taste.

Per ½ cup: 225 cal., 11g fat (6g sat. fat), 34mg chol., 629mg sod., 20g carb. (3g sugars, 1g fiber), 10g pro.

Greek-Style Stuffed Acorn Squash

With a truckload of acorn squash in my pantry, I wanted to make stuffed squash in lots of different ways. A bottle of Greek seasoning got my creativity flowing.
—**TERI RASEY** CADILLAC, MI

PREP: 45 MIN. • **BAKE:** 30 MIN.
MAKES: 12 SERVINGS

- 3 medium acorn squash, halved and seeds removed
- 1 cup lentils
- 2 cups chicken broth
- ¾ cup uncooked orzo pasta
- 1 pound bulk pork sausage
- ½ cup crumbled feta cheese
- 2 teaspoons Greek seasoning
- 2 tablespoons all-purpose flour
- 1 cup french-fried onions
  Additional crumbled feta cheese, optional

1. Preheat oven to 350°. Place squash, cut side up, on a baking sheet; roast until they can just be pierced with a fork, about 40 minutes. Cool on a wire rack. Meanwhile, place lentils in a large saucepan; add water to cover. Bring to a boil. Reduce heat; cook, covered, until tender, 20-25 minutes. Drain. Remove and set aside. In the same saucepan, bring broth to a boil. Add orzo; cook according to package directions for al dente. Drain, reserving broth.

2. In a large skillet, cook sausage, crumbling meat, until no longer pink, 6-8 minutes; drain. Add lentils and orzo to pan; remove from heat. Stir in ½ cup feta and the Greek seasoning.

3. Pour reserved chicken broth back into saucepan. Over medium heat, whisk in flour until thickened, then pour into sausage mixture.

4. When cool enough to handle, quarter squash and return to baking sheet. Top with sausage mixture. Bake until squash are tender, about 30 minutes. Before serving, sprinkle with french-fried onions and, if desired, additional feta.

Per serving: 335 cal., 14g fat (4g sat. fat), 29mg chol., 704mg sod., 41g carb. (5g sugars, 5g fiber), 13g pro.

JALAPENO POPPER MEXICAN STREET CORN

GREEK-STYLE STUFFED ACORN SQUASH

FAST FIX ▶ Jalapeno Popper Mexican Street Corn

One of the best things about summer is fresh sweet corn, and this recipe is a definite standout. We love its creamy dressing, crunchy panko and spicy jalapeno kick. If you're really feeling wild, sprinkle these with a bit of cooked bacon!
—**CRYSTAL SCHLUETER** NORTHGLENN, CO

START TO FINISH: 30 MIN.
MAKES: 4 SERVINGS

- 4 ears fresh sweet corn
- 2 jalapeno peppers
- 3 tablespoons canola oil, divided
- ¾ teaspoon salt, divided
- ¼ cup panko (Japanese) bread crumbs
- ½ teaspoon smoked paprika
- ½ teaspoon dried Mexican oregano
- 4 ounces cream cheese, softened
- ¼ cup media crema table cream or sour cream thinned with 1 teaspoon 2% milk
- 2 tablespoons lime juice
  Ground chipotle pepper or chili powder
  Chopped fresh cilantro, optional

1. Husk corn. Rub corn and jalapenos with 2 tablespoons canola oil. Grill, covered, on a greased grill rack over medium-high direct heat until lightly charred on all sides, 10-12 minutes. Remove from heat. When jalapenos are cool enough to handle, remove skin, seeds and membranes; chop finely. Set aside.

2. Sprinkle corn with ½ teaspoon salt. In a small skillet, heat remaining oil over medium heat. Add panko; cook and stir until starting to brown. Add paprika and oregano; cook until crumbs are toasted and fragrant.

3. Meanwhile, combine cream cheese, crema, lime juice and remaining salt; spread over corn. Sprinkle with bread crumbs, jalapenos, chipotle powder and, if desired, cilantro.

Note: This recipe was tested with Nestle crema; look for it in the international foods section.

Per 1 ear of corn: 339 cal., 26g fat (9g sat. fat), 39mg chol., 568mg sod., 25g carb. (8g sugars, 3g fiber), 6g pro.

Golden Beet Curry Risotto with Crispy Beet Greens

I was delighted to find golden beets at the farmers market and knew they'd be perfect in a risotto recipe I was working on. And please, don't forget the baked crispy beet greens...amazing! Move over, main dish! This vibrant side is sure to steal the show.

—MERRY GRAHAM NEWHALL, CA

PREP: 30 MIN. • **COOK:** 50 MIN.
MAKES: 6 SERVINGS

- 3 medium fresh golden beets and beet greens
- 3 tablespoons melted coconut oil, divided
- ¾ teaspoon sea salt, divided
- 5 cups reduced-sodium chicken broth
- 1 cup chopped leeks (white portion only)
- 1 teaspoon curry powder
- 1 teaspoon garlic salt
- 1 cup medium pearl barley
- ½ cup white wine or unsweetened apple juice
- 1 cup grated Manchego cheese
- 3 tablespoons lemon juice (Meyer lemons preferred)
- 4 teaspoons grated lemon peel, divided
- ¼ teaspoon coarsely ground pepper
- ¼ cup chopped fresh parsley
  Lemon slices

GOLDEN BEET CURRY RISOTTO WITH CRISPY BEET GREENS
Merry Graham
Newhall, CA

1. Preheat oven to 350°. Wash and trim beet greens, removing stems; dry with paper towels. Place greens in a single layer on parchment paper-lined baking sheets. Brush with 1 tablespoon coconut oil; sprinkle with ¼ teaspoon sea salt. Bake until dry and crisp, about 15-18 minutes. Set aside.

2. Meanwhile, peel and dice beets. In a large saucepan, bring broth to a boil. Add beets. Reduce heat; simmer, covered, until the beets are tender, 15-18 minutes. Remove beets with a slotted spoon. Keep broth hot.

3. In another large saucepan, heat remaining coconut oil over medium heat. Add leeks; cook and stir for 2-3 minutes. Add curry, garlic salt and remaining sea salt; cook, stirring, until leeks are tender, 2-3 minutes. Increase heat to medium-high. Add barley; stir constantly until lightly toasted, 2-3 minutes. Add the wine; stir until liquid has evaporated.

4. Add enough broth, about 1 cup, to cover barley. Reduce heat to medium; cook and stir until broth is absorbed. Add remaining broth, ½ cup at a time, cooking and stirring until broth is absorbed after each addition. Stir in beets with last addition of broth. Cook until barley is tender but firm to the bite and the risotto is creamy, about 25-30 minutes.

5. Remove from heat. Stir in cheese, lemon juice, 2½ teaspoons grated lemon peel and pepper. Transfer to a serving dish. Sprinkle with parsley and remaining lemon peel. Serve with crispy beet greens and lemon slices.

Per ⅔ cup: 314 cal., 14g fat (11g sat. fat), 19mg chol., 1238mg sod., 37g carb. (7g sugars, 8g fiber), 12g pro.

✳

DID YOU KNOW?
You don't have to waste those tough, fibrous leek tops. While they aren't typically used in recipes, they come in handy to enhance the flavor of homemade stock and broth. Rinse the tops well to remove any sand and cut them into large pieces so they'll be easy to discard after simmering.

FESTIVE RICE

Festive Rice

My mom and I transformed plain rice by adding feta, cranberries, pumpkin seeds and cayenne. We wound up with a sweet and spicy crowd-pleaser.

—**LISA DE PERIO** DALLAS, TX

PREP: 20 MIN. • **BAKE:** 30 MIN.
MAKES: 6 SERVINGS

- 2¼ cups water
- ¼ cup butter, cubed
- 1 teaspoon salt
- 1 teaspoon white vinegar
- ½ teaspoon garlic powder
- 1 cup uncooked jasmine rice
- ¼ cup salted pumpkin seeds or pepitas
- 2 teaspoons brown sugar
- ¼ to ½ teaspoon cayenne pepper
- ¼ cup crumbled feta cheese
- ¼ cup chopped fresh mint
- ¼ cup dried cranberries

1. Preheat oven to 325°. In a small saucepan, bring first five ingredients to a boil. Remove from heat. Pour over rice in a greased 8-in. square baking dish. Bake, covered, until all liquid is absorbed, 30-35 minutes.

2. Meanwhile, in a small nonstick skillet over medium-high heat, cook pumpkin seeds, brown sugar and cayenne pepper, stirring constantly until sugar melts and cayenne coats pumpkin seeds, about 4-5 minutes. Remove from heat; transfer to a plate, spreading out seeds to cool. Sprinkle rice with feta, mint, cranberries and spiced pumpkin seeds.

Per ⅔ cup: 244 cal., 11g fat (6g sat. fat), 23mg chol., 514mg sod., 32g carb. (5g sugars, 1g fiber), 5g pro.

SLOW COOKER

Slow Cooker Loaded Mashed Potatoes

Every holiday season, my mom could be counted on to deliver her cream cheese mashed potatoes. I keep the tradition going but boost the cheese factor.

—**ANN NOLTE** RIVERVIEW, FL

PREP: 25 MIN. + CHILLING • **COOK:** 3 HOURS
MAKES: 10 SERVINGS

- 3 pounds cubed peeled potatoes (about 9 medium)
- 1 package (8 ounces) cream cheese, softened
- 1 cup (8 ounces) sour cream
- ½ cup butter, cubed
- ¼ cup 2% milk
- ½ pound bacon strips, cooked and crumbled
- 1½ cups shredded cheddar cheese
- 1½ cups shredded pepper jack cheese
- 4 green onions, thinly sliced
- ½ teaspoon onion powder
- ½ teaspoon garlic powder
  Salt and pepper to taste

1. Place potatoes in a Dutch oven, adding water to cover. Bring to a boil; reduce heat and simmer, uncovered, until tender, 10-15 minutes. Drain potatoes; return to pan. Mash with the cream cheese, sour cream, butter and milk. Stir in bacon, cheeses, green onions and seasonings. Cover and refrigerate overnight.

2. Transfer to a greased 3- or 4-quart slow cooker. Cook, covered, on low for 3-3½ hours.

Per ¾ cup: 505 cal., 36g fat (20g sat. fat), 109mg chol., 530mg sod., 31g carb. (3g sugars, 3g fiber), 16g pro.

---

⑤ INGREDIENTS FAST FIX

Chard with Bacon-Citrus Sauce

Chard is a leafy veggie often used in Mediterranean cooking. I dress it up with orange juice and bacon, and the family gobbles it up.

—**TERI RASEY** CADILLAC, MI

START TO FINISH: 25 MIN.
MAKES: 6 SERVINGS

- ½ pound thick-sliced peppered bacon strips
- 2 pounds rainbow Swiss chard, chopped
- 1 cup orange juice
- 2 tablespoons butter
- 4 teaspoons grated orange peel
- ⅛ teaspoon salt
- ⅛ teaspoon pepper

1. In a large skillet, cook the bacon over medium heat until crisp; drain on paper towels. Discard all but 1 tablespoon of drippings. Cut bacon into small pieces.

2. Add chard to the drippings; cook and stir just until wilted, 5-6 minutes. Add remaining ingredients; cook for 1-2 minutes, stirring occasionally. Top with bacon.

Per ½ cup: 162 cal., 11g fat (5g sat. fat), 22mg chol., 655mg sod., 10g carb. (5g sugars, 3g fiber), 7g pro.

CHARD WITH BACON-CITRUS SAUCE

Twice-Baked Red Potatoes

Before my baby was born, I was in nesting mode and made lots of freezable recipes like these creamy red potatoes. The yogurt is a healthy swap for sour cream.
—**VALERIE COX** SECRETARY, MD

PREP: 30 MIN. • **BAKE:** 25 MIN. • **MAKES:** 1 DOZEN

- 6 large red potatoes (about 10 ounces each)
- ½ cup 1% milk
- ½ cup fat-free plain yogurt
- 3 tablespoons butter, softened
- 1½ teaspoons dried parsley flakes
- 1½ teaspoons garlic-herb seasoning blend
- 1 teaspoon salt
- ¼ teaspoon coarsely ground pepper
- 1 cup shredded Monterey Jack cheese

1. Preheat oven to 350°. Scrub potatoes; pierce several times with a fork. Microwave, uncovered, on high until just tender, 10-12 minutes, turning once.

2. When potatoes are cool enough to handle, cut each lengthwise in half. Scoop out pulp, leaving ¼-in.-thick shells. Mash pulp with all ingredients except cheese.

3. Spoon into potato shells. Top with cheese. Bake until heated through, 25-30 minutes. If desired, broil potatoes for 2-3 minutes until cheese is light golden brown.

Per ½ stuffed potato: 211 cal., 6g fat (4g sat. fat), 17mg chol., 322mg sod., 34g carb. (3g sugars, 4g fiber), 7g pro.
Diabetic Exchanges: 2 starch, 1 fat.

CHEESY CHEDDAR BROCCOLI CASSEROLE

TWICE-BAKED RED POTATOES

Cheesy Cheddar Broccoli Casserole

People who don't even like broccoli beg me to make this comforting recipe. It's similar to a classic green bean casserole, but the melted cheese just puts it over the top.
—**ELAINE HUBBARD** POCONO LAKE, PA

PREP: 15 MIN. • **BAKE:** 35 MIN. • **MAKES:** 8 SERVINGS

- 1 can (10¾ ounces) condensed cream of mushroom soup, undiluted
- 1 cup (8 ounces) sour cream
- 1½ cups shredded sharp cheddar cheese, divided
- 1 can (6 ounces) french-fried onions, divided
- 2 packages (16 ounces each) frozen broccoli florets, thawed

1. Preheat oven to 325°. In a large saucepan, combine soup, sour cream, 1 cup cheese and 1¼ cups onions; heat through over medium heat, stirring until blended, 4-5 minutes. Stir in broccoli. Transfer to a greased 2-qt. baking dish.

2. Bake, uncovered, until bubbly, 25-30 minutes. Sprinkle with the remaining cheese and onions. Bake until cheese is melted, 10-15 minutes.

Per ¾ cup: 359 cal., 26g fat (11g sat. fat), 30mg chol., 641mg sod., 19g carb. (4g sugars, 3g fiber), 8g pro.

Yellow Squash & Zucchini Gratin

This gratin is the perfect way to use up an abundance of summer squash. It's easy to prepare, takes just 10 minutes in the oven, and serves up bubbly and delicious.
—**JONATHAN LAWLER** GREENFIELD, IN

PREP: 25 MIN. • **BAKE:** 10 MIN. • **MAKES:** 6 SERVINGS

- 2 tablespoons butter
- 2 medium zucchini, cut into ¼-inch slices
- 2 medium yellow summer squash, cut into ¼-inch slices
- 2 shallots, minced
- ½ teaspoon sea salt
- ¼ teaspoon coarsely ground pepper
- 4 garlic cloves, minced
- ½ cup heavy whipping cream
- 1 cup panko (Japanese) bread crumbs, divided
- ½ cup grated Parmesan cheese, divided

1. Preheat oven to 450°. In a large skillet, melt butter over medium heat; add zucchini, yellow squash and shallots. Sprinkle with salt and pepper. Cook, stirring occasionally, until zucchini and squash are crisp-tender, 4-6 minutes. Add garlic; cook 1 minute more.
2. Add cream; cook until thickened, 3-5 minutes. Remove from heat; stir in ½ cup bread crumbs and ¼ cup cheese. Spoon mixture into a greased 11x7-in. or 2-qt. baking dish. Sprinkle with remaining bread crumbs and cheese. Bake until golden brown, 8-10 minutes.
Per 1 cup: 203 cal., 14g fat (8g sat. fat), 39mg chol., 357mg sod., 15g carb. (4g sugars, 2g fiber), 6g pro.

MUSHROOM & SPINACH SAUTE

EAT SMART **5 INGREDIENTS** FAST FIX

Mushroom & Spinach Saute

Mushrooms and spinach combine with plenty of garlic in this super-fast side dish for two. It takes a mere 10 minutes to whip up on the stovetop, so it's ideal for busy weeknights. I've found that the recipe is also easy to double or triple when you're having a dinner party.
—**PAULINE HOWARD** LAGO VISTA, TX

START TO FINISH: 10 MIN. • **MAKES:** 2 SERVINGS

- 2 teaspoons olive oil
- 2 cups sliced fresh mushrooms
- 2 garlic cloves, minced
- 1 package (5 to 6 ounces) fresh baby spinach
- ⅛ teaspoon salt
- ⅛ teaspoon pepper

In a large skillet, heat oil over medium-high heat. Add mushrooms; saute until tender, about 2 minutes. Add garlic; cook 1 minute longer. Add spinach in batches; cook and stir until wilted, about 1 minute. Season with salt and pepper. Serve immediately.
Per ¾ cup: 76 cal., 5g fat (1g sat. fat), 0mg chol., 208mg sod., 6g carb. (2g sugars, 2g fiber), 4g pro.
Diabetic Exchanges: 1 vegetable, 1 fat.

✱
TEST KITCHEN TIP
Using baby spinach saves prep time because you don't have to remove the tough stems of mature spinach. Some people prefer baby spinach's tender texture in salads.

YELLOW SQUASH & ZUCCHINI GRATIN

ROASTED HERBED SQUASH
WITH GOAT CHEESE

Roasted Herbed Squash with Goat Cheese

Cooking is a hobby I'm so happy to share with my toddler. She (and all our Christmas Eve party guests) heartily approved this new potluck favorite. Any type of winter squash works here.
—**LINDSAY OBERHAUSEN** LEXINGTON, KY

PREP: 25 MIN. • **COOK:** 30 MIN.
MAKES: 10 SERVINGS

- 2 medium acorn squash (about 1½ pounds each), peeled and cut into 2-inch cubes
- 1 large butternut squash (5 to 6 pounds), peeled and cut into 2-inch cubes
- 3 tablespoons olive oil
- 2 tablespoons minced fresh thyme
- 2 tablespoons minced fresh rosemary
- 1 tablespoon kosher salt
- 1 teaspoon coarsely ground pepper
- 1 log (11 ounces) fresh goat cheese, crumbled
- 2 tablespoons coarsely chopped fresh parsley
- 1 tablespoon maple syrup, warmed slightly

1. Preheat oven to 425°. Toss squashes with oil and seasonings. Transfer to foil-lined 15x10-in. rimmed pans. Roast squash, stirring once, until soft and some pieces are caramelized, 30-35 minutes. Switch position of pans midway through roasting to ensure even doneness. If darker color is desired, broil 3-4 in. from heat 2-4 minutes.

2. Cool slightly. To serve, add goat cheese to squash; gently toss. Sprinkle with parsley; drizzle with maple syrup.
Note: To save time, first cut squash into thick slices, then use a vegetable peeler to peel each slice.
Per 1 cup: 251 cal., 8g fat (3g sat. fat), 21mg chol., 715mg sod., 43g carb. (10g sugars, 10g fiber), 7g pro.

Spiced Cran-Apple & Grape Conserve

(PICTURED ON P. 115)
Faced with an abundance of grapes from my garden, I used them in various ways. This conserve was an afterthought, but I received so many great compliments from family and friends that I made sure to write down the recipe. I served it with crackers and Brie, but it would be great with pork, chicken, ham and cheesecake, too.
—**KALLEE KRONG-MCCREERY** ESCONDIDO, CA

PREP: 2 HOURS • **PROCESS:** 5 MIN./BATCH
MAKES: 10 HALF-PINTS

- 6 whole cloves
- 6 whole allspice berries
- 8 cups seedless red grapes
- 6 cups sugar
- 4 medium tart apples, peeled and chopped (about 4 cups)
- 4 cups coarsely chopped fresh cranberries
- 3 tablespoons lemon juice plus enough water to equal 1 cup
- 1½ teaspoons ground cinnamon
- 1 medium tart apple, peeled and shredded (about 1 cup)

1. Make a spice bag by placing cloves and allspice berries on a double thickness of cheesecloth. Gather corners of cloth to enclose seasonings; tie securely with string.
2. In a stockpot, combine next six ingredients. Add spice bag. Bring to a boil. Reduce heat; simmer, uncovered, until mixture begins to thicken, about 45 minutes. Add shredded apple; simmer until thickened, 35-45 minutes longer (mixture will thicken more after cooling). Discard spice bag.
3. Carefully ladle hot mixture into 10 hot sterilized half-pint jars, leaving ¼-in. headspace. Remove air bubbles and adjust headspace, if necessary, by adding hot mixture. Wipe rims. Center lids on jars; screw on bands until fingertip tight.
4. In batches, place jars into canner with simmering water, ensuring that they are completely covered with water. Bring to a boil; process for 5 minutes. Remove jars and cool.
Per 2 tablespoons: 77 cal., 0 fat (0 sat. fat), 0 chol., 2mg sod., 20g carb. (19g sugars, 0 fiber), 0 pro.

EAT SMART Asian Quinoa

I enjoy coming up with new recipes. I serve this Asian-style dish at least once a month and sometimes more. For a different twist, I might add a scrambled egg or use soy sauce instead of the rice vinegar.

—**SONYA LABBE** WEST HOLLYWOOD, CA

PREP: 20 MIN. • **COOK:** 20 MIN. + STANDING
MAKES: 4 SERVINGS

- 1 cup water
- 2 tablespoons rice vinegar
- 2 tablespoons plum sauce
- 2 garlic cloves, minced
- 1 teaspoon minced fresh gingerroot
- 1 teaspoon sesame oil
- ¼ teaspoon salt
- ¼ teaspoon crushed red pepper flakes
- ½ cup quinoa, rinsed
- 1 medium sweet red pepper, chopped
- ½ cup sliced water chestnuts, chopped
- ½ cup fresh sugar snap peas, trimmed and halved
- 2 green onions, thinly sliced

1. In a large saucepan, combine the first eight ingredients; bring to a boil. Add quinoa. Reduce heat; cover and simmer for 12-15 minutes or until water is absorbed.

2. Remove from the heat. Add the red pepper, water chestnuts, peas and onions; fluff with a fork. Cover and let stand for 10 minutes.

Per ⅔ cup: 138 cal., 3g fat (0 sat. fat), 0 chol., 205mg sod., 25g carb. (5g sugars, 3g fiber), 4g pro.
Diabetic Exchanges: 1 starch, 1 vegetable.

ASIAN QUINOA

Aunt Margaret's Sweet Potato Casserole

My great aunt made an incredible sweet potato casserole for our holiday dinners. I've lightened it up a bit, but we love it just the same.

—**BETH BRITTON** FAIRLAWN, OH

PREP: 50 MIN. • **BAKE:** 50 MIN.
MAKES: 12 SERVINGS

- 3 pounds sweet potatoes (about 3 large), peeled and cubed
- ½ cup sugar
- ½ cup 2% milk
- 2 large eggs, lightly beaten
- ¼ cup butter
- 1 teaspoon vanilla extract

TOPPING

- ¾ cup all-purpose flour
- ¾ cup packed brown sugar
- ¾ cup old-fashioned oats
- ⅛ teaspoon salt
- ⅓ cup cold butter, cubed
- 2 cups miniature marshmallows

1. Preheat oven to 350°. Place sweet potatoes in a 6-qt. stockpot; add water to cover. Bring to a boil. Reduce heat; cook, uncovered, 10-12 minutes or until tender. Meanwhile, make topping by combining flour, brown sugar, oats and salt; cut in butter until crumbly.

2. Drain potatoes; return to pan. Beat until mashed. Add sugar, milk, eggs, butter and vanilla; beat until combined. Transfer to a broiler-safe 13x9-in. baking dish. Sprinkle topping over potato mixture.

3. Bake, uncovered, until topping is golden brown, about 45 minutes; let stand 10 minutes. Sprinkle with marshmallows. If desired, broil for 4-5 inches from heat, 30-45 seconds or until the marshmallows are puffed and golden.

Per ½ cup: 373 cal., 11g fat (6g sat. fat), 56mg chol., 134mg sod., 66g carb. (39g sugars, 4g fiber), 5g pro.

Kale & Fennel Skillet

I love to mix different vegetables, herbs and spices to change things up. If you can't find apple sausage for this skillet, a mild Italian sausage would substitute just fine.
—**PATRICIA LEVENSON** SANTA ANA, CA

PREP: 10 MIN. • **COOK:** 25 MIN.
MAKES: 6 SERVINGS

- 2 tablespoons olive oil
- 1 small onion, thinly sliced
- 1 small fennel bulb, thinly sliced
- ½ pound cooked apple chicken sausage links or cooked Italian sausage links, halved lengthwise and sliced into half-moons
- 2 garlic cloves, minced
- 3 tablespoons dry sherry or dry white wine
- 1 tablespoon herbes de Provence
- ⅛ teaspoon salt
- ⅛ teaspoon pepper
- 1 bunch kale, trimmed and torn into bite-sized pieces

1. In a large skillet, heat olive oil over medium-high heat. Add onion and fennel; cook and stir until onion begins to brown, 6-8 minutes. Add sausage, garlic, sherry and seasonings; cook until sausage starts to caramelize, about 4-6 minutes.
2. Add kale; cook, covered, stirring occasionally, until the kale is tender, 15-17 minutes.
Note: Look for herbes de Provence in the spice aisle.
Per ¾ cup: 167 cal., 8g fat (2g sat. fat), 27mg chol., 398mg sod., 16g carb. (6g sugars, 3g fiber), 9g pro.
Diabetic Exchanges: 2 vegetable, 1 lean meat, 1 fat.

KALE & FENNEL SKILLET

BUTTERNUT, KALE & CASHEW SQUARES

Butternut, Kale & Cashew Squares

Butternut squash and kale are two of my favorite fall vegetables. Combined with cashews and feta in a puff pastry, it reminds me of a fall take on spanakopita! Serve it for brunch, lunch or dinner, or cut into smaller pieces for an appetizer.
—**ARLENE ERLBACH** MORTON GROVE, IL

PREP: 30 MIN. • **BAKE:** 15 MIN.
MAKES: 9 SERVINGS

- 4 bacon strips, cut into ½-inch pieces
- 1 shallot, thinly sliced
- 2½ cups peeled butternut squash, cut into ½-inch cubes
- 1 teaspoon minced fresh thyme, divided
- ⅛ teaspoon ground nutmeg
- 2 cups chopped fresh kale
- ¾ cup crumbled feta cheese
- ¼ cup plus 1 tablespoon chopped cashews, divided
- 1 package (17.3 ounces) frozen puff pastry, thawed
- 1 large egg, beaten
- 1 tablespoon water

1. Preheat oven to 450°. In a large skillet over medium heat, cook bacon until crisp. Remove with a slotted spoon. In same skillet, saute shallot until tender. Add squash, ¾ teaspoon thyme and nutmeg; cook, covered, until squash is almost tender, about 5 minutes. Combine squash mixture with bacon. Add kale, feta cheese and ¼ cup cashews; mix well.
2. Unfold one sheet of puff pastry on a parchment paper-lined baking sheet; roll out into a 10-in. square. Spoon squash mixture evenly over pastry sheet to within ¾ in. of edges. Whisk egg and water; brush edges of pastry. Unfold remaining pastry sheet; roll out into a 10-in. square. Place on top of squash mixture. Press edges of pastries together with a fork to seal. Brush top with egg mixture.
3. Cut slits in top. Bake until pastry is puffed and golden brown, 15-20 minutes, rotating halfway through cooking to ensure even browning. Sprinkle with remaining cashews and thyme. Cool on a wire rack 5 minutes before cutting into squares.
Per 1 piece: 403 cal., 24g fat (7g sat. fat), 34mg chol., 394mg sod., 39g carb. (2g sugars, 6g fiber), 9g pro.

Slow Cooker BBQ Baked Beans

I was under doctor's orders to reduce the amount of sodium I was eating, but I just couldn't part with some of my favorite foods. After many experiments I came up with this potluck favorite—and now everyone's happy!

—**SHERREL HENDRIX** ARKADELPHIA, AR

PREP: 10 MIN. + SOAKING
COOK: 8½ HOURS
MAKES: 12 SERVINGS (½ CUP EACH)

- 1 package (16 ounces) dried great northern beans
- 2 smoked ham hocks (about ½ pound each)
- 2 cups water
- 1 medium onion, chopped
- 2 teaspoons garlic powder, divided
- 2 teaspoons onion powder, divided
- 1 cup barbecue sauce
- ¾ cup packed brown sugar
- ½ teaspoon ground nutmeg
- ¼ teaspoon ground cloves
- 2 teaspoons hot pepper sauce, optional

1. Rinse and sort the beans; soak them according to package directions. Drain and rinse beans, discarding liquid.
2. In a 4-qt. slow cooker, combine the beans, ham hocks, water, onion, 1 teaspoon each of garlic powder and onion powder. Cook, covered, on low until beans are tender, 8-10 hours.
3. Remove ham hocks; cool slightly. Cut meat into small cubes, discarding bones; return meat to slow cooker. Stir in barbecue sauce, brown sugar, nutmeg, cloves, remaining garlic powder, remaining onion powder and, if desired, pepper sauce. Cook, covered, on high until heated through, about 30 minutes.
Per ½ cup: 238 cal., 1g fat (0 sat. fat), 4mg chol., 347mg sod., 48g carb. (22g sugars, 8g fiber), 10g pro.

✳

TEST KITCHEN TIP
Unless the recipe asks you to stir or add ingredients, do not lift the lid while a slow cooker is operating. Every time you lift the lid, steam escapes and you add cooking time.

GENTLEMAN'S WHISKEY BACON JAM

Gentleman's Whiskey Bacon Jam

You can slather this smoky jam on pretty much anything. It lasts only a week in the fridge, so I freeze small amounts for a quick snack with crackers.

—**COLLEEN DELAWDER** HERNDON, VA

PREP: 15 MIN. • **COOK:** 30 MIN.
MAKES: 3 CUPS

- 1½ pounds thick-sliced bacon strips, finely chopped
- 8 shallots, finely chopped
- 1 large sweet onion, finely chopped
- 2 garlic cloves, minced
- 1 teaspoon chili powder
- ½ teaspoon paprika
- ¼ teaspoon kosher salt
- ¼ teaspoon pepper
- ½ cup whiskey
- ½ cup maple syrup
- ¼ cup balsamic vinegar
- ½ cup packed brown sugar
  Assorted crackers

1. In a large skillet, cook bacon over medium heat until crisp; drain. Discard all but 2 tablespoons drippings. Add shallots and onion to drippings; cook until caramelized, stirring occasionally.
2. Stir in garlic; cook 30 seconds. Add seasonings. Remove from heat; stir in whiskey and maple syrup. Increase heat to high; bring to a boil, and cook 3 minutes, stirring constantly. Add vinegar and brown sugar; cook another 3 minutes, continuing to stir the mixture constantly.

3. Add crumbled bacon; reduce heat to low, and cook 12 minutes, stirring occasionally. Cool jam slightly. Pulse half of the jam in a food processor until smooth; stir puree into the remaining jam. Serve with crackers.
Per 2 tablespoons: 112 cal., 8g fat (3g sat. fat), 10mg chol., 118mg sod., 7g carb. (5g sugars, 0 fiber), 2g pro.

⑤INGREDIENTS SLOW COOKER
Cheddar Creamed Corn

I brought this super-easy recipe to a school potluck once and it was gone in no time. I've been asked to bring it to every function since.

—**JESSICA MAXWELL** ENGLEWOOD, NJ

PREP: 10 MIN. • **COOK:** 3 HOURS
MAKES: 9 SERVINGS

- 2 packages (one 16 ounces, one 12 ounces) frozen corn, thawed
- 1 package (8 ounces) cream cheese, cubed
- ¾ cup shredded cheddar cheese
- ¼ cup butter, melted
- ¼ cup heavy whipping cream
- ½ teaspoon salt
- ¼ teaspoon pepper

In a 3- or 4-qt. slow cooker, combine all ingredients. Cook, covered, on low 3 to 3½ hours or until cheese is melted and corn is tender. Stir just before serving.
Per ½ cup: 272 cal., 20g fat (12g sat. fat), 56mg chol., 317mg sod., 20g carb. (3g sugars, 2g fiber), 7g pro.

Chinese Chard with Almonds

The chard in my garden inspires all kinds of recipes. This one makes a great side dish, especially in spring and summer.
—**NANCY HEISHMAN** LAS VEGAS, NV

PREP: 20 MIN. • **COOK:** 15 MIN. • **MAKES:** 4 SERVINGS

- 1 bunch Swiss chard (about 1 pound), chopped
- 1 tablespoon olive oil
- 1 large sweet red pepper, cut into strips
- 1 large tomato, diced
- 1 small red onion, diced
- 3 garlic cloves, minced
- 1 tablespoon minced fresh gingerroot
- 1 tablespoon hoisin sauce
- ¾ teaspoon Chinese five-spice powder
- ¾ teaspoon kosher salt
  Dash crushed red pepper flakes
- 2 tablespoons lemon juice
- ½ cup sliced almonds, toasted

1. In a large saucepan over medium-high heat, bring 2 in. of water to a boil. Add the chard; cook it, covered, until crisp-tender, about 5 minutes. Drain; set aside.

2. In same saucepan, heat the oil over medium-high heat. Add pepper, tomato and onion; saute until the pepper is crisp-tender, 3-4 minutes. Add garlic; cook 1 minute more. Stir in next five ingredients; add cooked chard. Cook and stir until pepper is tender, 3-4 minutes ; add lemon juice. Top with the almonds.

Note: To toast nuts, bake in a shallow pan in a 350° oven for 5-10 minutes or cook in a skillet over low heat until lightly browned, stirring occasionally.

Per ¾ cup: 156 cal., 10g fat (1g sat. fat), 0 chol., 611mg sod., 15g carb. (6g sugars, 5g fiber), 5g pro.
Diabetic Exchanges: 2 fat, 1 starch.

CHINESE CHARD
WITH ALMONDS

SOUTHERN
HOPPIN' JOHN

Southern Hoppin' John

This cherished Southern dish of peas and rice is served on New Year's Day for good luck and prosperity. Make it an annual tradition for your family, too.
—**ANNE CREECH** KINSTON, NC

PREP: 10 MIN. • **COOK:** 30 MIN. • **MAKES:** 6 SERVINGS

- ½ pound sliced bacon, cut into 1-inch pieces
- 1 small green or sweet red pepper, chopped
- 2 celery ribs, chopped
- 6 green onions, sliced
- 1 cup uncooked long-grain rice
- 2 cups water
- ¼ teaspoon salt
- ½ to 1 teaspoon cayenne pepper
- ½ teaspoon dried basil
- ¼ teaspoon dried thyme
- ¼ teaspoon dried oregano
- 1 bay leaf
- 1 can (15 ounces) black-eyed peas, rinsed and drained

In a large skillet, cook bacon over medium heat until crisp. Drain on paper towels; discard all but 2 tablespoons drippings. Saute pepper, celery and onions in drippings until almost tender. Add rice, water and seasonings. Cover and simmer 10 minutes. Add peas and bacon; simmer for 10 minutes longer. Discard bay leaf.

Per 1 cup: 343 cal., 15g fat (5g sat. fat), 25mg chol., 448mg sod., 39g carb. (2g sugars, 3g fiber), 11g pro.

Summer Squash Mushroom Casserole

With its crunchy topping, this rich and creamy side is a wonderful dish to take to potlucks and picnics. It pairs well with a wide variety of entrees.

—JENNIFER WALLACE CANAL WINCHESTER, OH

PREP: 20 MIN. • **BAKE:** 25 MIN. • **MAKES:** 10 SERVINGS

- 2 medium yellow summer squash, diced
- 1 large zucchini, diced
- ½ pound sliced fresh mushrooms
- 1 cup chopped onion
- 2 tablespoons olive oil
- 2 cups shredded cheddar cheese
- 1 can (10¾ ounces) condensed cream of mushroom soup, undiluted
- ½ cup sour cream
- ½ teaspoon salt
- 1 cup crushed butter-flavored crackers (about 25 crackers)
- 1 tablespoon butter, melted

1. In a large skillet, saute the summer squash, zucchini, mushrooms and onion in oil until tender; drain.
2. In a large bowl, combine the vegetable mixture, cheese, soup, sour cream and salt. Transfer to a greased 11x7-in. baking dish. Combine cracker crumbs and butter. Sprinkle over vegetable mixture.
3. Bake casserole, uncovered, at 350° for 25-30 minutes or until bubbly.
Per ⅔ cup: 234 cal., 16g fat (8g sat. fat), 36mg chol., 564mg sod., 14g carb. (4g sugars, 2g fiber), 8g pro.

RIGATONI
CHARD TOSS

EAT SMART Rigatoni Chard Toss

I had to get my firefighter husband to eat more fruits and veggies to lower his cholesterol and triglycerides. Fresh chard and tomatoes add fiber and vitamins, but we love it for the flavor. While he would never admit to eating health food around the firehouse, this dish is one of many that made his trips to the doctor much more pleasant!

—CAROLYN KUMPE EL DORADO, CA

PREP: 25 MIN. • **COOK:** 20 MIN. • **MAKES:** 10 SERVINGS

- 8 ounces uncooked rigatoni or large tube pasta
- 2 tablespoons olive oil
- 1 bunch Swiss chard, coarsely chopped
- 1 small onion, thinly sliced
- 2 garlic cloves, minced
- 3 medium tomatoes, chopped
- 1 can (15 ounces) cannellini beans, rinsed and drained
- ½ teaspoon salt
- ⅛ teaspoon crushed red pepper flakes
- ⅛ teaspoon fennel seed, crushed
- ⅛ teaspoon pepper
- ¼ cup minced fresh basil
- ½ cup grated Parmesan cheese

1. Cook rigatoni according to package directions.
2. Meanwhile, in a large skillet, heat oil over medium-high heat. Add Swiss chard and onion; cook and stir 4 minutes. Add garlic; cook 2 minutes longer. Stir in tomatoes, beans, salt, pepper flakes, fennel and pepper. Cook 3-4 minutes longer or until chard is tender.
3. Drain rigatoni, reserving ¼ cup pasta water. Add rigatoni, pasta water and basil to skillet; toss to combine. Serve with cheese.
Per ¾ cup: 159 cal., 4g fat (1g sat. fat), 3mg chol., 291mg sod., 24g carb. (2g sugars, 3g fiber), 7g pro.
Diabetic Exchanges: 1½ starch, ½ fat.

SUMMER SQUASH MUSHROOM CASSEROLE

**HOLLY JONES'
BACON-PIMIENTO CHEESE
CORN MUFFINS** PAGE 136

Breads, Rolls & Muffins

Savor the aroma of **fresh-baked bread** when you treat yourself and the ones you love to homemade muffins, loaves, sweet rolls and biscuits. Nothing **warms the heart** like oven-fresh **goodness.**

**VELMA HORTON'S
FROSTED CINNAMON ROLLS**

PAGE 137

**CHARLENE CHAMBERS'
APRICOT-ROSEMARY SCONES**

PAGE 138

**BONNIE APPLETON'S
SOUR CREAM-LEEK BISCUITS**

PAGE 140

SOFT OATMEAL BREAD

Honey-Coconut Sticky Buns

Thanks to a friend, I got my hands on this easy recipe for sticky buns—and then I tweaked it. Sprinkle them with coconut for the crowning touch.

—**DIANE NEMITZ** LUDINGTON, MI

PREP: 20 MIN. + RISING • **BAKE:** 30 MIN.
MAKES: 16 SERVINGS

- 1 loaf (1 pound) frozen bread dough, thawed
- 4 ounces (½ cup) cream cheese, softened
- ½ cup sweetened shredded coconut
- 3 tablespoons thawed orange juice concentrate
- ½ cup butter
- ½ cup honey
  Toasted sweetened shredded coconut, optional

1. Grease two 8-in. round baking pans. Cut thawed bread dough in half; roll each half into a 10x8-in. rectangle. Combine cream cheese, coconut and orange juice concentrate; spread mixture on dough. Roll up jelly-roll style, starting with long side. Cut each roll crosswise into eight slices; place in prepared pans. Cover with plastic wrap; let rise until almost doubled, about 1 hour.
2. Preheat oven to 350°. In a microwave, melt butter and honey. Spoon 1 tablespoon butter-honey mixture over each bun. Bake until tops are golden brown, about 30 minutes. Immediately invert onto a serving plate. If desired, top with toasted coconut.
Note: To toast coconut, bake in a shallow pan in a 350° oven for 5-10 minutes or cook in a skillet over low heat until golden brown, stirring occasionally. Keep an eye on it because it browns very quickly.
Per 1 bun: 206 cal., 10g fat (6g sat. fat), 23mg chol., 239mg sod., 25g carb. (12g sugars, 1g fiber), 4g pro.

✳

TEST KITCHEN TIP
An oven is a great place to raise dough. Turn on the oven light, place the bowl of dough inside and close the door. Ovens are draft-free, and with the light on, the temperature will hover around 90°.

FREEZE IT (5) INGREDIENTS
Soft Oatmeal Bread

My husband loves to make this bread. With its mild oat taste and soft texture, it's sure to be a hit with the whole family. Slices are delicious for sandwiches or toasted up at breakfast time.

—**NANCY MONTGOMERY** PLAINWELL, MI

PREP: 10 MIN. • **BAKE:** 3 HOURS
MAKES: 1 LOAF (2 POUNDS, 20 SLICES)

- 1½ cups water (70° to 80°)
- ¼ cup canola oil
- 1 teaspoon lemon juice
- ¼ cup sugar
- 2 teaspoons salt
- 3 cups all-purpose flour
- 1½ cups quick-cooking oats
- 2½ teaspoons active dry yeast

1. In bread machine pan, place all ingredients in order suggested by manufacturer. Select basic bread setting. Choose crust color and loaf size if available.
2. Bake according to manufacturer directions (check the dough after 5 minutes of mixing and add 1-2 tablespoons of water or flour if needed).
To freeze: Securely wrap cooled loaf in foil and place in a resealable plastic freezer bag; freeze. To use, thaw at room temperature.
Per 1 slice: 127 cal., 3g fat (0 sat. fat), 0 chol., 237mg sod., 21g carb. (3g sugars, 1g fiber), 3g pro.

**HONEY-COCONUT
STICKY BUNS**
Diane Nemitz
Ludington, MI

FAST FIX ▸ Bacon-Pimiento Cheese Corn Muffins

Corn bread is essential at our family dinners, and with the additions of bacon and pimiento cheese, you'll have recipe requests long after the get-together!

—HOLLY JONES KENNESAW, GA

START TO FINISH: 25 MIN.
MAKES: 10 MUFFINS

- 1 jar (5 ounces) pimiento cheese spread
- ¼ cup butter, melted
- ¼ cup sour cream
- 1 large egg
- 1 package (8½ ounces) corn bread/muffin mix
- 4 bacon strips, cooked and crumbled

1. Preheat oven to 400°. Whisk together cheese spread, butter, sour cream and egg until blended. Add corn bread mix; stir just until moistened. Fold in bacon.

2. Fill 10 greased or paper-lined muffin cups three-fourths full. Bake until a toothpick inserted in center comes out clean, 10-12 minutes. Cool 5 minutes before removing from pan to a wire rack. Serve warm.

Per 1 muffin: 212 cal., 13g fat (7g sat. fat), 47mg chol., 376mg sod., 18g carb. (6g sugars, 2g fiber), 5g pro.

BACON-PIMIENTO
CHEESE CORN MUFFINS

ITALIAN RICOTTA
EASTER BREAD
Tina Mirilovich
Johnstown, PA

Italian Ricotta Easter Bread

I changed our family's traditional Easter bread by adding ricotta cheese and a few other ingredients. The almond extract works wonders!

—TINA MIRILOVICH JOHNSTOWN, PA

PREP: 30 MIN. • **BAKE:** 45 MIN.
MAKES: 18 SERVINGS

- ¾ cup plain or butter-flavored shortening, room temperature
- 1½ cups granulated sugar
- 3 large eggs, room temperature
- 3 large egg yolks, room temperature
- 1 cup whole-milk ricotta cheese
- 1 teaspoon almond extract (or flavor of choice)
- 6 cups all-purpose flour
- 1 tablespoon baking powder
- 1 teaspoon salt
- ½ cup 2% milk

GLAZE
- 1½ cups confectioners' sugar
- 3 tablespoons 2% milk
- ½ teaspoon almond extract (or flavor of choice)
  - Sliced toasted almonds or assorted sprinkles

1. Preheat oven to 350°. Cream shortening and sugar until light and fluffy. Add eggs and egg yolks, one at a time, beating well after each addition. Beat in ricotta and extract. In another bowl, whisk flour, baking powder and salt; add to the creamed mixture alternately with milk, beating well after each addition, stirring in final 1 cup flour by hand.

2. Turn dough onto a lightly floured surface; divide into thirds. Roll each into an 18-in. rope. Place ropes on a parchment paper-lined baking sheet and braid. Pinch ends to seal; tuck under braid. Bake until a toothpick inserted in center comes out clean, 45-55 minutes (do not overbake). Remove to wire racks to cool.

3. Meanwhile, beat confectioners' sugar, milk and extract until smooth. Brush on bread while still warm; top with sliced almonds or sprinkles.

Note: To toast nuts, bake in a shallow pan in a 350° oven for 5-10 minutes or cook in a skillet over low heat until lightly browned, stirring occasionally.

Per 1 piece: 376 cal., 11g fat (4g sat. fat), 68mg chol., 247mg sod., 60g carb. (28g sugars, 1g fiber), 8g pro.

Frosted Cinnamon Rolls

(PICTURED ON P. 133)

These marvelous cinnamon rolls taste just like the ones sold at the mall! Topped with a sweet cream cheese frosting, they're best served warm with coffee. Reheat leftover rolls in the microwave and enjoy any time of day.

—VELMA HORTON LAGRANGE, CA

PREP: 35 MIN. + RISING • **BAKE:** 20 MIN.
MAKES: 21 ROLLS

- 1 cup warm milk (70° to 80°)
- ¼ cup water (70° to 80°)
- ¼ cup butter, softened
- 1 large egg
- 1 teaspoon salt
- 4 cups bread flour
- ¼ cup instant vanilla pudding mix
- 1 tablespoon sugar
- 1 tablespoon active dry yeast

FILLING
- ¼ cup butter, softened
- 1 cup packed brown sugar
- 2 teaspoons ground cinnamon

FROSTING
- 4 ounces cream cheese, softened
- ¼ cup butter, softened
- 1½ cups confectioners' sugar
- 1½ teaspoons milk
- ½ teaspoon vanilla extract

1. In bread machine pan, place first nine ingredients in order suggested by manufacturer. Select dough setting (check dough after 5 minutes of mixing; add 1-2 tablespoons water or flour if needed).
2. When cycle is completed, turn dough onto lightly floured surface. Roll into a 17x10-in. rectangle. Spread with butter; sprinkle with brown sugar and cinnamon. Roll up, jelly-roll style, starting from a long side; pinch seam to seal. Cut into 21 slices.
3. Place 12 slices, cut side down, in a greased 13x 9-in. baking pan and nine slices in a 9-in. square baking pan. Cover; let rise in a warm place until doubled, about 45 minutes.
4. Bake cinnamon rolls at 350° for 20-25 minutes or until golden brown. Cool for 10 minutes on wire racks.
5. In a large bowl, beat the frosting ingredients until smooth. Frost rolls while they are still warm. Store in the refrigerator.

CREOLE CORN BREAD

Note: We recommend you do not use a bread machine's time-delay feature for this recipe.
Per 1 roll: 266 cal., 10g fat (6g sat. fat), 33mg chol., 208mg sod., 41g carb. (21g sugars, 1g fiber), 4g pro.

Creole Corn Bread

Corn bread is a staple of Cajun and Creole cuisine. This is an old favorite that I found in the bottom of my recipe drawer, and it really tastes wonderful.

—ENID HEBERT LAFAYETTE, LA

PREP: 15 MIN. • **BAKE:** 45 MIN.
MAKES: 12 SERVINGS

- 2 cups cooked rice
- 1 cup yellow cornmeal
- ½ cup chopped onion
- 1 to 2 tablespoons seeded chopped jalapeno peppers
- 1 teaspoon salt
- ½ teaspoon baking soda
- 2 large eggs
- 1 cup whole milk
- ¼ cup canola oil
- 1 can (16½ ounces) cream-style corn
- 3 cups shredded cheddar cheese
  Additional cornmeal

1. In a large bowl, combine rice, cornmeal, onion, peppers, salt and baking soda.
2. In another bowl, beat the eggs, milk and oil. Add corn; mix well. Stir into rice mixture until blended. Fold in cheese. Sprinkle a well-greased 10-in. ovenproof skillet with cornmeal. Pour batter into skillet.
3. Bake at 350° for 45-50 minutes or until bread tests done. Cut into wedges and serve warm.
Note: Wear disposable gloves when cutting hot peppers; the oils can burn skin. Avoid touching your face.
Per 1 piece: 293 cal., 16g fat (6g sat. fat), 61mg chol., 557mg sod., 27g carb. (3g sugars, 1g fiber), 11g pro.

I Like to Eat Apples & Bananas Bread

My children love to bake (and eat) all kinds of homemade banana bread. They make this all by themselves, with just a little help from me to put it in the oven.
—**KRISTIN METCALF** CHARLTON, MA

PREP: 20 MIN. • **BAKE:** 50 MIN. + COOLING
MAKES: 1 LOAF (16 SLICES)

- 1½ cups mashed ripe bananas (4-5 medium)
- 1½ cups chopped peeled apples (2 medium)
- ½ cup granulated sugar
- ½ cup packed brown sugar
- 2 tablespoons water
- 2 tablespoons butter, melted
- 1½ cups all-purpose flour
- 1 teaspoon baking soda
- 1 teaspoon baking powder
- ¼ teaspoon salt
- 1 cup sweetened shredded coconut
- ½ cup caramel sundae syrup
- ¼ teaspoon sea salt

1. Preheat oven to 350°. Combine bananas, apples, sugars and water. Stir in melted butter. In another bowl, whisk flour, baking soda, baking powder and salt. Stir into banana mixture. Transfer to a greased and floured 9x5-in. loaf pan.
2. Bake until a toothpick inserted in center comes out clean, 50-60 minutes. Cool in pan 10 minutes before removing to a wire rack to cool completely.
3. Meanwhile, toast coconut, stirring occasionally, in a shallow pan at 350° until golden brown, 4-6 minutes. Cool slightly. Mix coconut with caramel syrup and sea salt; spread over loaf.
Per 1 slice: 187 cal., 4g fat (3g sat. fat), 4mg chol., 232mg sod., 38g carb. (25g sugars, 1g fiber), 2g pro.

I LIKE TO EAT
APPLES & BANANAS BREAD

APRICOT-ROSEMARY SCONES

FREEZE IT ## Apricot-Rosemary Scones

Make these easy sweet-savory scones a family project. Baking them is a delightful way to show your love on Mother's Day.
—**CHARLENE CHAMBERS** ORMOND BEACH, FL

PREP: 25 MIN. • **BAKE:** 15 MIN. • **MAKES:** 16 SCONES

- 4 cups all-purpose flour
- 2 tablespoons sugar
- 2 tablespoons baking powder
- ¾ teaspoon salt
- 1½ cups cold butter, cubed
- 1 cup chopped dried apricots
- 1 tablespoon minced fresh rosemary
- 4 large eggs, lightly beaten
- 1 cup cold heavy whipping cream

TOPPING
- 1 large egg, lightly beaten
- 2 tablespoons 2% milk
- 2 teaspoons sugar

1. Preheat oven to 400°. Whisk together flour, sugar, baking powder and salt. Cut in cold butter until the size of peas. Stir in apricots and rosemary.
2. In a separate bowl, whisk eggs and whipping cream until blended. Stir into flour-butter mixture just until moistened.
3. Turn onto a well-floured surface. Roll dough into a 10-in. square. Cut into four squares; cut each square into four triangles. Place on baking sheets lined with parchment paper.
4. For topping, combine egg and milk. Brush tops of scones with egg mixture; sprinkle with sugar. Bake until golden brown, 12-15 minutes.
To freeze: Freeze cooled scones in resealable plastic freezer bags. To use, reheat in a preheated 350° oven 20-25 minutes, adding time as necessary to heat through.
Per 1 scone: 372 cal., 25g fat (15g sat. fat), 121mg chol., 461mg sod., 32g carb. (7g sugars, 1g fiber), 6g pro.

Tender Whole Wheat Muffins

Want oven-baked treats but need something lighter? Simple whole wheat muffins are wonderful paired with soup or spread with a little jam for breakfast.

—**KRISTINE CHAYES** SMITHTOWN, NY

START TO FINISH: 30 MIN. • **MAKES:** 10 MUFFINS

- 1 cup all-purpose flour
- 1 cup whole wheat flour
- 2 tablespoons sugar
- 2½ teaspoons baking powder
- 1 teaspoon salt
- 1 large egg
- 1¼ cups milk
- 3 tablespoons butter, melted

1. Preheat oven to 400°. In a large bowl, whisk flours, sugar, baking powder and salt. In another bowl, whisk egg, milk and melted butter until blended. Add to flour mixture; stir just until moistened.

2. Fill 10 greased muffin cups three-fourths full. Bake for 15-17 minutes or until a toothpick inserted in center comes out clean. Cool 5 minutes before removing from pan to a wire rack. Serve warm.

Per 1 muffin: 152 cal., 5g fat (3g sat. fat), 35mg chol., 393mg sod., 22g carb. (4g sugars, 2g fiber), 5g pro.
Diabetic Exchanges: 1½ starch, 1 fat.

CARAWAY CHEESE BREAD

TENDER WHOLE WHEAT MUFFINS

Caraway Cheese Bread

We enjoy cheese in lots of ways. In this bread, cheddar blends with just the right amount of caraway.

—**HOMER WOOTEN** RIDGETOWN, ON

PREP: 10 MIN. • **BAKE:** 30 MIN. + COOLING • **MAKES:** 1 LOAF

- 2½ cups all-purpose flour
- 2 cups shredded cheddar cheese
- 1½ to 2 teaspoons caraway seeds
- ¾ teaspoon salt
- ½ teaspoon baking powder
- ½ teaspoon baking soda
- 2 large eggs
- 1 cup (8 ounces) plain yogurt
- ½ cup butter, melted
- 1 tablespoon Dijon mustard

Preheat oven to 375°. Combine the first six ingredients. In another bowl, combine remaining ingredients. Stir into dry ingredients just until moistened. Pour into a greased 9x5-in. loaf pan. Bake until a toothpick comes out clean, 30-35 minutes. Cool 10 minutes before removing from pan to a wire rack. Serve warm. Refrigerate leftovers.

Per 1 slice: 199 cal., 12g fat (7g sat. fat), 55mg chol., 338mg sod., 16g carb. (1g sugars, 1g fiber), 7g pro.

Sour Cream-Leek Biscuits

I've made these biscuits with whole grain flour as well as all-purpose white, and both work equally well. No matter how you make them, they're great with soup!

—**BONNIE APPLETON** CANTERBURY, CT

START TO FINISH: 30 MIN.
MAKES: ABOUT 1 DOZEN

- ⅓ cup cold unsalted butter, divided
- 1½ cups finely chopped leeks (white portion only)
- 2 cups white whole wheat flour
- 2½ teaspoons baking powder
- ½ teaspoon salt
- ¼ teaspoon baking soda
- ¾ cup reduced-fat sour cream
- ¼ cup water

1. Preheat the oven to 400°. In a small skillet over medium heat, melt 1 tablespoon butter. Add leeks; cook until tender, 6-7 minutes. Cool.
2. Whisk together flour, baking powder, salt and baking soda. Cut in remaining butter until mixture resembles coarse crumbs. Stir in the leeks, sour cream and water just until moistened. Turn onto a lightly floured surface; knead 8-10 times.

SOUR CREAM-LEEK BISCUITS

3. Pat or roll out to ½-in. thickness; cut with a floured 2½-in. biscuit cutter. Place biscuits 2 in. apart on an ungreased baking sheet; bake until golden brown, 12-16 minutes. Serve warm.
Per 1 biscuit: 166 cal., 7g fat (4g sat. fat), 20mg chol., 241mg sod., 20g carb. (2g sugars, 3g fiber), 4g pro.
Diabetic Exchanges: 1½ fat, 1 starch.

Poppy Seed Cheese Bread

This easy-to-make bread goes equally well with a salad luncheon or a casserole dinner. I especially like to serve it with spaghetti and pasta dishes. The cheese topping is its crowning glory!

—**ELAINE MUNDT** DETROIT, MI

PREP: 20 MIN. + RISING • **BAKE:** 15 MIN.
MAKES: 15 SERVINGS

- 1 package (¼ ounce) active dry yeast
- 2 teaspoons sugar
- ¼ cup warm water (110° to 115°)
- ¾ cup warm milk (110° to 115°)
- 2 tablespoons shortening
- 1 teaspoon salt
- 2¼ to 2½ cups all-purpose flour

TOPPING

- 2 cups shredded cheddar cheese
- 1 large egg
- ⅓ cup whole milk
- 1 teaspoon finely chopped onion
  Poppy seeds

1. Dissolve yeast and sugar in water. Combine milk, shortening and salt; stir into yeast mixture. Add enough flour to form a soft dough. Turn onto a floured surface; knead until smooth and elastic, about 3 minutes. Place in a greased bowl, turning once to grease top. Cover and let rise in a warm place until doubled, about 1½ hours.
2. Punch down dough; press into a greased 13x9-in. baking pan. Cover and let rise in a warm place until doubled, about 45 minutes.
3. Preheat oven to 425°. Combine cheese, egg, milk and onion; spread over dough. Sprinkle with poppy seeds. Bake 15-20 minutes. Cut into squares; serve warm.
Per 1 piece: 163 cal., 8g fat (4g sat. fat), 30mg chol., 267mg sod., 16g carb. (2g sugars, 1g fiber), 7g pro.

POPPY SEED
CHEESE BREAD

Lemon Blueberry Muffins

When my sister and I spent the night at our grandma's, we often requested these muffins. Today, I bake them for my kids. The aroma is a trip down memory lane.

—**KRIS MICHELS** WALLED LAKE, MI

START TO FINISH: 30 MIN.
MAKES: 1 DOZEN

- 2 cups biscuit/baking mix
- ½ cup plus 2 tablespoons sugar, divided
- 1 large egg
- 1 cup (8 ounces) sour cream
- 1 cup fresh or frozen blueberries
- 2 teaspoons grated lemon peel

1. In a large bowl, combine biscuit mix and ½ cup sugar. Whisk egg and sour cream; stir into dry ingredients just until moistened. Fold in blueberries.

2. Fill greased or paper-lined muffin cups half full. Combine lemon peel and remaining sugar; sprinkle over batter.

3. Bake at 400° for 20-25 minutes or until a toothpick inserted in the center comes out clean. Cool the muffins for 5 minutes before removing from pan to a wire rack. Serve warm.

Note: If using frozen blueberries, use without thawing to avoid discoloring the batter.

Per 1 muffin: 174 cal., 7g fat (3g sat. fat), 20mg chol., 260mg sod., 26g carb. (13g sugars, 1g fiber), 3g pro.

★ ★ ★ ★ ★ **READER REVIEW**

"My kids INHALED these! Doubled the recipe so that I could keep extras in the freezer for a quick on-the-go breakfast. After baking, I also drizzled them with a glaze of lemon juice and powdered sugar for an extra citrus punch. This one is a keeper for sure!"

MY4SWEETYS TASTEOFHOME.COM

POTATO PAN ROLLS

⑤INGREDIENTS
Potato Pan Rolls

My family loves these rolls, so I prepare them often. They don't take long to make because of the quick-rise yeast.

—**CONNIE STORCKMAN** EVANSTON, WY

PREP: 15 MIN. + RISING • **BAKE:** 20 MIN.
MAKES: 16 ROLLS

- 4½ to 5 cups all-purpose flour
- 3 tablespoons sugar
- 2 packages (¼ ounce each) quick-rise yeast
- 1½ teaspoons salt
- 1¼ cups water
- 3 tablespoons butter
- ½ cup mashed potatoes (without added milk and butter)
  Additional all-purpose flour

1. In a large bowl, combine 2 cups flour with the sugar, yeast and salt. In a small saucepan, heat water and butter to 120°-130°. Add to dry ingredients; beat until smooth. Stir in mashed potatoes and enough remaining flour to form a soft dough.

2. Turn onto a floured surface; knead until smooth and elastic, 6-8 minutes. Cover dough and let rest 10 minutes. Divide into 16 pieces. Shape each into a ball. Place in two greased 8- or 9-in. round baking pans or ovenproof skillets. Cover and let rise in a warm place until doubled, about 30 minutes.

3. Preheat oven to 400°. Sprinkle tops of rolls with additional flour. Bake 18-22 minutes or until golden brown. Remove from pans to wire racks.

Per 1 roll: 163 cal., 3g fat (1g sat. fat), 6mg chol., 239mg sod., 30g carb. (3g sugars, 1g fiber), 4g pro.

**JOAN ELBOURN'S
PEAR-BERRY BREAKFAST TARTS**
PAGE 149

Breakfast & Brunch

These **rise-and-shine recipes** make a hot **homemade breakfast** as easy as can be. Whether you crave convenient **overnight oats,** buttery **sweet rolls** or grab-and-go **avocado toast,** dozens of morning specialties are sure to **tempt your taste buds.**

SHARON BICKETT'S BROWN SUGAR OATMEAL PANCAKES *PAGE 145*

JOYCE MUMMAU'S MORNING ORANGE DRINK *PAGE 148*

ANUJA ARGADE'S HASH BROWN MAPLE SAUSAGE CASSEROLE *PAGE 155*

HAM STEAKS WITH GRUYERE, BACON & MUSHROOMS

⑤ INGREDIENTS
Easy Orange Rolls

Life on a dairy farm is busy, so I need breakfast recipes that are simple yet delicious. My teenager daughter has been helping in the kitchen for years. In fact, this was probably one of the first recipes she made herself.

—**PEGGY KRAEMER** THIEF RIVER, MN

PREP: 15 MIN. • **BAKE:** 25 MIN. • **MAKES:** 16 SERVINGS

- 1 cup sugar
- ½ cup butter, cubed
- ¼ cup orange juice
- 2 tablespoons grated orange peel
- 3 tubes (10 ounces each) refrigerated biscuits

1. In a small saucepan, combine the sugar, butter, orange juice and peel. Heat until sugar is dissolved and butter is melted. Pour into a greased 10-in. fluted tube pan.

2. Place 12 biscuits on their sides along the perimeter of the pan, overlapping slightly. Arrange the remaining biscuits in the same manner, creating two concentric rings, using 10 biscuits for the middle ring and eight biscuits for the inside ring.

3. Bake at 350° for 25-30 minutes or until golden brown. Immediately invert onto a serving platter. Serve warm.

Per 1 piece: 159 cal., 8g fat (4g sat. fat), 15mg chol., 226mg sod., 20g carb. (13g sugars, 0 fiber), 1g pro.

EASY ORANGE ROLLS

Ham Steaks with Gruyere, Bacon & Mushrooms

This meat lover's breakfast has a big wow factor. The Gruyere, bacon and fresh mushrooms in the topping are a great combination.

—**LISA SPEER** PALM BEACH, FL

START TO FINISH: 25 MIN. • **MAKES:** 4 SERVINGS

- 2 tablespoons butter
- ½ pound sliced fresh mushrooms
- 1 shallot, finely chopped
- 2 garlic cloves, minced
- ⅛ teaspoon coarsely ground pepper
- 1 fully cooked boneless ham steak (about 1 pound), cut into four pieces
- 1 cup shredded Gruyere cheese
- 4 bacon strips, cooked and crumbled
- 1 tablespoon minced fresh parsley, optional

1. In a large nonstick skillet, heat butter over medium-high heat. Add the mushrooms and shallot; cook and stir for 4-6 minutes or until tender. Add garlic and pepper; cook 1 minute longer. Remove from pan; keep warm.

2. Wipe skillet clean. In same pan, cook ham over medium heat 3 minutes. Turn; sprinkle with the cheese and bacon. Cook, covered, 2-4 minutes longer or until cheese is melted and ham is heated through. Serve with mushroom mixture. If desired, sprinkle with parsley.

Per 1 serving: 352 cal., 22g fat (11g sat. fat), 113mg chol., 1576mg sod., 5g carb. (2g sugars, 1g fiber), 34g pro.

Brown Sugar Oatmeal Pancakes

(PICTURED ON P. 143)

These pancakes are a favorite at my house. If I don't make them every Saturday and Sunday, the family won't believe it's the weekend! My son's friends often spend the night, and I think it's because they like the pancakes so much.

—SHARON BICKETT CHESTER, SC

START TO FINISH: 15 MIN. • **MAKES:** ABOUT 10 PANCAKES

- ½ cup plus 2 tablespoons quick-cooking oats
- ½ cup whole wheat flour
- ½ cup all-purpose flour
- ½ teaspoon baking soda
- ½ teaspoon salt
- ⅓ cup packed brown sugar
- 1 large egg
- 2 tablespoons oil
- 1 cup buttermilk

In a small bowl, combine the oats, flours, baking soda, salt and sugar. Beat the egg, oil and buttermilk; stir into dry ingredients just until moistened. Pour batter by ⅓ cupfuls onto a greased hot griddle. Turn when bubbles form on top; cook until the second side is golden brown.

To freeze: Freeze cooled pancakes between layers of waxed paper in a resealable plastic freezer bag. To use, place pancakes on an ungreased baking sheet, cover with foil and reheat in a 375° oven 5-10 minutes. Or, place a stack of three pancakes on a microwave-safe plate and microwave on high 1¼-1½ minutes.

Per 2 pancakes: 263 cal., 8g fat (1g sat. fat), 44mg chol., 433mg sod., 42g carb. (17g sugars, 3g fiber), 7g pro.

Fruity Frappe

Making a taste-alike of a restaurant drink is fun, but better yet, I know exactly what's in this one. My frappe gets its sweetness from berries, juice and honey.

—PATTY CROUSE WARREN, PA

START TO FINISH: 10 MIN. • **MAKES:** 4 SERVINGS

- 1 cup water
- 1 cup fat-free milk
- ⅔ cup thawed orange juice concentrate
- 3 tablespoons honey
- ½ teaspoon vanilla extract
- 1 cup ice cubes
- 1 cup frozen unsweetened mixed berries

Place all ingredients in a blender; cover and process until blended. Serve immediately.

Per 1¼ cups: 166 cal., 0 fat (0 sat. fat), 1mg chol., 28mg sod., 39g carb. (37g sugars, 1g fiber), 3g pro.

PORK SAUSAGE PATTIES

Pork Sausage Patties

With pork sausage patties, any breakfast gets a boost. These little beauties will certainly have them coming back for seconds.

—CAROLE THOMSON KOMARNO, MB

START TO FINISH: 25 MIN. • **MAKES:** 6 SERVINGS

- 1 large egg, beaten
- ⅓ cup milk
- ½ cup chopped onion
- 2 tablespoons all-purpose flour
- ⅛ teaspoon salt
  Dash pepper
- 1 pound sage bulk pork sausage

1. In a large bowl, combine the first six ingredients. Crumble sausage over mixture and mix well. Shape into six patties.

2. In a large skillet, cook patties over medium heat for 6 minutes on each side or until meat is no longer pink, turning occasionally.

To freeze: Prepare uncooked patties and freeze, covered, on a plastic wrap-lined baking sheet until firm. Transfer patties to a resealable plastic bag; return to freezer. To use, cook frozen patties as directed, increasing time as necessary for a thermometer to read 160°.

Per 1 patty: 219 cal., 18g fat (6g sat. fat), 73mg chol., 527mg sod., 5g carb. (1g sugars, 0 fiber), 10g pro.

FREEZE IT | SLOW COOKER

Pot Roast Hash

I love to cook a Sunday-style pot roast for weeknights, then make it into pot roast hash for any day of the week.

—**GINA JACKSON** OGDENSBURG, NY

PREP: 6¼ HOURS • **COOK:** 15 MIN.
MAKES: 10 SERVINGS

- 1 cup warm water
- 1 tablespoon beef base
- ½ pound sliced fresh mushrooms
- 1 large onion, coarsely chopped
- 3 garlic cloves, minced
- 1 boneless beef chuck roast (3 pounds)
- ½ teaspoon pepper
- 1 tablespoon Worcestershire sauce
- 1 package (28 ounces) frozen O'Brien potatoes

EGGS
- 2 tablespoons butter
- 10 large eggs
- ½ teaspoon salt
- ½ teaspoon pepper
  Minced chives

1. In a 5- or 6-qt. slow cooker, whisk water and beef base; add mushrooms, onion and garlic. Sprinkle roast with pepper; transfer to slow cooker. Drizzle with Worcestershire sauce. Cook, covered, on low 6-8 hours or until meat is tender.

2. Remove roast; cool slightly. Shred meat with two forks. In a large skillet, cook potatoes according to package directions; stir in shredded beef. Using a slotted spoon, add vegetables from slow cooker to skillet; heat through. Discard cooking juices.

3. For eggs, in another skillet, heat 1 tablespoon butter over medium-high heat. Break five eggs, one at a time, into pan. Sprinkle with half of the salt and pepper. Reduce heat to low. Cook until desired doneness, turning after the whites are set if desired. Repeat with the remaining butter, eggs, salt and pepper. Serve eggs over hash; sprinkle with chives.

To freeze: Place shredded pot roast and vegetables in a freezer container; top with cooking juices. Cool and freeze. To use, partially thaw in refrigerator overnight. Heat through in a covered saucepan.
Note: Look for beef base near the broth and bouillon.
Per ⅔ cup hash with 1 egg: 429 cal., 24g fat (8g sat. fat), 281mg chol., 306mg sod., 15g carb. (2g sugars, 2g fiber), 35g pro.

---

⑤ INGREDIENTS | FAST FIX

English Muffins with Bacon Butter

For a change from the usual breakfast bread, I toast up a batch of English muffins with a bacony butter. The hint of Dijon mustard in this hearty spread really dresses up the English muffins.

—**EDNA HOFFMAN** HEBRON, IN

START TO FINISH: 10 MIN.
MAKES: 6 SERVINGS

- ½ cup butter, softened
- ½ to ¾ teaspoon Dijon mustard
- 4 bacon strips, cooked and crumbled
- 6 English muffins, split

In a bowl, combine butter and mustard; stir in bacon. Toast the English muffins; spread with bacon butter. Refrigerate any leftover butter.
Per 1 serving: 248 cal., 18g fat (10g sat. fat), 44mg chol., 408mg sod., 18g carb. (1g sugars, 1g fiber), 4g pro.

Homemade Biscuits & Maple Sausage Gravy

I remember digging into flaky, gravy-smothered biscuits on Christmas morning and other special occasions when I was a child. What a satisfying way to start the day!

—**JENN TIDWELL** FAIR OAKS, CA

PREP: 30 MIN. • **BAKE:** 15 MIN.
MAKES: 8 SERVINGS

- 2 cups all-purpose flour
- 3 teaspoons baking powder
- 1 tablespoon sugar
- 1 teaspoon salt
- ¼ teaspoon pepper, optional
- 3 tablespoons cold butter, cubed
- 1 tablespoon shortening
- ¾ cup 2% milk

SAUSAGE GRAVY
- 1 pound bulk maple pork sausage
- ¼ cup all-purpose flour
- 3 cups 2% milk
- 2 tablespoons maple syrup
- ½ teaspoon salt
- ¼ teaspoon ground sage
- ¼ teaspoon coarsely ground pepper

1. Preheat oven to 400°. In a large bowl, whisk flour, baking powder, sugar, salt and, if desired, pepper. Cut in butter and shortening until mixture resembles coarse crumbs. Add milk; stir just until moistened. Turn onto a lightly floured surface; knead gently 8-10 times.

2. Pat or roll dough to 1-in. thickness; cut with a floured 2-in. biscuit cutter. Place 1 in. apart on an ungreased baking sheet. Bake 15-17 minutes or until golden brown.

3. Meanwhile, in a large skillet, cook the sausage over medium heat for 6-8 minutes or until no longer pink, breaking into crumbles. Stir in flour until blended; gradually stir in milk. Bring to a boil, stirring constantly; cook and stir 4-6 minutes or until sauce is thickened. Stir in remaining ingredients. Serve with warm biscuits.
Per 1 biscuit with ½ cup gravy: 371 cal., 19g fat (8g sat. fat), 41mg chol., 915mg sod., 38g carb. (11g sugars, 1g fiber), 11g pro.

POT ROAST HASH

SMOOTH OPERATORS

MAKE YOURS TROPICAL, BERRY-PACKED OR PEACHY AND CREAMY. FACEBOOK FRIENDS SHARE THEIR SECRETS FOR ADDING WHOLESOME INGREDIENTS TO THEIR SWEET SMOOTHIES.

1 FRESH PEACH
My smoothies use vanilla almond milk, orange juice, peaches, Greek yogurt and a surprise ingredient: English cucumber.
—*Angela Lively, Conroe, TX*

2 GREEN GOODNESS
I make smoothies with frozen or fresh fruit, kefir, spinach and unsweetened almond milk, plus flax and chia seeds. Yummy!
—*Jami Kruse, Baltic, SD*

3 PEACH MELBA
I use frozen peaches, raspberries, yogurt, peach nectar, wheat germ and vanilla to make mine taste like this old-school dessert.
—*Mari Lizzt, Kalamazoo, MI*

4 STRAWBERRY-BANANA
I make a smoothie almost every day for my oldest granddaughter using 1 banana, ½ cup strawberry yogurt, a splash of coconut water and a handful of frozen strawberries.
—*Don Mellott, Durand, MI*

5 SWEET POTATO-CHERRY
There's nothing like a blend of sweet potatoes, banana and cherries.
—*Brenda Nora, Memphis, TN*

6 COCONUT-MANGO
My favorite smoothie combines coconut milk, mango, pineapple, Greek yogurt and ice.
—*Megan Worthington, Birmingham, AL*

7 PEANUTTY CHOCOLATE
With baby spinach, banana, dark chocolate soy milk, dairy-free yogurt, powdered peanut butter, instant coffee granules and ice, this tasty combo is gluten- and dairy-free.
—*Tricia Barlow Walker, Oshkosh, WI*

8 BROCCOLI-BERRY
My favorite smoothie includes frozen broccoli, frozen berries, a banana, kiwi, Greek yogurt, fruit juice of some kind and hemp protein powder.
—*Lisa Kydyk McGann, Peterborough, ON*

9 MANGO-CARROT
You can't go wrong with frozen mango chunks, almonds, cinnamon, raw carrot, milk and water. Blend all until smooth.
—*Ian Crawford, Deux-Montagnes, QC*

10 PUMPKIN SPICE
This tastes just like fall: pumpkin puree, vanilla Greek yogurt, orange juice, cinnamon, nutmeg and ice.
—*Syndee Yurkanin Mears, Round Lake, IL*

1/ FRESH PEACH

2/ GREEN GOODNESS

4/ STRAWBERRY-BANANA

6/ COCONUT-MANGO

7/ PEANUTTY CHOCOLATE

Spring Onion Pimiento Cheese Grits

Grits were a breakfast staple when I was growing up. Even today, we still have them about three times a week. The trick with grits is the more you whisk, the creamier they'll be.

—**MELISSA PELKEY HASS** WALESKA, GA

PREP: 15 MIN. • **COOK:** 20 MIN.
MAKES: 16 SERVINGS

- 2 cups uncooked stone-ground yellow grits
- 1 package (8 ounces) cream cheese, softened
- ½ cup mayonnaise
- 3 cups shredded Monterey Jack cheese
- 1 jar (4 ounces) diced pimientos, drained
- 3 green onions, diced
- 1 teaspoon sugar
  Dash cayenne pepper
- ¼ cup butter, softened
  Salt and pepper to taste

1. Prepare grits according to package directions. Keep warm.
2. Meanwhile, using a mixer, beat cream cheese. Add mayonnaise; continue beating until creamy. Add next five ingredients, mixing until well blended.
3. Stir butter and pimiento cheese mixture into the warm grits; season to taste. Mix well.
Per ¾ cup: 281 cal., 20g fat (10g sat. fat), 41mg chol., 231mg sod., 19g carb. (1g sugars, 1g fiber), 8g pro.

SPRING ONION
PIMIENTO CHEESE GRITS

CORNMEAL
PANCAKES

FAST FIX

Cornmeal Pancakes

I like to joke that these pancakes are so light, you have to hold them down! When we can, we make them with freshly ground cornmeal bought at one of the local festivals.

—**BETTY CLAYCOMB** ALVERTON, PA

START TO FINISH: 30 MIN.
MAKES: 6 SERVINGS

- 1⅓ cups all-purpose flour
- ⅔ cup cornmeal
- 2 tablespoons sugar
- 4 teaspoons baking powder
- 1 teaspoon salt
- 2 large eggs
- 1⅓ cups 2% milk
- ¼ cup canola oil
  Pancake syrup

Combine the first five ingredients. In another bowl, whisk eggs, milk and oil; stir into dry ingredients just until moistened. Pour batter by ¼ cupfuls onto a lightly greased hot griddle. Turn when bubbles on top begin to pop; cook until second side is golden brown. Serve with syrup.
Per 2 pancakes: 321 cal., 13g fat (2g sat. fat), 67mg chol., 709mg sod., 42g carb. (7g sugars, 1g fiber), 8g pro.
Cranberry-Orange Pancakes: Stir ¾ cup of chopped fresh cranberries and 1 teaspoon orange zest into the prepared batter.

Blueberry-Lemon Pancakes: Stir ¾ cup of fresh blueberries and 1 teaspoon lemon zest into prepared batter.
Bacon Flapjacks: Stir 4-6 cooked and crumbled bacon strips into prepared batter.

⑤ INGREDIENTS FAST FIX

Morning Orange Drink

(PICTURED ON P. 143)

Although it takes just a few basic ingredients and little preparation, this drink always draws raves from overnight guests, who love its wake-up taste.

—**JOYCE MUMMAU** MOUNT AIRY, MD

START TO FINISH: 10 MIN.
MAKES: 4-6 SERVINGS

- 1 can (6 ounces) frozen orange juice concentrate
- 1 cup cold water
- 1 cup milk
- ⅓ cup sugar
- 1 teaspoon vanilla extract
- 10 ice cubes

Combine the first five ingredients in a blender; process at high speed. Add ice cubes, a few at a time, blending until smooth. Serve immediately.
Per ¾ cup: 115 cal., 1g fat (1g sat. fat), 6mg chol., 21mg sod., 24g carb. (23g sugars, 0 fiber), 2g pro.
Diabetic Exchanges: 1 fruit, ½ reduced-fat milk.

Pear-Berry Breakfast Tarts

(PICTURED ON P. 142)

When my kids were small, I could never get pancakes on the table while they were all still hot. Then I got the idea for these breakfast tarts. They're a good and simple recipe for any busy family.

—JOAN ELBOURN GARDNER, MA

PREP: 45 MIN. + CHILLING • **BAKE:** 20 MIN.
MAKES: 10 SERVINGS

- ½ cup butter, softened
- 1 cup granulated sugar, divided
- 2 large eggs
- 2½ cups all-purpose flour
- 2 teaspoons baking powder
- 2 cups chopped peeled pears (about 2 large)
- 2 tablespoons cornstarch
- 2 tablespoons water
- ½ cup fresh raspberries
- 1 large egg white
- 3 to 5 tablespoons 2% milk, divided
- 1⅓ cups confectioners' sugar
  Food coloring, optional

1. Cream the butter and ½ cup granulated sugar until light and fluffy. Add eggs, one at a time, beating well after each addition. In another bowl, whisk flour and baking powder; gradually beat into creamed mixture to form a dough. Divide dough in half; shape each into a rectangle. Wrap in plastic; refrigerate 1 hour.
2. Meanwhile, in a small saucepan over medium heat, combine pears and remaining granulated sugar. Cook and stir until sugar is dissolved and pears are softened, 6-8 minutes. In a small bowl, mix cornstarch and water until smooth; stir into pear mixture. Bring to a boil, stirring constantly; cook and stir 1-2 minutes or until thickened. Remove from heat; cool. Stir in the raspberries.
3. Preheat oven to 350°. On a lightly floured surface, roll one half of the dough into a 15x8-in. rectangle. Cut into ten 4x3-in. rectangles. Transfer to parchment paper-lined baking sheets; spoon about 2 tablespoons filling over each pastry to within ½ in. of edges. Roll the remaining dough into a 15x8-in. rectangle; cut into ten 4x3-in. rectangles and place over filling. Press

edges with a fork to seal. Whisk egg white and 1 tablespoon milk; brush over pastries. Bake until golden brown and filling is bubbly, 20-25 minutes.
4. Remove from baking sheets to wire racks to cool. For icing, mix the confectioners' sugar and enough of the remaining milk to reach desired consistency; tint with food coloring if desired. Spread or drizzle on pastries.
Per 1 tart: 379 cal., 11g fat (6g sat. fat), 62mg chol., 193mg sod., 67g carb. (39g sugars, 2g fiber), 5g pro.

Italian Baked Eggs & Sausage

This isn't your typical egg bake! I serve this robust casserole of eggs, Italian sausage and fire-roasted tomatoes in bowls with warm artisan bread, spread with butter.

—SHELLY L. BEVINGTON HERMISTON, OR

PREP: 15 MIN. • **BAKE:** 30 MIN.
MAKES: 8 SERVINGS

- 1 pound bulk Italian sausage
- 1 jar (24 ounces) fire-roasted tomato and garlic pasta sauce
- 1 can (14½ ounces) fire-roasted diced tomatoes, drained
- ¾ cup part-skim ricotta cheese
- 8 large eggs
- ¼ teaspoon salt
- ¼ teaspoon pepper
- ¼ cup shredded Parmesan cheese
- 1 tablespoon minced fresh basil
- 1 French bread demi-baguette (4 ounces), cut into 1-inch slices
- ¼ cup butter, softened

1. Preheat oven to 350°. In a large skillet over medium heat, cook sausage, crumbling meat, until no longer pink, 3-4 minutes; drain. Stir in pasta sauce and tomatoes. Transfer to a 13x9-in. baking dish.
2. Dollop ricotta cheese on top of meat mixture. Gently break an egg into a small bowl; slip egg onto ricotta. Repeat with remaining eggs. Sprinkle salt, pepper and Parmesan over top.
3. Bake 30-35 minutes or until egg whites are completely set and yolks have begun to thicken but are not hard. Remove from oven; sprinkle with basil.
4. Meanwhile, spread bread slices with butter; place on an ungreased baking sheet. Preheat broiler. Broil 3-4 in. from heat 1-2 minutes on each side or until golden brown. Serve immediately with baked eggs.
Per 1 serving: 408 cal., 27g fat (11g sat. fat), 241mg chol., 1183mg sod., 22g carb. (8g sugars, 3g fiber), 19g pro.

ITALIAN BAKED
EGGS & SAUSAGE

Raised Yeast Waffles

These terrific waffles are crispy on the outside and tender on the inside. Never too filling, they leave room for sampling the rest of the brunch buffet.

—**HELEN KNAPP** NORTH POLE, AK

PREP: 15 MIN. + RISING • **BAKE:** 5 MIN./BATCH • **MAKES:** 10 WAFFLES

- 1 package (¼ ounce) active dry yeast
- 1 teaspoon sugar
- ½ cup warm water (110° to 115°)
- 2 cups warm 2% milk (110° to 115°)
- 2 large eggs
- ½ cup butter, melted
- 2¼ cups all-purpose flour
- 1 teaspoon salt
- ⅛ teaspoon baking soda

Dissolve yeast and sugar in warm water; let stand 5 minutes. Beat in milk, eggs and butter. In another bowl, combine flour, salt and baking soda; stir into yeast mixture just until combined. Cover and let rise in a warm place until doubled, about 45 minutes. Stir batter. Bake in a preheated waffle iron according to manufacturer's directions until golden brown.

Per 2 waffles: 453 cal., 23g fat (14g sat. fat), 131mg chol., 726mg sod., 49g carb. (6g sugars, 2g fiber), 12g pro.

Spiced Yeast Waffles: Add ¼ teaspoon vanilla extract to the milk and stir in ¼ teaspoon ground nutmeg or cinnamon along with the flour.

EAT SMART ⑤ INGREDIENTS FAST FIX ▶

Makeover Hash & Eggs

Our lightened-up version of the diner classic delivers fresh flavors with a healthy dose of fiber.

—**TASTE OF HOME** TEST KITCHEN

START TO FINISH: 30 MIN. • **MAKES:** 4 SERVINGS

- 1 large onion, chopped
- 1 tablespoon canola oil
- 6 medium red potatoes (about 1½ pounds), cubed
- ¼ cup water
- 3 packages (2 ounces each) thinly sliced deli corned beef, coarsely chopped
- ¼ teaspoon pepper
- 4 large eggs

1. In a large nonstick skillet, saute onion in oil until tender. Stir in potatoes and water. Bring to a boil. Reduce heat; cover and simmer for 15-20 minutes or until potatoes are tender. Stir in corned beef and pepper; heat through.

2. Meanwhile, in a large nonstick skillet coated with cooking spray, fry eggs as desired. Serve with hash.

Per 1 serving: 301 cal., 12g fat (3g sat. fat), 239mg chol., 652mg sod., 31g carb. (4g sugars, 4g fiber), 18g pro.

Diabetic Exchanges: 2 starch, 2 medium-fat meat, ½ fat.

TWISTED EGGS BENEDICT SALAD

EAT SMART **Twisted Eggs Benedict Salad**

Salad for breakfast? Absolutely. You can prepare everything but the dressing and chill it overnight; in the morning dress the salad and poach the eggs.

—**NOELLE MYERS** GRAND FORKS, ND

PREP: 20 MIN. • **COOK:** 20 MIN. • **MAKES:** 8 SERVINGS

- 4 tablespoons olive oil, divided
- 1½ pounds fresh asparagus, trimmed and chopped
- 1⅓ cups chopped fennel bulb
- 8 ounces diced deli ham or Canadian bacon
- 6 cups baby kale salad blend (about 4 ounces)
- 1 cup chopped roasted sweet red peppers
- 3 tablespoons chopped green onion tops
- 3 tablespoons Dijon mustard
- 2 tablespoons cider vinegar
- ¼ teaspoon salt
- ¼ teaspoon pepper
- 2 quarts water
- 8 large eggs

1. In a large nonstick skillet, heat 1 tablespoon olive oil over medium heat. Add asparagus, fennel and ham; saute until vegetables are crisp-tender, about 8 minutes. Cool for 3 minutes.

2. Toss vegetable mixture with salad blend, peppers and green onions. Whisk together mustard, vinegar, salt, pepper and remaining oil until smooth.

3. In a large saucepan, bring water to a boil; reduce heat to a gentle simmer. Break eggs, one at a time, into a small bowl; slip eggs into water. Poach, uncovered, until whites are completely set and yolks begin to thicken, 3-5 minutes.

4. Meanwhile, toss salad with dressing. Divide salad among eight plates. Using a slotted spoon, remove eggs from water; place one on top of each salad.

Per 1 cup salad with 1 egg: 199 cal., 13g fat (3g sat. fat), 200mg chol., 710mg sod., 5g carb. (3g sugars, 2g fiber), 14g pro.

Diabetic Exchanges: 2 lean meat, 2 fat, 1 vegetable.

Vanilla French Toast

We discovered this recipe in Mexico. We couldn't figure out what made the French toast so delicious until we learned the secret was vanilla—one of Mexico's most popular flavorings. Since then, we've added a touch of vanilla to our waffle and pancake recipes, and it makes all the difference.

—JOE & BOBBI SCHOTT CASTROVILLE, TX

START TO FINISH: 15 MIN. • **MAKES:** 6 SERVINGS

- 4 large eggs, lightly beaten
- 1 cup 2% milk
- 2 tablespoons sugar
- 2 teaspoons vanilla extract
- ⅛ teaspoon salt
- 12 slices day-old sandwich bread
  Optional toppings: butter, maple syrup, fresh berries and confectioners' sugar

1. In a shallow dish, whisk together first five ingredients. Preheat a greased griddle over medium heat.
2. Dip bread in egg mixture, allowing to soak 30 seconds on each side. Cook on griddle until golden brown on both sides. Serve with toppings as desired.
Per 2 slices: 218 cal., 6g fat (3g sat. fat), 127mg chol., 376mg sod., 30g carb. (9g sugars, 1g fiber), 10g pro.
Diabetic Exchanges: 2 starch, 1 medium-fat meat.
Whole Wheat Cinnamon French Toast: Omit the vanilla. Substitute 1½ teaspoons honey for sugar and whole wheat bread for the day-old bread. Add ¼ teaspoon ground cinnamon to the milk mixture.

CANADIAN BACON WITH APPLES

VANILLA FRENCH TOAST

⑤ INGREDIENTS FAST FIX
Canadian Bacon with Apples

At the holidays, I'd rather spend time with family than in the kitchen, so I rely on easy-to-fix recipes like this. No one can resist Canadian bacon and apples coated with a brown sugar glaze.

—PAULA MARCHESI LENHARTSVILLE, PA

START TO FINISH: 20 MIN. • **MAKES:** 6 SERVINGS

- ½ cup packed brown sugar
- 1 tablespoon lemon juice
- ⅛ teaspoon pepper
- 1 large unpeeled red apple
- 1 large unpeeled green apple
- 1 pound sliced Canadian bacon

1. In a large skillet, mix brown sugar, lemon juice and pepper. Cook and stir over medium heat until sugar is dissolved. Cut each apple into 16 wedges; add to brown sugar mixture. Cook over medium heat until apples are tender, 5-7 minutes, stirring occasionally. Remove apples to a platter with a slotted spoon; keep warm.
2. Add bacon to skillet; cook over medium heat, turning once, until heated through, about 3 minutes. Transfer to platter. Pour remaining brown sugar mixture over apples and bacon.
Per 1 serving: 199 cal., 4g fat (1g sat. fat), 28mg chol., 744mg sod., 30g carb. (27g sugars, 2g fiber), 12g pro.

Hash Brown Pancakes with Smoked Salmon & Dill Cream

On weekends when I was growing up, pancakes, salmon and bagels were our brunch staples. I've combined the concepts in this dish. I use whipped cream instead of cream cheese.

—**ARLENE ERLBACH** MORTON GROVE, IL

PREP: 15 MIN. • **COOK:** 20 MIN.
MAKES: 4 SERVINGS

- ⅓ cup heavy whipping cream
- 1⅛ teaspoons dill weed, divided
- 4 cups frozen shredded hash brown potatoes, thawed
- 2 large eggs, beaten
- 2 tablespoons minced chives
- ¼ teaspoon salt
- 1 package (3 to 4 ounces) smoked salmon or lox

1. Beat heavy whipping cream and 1 teaspoon dill on high until stiff peaks form. Cover and refrigerate.
2. Preheat griddle over medium heat. Stir together potatoes, eggs, chives and salt until well combined. Grease griddle. Drop potato mixture by heaping ½ cupfuls onto griddle; flatten to ½-inch thick. Cook until bottoms are golden brown, about 10 minutes. Turn; cook until second side is golden brown. Keep warm.
3. To serve, place salmon slices on pancakes. Top with whipped cream; sprinkle with remaining dill.
Per 1 serving: 187 cal., 11g fat (6g sat. fat), 125mg chol., 350mg sod., 14g carb. (1g sugars, 1g fiber), 9g pro.

ASPARAGUS, BACON & SHALLOT TART

HASH BROWN PANCAKES WITH SMOKED SALMON & DILL CREAM

Asparagus, Bacon & Shallot Tart

My tart is adapted from my mom's quiche recipe. She lives thousands of miles away from me in the U.K., so whenever I make it, happy memories of home come flooding back.

—**PAULA NOLAN** GRANITE BAY, CA

PREP: 40 MIN. + CHILLING
BAKE: 25 MIN. + STANDING
MAKES: 12 SERVINGS

- Pastry for single-crust pie
- 1 pound fresh asparagus
- 6 thick-sliced center cut bacon strips, coarsely chopped
- 1 tablespoon extra virgin olive oil
- 1 medium red onion, thinly sliced
- 1 shallot, thinly sliced
- 1 tablespoon red wine vinegar
- ⅓ cup oil-packed sun-dried tomatoes, coarsely chopped
- 1 tablespoon chopped fresh parsley
- 1 teaspoon grated lemon peel
- ¼ teaspoon salt
- ¼ teaspoon pepper
- 3 large eggs, lightly beaten
- 1¼ cups half-and-half cream
- 1½ cups shredded sharp cheddar cheese
- ¼ cup shredded Gruyere cheese

1. Preheat oven to 400°. On a lightly floured surface, roll pie pastry to a ⅛-in.-thick circle; transfer to an 11-in. tart pan and press into edges. Refrigerate 30 minutes. Prick pastry with a fork 5 or 6 times; line with a double thickness of foil. Fill with dried beans or pie weights. Bake for 12-15 minutes. Remove foil and beans (or weights); bake until light golden brown, 5 minutes more. Cool on a wire rack. Reduce oven setting to 375°.
2. Trim tough ends from asparagus. Reserve 12 spears; cut remaining asparagus into ½-in. pieces.
3. In a large skillet, cook bacon over medium heat until crisp, 6-8 minutes; remove and drain. Add olive oil to skillet, then red onion, shallot and chopped asparagus; cook and stir until softened, 6-8 minutes. Stir in vinegar; cook 3 minutes. Reduce heat to low. Return bacon to pan; stir in tomatoes, parsley, lemon peel, salt and pepper. Spoon into pastry shell.
4. Whisk eggs and cream; stir in cheddar cheese until blended. Pour over top. Arrange reserved asparagus spears in a spoke pattern with tips facing outward. Sprinkle with the Gruyere cheese. Bake until a knife inserted in center comes out clean, 25-30 minutes. Let stand 10 minutes before cutting.
Pastry for single-crust pie: Combine 1¼ cups all-purpose flour and ¼ tsp. salt; cut in ½ cup cold butter until crumbly. Gradually add 3-5 Tbsp. ice water, tossing with a fork until dough holds together when pressed. Wrap in plastic and refrigerate 1 hour.
Per 1 slice: 367 cal., 30g fat (14g sat. fat), 109mg chol., 441mg sod., 14g carb. (2g sugars, 1g fiber), 11g pro.

Confetti Bubble Ring

My daughters made this addictive pull-apart bread when they were in 4-H, and we've shared it many times over the years. With refrigerated biscuits, it's easy breezy.
—**VIRGINIA KRITES** CRIDERSVILLE, OH

PREP: 15 MIN. • **BAKE:** 30 MIN.
MAKES: 12 SERVINGS

- ½ pound bacon strips, diced
- ¼ cup grated Parmesan cheese
- ¼ cup chopped onion, optional
- ¼ cup chopped green pepper, optional
- 1 tube (16.3 ounces) large refrigerated flaky biscuits
- ⅓ cup butter, melted

1. Preheat oven to 350°. In a large skillet, cook bacon until crisp; drain. Combine bacon with cheese and, if desired, onion and green pepper. Cut biscuits into quarters; add to bacon mixture. Stir in butter and toss to coat. Transfer to a greased 10-in. tube pan.
2. Bake until browned, about 30 minutes. Cool 10 minutes before inverting onto a serving platter. Refrigerate leftovers.
Per 1 piece: 214 cal., 14g fat (6g sat. fat), 22mg chol., 557mg sod., 17g carb. (4g sugars, 1g fiber), 6g pro.

EAT SMART (5)INGREDIENTS FAST FIX
Classic Avocado Toast

This is such an easy way to add avocados to your diet. Use healthy multi-grain bread and top with sliced radishes and cracked pepper or lime zest, chipotle peppers and cilantro for extra flavor.
—*TASTE OF HOME* TEST KITCHEN

START TO FINISH: 5 MIN.
MAKES: 1 SERVING

- 1 slice hearty bread, toasted
- 1 to 2 teaspoons extra virgin olive oil or coconut oil
- ¼ medium ripe avocado, sliced
- ⅛ teaspoon sea salt

Spread toast with olive oil; top with avocado slices. If desired, mash avocado slightly and drizzle with additional oil. Sprinkle with salt.
Per 1 slice: 160 cal., 11g fat (2g sat. fat), 0 chol., 361mg sod., 15g carb. (1g sugars, 3g fiber), 3g pro.
Diabetic Exchanges: 2 fat, 1 starch.

BREAKFAST BURGER
Tina Janssen
Walworth, WI

Breakfast Burger

My husband is big on eggs and bacon, so I wanted to merge his breakfast favorites with a grilled burger for an over-the-top treat. Topping it with my homemade blackberry jam sealed the deal.
—**TINA JANSSEN** WALWORTH, WI

PREP: 25 MIN. • **GRILL:** 30 MIN.
MAKES: 4 SERVINGS

- 1 pound ground beef
- 1 tablespoon Worcestershire sauce
- 1 teaspoon Montreal steak seasoning
- ½ teaspoon salt, divided
- ½ teaspoon pepper, divided
- 3 tablespoons butter, softened and divided
- 8 slices Texas toast
- 2 tablespoons canola oil
- 2½ cups frozen shredded hash brown potatoes, thawed
- 4 large eggs
- ¼ cup seedless blackberry spreadable fruit
- 4 slices American cheese
- 8 cooked bacon strips

1. Combine the ground beef, Worcestershire sauce, steak seasoning, ¼ teaspoon salt and ¼ teaspoon pepper, mixing lightly but thoroughly.

Shape into four ½-in.-thick patties. Grill burgers, covered, on a greased grill rack over medium heat for 4-5 minutes on each side or until a thermometer reads 160°. Meanwhile, spread 2 tablespoons butter over one side of Texas toast slices; grill with burgers until golden brown. Remove burgers and toast from the heat and keep warm.
2. Increase heat to high. In a large skillet on grill rack, heat oil. Drop hash browns by ½ cupfuls into oil; press to flatten. Sprinkle with remaining salt and pepper. Fry, covered, until golden brown on each side and crisp, 12-15 minutes, adding more oil as needed. Remove and keep warm.
3. Reduce heat to medium. In same skillet, heat remaining butter. Add eggs; fry over easy.
4. To assemble, spread blackberry preserves over four slices of Texas toast. Layer each slice with one hash brown patty, one burger, one fried egg, one cheese slice and two bacon strips. Top with remaining toast slices.
Per 1 burger: 859 cal., 49g fat (19g sat. fat), 307mg chol., 1703mg sod., 55g carb. (13g sugars, 2g fiber), 45g pro.

Fall & Oats

CRISP MORNINGS CALL FOR BIG BOWLS OF COZY. SNUGGLE UP WITH THESE SWEET AND SAVORY OATMEAL TOPPERS FROM OUR FACEBOOK PALS.

1 I like mine with plain ol' sugar and butter. However, my boys love it with **banana slices, mini chocolate chips** and a spoonful of **peanut butter.**
—*Angela Lively, Conroe, TX*

2 Poached **eggs, roasted red peppers, avocado, spinach** and **herbed cheese,** then top with **hot sauce, salt** and **pepper.**
—*Rachel Long, Firestone, CO*

3 I stir in **butter, brown sugar** and crumbled **pork sausage.** I love the flavor combo of sweet and slightly salty.
—*Melanie Lindsey, Springtown, TX*

4 Make it savory with **chicken broth, mushrooms** and **Parmesan cheese.**
—*Jane Stewart, Sanford, NC*

5 Stir in **Nutella** and top with **raspberries.**
—*Lora Tucker Schmelz, New Salisbury, IN*

6 Add **pumpkin puree** and sprinkle on some **brown sugar, pumpkin pie spice** and **cinnamon.** It's like eating a bowl of warm pumpkin pie.
—*Julie Circello, Iowa City, IA*

7 I heat up a **baked apple** (bake a dishful and refrigerate beforehand) with a little of the juice, then pour the oatmeal all around it when cooked.
—*Susan Franco, Allentown, PA*

8 **Huckleberries:** hand-picked.
—*Doretta Timentwa, Omak, WA*

9 My favorite is **dried cranberries, cinnamon,** a drizzle of **honey, walnuts** and a squeeze of **orange.**
—*Tammy Bazinski, Rochester Hills, MI*

10 **Peanut butter...** it's like a no-bake cookie for breakfast!
—*Gretchen Schneider, Muskegon, MI*

Hash Brown Maple Sausage Casserole

(PICTURED ON P. 143)

This crave-worthy casserole has a golden hash-brown crust that's topped with sausage and veggies. My favorite part is the surprise layer of gooey Gruyere.

—ANUJA ARGADE FOSTER CITY, CA

PREP: 15 MIN. • **BAKE:** 45 MIN. + STANDING
MAKES: 8 SERVINGS

- 1 pound maple pork sausage
- ½ cup cubed peeled sweet potato
- 2 tablespoons olive oil
- 1 package (30 ounces) frozen shredded hash brown potatoes, thawed
- 1½ cups shredded Gruyere or cheddar cheese
- 2 cups coarsely chopped fresh kale (tough stems removed)
- ¾ cup fresh or frozen corn
- 5 large eggs, lightly beaten
- 2 cups half-and-half cream
- 1 teaspoon salt
- ½ teaspoon pepper
  Maple syrup, optional

1. Preheat oven to 375°. In a large skillet, cook sausage and sweet potato over medium-high heat 5-7 minutes or until sausage is no longer pink, breaking up sausage into crumbles. Remove with a slotted spoon; drain on paper towels.
2. Meanwhile, coat bottom of a 12-in. ovenproof skillet with oil. Reserve ½ cup hash browns for topping; add remaining potatoes to the skillet, pressing firmly with a spatula to form an even layer.
3. Layer with cheese, kale and corn; top with sausage mixture and reserved hash browns. In a bowl, whisk eggs, cream, salt and pepper until blended; pour over top.
4. Bake, uncovered, 45-55 minutes or until edges are golden brown and egg portion is set. Cover loosely with foil during the last 10 minutes if needed to prevent overbrowning. Let stand for 20 minutes before serving. If desired, serve with syrup.
Per 1¼ cups: 487 cal., 32g fat (13g sat. fat), 200mg chol., 899mg sod., 27g carb. (5g sugars, 2g fiber), 22g pro.

HERBED VEGETABLE STRATA

FREEZE IT
Herbed Vegetable Strata

We always serve food at our bunco games, and since one of us is a vegetarian, we're always coming up with fun meatless dishes we can all enjoy. This strata can easily be doubled and tastes fantastic hot or at room temperature.

—DORIS MANCINI PORT ORCHARD, WA

PREP: 40 MIN. + CHILLING
BAKE: 40 MIN. + STANDING
MAKES: 12 SERVINGS

- 3 teaspoons olive oil, divided
- 1 pound fresh asparagus, trimmed and cut into 2-inch pieces
- 2 medium zucchini, quartered and sliced
- 1 cup fresh or frozen corn
- 2 shallots, chopped
- 3 garlic cloves, minced
- 4 teaspoons each minced fresh sage, basil and parsley
- ½ teaspoon salt
- ½ teaspoon pepper
- 1 loaf (1 pound) Italian bread, cut into 1-inch cubes
- 3 cups shredded Gruyere or Swiss cheese
- 5 large eggs
- 1¾ cups 2% milk
- ½ cup chopped pecans

1. Preheat oven to 350°. In a large skillet, heat 1 teaspoon oil over medium-high heat. Add asparagus; cook and stir until crisp-tender. Transfer to a large bowl.
2. Repeat with an additional 1 teaspoon oil and zucchini; add to asparagus. In same pan, cook and stir corn, shallots and garlic in remaining oil until shallots are tender; stir in herbs, salt and pepper. Add to the asparagus mixture; stir in bread cubes.
3. Place half of mixture in a greased 13x9-in. baking dish. Sprinkle with 1½ cups cheese. Repeat layers. In another bowl, whisk eggs and milk; pour over casserole. Sprinkle with pecans. Refrigerate, covered, at least 1 hour.
4. Bake, uncovered, 40-50 minutes or until a knife inserted in the center comes out clean. Let stand 10 minutes before serving.
To freeze: After assembling, cover and freeze. To use, partially thaw in refrigerator overnight. Remove from refrigerator 30 minutes before baking. Preheat oven to 350°. Bake strata, covered, 45 minutes. Uncover; bake 10-15 minutes longer or until a knife inserted in the center comes out clean. Let stand 10 minutes before serving.
Per 1 piece: 677 cal., 36g fat (15g sat. fat), 244mg chol., 940mg sod., 55g carb. (8g sugars, 5g fiber), 35g pro.

BLT WAFFLE SLIDERS

EAT SMART Overnight Oatmeal

Start this breakfast the night before so you can catch a few extra winks in the morning. My husband adds coconut to his, and I stir in dried fruit.
—JUNE THOMAS CHESTERTON, IN

PREP: 10 MIN. + CHILLING • **MAKES:** 1 SERVING

- ⅓ cup old-fashioned oats
- 3 tablespoons fat-free milk
- 3 tablespoons reduced-fat plain yogurt
- 1 tablespoon honey
- ½ cup assorted fresh fruit
- 2 tablespoons chopped walnuts, toasted

In a small container or mason jar, combine oats, milk, yogurt and honey. Top with fruit and nuts. Seal; refrigerate overnight.

Note: To toast nuts, bake in a shallow pan in a 350° oven for 5-10 minutes or cook in a skillet over low heat until lightly browned, stirring occasionally.

Per serving: 345 cal., 13g fat (2g sat. fat), 4mg chol., 53mg sod., 53g carb. (31g sugars, 5g fiber), 10g pro.

Chocolate-Cherry Oats: Use cherry-flavored yogurt; add 1 tablespoon cocoa powder, and top with fresh or frozen pitted cherries.

Banana Bread Oats: Replace honey with maple syrup and stir in ½ mashed banana and ½ teaspoon cinnamon. Top with toasted pecans.

Carrot Cake Oats: Add 2 tablespoons grated carrots and substitute spreadable cream cheese for the yogurt.

Pina Colada Oats: Add ½ mashed banana, 2 tablespoons crushed pineapple and 1 tablespoon shredded coconut to oats.

OVERNIGHT OATMEAL

FAST FIX ▶ BLT Waffle Sliders

My breakfast BLTs are deliciously different. Make and freeze the waffles, then reheat them in the toaster.
—STACY JOURA STONEBORO, PA

START TO FINISH: 30 MIN. • **MAKES:** 12 SERVINGS

- ¾ cup all-purpose flour
- ¾ cup cornmeal
- 3 teaspoons baking powder
- 1 tablespoon sugar
- 1 teaspoon salt
- 2 large eggs, separated
- 1 cup 2% milk
- 3 tablespoons butter, melted
- ½ cup shredded cheddar cheese
- 6 tablespoons mayonnaise
- 12 bacon strips, cooked and drained
- 2 small tomatoes, sliced
- 6 lettuce leaves
  Salt and pepper to taste

1. Preheat waffle maker. Whisk together first five ingredients. In another bowl, whisk egg yolks, milk and butter. Stir into dry ingredients just until moistened. Stir in cheese.

2. In a separate bowl, beat egg whites until stiff but not dry. Fold into batter. Drop 1 heaping tablespoon of batter in the center of each waffle iron quadrant; bake according to manufacturer's directions until golden brown, about 5 minutes. Cool on wire rack. Repeat with remaining batter.

3. Spread mayonnaise evenly over half of the waffle pieces; top with bacon, tomatoes, lettuce, salt and pepper and remaining waffle pieces to make sliders. Serve immediately.

Per 1 slider: 224 cal., 14g fat (5g sat. fat), 54mg chol., 574mg sod., 17g carb. (3g sugars, 1g fiber), 7g pro.

For regular-size BLT Waffle Sandwiches: Prepare batter as instructed. Bake 3 waffles according to manufacturer's directions until golden brown. Cut waffles into fourths. Spread mayonnaise on six; top with bacon, tomatoes, lettuce, seasonings and remaining waffle pieces to make sandwiches. Serve immediately.

FAST FIX ▶ Old-World Puff Pancake

My mom told me her mother-in-law showed her how to make this dish, which became popular during the Depression, on their "get acquainted" visit long ago. Back then, cooks measured ingredients in pinches, dashes and dabs. Over the years, accurate amounts were noted. My wife and I continue to enjoy this dish today, particularly for brunch.
—**AUTON MILLER** PINEY FLATS, TN

START TO FINISH: 30 MIN. • **MAKES:** 4 SERVINGS

- 2 tablespoons butter
- 3 large eggs
- ¾ cup whole milk
- ¾ cup all-purpose flour
- 2 teaspoons sugar
- 1 teaspoon ground nutmeg
  Confectioners' sugar
  Lemon wedges
  Syrup, optional
  Fresh raspberries, optional

1. Place butter in a 10-in. ovenproof skillet; place in a 425° oven for 2-3 minutes or until melted. In a blender, process the eggs, milk, flour, sugar and nutmeg until smooth. Pour into prepared skillet.
2. Bake at 425° for 16-18 minutes or until puffed and browned. Dust with confectioners' sugar. Serve with lemon wedges and, if desired, syrup and raspberries.
Per 1 piece: 178 cal., 5g fat (2g sat. fat), 144mg chol., 74mg sod., 23g carb. (5g sugars, 1g fiber), 9g pro.

EAT SMART FAST FIX ▶ Fruit Smoothies

My kids like smoothies so I make them often. They're just right for breakfast, dessert or an afternoon snack. It's fun to experiment with different fruits and berries.
—**SUSAN McCARTNEY** ONALASKA, WI

START TO FINISH: 10 MIN. • **MAKES:** 4 SERVINGS

- 1 cup fat-free milk
- ½ cup plain yogurt
- ¼ teaspoon vanilla extract
- 1½ cups fresh or frozen strawberries, thawed
- ½ cup canned unsweetened pineapple chunks
- ¼ cup nonfat dry milk powder
- 4 ice cubes
- 2 tablespoons sugar

In a blender, combine all ingredients; cover and process for 30-45 seconds or until blended. Stir if necessary. Pour into chilled glasses; serve immediately.
Per 1 cup: 122 cal., 1g fat (1g sat. fat), 7mg chol., 81mg sod., 22g carb. (20g sugars, 1g fiber), 6g pro.
Diabetic Exchanges: 1 starch, ½ fruit.

BROCCOLI HAM QUICHE

Broccoli Ham Quiche

This rich quiche is featured in a family cookbook that I put together. My husband is proof that quiche can satisfy even a very healthy appetite.
—**MARILYN DAY** NORTH FORT MYERS, FL

PREP: 20 MIN. + COOLING • **BAKE:** 55 MIN. + STANDING
MAKES: 8 SERVINGS

- 1 unbaked deep-dish pastry shell (9 inches)
- 1 cup shredded Swiss cheese
- 1 cup shredded part-skim mozzarella cheese
- 2 tablespoons all-purpose flour
- 4 large eggs, lightly beaten
- 1½ cups milk
- 2 tablespoons chopped green onion
- ¼ teaspoon salt
- ⅛ teaspoon pepper
- ⅛ teaspoon dried thyme
- ⅛ teaspoon dried rosemary, crushed
- ½ cup diced fully cooked ham
- ½ cup chopped fresh broccoli

1. Line unpricked pastry shell with a double thickness of heavy-duty foil. Bake at 450° for 8 minutes. Remove foil; bake 5 minutes longer. Cool on a wire rack while preparing the filling.
2. Toss cheeses with flour; set aside. In a large bowl, combine the eggs, milk, onion and seasonings. Stir in the ham, broccoli and cheese mixture. Pour into prepared crust.
3. Bake at 350° for 55-60 minutes or until set. Let stand 10 minutes before cutting.
Per 1 slice: 269 cal., 17g fat (7g sat. fat), 140mg chol., 408mg sod., 16g carb. (3g sugars, 0 fiber), 14g pro.

**JUDY OLSON'S
CHERRY-COCONUT SLICES**
PAGE 164

Cookies, Bars & Candies

Here's a roundup of **the year's best sweets,** sure to disappear fast everywhere they go. It's tough to eat just one of these **scrumptious** cookies, **melt-in-your-mouth** candies or **crowd-pleasing** bars.

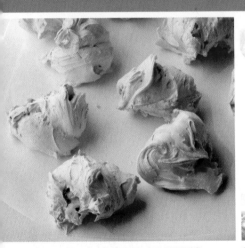

CRYSTAL RALPH-HAUGHN'S CHERRY DIVINITY
PAGE 161

SARAH KNOBLOCK'S ITALIAN HONEY BALL COOKIES
PAGE 169

NOT YOUR MAMA'S SEVEN-LAYER BARS FROM ANDREA BARLOW
PAGE 168

CALGARY
NANAIMO
BARS

Calgary Nanaimo Bars

This version may claim roots in Alberta, but the original is said to have been dreamed up in a kitchen in Nanaimo, British Columbia. Regardless, they're three delicious layers of Canadian goodness.
—**CAROL HILLIER** CALGARY, AB

PREP: 25 MIN. + CHILLING • **MAKES:** 3½ DOZEN

- ¼ cup sugar
- ¼ cup baking cocoa
- ¾ cup butter, cubed
- 2 large eggs, beaten
- 2 cups graham cracker crumbs
- 1 cup sweetened shredded coconut
- ½ cup chopped almonds, optional

FILLING
- 2 cups confectioners' sugar
- 2 tablespoons instant vanilla pudding mix
- ¼ cup butter, melted
- 3 tablespoons 2% milk

GLAZE
- 3 ounces semisweet chocolate, chopped
- 1 tablespoon butter

1. Line an 8-in. square baking pan with foil, letting ends extend over sides by 1 in. In a large heavy saucepan, combine sugar and cocoa; add butter. Cook and stir over medium-low heat until butter is melted. Whisk a small amount of hot mixture into eggs. Return all to the pan, whisking constantly. Cook and stir until mixture reaches 160°. Remove from heat.
2. Stir in cracker crumbs, coconut and, if desired, almonds. Press into prepared pan. Chill 30 minutes or until set.
3. For filling, in a small bowl, beat confectioners' sugar, pudding mix, butter and milk until smooth; spread over the crust.
4. In a microwave, melt chocolate and butter; stir until smooth. Spread over top. Refrigerate until set. Using foil, lift bars out of pan. Discard foil; cut into bars.
Per 1 bar without almonds: 116 cal., 7g fat (4g sat. fat), 21mg chol., 72mg sod., 14g carb. (11g sugars, 0 fiber), 1g pro.

⑤ INGREDIENTS
Oreos & Candy Cane Chocolate Bark

This brilliant sweet, perfect for sharing with teachers, neighbors and friends, stars two super-duper treats—Oreos and candy canes. We keep a big supply ready for gift-giving.
—**ROBIN TURNER** LAKE ELSINORE, CA

PREP: 15 MIN. + CHILLING • **MAKES:** ABOUT 1½ POUNDS

- 2 packages (10 ounces each) dark chocolate chips
- 10 candy cane or chocolate mint creme Oreo cookies, split and chopped
- ⅓ cup white baking chips
- ⅛ teaspoon peppermint extract
- 2 candy canes, crushed

1. Line a 15x10x1-in. baking pan with parchment paper. In the top of a double boiler or a metal bowl over hot water, melt dark chocolate; stir until smooth. Remove from heat. Stir in cookies; spread over prepared pan.
2. Microwave white baking chips on high until melted, stirring every 30 seconds. Stir in extract. Drizzle over dark chocolate mixture; sprinkle with crushed candy canes. Cool. Refrigerate 1 hour or until set.
3. Break into pieces. Store in an airtight container.
Per 1 ounce: 141 cal., 8g fat (5g sat. fat), 0 chol., 32mg sod., 19g carb. (16g sugars, 2g fiber), 2g pro.

OREOS & CANDY CANE
CHOCOLATE BARK

Cherry Divinity

(PICTURED ON P. 159)

It's not a Valentine's Day party without these light and airy confections on my dessert platter. The recipe is versatile in that you can replace the cherry gelatin with any flavor to suit your tastes.

—CRYSTAL RALPH-HAUGHN BARTLESVILLE, OK

PREP: 35 MIN. • **COOK:** 25 MIN. + STANDING
MAKES: 5 DOZEN

- 2 large egg whites
- 3 cups sugar
- ¾ cup water
- ¾ cup light corn syrup
- 1 package (3 ounces) cherry gelatin
- 1 cup chopped walnuts

1. Place egg whites in the bowl of a large stand mixer; let stand at room temperature for 30 minutes. Meanwhile, line three 15x10x1-in. baking pans with waxed paper.

2. In a heavy saucepan, combine the sugar, water and corn syrup; cook and stir until sugar is dissolved and mixture comes to a boil. Cook over medium heat, without stirring, until a candy thermometer reads 250° (hard-ball stage).

3. Just before the temperature is reached, beat egg whites until foamy. Gradually beat in gelatin. Beat until stiff peaks form. With mixer running on high speed, carefully pour hot syrup in a slow, steady stream into the bowl. Beat just until candy loses its gloss and holds its shape, about 5 minutes. Immediately stir in walnuts.

4. Quickly drop by tablespoonfuls onto prepared pans. Let stand at room temperature overnight or until dry to the touch. Store in an airtight container at room temperature.
Note: We recommend that you test your candy thermometer before each use by bringing water to a boil; the thermometer should read 212°. Adjust the recipe temperature up or down based on your test.
Per 1 piece: 69 cal., 1g fat (0 sat. fat), 0 chol., 8mg sod., 15g carb. (12g sugars, 0 fiber), 1g pro.

EAT SMART

Easy Pecan Pie Bars

I am always searching for fast and easy recipes to take to the teachers' lounge. The staff goes nuts for these shortcut pecan pie bars.

—KATHRO YODER DEFIANCE, OH

PREP: 10 MIN. • **BAKE:** 40 MIN. + COOLING
MAKES: 2 DOZEN

- 1 package yellow cake mix (regular size)
- ⅓ cup butter, softened
- 1 large egg
- **FILLING**
- 1½ cups corn syrup
- ½ cup packed brown sugar
- 1 teaspoon vanilla extract

EASY PECAN PIE BARS

- 3 large eggs
- 1 cup chopped pecans

1. Preheat oven to 350°. Line a 13x9-in. baking pan with foil; grease foil.

2. Reserve ⅔ cup cake mix; set aside. Combine remaining cake mix, butter and 1 egg; beat on low speed until blended. Press onto bottom of prepared pan. Bake 15 minutes. Cool on a wire rack.

3. For filling, beat corn syrup, brown sugar, vanilla and reserved cake mix until blended. Add 3 eggs; beat on low speed just until combined. Pour over warm crust; sprinkle with pecans.

4. Bake until center is set, 25-30 minutes longer. Cool completely in pan on a wire rack. To serve, refrigerate at least 15 minutes. Lift out of pan; discard foil. Cut into bars.
Per 1 bar: 223 cal., 8g fat (3g sat. fat), 38mg chol., 174mg sod., 38g carb. (30g sugars, 0 fiber), 2g pro.

✱

DID YOU KNOW?

Corn syrup is a key ingredient in pecan pie. A thick liquid, it helps give the dessert its rich, custardy consistency. Unless the recipe specifies, you can use either light or dark corn syrup according to your tastes. Light corn syrup is more refined, colorless and lightly flavored with vanilla. Dark corn syrup may contain molasses and/or caramel color and flavor. Use it for a more robust taste.

Chocolate-Coconut Layer Bars

I'm a huge fan of Nanaimo bars, the no-bake layered dessert named for the city in British Columbia. For fun, I reinvented the treat with coconut lovers in mind.
—**SHANNON DOBOS** CALGARY, AB

PREP: 20 MIN. + CHILLING
MAKES: 3 DOZEN

- ¾ cup butter, cubed
- 3 cups Oreo cookie crumbs
- 2 cups sweetened shredded coconut
- ½ cup cream of coconut

FILLING

- ⅓ cup butter, softened
- 3 tablespoons cream of coconut
- ¼ teaspoon coconut extract
- 3 cups confectioners' sugar
- 1 to 2 tablespoons 2% milk

TOPPING

- 1½ cups semisweet chocolate chips
- 4 teaspoons canola oil
- 3 Mounds candy bars (1¾ ounces each), coarsely chopped, optional

1. Microwave butter on high until melted; stir until smooth. Stir in cookie crumbs, coconut and cream of coconut until blended (mixture will be wet). Spread onto bottom of an ungreased 13x9-in. baking pan. Chill until set, about 30 minutes.
2. For filling, beat butter, cream of coconut and extract until smooth. Gradually beat in confectioners' sugar and enough milk to reach a spreading consistency. Spread over crust.

CHOCOLATE-COCONUT
LAYER BARS

3. For topping, microwave chocolate chips and oil until melted; stir until smooth. Cool slightly; spread over filling. If desired, sprinkle with chopped candy bars. Refrigerate.
Per 1 bar without chopped candies: 229 cal., 13g fat (8g sat. fat), 15mg chol., 124mg sod., 28g carb. (23g sugars, 1g fiber), 1g pro.

Mole New Mexican Wedding Cookies

Heat and sweet is such an amazing combo. The addition of red chili and chocolate chips makes these traditional Mexican Wedding Cookies a fiesta for your senses!
—**MARLA CLARK** ALBUQUERQUE, NM

PREP: 30 MIN. • **BAKE:** 15 MIN./BATCH
MAKES: 2½ DOZEN

- ½ cup butter, softened
- ¾ cup confectioners' sugar, divided
- 1 teaspoon vanilla extract
- 1 cup all-purpose flour

**MOLE NEW MEXICAN
WEDDING COOKIES**
Marla Clark
Albuquerque, NM

- ½ cup ground pecans
- 1 teaspoon chili powder
- ¼ teaspoon ground cinnamon
- ¼ teaspoon ground cloves
- ¼ teaspoon ground allspice
- ½ cup miniature semisweet chocolate chips

1. Preheat oven to 350°. Cream butter and ⅓ cup confectioners' sugar until light and fluffy; beat in vanilla. Whisk together the next six ingredients. Gradually beat into creamed mixture. Fold in chocolate chips.
2. Shape dough into 1-in. balls. Place 1 in. apart on ungreased baking sheets. Bake until the bottoms are lightly browned, 12-15 minutes. Remove from pans to wire racks to cool 5 minutes. Roll in remaining confectioners' sugar. Cool completely.
Per 1 cookie: 81 cal., 5g fat (3g sat. fat), 8mg chol., 27mg sod., 8g carb. (5g sugars, 1g fiber), 1g pro.

Turtle Cookies

Our special education class developed these fudgy turtle cookies. The class has a cookie club teachers can pay to join, and members give this cookie two thumbs up.

—**DEBBIE ETHRIDGE** BENTONVILLE, AR

PREP: 20 MIN.
BAKE: 10 MIN./BATCH + COOLING
MAKES: 5 DOZEN

- 4 tablespoons unsalted butter
- 1 package (12 ounces) semisweet chocolate chips
- 1 can (14 ounces) sweetened condensed milk
- 1 teaspoon vanilla extract
- 1 cup all-purpose flour
- 1½ cups chopped pecans, toasted
- 1¼ cups caramel bits

ICING

- 1 cup (6 ounces) semisweet chocolate chips
- 2 teaspoons shortening

1. Preheat oven to 350°. Microwave butter until melted. Add chocolate chips and milk; microwave until chips are melted, stirring every 30 seconds. Stir in vanilla. Add flour; mix well. Stir in pecans and caramel bits.

TURTLE COOKIES

2. Drop dough by tablespoonfuls 2 in. apart onto parchment paper-lined baking sheets. Bake until edges are set, 7-9 minutes. Cool on pans 2 minutes. Remove cookies to wire racks to cool completely.

3. For icing, microwave chocolate chips and shortening on high until melted. Drizzle over cooled cookies. Store in an airtight container.

Note: To toast nuts, bake in a shallow pan in a 350° oven for 5-10 minutes or cook in a skillet over low heat until lightly browned, stirring occasionally.

Per 1 cookie: 121 cal., 7g fat (3g sat. fat), 5mg chol., 24mg sod., 16g carb. (13g sugars, 1g fiber), 2g pro.

Peanut Butter Brownies

The combination of chocolate and peanut butter makes these brownies a real crowd-pleaser. They're so good, they earned a ribbon at a local fair.

—**MARGARET McNEIL** GERMANTOWN, TN

PREP: 15 MIN. • **BAKE:** 35 MIN. + COOLING
MAKES: 3 DOZEN

- 3 large eggs
- 1 cup butter, melted
- 2 teaspoons vanilla extract
- 2 cups sugar
- 1¼ cups all-purpose flour
- ¾ cup baking cocoa
- ½ teaspoon baking powder
- ¼ teaspoon salt
- 1 cup milk chocolate chips

FILLING

- 2 packages (8 ounces each) cream cheese, softened
- ½ cup creamy peanut butter
- ¼ cup sugar
- 1 large egg
- 2 tablespoons 2% milk

1. In a large bowl, beat the eggs, butter and vanilla until smooth. Combine the dry ingredients; gradually add to egg mixture. Stir in chocolate chips. Set aside 1 cup for topping. Spread the remaining batter into a greased 13x9-in. baking pan.

2. In a small bowl, beat the cream cheese, peanut butter and sugar until smooth. Beat in egg and milk on low just until combined. Carefully spread cream cheese mixture over batter. Drop reserved batter by

tablespoonfuls over filling. Cut through batter with a knife to swirl.

3. Bake at 350° for 35-40 minutes or until a toothpick inserted in the center comes out clean (do not overbake). Cool on a wire rack. Chill until serving.

Note: Reduced-fat peanut butter is not recommended for this recipe.

Per 1 brownie: 190 cal., 11g fat (6g sat. fat), 45mg chol., 120mg sod., 21g carb. (15g sugars, 1g fiber), 3g pro.

Jumbo Chocolate Chip Cookies

These enormous cookies are a family favorite. No one can resist their sweet chocolaty taste.

—**LORI SPORER** OAKLEY, KS

PREP: 15 MIN. + CHILLING
BAKE: 15 MIN./BATCH • **MAKES:** 2 DOZEN

- ⅔ cup shortening
- ⅔ cup butter, softened
- 1 cup sugar
- 1 cup packed brown sugar
- 2 large eggs
- 2 teaspoons vanilla extract
- 3½ cups all-purpose flour
- 1 teaspoon baking soda
- 1 teaspoon salt
- 2 cups (12 ounces) semisweet chocolate chips
- 1 cup chopped pecans

1. In a large bowl, cream the shortening, butter and sugars until light and fluffy. Beat in eggs and vanilla. Combine flour, baking soda and salt; add to creamed mixture and mix well. Fold in chocolate chips and pecans. Chill for at least 1 hour.

2. Preheat oven to 375°. Drop dough by ¼ cupfuls 2 in. apart onto greased baking sheets. Bake 13-15 minutes or until golden brown. Cool 5 minutes before removing to wire racks.

Per 1 cookie: 335 cal., 19g fat (7g sat. fat), 31mg chol., 213mg sod., 41g carb. (26g sugars, 2g fiber), 3g pro.

FUDGE PUDDLES

Cherry-Coconut Slices

My mother got this recipe from a woman named Emmie Oddie, a well-known home economist in Canada who had a column in a farming newspaper. She would test reader recipes in her own kitchen and write about her experiences. These tasty sweets are so rich that you only need a small piece.

—**JUDY OLSON** WHITECOURT, AB

PREP: 15 MIN. + CHILLING • **COOK:** 5 MIN. + COOLING
MAKES: 32 BARS

- 3 cups graham cracker crumbs
- 1½ cups miniature marshmallows
- 1 cup unsweetened finely shredded coconut
- ½ cup chopped maraschino cherries
- 1 can (14 ounces) sweetened condensed milk
- 1 teaspoon maple flavoring

FROSTING
- 1 cup packed brown sugar
- ⅓ cup butter, cubed
- ¼ cup 2% milk
- 1 cup confectioners' sugar

1. In a large bowl, mix cracker crumbs, marshmallows, coconut and cherries; stir in condensed milk and flavoring. Press into a greased 8-in. square baking pan.

2. For frosting, in a small saucepan, combine brown sugar, butter and milk. Bring to a boil, stirring constantly; cook and stir 3 minutes. Transfer to a small bowl; cool until lukewarm, about 15 minutes. Stir in confectioners' sugar until smooth. Spread over crumb mixture; refrigerate until set, about 1½ hours.

3. Cut into bars. Store in an airtight container in the refrigerator.

Note: Look for unsweetened coconut in the baking or health food section.

Per 1 slice: 169 cal., 6g fat (4g sat. fat), 9mg chol., 82mg sod., 28g carb. (22g sugars, 1g fiber), 2g pro.

Fudge Puddles

I was inspired to make these cookies after trying something like them at a cafe during a break from my Christmas shopping. I changed a few things when I got home. They were an instant hit with my family.

—**KIMARIE MAASSEN** AVOCA, IA

PREP: 25 MIN. + CHILLING • **BAKE:** 15 MIN./BATCH + COOLING
MAKES: 4 DOZEN

- ½ cup butter, softened
- ½ cup creamy peanut butter
- ½ cup sugar
- ½ cup packed light brown sugar
- 1 large egg
- ½ teaspoon vanilla extract
- 1¼ cups all-purpose flour
- ¾ teaspoon baking soda
- ½ teaspoon salt

FUDGE FILLING
- 1 cup milk chocolate chips
- 1 cup semisweet chocolate chips
- 1 can (14 ounces) sweetened condensed milk
- 1 teaspoon vanilla extract
  Chopped peanuts

1. In a large bowl, cream butter, peanut butter and sugars until blended. Beat in egg and vanilla. In a small bowl, whisk flour, baking soda and salt; gradually beat into creamed mixture. Refrigerate, covered, 1 hour or until easy to handle.

2. Preheat oven to 325°. Shape into forty-eight 1-in. balls. Place in greased mini-muffin cups. Bake 14-16 minutes or until light brown. Immediately press a ½-in.-deep indentation in center of each cookie with the end of a wooden spoon handle. Cool in pans 5 minutes. Remove to wire racks to cool completely.

3. For filling, in a microwave, melt chocolate chips; stir until smooth. Whisk in milk and vanilla until smooth. Fill each cookie with filling; sprinkle with peanuts. (If desired, refrigerate remaining filling; serve warm with ice cream.)

Per 1 cookie: 248 cal., 12g fat (6g sat. fat), 26mg chol., 184mg sod., 32g carb. (26g sugars, 1g fiber), 4g pro.

CHERRY-COCONUT SLICES

MEXICAN CRINKLE COOKIES

Mexican Crinkle Cookies

When it's baking time, my family lobbies for these Mexican crinkle cookies. You can replace 1 ounce unsweetened chocolate with 3 tablespoons cocoa powder plus 1 tablespoon shortening, butter or oil.

—**KIM KENYON** GREENWOOD, MO

PREP: 25 MIN. + CHILLING • **BAKE:** 10 MIN./BATCH
MAKES: ABOUT 2 DOZEN

- ¾ cup butter, cubed
- 2 ounces unsweetened chocolate, chopped
- 1 cup packed brown sugar
- ¼ cup light corn syrup
- 1 large egg
- 2 cups all-purpose flour
- 2 teaspoons baking soda
- 1½ teaspoons ground cinnamon, divided
- ¼ teaspoon salt
- ½ cup confectioners' sugar

1. In a microwave, melt butter and chocolate; stir until smooth. Beat in brown sugar and corn syrup until blended. Beat in egg. In another bowl, whisk flour, baking soda, 1 teaspoon cinnamon and salt; gradually beat into brown sugar mixture. Refrigerate, covered, until firm, about 1 hour.

2. Preheat oven to 350°. In a shallow bowl, mix the confectioners' sugar and remaining cinnamon. Shape dough into 1½-in. balls; roll in confectioners' sugar mixture. Place 2 in. apart on greased baking sheets.

3. Bake until set and tops are cracked, 10-12 minutes. Cool on pans 2 minutes. Remove to wire racks to finish cooling.

Per 1 cookie: 158 cal., 7g fat (4g sat. fat), 23mg chol., 184mg sod., 22g carb. (13g sugars, 1g fiber), 2g pro.

Potato Chip Clusters

Just three offbeat ingredients add up to one unique, delectable, no-bake treat. These easy sweet-and-salty candy clusters make for great munching on road trips and at parties. They travel well in containers without melting or getting soft.

—**DONNA BROCKETT** KINGFISHER, OK

PREP: 15 MIN. + CHILLING • **MAKES:** ABOUT 3 DOZEN

- 9 ounces white baking chocolate, chopped
- 2 cups coarsely crushed ridged potato chips
- ½ cup chopped pecans

In a large microwave-safe bowl, melt white chocolate. Stir in potato chips and pecans. Drop by tablespoonfuls onto waxed paper-lined baking sheets. Refrigerate until set.

Per 1 cluster: 33 cal., 3g fat (1g sat. fat), 0 chol., 19mg sod., 2g carb. (1g sugars, 0 fiber), 0 pro.

Chocolate Crunch Patties: Substitute 4 cups butterscotch chips and 2 cups milk chocolate chips for the white chocolate. Substitute 3 cups dry roasted peanuts for pecans. Proceed as directed. Makes about 8 dozen.

Peanut Butter Clusters: Substitute 4 cups peanut butter chips and 2 cups milk chocolate chips for the white chocolate. Substitute 3 cups dry roasted peanuts for pecans. Proceed as directed. Makes about 8 dozen.

POTATO CHIP CLUSTERS

COCONUT
BANANA
COOKIES

Coconut Banana Cookies

This is a springtime variation of my grandma's banana drop cookies. With tons of coconut flavor, my spin is perfect for Easter.

—**ELYSE BENNER** SOLON, OH

PREP: 20 MIN. • **BAKE:** 15 MIN./BATCH
MAKES: ABOUT 1½ DOZEN

- ½ cup shortening, room temperature
- ¼ cup creamy cashew butter
- 1 cup sugar
- 1 cup mashed ripe banana (about 2 medium)
- 1 large egg
- 1 tablespoon grated lime peel
- 1 teaspoon salt
- ½ teaspoon baking soda
- 1¾ cups unsweetened finely shredded coconut
- 1½ cups all-purpose flour
- ½ cup sweetened flaked coconut

1. Preheat oven to 375°. Cream shortening, cashew butter and sugar until light and fluffy. Beat in next five ingredients until thoroughly mixed. In a separate bowl, mix unsweetened coconut and flour. Beat into creamed mixture just until combined.
2. Using a medium cookie scoop, drop dough 2 in. apart on parchment paper-lined baking sheets. Sprinkle with sweetened coconut. Bake until the edges are golden brown, 15-20 minutes (cookies will have a cake-like texture). Remove from pans to wire racks to cool. Serve warm or at room temperature.
Note: Look for unsweetened coconut in the baking or health food section.
Per 1 cookie: 232 cal., 14g fat (7g sat. fat), 10mg chol., 192mg sod., 26g carb. (15g sugars, 2g fiber), 3g pro.

Grandma Brubaker's Orange Cookies

At least two generations of my family have enjoyed the recipe for these light, delicate, orange-flavored cookies. Perhaps your family will like them just as much.

—**SHERI DEBOLT** HUNTINGTON, IN

PREP: 20 MIN.
BAKE: 10 MIN./BATCH + COOLING
MAKES: ABOUT 6 DOZEN

- 1 cup shortening
- 2 cups sugar
- 2 large eggs, separated
- 1 cup buttermilk
- 5 cups all-purpose flour
- 2 teaspoons baking powder
- 2 teaspoons baking soda
  Pinch salt
  Juice and grated peel of 2 medium navel oranges

ICING

- 2 cups confectioners' sugar
- ¼ cup orange juice
- 1 tablespoon butter
- 1 tablespoon grated orange peel

1. In a bowl, cream the shortening and sugar. Beat in the egg yolks and buttermilk. Sift together flour, baking powder, soda and salt; add to creamed mixture alternately with orange juice and peel. Add the egg whites and beat until smooth.
2. Drop by rounded teaspoonfuls onto greased cookie sheets. Bake at 325° for 10 minutes.
3. For icing, combine all ingredients and beat until smooth. Frost cookies when cool.
Per 1 cookie: 97 cal., 3g fat (1g sat. fat), 6mg chol., 58mg sod., 16g carb. (9g sugars, 0 fiber), 1g pro.

Almond Cream Spritz

Love spritz cookies during the holidays? Sample this version featuring almond-flavored dough and colored sugars sprinkled on top.

—**JO-ANNE COOPER** BONNYVILLE, AB

PREP: 25 MIN. + CHILLING
BAKE: 10 MIN./BATCH
MAKES: ABOUT 3 DOZEN

- 1 cup butter, softened
- 3 ounces cream cheese, softened
- ½ cup sugar
- ½ teaspoon almond extract
- ¼ teaspoon vanilla extract
- 2 cups all-purpose flour
  Colored sugar or finely chopped almonds

1. Cream butter, cream cheese and sugar until light and fluffy. Beat in extracts. Gradually beat in flour. Refrigerate, covered, 30 minutes.
2. Preheat oven to 375°. Using a cookie press fitted with a disk of your choice, press dough 2 in. apart onto ungreased baking sheets. Sprinkle with colored sugar.
3. Bake until set, 8-10 minutes. Cool on pans 1 minute. Remove to wire racks to cool.
Per 1 cookie: 100 cal., 7g fat (4g sat. fat), 16mg chol., 48mg sod., 9g carb. (3g sugars, 0 fiber), 1g pro.

ALMOND CREAM SPRITZ
Jo-Anne Cooper
Bonnyville, AB

Chocolate-Peanut Butter Cup Cookies

If you want to enjoy one of these soft, fully loaded treats the day after you make them, you'd better find a good hiding spot.
—**JENNIFER KREY** CLARENCE, NY

PREP: 25 MIN. • **BAKE:** 10 MIN./BATCH
MAKES: 4 DOZEN

- 1 cup butter, softened
- ¾ cup creamy peanut butter
- 1 cup packed brown sugar
- ½ cup sugar
- 2 large egg yolks
- ¼ cup 2% milk
- 2 teaspoons vanilla extract
- 2⅓ cups all-purpose flour
- ⅓ cup baking cocoa
- 1 teaspoon baking soda
- 1 cup milk chocolate chips
- 1 cup peanut butter chips
- 6 packages (1½ ounces each) peanut butter cups, chopped

1. Preheat oven to 350°. In a large bowl, cream butter, peanut butter and sugars until light and fluffy. Beat in egg yolks, milk and vanilla. Combine flour, cocoa and baking soda; gradually add to creamed mixture and mix well. Stir in chips and peanut butter cups.
2. Drop heaping tablespoonfuls 2 in. apart onto ungreased baking sheets. Bake 8-10 minutes or until set (do not overbake). Cool 2 minutes before removing from pans to wire racks. Store in an airtight container.
Per 1 cookie: 170 cal., 10g fat (4g sat. fat), 20mg chol., 100mg sod., 18g carb. (12g sugars, 1g fiber), 3g pro.

CHOCOLATE-PEANUT BUTTER CUP COOKIES

NOT YOUR MAMA'S SEVEN-LAYER BARS

Not Your Mama's Seven-Layer Bars

The addition of dulce de leche makes this a decadent new take on traditional seven-layer bars. If you want to cut this recipe in half, just make it in an 8x8-in. pan.
—**ANDREA BARLOW** HOT SPRINGS, AR

PREP: 10 MIN. • **BAKE:** 30 MIN. + COOLING
MAKES: 2 DOZEN

- 24 Oreo cookies
- ½ cup butter, melted
- 1 cup flaked coconut
- 1½ cups crisp brown rice cereal
- 1 can (13.4 ounces) dulce de leche
- 6 tablespoons warm water
- 1½ cups coarsely chopped pecans
- ¼ teaspoon sea salt

1. Preheat oven to 350°. Pulse cookies in food processor until finely chopped. Combine cookie crumbs and melted butter; press onto bottom of greased, foil-lined 13x9-in. baking pan. Spread coconut over crust; sprinkle with crisp rice cereal.
2. Combine dulce de leche and water until smooth. Pour over the cereal. Sprinkle pecans over dulce de leche; press down lightly.
3. Bake until edges are set but center is still soft, about 30 minutes. (Do not overbake.) Remove from oven; immediately sprinkle with sea salt. Cool completely on a wire rack before cutting into 24 squares.
Note: This recipe was tested with Nestle La Lechera dulce de leche; look for it in the international foods section. If using Eagle Brand dulce de leche (caramel flavored sauce), thicken according to package directions before using.
Per 1 bar: 228 cal., 14g fat (6g sat. fat), 16mg chol., 156mg sod., 24g carb. (18g sugars, 1g fiber), 2g pro.

Italian Honey Ball Cookies

(PICTURED ON P. 159)

My mother made these treats flavored with cinnamon and anise for neighbors, teachers and anyone who stopped by. Make sure the honey doesn't boil longer than a minute or it could burn.

—**SARAH KNOBLOCK** HYDE PARK, IN

PREP: 45 MIN. + STANDING
COOK: 5 MIN./BATCH
MAKES: ABOUT 2 DOZEN

- 3 cups all-purpose flour
- ½ teaspoon ground cinnamon
- ½ teaspoon aniseed, crushed
- ⅛ teaspoon salt
- 4 large eggs, lightly beaten
- ⅓ cup 2% milk
  Oil for deep-fat frying
- 1 cup honey
- ¼ cup sugar
- ½ cup pine nuts, toasted
  Nonpareils, optional

1. Line 24 muffin cups with paper or foil liners. In a large bowl, whisk flour, cinnamon, aniseed and salt. Stir in eggs and milk. Turn dough onto a floured surface; knead until smooth and elastic, 6-8 minutes. Shape into a disk; wrap in plastic. Let stand for 1 hour.
2. Divide dough into six portions. Roll each portion into ½-in.-thick ropes; cut crosswise into ½-in. pieces. In an electric skillet or deep-fat fryer, heat oil to 350°. Fry pieces, a few at a time, for 2-3 minutes on each side or until golden brown. Drain on paper towels. Place dough pieces in a large heatproof bowl and keep warm in a 200° oven.
3. In a large heavy saucepan, bring honey and sugar to a boil over medium heat; boil for 1 minute. Immediately remove from the heat and drizzle over dough pieces. Stir to coat. Immediately spoon into prepared cups. Sprinkle with pine nuts and, if desired, the nonpareils.

Per 1 cluster: 161 cal., 5g fat (1g sat. fat), 31mg chol., 27mg sod., 26g carb. (14g sugars, 1g fiber), 3g pro.

GINGERBREAD OATMEAL COOKIES

Gingerbread Oatmeal Cookies

Creamy cookie butter is the secret ingredient in these old-fashioned treats. The recipe makes about 18 cookies. They go fast, so you may want to prepare a double batch.

—**CAROLE RESNICK** CLEVELAND, OH

PREP: 10 MIN. + CHILLING
BAKE: 15 MIN./BATCH + COOLING
MAKES: ABOUT 1½ DOZEN

- ¾ cup all-purpose flour
- ½ teaspoon baking soda
- ½ teaspoon salt
- ½ teaspoon ground ginger
- ¼ teaspoon baking powder
- 1 cup Biscoff creamy cookie spread, room temperature
- ½ cup unsalted butter
- ½ cup granulated sugar
- ½ cup packed brown sugar
- 1 large egg
- 1 teaspoon vanilla extract
- 1 cup quick-cooking oats

1. Preheat oven to 350°. Whisk together first five ingredients. In another bowl, cream cookie spread, butter and sugars until light and fluffy. Beat in egg and vanilla. Gradually beat in the flour mixture; stir in the oats. Refrigerate at least 3 hours.
2. Bring dough to room temperature. Using a medium cookie scoop, drop mounds of dough onto baking sheets lined with parchment paper or baking mats. Bake until lightly browned, 15-18 minutes, rotating pans halfway through baking time. Cool on pans 5 minutes. Remove to wire racks to cool completely.
Note: Look for Biscoff creamy cookie spread near the peanut butter.
Per 1 cookie: 210 cal., 11g fat (4g sat. fat), 24mg chol., 113mg sod., 26g carb. (17g sugars, 1g fiber), 2g pro.

**FAY MORELAND'S
PEANUT BUTTER CHOCOLATE POKE CAKE**
PAGE 179

Cakes & Pies

From dazzling **confetti pie** in a sugar-cone crust to old-fashioned **apple cake** baked up in a loaf pan—and for **cupcakes, layer cakes, tarts** and more—turn here for the **show-stopping sweets** you'll be proud to serve every time.

SUSAN FRISCH'S UPSIDE-DOWN APPLE PIE
PAGE 172

ELIZABETH LARSEN'S FRESH RASPBERRY ICEBOX CAKE
PAGE 183

MARCIA WHITNEY'S MILE-HIGH CRANBERRY MERINGUE PIE
PAGE 181

Upside-Down Apple Pie

(PICTURED ON P. 171)

This pie has won eight ribbons at area fairs. People say it looks and tastes like a giant apple-cinnamon bun. The recipe is a great favorite with apple and spice lovers.

—**SUSAN FRISCH** GERMANSVILLE, PA

PREP: 30 MIN. + CHILLING • **BAKE:** 50 MIN. + COOLING
MAKES: 8 SERVINGS

- 2 cups all-purpose flour
- ½ teaspoon salt
- 6 tablespoons shortening
- 2 tablespoons cold butter
- 5 to 7 tablespoons orange juice

FILLING

- 6 tablespoons butter, melted, divided
- ½ cup packed brown sugar
- ½ cup chopped pecans
- 8 cups thinly sliced peeled tart apples (about ⅛ inch thick)
- 1 cup sugar
- ⅓ cup all-purpose flour
- ¾ teaspoon ground cinnamon
- ¼ teaspoon ground nutmeg

GLAZE

- ½ cup confectioners' sugar
- 2 to 3 teaspoons orange juice

1. In a large bowl, combine flour and salt; cut in shortening and butter until crumbly. Gradually add orange juice, tossing with a fork until dough forms a ball. Divide dough into two balls. Wrap in plastic; refrigerate for at least 30 minutes.

2. Line a 9-in. deep-dish pie plate with heavy-duty foil, leaving 1½ in. beyond edge; coat the foil with cooking spray. Combine 4 tablespoons butter, brown sugar and pecans; spoon into prepared pie plate.

3. In a large bowl, combine the apples, sugar, flour, cinnamon, nutmeg and remaining butter; toss gently.

4. On waxed paper, roll out one ball of pastry to fit pie plate. Place pastry over nut mixture, pressing firmly against mixture and sides of plate; trim to 1 in. beyond plate edge. Fill with apple mixture.

5. Roll out remaining pastry to fit top of pie; place over filling. Trim to ¼ in. beyond plate edge. Fold bottom pastry over top pastry; seal and flute edges. Cut four 1-in. slits in top pastry.

6. Bake at 375° for 50-55 minutes or until apples are tender and crust is golden brown (cover edges with foil during the last 20 minutes to prevent overbrowning if necessary).

7. Cool for 15 minutes on a wire rack. Invert onto a serving platter; carefully remove foil. Combine glaze ingredients; drizzle over pie.

Per 1 slice: 613 cal., 26g fat (10g sat. fat), 31mg chol., 270mg sod., 92g carb. (60g sugars, 4g fiber), 5g pro.

DUTCH APPLE CAKE

Dutch Apple Cake

My husband and I came to Canada more than 50 years ago from Holland. This recipe, a family favorite, is one I found in a Dutch cookbook. It frequently goes along with me to potluck suppers.

—**ELIZABETH PETERS** MARTINTOWN, ON

PREP: 15 MIN. + STANDING • **BAKE:** 1½ HOURS + COOLING
MAKES: 10-12 SERVINGS

- 3 medium tart apples, peeled and cut into ¼-inch slices (3 cups)
- 3 tablespoons plus 1 cup sugar, divided
- 1 teaspoon ground cinnamon
- ⅔ cup butter, softened
- 4 large eggs
- 1 teaspoon vanilla extract
- 2 cups all-purpose flour
- ⅛ teaspoon salt

1. In a large bowl, combine the apples, 3 tablespoons sugar and cinnamon; let stand for 1 hour.

2. In another bowl, cream butter and remaining sugar until light and fluffy. Add eggs, one at a time, beating well after each addition. Add vanilla. Combine flour and salt; gradually add to creamed mixture and beat until smooth.

3. Transfer to a greased 9x5-in. loaf pan. Push apple slices vertically into batter, placing them close together.

4. Bake at 300° for 1½-1¾ hours or until a toothpick inserted near the center comes out clean. Cool 10 minutes before removing from pan to a wire rack. Serve warm.

Per 1 slice: 282 cal., 12g fat (7g sat. fat), 97mg chol., 120mg sod., 40g carb. (24g sugars, 1g fiber), 4g pro.

Chocolate Zucchini Cupcakes

Our grandkids love these cupcakes and don't believe us when we tell them there are veggies in them! The recipe is a must-make every summer.

—**CAROLE FRASER** NORTH YORK, ON

PREP: 25 MIN. • **BAKE:** 20 MIN. + COOLING • **MAKES:** 21 CUPCAKES

- 1¼ cups butter, softened
- 1½ cups sugar
- 2 large eggs
- 1 teaspoon vanilla extract
- 2½ cups all-purpose flour
- ¾ cup baking cocoa
- 1 teaspoon baking powder
- 1 teaspoon baking soda
- ½ teaspoon salt
- ½ cup plain yogurt
- 1 cup grated zucchini
- 1 cup grated carrots
- 1 can (16 ounces) chocolate frosting

1. In a large bowl, cream butter and sugar until light and fluffy. Add eggs, one at a time, beating well after each addition. Stir in vanilla. Combine the flour, baking cocoa, baking powder, baking soda and salt; add to the creamed mixture alternately with yogurt, beating well after each addition. Fold in zucchini and carrots.

2. Fill paper-lined muffin cups two-thirds full. Bake at 350° for 18-22 minutes or until a toothpick inserted near the center comes out clean. Cool for 10 minutes before removing the cupcakes from pans to wire racks to cool completely. Frost cupcakes.

Per 1 cupcake: 326 cal., 17g fat (9g sat. fat), 50mg chol., 288mg sod., 40g carb. (25g sugars, 1g fiber), 3g pro.

PISTACHIO & COCONUT CAKE

Pistachio & Coconut Cake

This coconut cake is good any time of the year, but the color is perfect for St. Patrick's Day. The secret is adding instant pistachio pudding mix into the cake mix and the frosting.

—**D. MEREDITH** ROCKFORD, IL

PREP: 20 MIN. • **BAKE:** 40 MIN. + COOLING • **MAKES:** 16 SERVINGS

- 1 white cake mix (regular size)
- 1 package (3.4 ounces) instant pistachio pudding mix
- 1 cup lemon-lime soda
- ¾ cup canola oil
- 3 large eggs
- ½ cup flaked coconut
- ½ cup toasted shelled pistachios, chopped

FROSTING
- 1¼ cups cold 2% milk
- 1 package (3.4 ounces) instant pistachio pudding mix
- 1 carton (8 ounces) frozen whipped topping, thawed

TOPPINGS
- ¼ cup flaked coconut, toasted
- ¼ cup toasted shelled pistachios, chopped

1. Preheat oven to 350°. Combine the first five ingredients; beat on low speed until moistened, about 30 seconds. Beat on medium for 2 minutes; stir in coconut and pistachios.

2. Pour into two greased 8-in. round baking pans or a greased 13x9-in. baking pan. Bake until a toothpick inserted in the center comes out clean, 40-45 minutes. Cool on a wire rack.

3. For frosting, beat milk and pudding mix on low speed for 2 minutes. Fold in whipped topping. Spread frosting over top of cake, and, if using round pans, between layers. Top with toasted coconut and pistachios. Chill until serving.

Note: To toast nuts and coconut, bake in separate shallow pans in a 350° oven for 5-10 minutes or until golden brown, stirring occasionally.

Per 1 slice: 380 cal., 21g fat (6g sat. fat), 36mg chol., 431mg sod., 41g carb. (28g sugars, 1g fiber), 5g pro.

CHOCOLATE ZUCCHINI CUPCAKES

Pumpkin Caramel Cupcakes

Not only do kids love to eat these cupcakes; they can help bake them, too. To make things even easier, we like to dunk them in caramel apple dip instead of using frosting.

—**DONNA SCHAAB** BELLEVILLE, IL

PREP: 25 MIN. • **BAKE:** 20 MIN.+ COOLING • **MAKES:** 2 DOZEN

- 1 package yellow cake mix (regular size)
- 1 can (15 ounces) pumpkin
- ⅔ cup water
- ¼ cup maple syrup
- 3 large eggs
- 4 teaspoons sugar
- 4 teaspoons ground cinnamon
  Dash salt
- 1 carton (16 ounces) caramel apple dip
  Chocolate frosting and decorating icing, optional

1. Preheat oven to 350°. Line 24 muffin cups with paper liners. Combine the first eight ingredients. Beat on low speed 30 seconds; beat on medium 2 minutes.
2. Fill prepared cups three-fourths full. Bake until a toothpick inserted in center comes out clean, about 18-22 minutes. Cool in pans 10 minutes before removing to wire racks to cool completely.
3. Frost cupcakes with caramel apple dip. Decorate, if desired, with frosting and decorating icing. Refrigerate leftovers.
Per 1 cupcake: 178 cal., 5g fat (2g sat. fat), 26mg chol., 242mg sod., 31g carb. (22g sugars, 1g fiber), 2g pro.

PUMPKIN CARAMEL CUPCAKES

TOFFEE-PEACH ICE CREAM PIE
Kim Ciepluch
Kenosha, WI

Toffee-Peach Ice Cream Pie

A sugar cone and toffee crust, fresh peaches and ice cream—you can't go wrong with this winning combo! Top with hot caramel for a delectable frozen treat.

—**KIM CIEPLUCH** KENOSHA, WI

PREP: 15 MIN. + FREEZING • **COOK:** 5 MIN. • **MAKES:** 8 SERVINGS

- 6 ice cream sugar cones
- ½ cup brickle toffee bits
- 3 tablespoons butter, melted

FILLING
- 2 cups finely chopped peeled fresh peaches (about 2 large), divided
- ½ cup sugar
- 2 tablespoons lemon juice
- 1 tablespoon cornstarch
- 4 cups vanilla ice cream, softened if necessary

TOPPINGS
- 1 tablespoon hot caramel ice cream topping
- 2 tablespoons brickle toffee bits

1. Pulse sugar cones and toffee bits in a food processor until coarsely ground. Drizzle with butter; pulse just until blended. Press onto bottom and up sides of an ungreased 9-in. pie plate. Freeze at least 30 minutes.
2. In a small saucepan, mix 1 cup peaches, sugar, lemon juice and cornstarch; cook and stir over medium heat until thickened and bubbly. Reduce heat to low; cook and stir 2 minutes longer. Remove from heat; cool slightly. Stir in remaining peaches; cool completely.
3. Reserve ½ cup peach mixture for topping; refrigerate, covered. Beat ice cream and remaining peach mixture just until blended. Pour into crust. Freeze, covered, overnight. To serve, top with caramel topping, reserved peach mixture and toffee bits.
Per 1 piece: 379 cal., 18g fat (10g sat. fat), 47mg chol., 225mg sod., 52g carb. (44g sugars, 1g fiber), 3g pro.

Maple Carrot Cupcakes

I come from a line of family cooks: Mother and Grandmom were always in the kitchen cooking up something delicious. So it's no surprise I have liked to cook and bake since I was young. These carrot cupcakes were Grandmom's specialty, and we always have them at family gatherings.

—**LISA ANN PANZINO DINUNZIO** VINELAND, NJ

PREP: 15 MIN. • **BAKE:** 20 MIN. + COOLING • **MAKES:** 1½ DOZEN

- 2 cups all-purpose flour
- 1 cup sugar
- 1 teaspoon baking powder
- 1 teaspoon baking soda
- 1 teaspoon ground cinnamon
- ½ teaspoon salt
- 4 large eggs
- 1 cup canola oil
- ½ cup maple syrup
- 3 cups grated carrots (about 6 medium)

FROSTING
- 1 package (8 ounces) cream cheese, softened
- ¼ cup butter, softened
- ¼ cup maple syrup
- 1 teaspoon vanilla extract
  Chopped walnuts, optional

1. In a large bowl, combine the first six ingredients. Beat the eggs, oil and syrup; stir into dry ingredients just until moistened. Fold in carrots.

2. Fill 18 greased or paper-lined muffin cups two-thirds full. Bake at 350° for 20-25 minutes or until a toothpick inserted near the center comes out clean. Cool for 5 minutes before removing from pans to wire racks.

3. For frosting, combine the cream cheese, butter, syrup and vanilla in a bowl; beat until smooth. Frost cooled cupcakes. Sprinkle with nuts if desired. Store cupcakes in the refrigerator.

Per 1 cupcake: 327 cal., 20g fat (6g sat. fat), 68mg chol., 243mg sod., 33g carb. (21g sugars, 1g fiber), 4g pro.

MAPLE CARROT CUPCAKES

BANANA CREAM PIE WITH CAKE MIX CRUST

Banana Cream Pie with Cake Mix Crust

I added an extra layer to the classic banana cream pie, topping it off with a crunchy peanut-buttery streusel.

—**MATTHEW HASS** FRANKLIN, WI

PREP: 15 MIN. • **BAKE:** 30 MIN. + CHILLING • **MAKES:** 10 SERVINGS

- 1 package yellow cake mix (regular size), divided
- 1 large egg, lightly beaten
- 3 tablespoons butter, softened and divided
- 1 cup cold 2% milk
- 1 package (3.4 ounces) instant banana cream pudding mix
- 1 medium banana, sliced
- 1 carton (8 ounces) frozen whipped topping, thawed and divided
- ⅓ cup creamy peanut butter
  Additional sliced ripe banana

1. Preheat oven to 350°. Grease a 9-in. pie plate. Stir together 1¾ cups cake mix, egg and 1 tablespoon butter until combined. Turn onto a floured surface; knead until a smooth dough forms. Roll dough to fit prepared pie plate. Flute edge. Prick bottom several times with a fork. Bake until golden brown, 12-15 minutes. Cool on a wire rack.

2. Whisk milk and pudding mix 2 minutes. Fold in banana and 1 cup whipped topping. Transfer to cooled crust. Top with remaining whipped topping. Refrigerate for at least 3 hours.

3. Meanwhile, mix remaining cake mix, peanut butter and remaining butter until crumbly. Transfer to a parchment paper-lined rimmed baking pan. Bake until golden brown, 14-18 minutes, stirring once. Cool completely.

4. Top pie with additional sliced banana and some of the crumb topping (save remaining topping for another use).

Per 1 piece: 394 cal., 16g fat (8g sat. fat), 30mg chol., 526mg sod., 55g carb. (35g sugars, 1g fiber), 6g pro.

Oma's Apfelkuchen (Grandma's Apple Cake)

Oma's Apfelkuchen has been shared by members of my husband's German family for more than 150 years. It's that scrumptious! Try it with any apples you have on hand. I use Granny Smith.

—AMY KIRCHEN LOVELAND, OH

PREP: 20 MIN. • **BAKE:** 45 MIN. + COOLING • **MAKES:** 10 SERVINGS

- 5 large egg yolks
- 2 medium tart apples, peeled, cored and halved
- 1 cup plus 2 tablespoons unsalted butter, softened
- 1¼ cups sugar
- 2 cups all-purpose flour
- 2 tablespoons cornstarch
- 2 teaspoons cream of tartar
- 1 teaspoon baking powder
- ½ teaspoon salt
- ¼ cup 2% milk
  Confectioners' sugar

1. Preheat oven to 350°. Let egg yolks stand at room temperature for 30 minutes. Starting at ½-in. from one end, cut apple halves lengthwise into ¼-in. slices, leaving them attached at the top so they fan out slightly. Set aside.
2. Cream butter and sugar until light and fluffy. Add egg yolks, one at a time, beating well after each addition. In another bowl, sift flour, cornstarch, cream of tartar, baking powder and salt twice. Gradually beat into creamed mixture. Add milk; mix well (batter will be thick).
3. Spread batter into a greased 9-in. springform pan wrapped in a sheet of heavy-duty foil. Gently press apples, round side up, into batter. Bake until a toothpick inserted in the center comes out with moist crumbs, 45-55 minutes. Cool on a wire rack 10 minutes. Loosen sides from pan with a knife; remove foil. Cool 1 hour longer. Remove rim from pan. Dust with confectioners' sugar.

Per 1 slice: 422 cal., 23g fat (14g sat. fat), 148mg chol., 177mg sod., 50g carb. (28g sugars, 1g fiber), 4g pro.

OMA'S APFELKUCHEN

BLUE-RIBBON BUTTER CAKE

Blue-Ribbon Butter Cake

I found this recipe in an old cookbook I bought at a garage sale, and I couldn't wait to try it. I knew it had been someone's favorite because of the well-worn page.

—JOAN GERTZ PALMETTO, FL

PREP: 20 MIN. • **BAKE:** 65 MIN. + COOLING • **MAKES:** 16 SERVINGS

- 1 cup butter, softened
- 2 cups sugar
- 4 large eggs
- 2 teaspoons vanilla extract
- 3 cups all-purpose flour
- 1 teaspoon baking powder
- ½ teaspoon baking soda
- ½ teaspoon salt
- 1 cup buttermilk

BUTTER SAUCE

- 1 cup sugar
- ½ cup butter, cubed
- ¼ cup water
- 1½ teaspoons almond extract
- 1½ teaspoons vanilla extract

1. In a large bowl, cream butter and sugar until light and fluffy. Add eggs, one at a time, beating well after each addition. Beat in vanilla. Combine the flour, baking powder, baking soda and salt; add to creamed mixture alternately with buttermilk, beating well after each addition.
2. Pour into a greased and floured 10-in. tube pan. Bake at 350° for 65-70 minutes or until a toothpick inserted in center comes out clean. Cool 10 minutes. Run a knife around edges and center tube of pan. Invert cake onto a wire rack over waxed paper.
3. For sauce, combine the sugar, butter and water in a small saucepan. Cook over medium heat just until butter is melted and sugar is dissolved. Remove from the heat; stir in the extracts.
4. Poke holes in the top of the warm cake; spoon ¼ cup sauce over cake. Let stand until absorbed. Repeat twice. Poke holes into sides of cake; brush remaining sauce over sides. Cool completely.

Per 1 slice: 410 cal., 19g fat (11g sat. fat), 100mg chol., 344mg sod., 56g carb. (38g sugars, 1g fiber), 5g pro.

Ozark Mountain Berry Pie

I think the best berries in the world are grown in the Ozarks. We own a small berry farm, and this is one of my favorite recipes. It's delicious served warm.
—**ELAINE MOODY** CLEVER, MO

PREP: 15 MIN. • **BAKE:** 55 MIN. + COOLING • **MAKES:** 8 SERVINGS

- 1 cup sugar
- ¼ cup cornstarch
- ½ teaspoon ground cinnamon, optional
  Dash salt
- ⅓ cup water
- 1 cup fresh blueberries
  Pastry for a double-crust pie (9 inches)
- 1 cup halved fresh strawberries
- 1 cup fresh raspberries
- ¾ cup fresh blackberries
- 1 tablespoon lemon juice
- 2 tablespoons butter

1. In a large saucepan, combine the sugar, cornstarch, cinnamon if desired, salt and water until smooth; add the blueberries. Bring to a boil; cook and stir for 2 minutes or until thickened. Set aside to cool slightly.
2. Line a 9-in. pie plate with bottom crust; trim pastry even with edge. Gently fold the strawberries, raspberries, blackberries and lemon juice into the blueberry mixture. Pour into pastry; dot with butter. Roll out remaining pastry; make a lattice crust. Trim, seal and flute edges.
3. Bake at 400° for 10 minutes. Reduce heat to 350°; bake for 45-50 minutes or until the crust is golden brown and filling is bubbly. Cool on a wire rack. Refrigerate leftovers.
Per 1 piece: 406 cal., 17g fat (8g sat. fat), 18mg chol., 248mg sod., 62g carb. (31g sugars, 2g fiber), 3g pro.

EASY CONFETTI PIE

OZARK MOUNTAIN BERRY PIE

Easy Confetti Pie

Sugar cone crust makes a pie that tastes like birthday cake when you add a dreamy, creamy no-bake confetti filling. Buy two boxes of cones to get the job done.
—**TASTE OF HOME** TEST KITCHEN

PREP: 10 MIN. • **BAKE:** 15 MIN. + CHILLING • **MAKES:** 10 SERVINGS

- 2¾ cups crushed ice cream sugar cones
- 2 tablespoons plus ½ cup sugar, divided
- ½ cup butter, melted
- 1 envelope unflavored gelatin
- ¼ cup cold water
- 2 packages (8 ounces each) cream cheese, softened
- 2 cups heavy whipping cream
- 2 teaspoons butter flavoring
- 1 teaspoon almond extract
- ⅓ cup assorted sprinkles

1. Preheat oven to 350°. Combine crushed sugar cones and 2 tablespoons sugar with melted butter. Using the bottom of a glass, press cone mixture onto bottom and up the sides of a greased 9-in. deep-dish pie plate. Bake until set, about 12-15 minutes. Cool completely on a wire rack.
2. Meanwhile, sprinkle gelatin over cold water; let stand 5 minutes. Beat cream cheese and remaining sugar until smooth. Slowly beat in cream, butter flavoring and extract. In a microwave, heat gelatin on high until melted, about 10 seconds; beat into the cream cheese mixture. Fold in sprinkles. Add filling to crust. Chill until set, about 3 hours.
3. Top with additional sprinkles.
Per 1 piece: 568 cal., 44g fat (26g sat. fat), 125mg chol., 290mg sod., 38g carb. (24g sugars, 0 fiber), 7g pro.

FREEZE IT

Chocolate & Cardamom Coconut Tart

This tart with a cardamom-scented crust is my nod to our family's Scandinavian heritage. The filling is rich in all the right ways: coconut, cranberries and chocolate.

—**CAROLE HOLT** MENDOTA HEIGHTS, MN

PREP: 20 MIN. + CHILLING
BAKE: 50 MIN. + COOLING
MAKES: 16 SERVINGS

- 1⅓ cups butter, softened
- 1⅓ cups sugar
- 4 teaspoons grated orange peel, divided
- 1 large egg
- 2⅔ cups all-purpose flour
- ¾ teaspoon ground cardamom
- ¾ cup pistachios
- ½ cup fresh cranberries
- ¾ cup sweetened shredded coconut
- ⅓ cup plus ½ cup 60% cacao bittersweet chocolate baking chips, divided
- ⅔ cup sweetened condensed milk
- ½ cup white baking chips

1. Preheat oven to 325°. Cream butter, sugar and 2 teaspoons orange peel until light and fluffy. Beat in egg. Add flour and cardamom, mixing well. Refrigerate dough 30 minutes.

2. Meanwhile, pulse pistachios in a food processor until finely chopped; remove. Repeat with cranberries. Mix together ⅓ cup of the pistachios, cranberries, coconut, ⅓ cup of the bittersweet chocolate chips and milk.

3. Press half the dough onto bottom and ¼ in. up sides of a greased 9-in. springform pan. Spread pistachio mixture over dough. Between sheets of waxed paper, roll remaining dough into a 9-in. circle. Remove top sheet of paper. Gently flip dough and place over pistachio filling; remove remaining paper. Press dough around edge to seal. Place pan on a 15x10-in. rimmed baking pan.

4. Bake until golden brown, about 50-60 minutes. Cool in pan for 15 minutes. Loosen sides from pan with a knife; cool completely. Remove rim from pan. Microwave white baking chips on high until melted, stirring every 30 seconds; remove. Repeat with remaining bittersweet chips. Drizzle tart with white and bittersweet melted chocolate. Sprinkle with remaining pistachios and orange peel.

To freeze: Cover and freeze unbaked tart. To use, remove from freezer 30 minutes before baking (do not thaw). Preheat oven to 325°. Place tart on a baking sheet; cover edge loosely with foil. Bake as directed, increasing time as necessary. Cool and top as directed.

Per 1 slice: 449 cal., 25g fat (15g sat. fat), 58mg chol., 185mg sod., 53g carb. (34g sugars, 2g fiber), 6g pro.

CHOCOLATE & CARDAMOM
COCONUT TART

Peanut Butter Chocolate Poke Cake

(PICTURED ON P. 170)

When my family is planning a get-together, I can count on three or four people asking if I'm bringing this. If you don't have a chocolate cake mix, you can use a white or yellow one and stir in 3 tablespoons of baking cocoa.

—**FAY MORELAND** WICHITA FALLS, TX

PREP: 20 MIN. • **BAKE:** 25 MIN. + CHILLING
MAKES: 20 SERVINGS

- 1 package chocolate cake mix (regular size)
- 2 teaspoons vanilla extract, divided
  Dash salt
- ⅔ cup creamy peanut butter
- 2 cans (14 ounces each) sweetened condensed milk
- 1 cup confectioners' sugar
  TOPPINGS: chopped peanut butter-filled sandwich cookies or peanut butter cups or a combination of the two

1. Preheat oven to 350°. Prepare cake mix according to package directions, adding 1 teaspoon vanilla and salt before mixing batter. Transfer to a greased 13x9-in. baking pan. Bake and cool completely as package directs.
2. Whisk peanut butter and milk until blended. Using the end of a wooden spoon handle, poke holes in cake 2 in. apart. Slowly pour 2 cups peanut butter mixture over cake, filling each hole. Refrigerate cake and remaining peanut butter mixture, covered, until cake is cold, 2-3 hours.
3. Combine the remaining vanilla and the remaining peanut butter mixture; gradually beat in enough confectioners' sugar to reach a spreading consistency. Spread over cake. Add toppings as desired. Refrigerate leftovers.
Per 1 piece: 360 cal., 16g fat (4g sat. fat), 41mg chol., 312mg sod., 49g carb. (40g sugars, 1g fiber), 7g pro.

Blueberry Pie

During blueberry season, this pie always makes an appearance. It has a wonderful fresh berry flavor and a bit of tang from the lemon peel.

—**RICHARD CASE** JOHNSTOWN, PA

PREP: 30 MIN. • **BAKE:** 1 HOUR + COOLING
MAKES: 8 SERVINGS

- 4 cups fresh blueberries
- 1 tablespoon lemon juice
- ½ teaspoon grated lemon peel
- 1¼ to 1½ cups sugar
- ¼ cup quick-cooking tapioca
- 1 tablespoon cornstarch
- ½ teaspoon ground cinnamon
  Pastry for a double-crust pie (9 inches)
- 1 tablespoon butter, softened
- 1 large egg
- 1 tablespoon 2% milk
  Coarse sugar, optional

1. Preheat oven to 350°. Combine blueberries, lemon juice and lemon peel. In another bowl, combine sugar, tapioca, cornstarch and cinnamon. Add to berries; toss gently to coat.
2. On a lightly floured surface, roll half of pie dough to a ⅛-in.-thick circle; transfer to a 9-in. pie plate. Trim pastry to ½ in. beyond rim of plate. Add blueberry mixture. Dot filling with butter.
3. Roll remaining dough to a ⅛-in.-thick circle; cut into 1-in.-wide strips. Arrange over filling in a lattice pattern. Trim and seal strips to edge of bottom pastry; flute edge. Whisk egg and milk; brush over pastry. If desired, sprinkle with coarse sugar.
4. Bake 30 minutes. Cover edge loosely with foil. Bake until crust is golden brown and berries have burst, about 30-35 minutes more. Cool on a wire rack.

Pastry for double-crust pie (9 inches): Combine 2½ cups all-purpose flour and ½ tsp. salt; cut in 1 cup cold butter until crumbly. Gradually add ⅓ to ⅔ cup ice water, tossing with fork until dough holds together when pressed. Divide dough in half. Shape each into a disk; wrap in plastic wrap. Refrigerate 1 hour or overnight.
Per 1 slice: 553 cal., 25g fat (16g sat. fat), 87mg chol., 332mg sod., 78g carb. (40g sugars, 3g fiber), 6g pro.
Rhubarb Cherry Pie: Substitute 3 cups sliced rhubarb and 1 drained 16-ounce can of tart cherries for the blueberries. Omit lemon peel and cinnamon. Bake as directed until filling is bubbly.

...g and desserts that
...ts and minimal effort.
...e is a holiday lifesaver.
...NE BANFIELD BASKING RIDGE, NJ

PREP: 20 MIN. + CHILLING
MAKES: 12 SERVINGS

- 1 package (8 ounces) cream cheese, softened
- 2 teaspoons grated lemon peel
- 1 jar (10 ounces) lemon curd
- 2 cups heavy whipping cream
- 2 packages (5¼ ounces each) thin ginger cookies
- 2 tablespoons chopped crystallized ginger

1. In a large bowl, beat cream cheese and lemon peel until creamy. Beat in lemon curd until smooth. Gradually add cream, beating on medium-high speed until soft peaks form.

2. Line bottom of an 8-in. square dish with nine cookies; spread with about ⅔ cup cream cheese mixture. Repeat the layers six times. Sprinkle with crystallized ginger. Refrigerate cake, covered, 2 hours or overnight.

Note: This recipe was tested with Anna's Ginger Thins Swedish cookies.

Per 1 square: 521 cal., 31g fat (19g sat. fat), 93mg chol., 340mg sod., 54g carb. (34g sugars, 0 fiber), 4g pro.

LEMON GINGER ICEBOX CAKE

GRILLED FIGGY PIES
Renee Murby
Johnston, RI

Grilled Figgy Pies

Delicious figs combined with maple, walnuts and creamy mascarpone make a decadent treat that's easy to enjoy at a backyard cookout. These unique hand pies always disappear quickly.

—**RENEE MURBY** JOHNSTON, RI

PREP: 50 MIN. + FREEZING • **GRILL:** 10 MIN.
MAKES: 1 DOZEN

- 1 package refrigerated pie pastry
- 12 dried figs
- ¼ cup bourbon
- ½ cup chopped walnuts
- ¼ cup plus 1 tablespoon maple syrup, divided
- 1 teaspoon ground cinnamon
- ½ teaspoon ground nutmeg
- ½ teaspoon vanilla extract
- ⅔ cup (about 5 ounces) mascarpone cheese
- 1 large egg
- 1 tablespoon water

1. Warm the pie pastry to room temperature according to package directions. Meanwhile, in a small saucepan, combine figs and bourbon; add enough water to cover by 1 in. Cook, covered, over low heat until figs are plump, 15-20 minutes. Remove from heat; drain. Cool 15 minutes and pat dry. Cut each fig into quarters. Set aside.

2. In same saucepan over medium-low heat, combine walnuts with ¼ cup maple syrup, cinnamon and nutmeg. Cook, stirring constantly, until liquid is almost evaporated, 5-7 minutes. Spread nuts on a baking sheet lined with parchment paper; freeze until set, about 10 minutes.

3. Unroll pastry sheets. Using a 4-in. round cutter, cut 12 circles, rolling and cutting scraps as necessary. Stir vanilla and remaining maple syrup into mascarpone cheese. Spread 1 scant tablespoon mascarpone mixture over half of each circle to within ¼ in. of edge; layer with 2 teaspoons maple walnuts and four fig pieces. Make an egg wash by whisking egg and water; use to moisten edge of pastry. Fold dough over filling; press edges with a fork to seal. Repeat with remaining dough and filling. Brush egg wash over pies. Freeze pies on a parchment paper-lined baking sheet 10 minutes.

4. Remove from baking sheet. Grill pies, covered, on a well-greased grill rack over medium direct heat until golden brown, 5-7 minutes per side.

Per 1 hand pie: 280 cal., 17g fat (7g sat. fat), 35mg chol., 137mg sod., 28g carb. (10g sugars, 1g fiber), 4g pro.

Mile-High Cranberry Meringue Pie

(PICTURED ON P. 171)

Your crowd will be blown away when they see this pie with towering meringue on top. Let it chill in the fridge for at least four hours for best results.

—**MARCIA WHITNEY** GAINESVILLE, FL

PREP: 1 HOUR • **BAKE:** 25 MIN. + CHILLING
MAKES: 8 SERVINGS

- 4 large eggs, separated
  Pastry for single-crust pie (9 inches)
- 4 cups fresh or frozen cranberries, thawed
- 2¼ cups sugar, divided
- ¾ cup water
- 2 tablespoons all-purpose flour
- ¼ teaspoon salt
- 2 tablespoons butter
- 2 teaspoons vanilla extract, divided
- ½ teaspoon cream of tartar

1. Preheat oven to 425°. Let egg whites stand 30 minutes at room temperature.

2. On a lightly floured surface, roll dough to a ⅛-in.-thick circle; transfer to a 9-in. pie plate. Trim pastry to ½ in. beyond rim of plate; flute edge. Refrigerate 30 minutes.

3. Line unpricked pastry with a double thickness of foil. Fill with pie weights, dried beans or uncooked rice. Bake on a lower oven rack 15-20 minutes or until edges are light golden brown. Remove foil and weights; bake 3-6 minutes longer or until bottom is golden brown. Cool on a wire rack. Reduce heat to 325°.

4. In a large saucepan, combine cranberries, 1½ cups sugar and water. Bring to a boil, stirring to dissolve sugar. Reduce heat to medium; cook, uncovered, 4-6 minutes or until the berries stop popping, stirring mixture occasionally. Remove from heat. In a small bowl, whisk egg yolks, ¼ cup sugar, flour and salt until blended. Gradually whisk in ½ cup of the hot cranberry liquid; return all to the saucepan, stirring constantly. Bring to a gentle boil; cook and stir 2 minutes. Remove from heat; stir in butter and 1 teaspoon vanilla.

5. For meringue, beat egg whites with cream of tartar and remaining vanilla

on medium speed until foamy. Add remaining sugar, 1 tablespoon at a time, beating on high after each addition until sugar is dissolved. Continue beating until stiff glossy peaks form. Transfer hot filling to pastry. Spread meringue evenly over hot filling, sealing to edge of pastry. Bake 25-30 minutes or until meringue is golden brown. Cool 1 hour on a wire rack. Refrigerate at least 4 hours before serving.

Pastry for single-crust pie (9 inches): Combine 1¼ cups all-purpose flour and ¼ tsp. salt; cut in ½ cup cold butter until crumbly. Gradually add 3-5 Tbsp. ice water, tossing with a fork until dough holds together when pressed. Wrap in plastic wrap and refrigerate 1 hour.
Per 1 piece: 486 cal., 17g fat (10g sat. fat), 131mg chol., 289mg sod., 80g carb. (59g sugars, 3g fiber), 6g pro.

Grandma's Red Velvet Cake

No one believes it's Christmas at our house until this jolly cake appears. It's different from other red velvets I've tasted; the icing is as light as snow.

—**KATHRYN DAVISON** CHARLOTTE, NC

PREP: 30 MIN. • **BAKE:** 20 MIN. + COOLING
MAKES: 14 SERVINGS

- ½ cup butter, softened
- 1½ cups granulated sugar
- 2 large eggs
- 2 bottles (1 ounce each) red food coloring
- 1 tablespoon white vinegar
- 1 teaspoon vanilla extract

GRANDMA'S RED VELVET CAKE

- 2¼ cups cake flour
- 2 tablespoons baking cocoa
- 1 teaspoon baking soda
- 1 teaspoon salt
- 1 cup buttermilk

FROSTING

- 1 tablespoon cornstarch
- ½ cup cold water
- 2 cups butter, softened
- 2 teaspoons vanilla extract
- 3½ cups confectioners' sugar

1. Preheat oven to 350°. Cream butter and sugar until light and fluffy. Add eggs, one at a time, beating well after each addition. Beat in food coloring, vinegar and vanilla. In another bowl, whisk together flour, cocoa, baking soda and salt; add to creamed mixture alternately with buttermilk, beating well after each addition.

2. Pour into two greased and floured 9-in. round baking pans. Bake until a toothpick inserted in the center comes out clean, 20-25 minutes. Cool layers 10 minutes before removing from pans to wire racks to cool completely.

3. For frosting, combine water and cornstarch in a small saucepan over medium heat. Stir until thickened and opaque, 2-3 minutes. Cool to room temperature. Beat butter and vanilla until light and fluffy. Beat in the cornstarch mixture. Gradually add confectioners' sugar; beat until light and fluffy. Spread between layers and over top and sides of cake.
Per 1 slice: 595 cal., 34g fat (21g sat. fat), 115mg chol., 564mg sod., 71g carb. (52g sugars, 1g fiber), 4g pro.

APPLE-PUMPKIN UPSIDE-DOWN CAKE

Apple-Pumpkin Upside-Down Cake

We love the combination of classic fall fruits in this yummy cake. I bake the apples on the bottom to keep them plump and moist, then flip the cake so we can dig in. It's best served warm with ice cream.

—**CHRISTINA YAHRAES** SAN FRANCISCO, CA

PREP: 15 MIN. • **BAKE:** 30 MIN. + COOLING
MAKES: 8 SERVINGS

- 2 large eggs
- 2 tablespoons plus ¼ cup softened butter, divided
- 2 tablespoons plus ¾ cup sugar, divided
- 1 teaspoon ground cinnamon, divided
- 2 medium apples (about 10 ounces), peeled and thinly sliced
- ½ cup canned pumpkin
- 1¼ cups all-purpose flour
- 1 teaspoon baking soda
- ½ teaspoon salt
- ½ cup buttermilk
  Vanilla ice cream, optional

1. Preheat oven to 350°. Let eggs stand at room temperature for 30 minutes. In a microwave, melt 2 tablespoons butter. Stir in 2 tablespoons sugar and ½ teaspoon cinnamon; spread mixture into a 9-in. pie plate. Arrange apples in a single layer over butter mixture.
2. Cream remaining butter and remaining sugar until light and fluffy. Beat in pumpkin. Add eggs, one at a time, beating well after each addition. In another bowl, whisk together flour, baking soda, salt and remaining cinnamon; add to creamed mixture alternately with buttermilk, beating well after each addition.
3. Spread batter evenly over apples. Bake until a toothpick inserted in the center comes out clean, about 30-35 minutes. Loosen sides of cake from pie plate with a knife. Cool for 10 minutes before inverting onto a serving plate. Serve warm and, if desired, with vanilla ice cream.
Per 1 slice: 278 cal., 10g fat (6g sat. fat), 70mg chol., 422mg sod., 43g carb. (27g sugars, 2g fiber), 4g pro.

FRESH RASPBERRY ICEBOX CAKE

Fresh Raspberry Icebox Cake

(PICTURED ON P. 171)

Layered icebox cakes are so fun because they look impressive but couldn't be easier. Fresh raspberries make this one really special. Use Anna's Ginger Thins to get the scalloped edges, or regular gingersnaps if those are not available.

—**ELISABETH LARSEN** PLEASANT GRV, UT

PREP: 25 MIN. + CHILLING
MAKES: 12 SERVINGS

- 1 carton (8 ounces) mascarpone cheese
- 3 cups cold heavy whipping cream
- 2 tablespoons sugar
- 2 tablespoons grated lemon peel (about 2 lemons)
- 2 packages (5¼ ounces each) thin ginger cookies
- 5 cups fresh raspberries (about 20 ounces), divided

1. Stir mascarpone cheese; let stand at room temperature 30 minutes. Meanwhile, beat cream until it begins to thicken. Add sugar; beat until soft peaks form. Reserve ½ cup cream; cover and refrigerate. Add lemon peel and mascarpone to remaining whipped cream; beat until stiff peaks form, 30-60 seconds.
2. On a serving plate, spread ½ cup of the cream mixture in a 7-in.-diameter circle. Arrange six cookies in a circle on top of the cream, placing a seventh cookie in the center. Gently fold 4 cups of raspberries into remaining cream mixture. Spoon about 1 cup raspberry cream mixture over the cookies. Repeat layers six times, ending with cookies (there will be eight cookie layers in all). Spread reserved whipped cream over cookies; top with remaining raspberries. Refrigerate, covered, overnight.
Note: This recipe was tested with Anna's Ginger Thins Swedish cookies.
Per 1 slice: 421 cal., 35g fat (21g sat. fat), 91mg chol., 132mg sod., 25g carb. (13g sugars, 3g fiber), 4g pro.

Blueberry Pan-Cake with Maple Frosting

Here's your excuse to have cake for breakfast. The batter is made with pancake mix!

—MATTHEW HASS FRANKLIN, WI

PREP: 10 MIN. • **BAKE:** 15 MIN. + COOLING • **MAKES:** 12 SERVINGS

- 3 cups complete buttermilk pancake mix
- 1¾ cups water
- 1 cup fresh blueberries
- 2 teaspoons all-purpose flour

FROSTING
- 2 cups confectioners' sugar
- ⅓ cup maple syrup
- ¼ cup butter, softened

1. Preheat oven to 350°. Stir pancake mix and water just until moistened. In another bowl, toss blueberries with flour. Fold into batter.

2. Transfer to a greased 13x9-in. baking pan. Bake until a toothpick inserted in center comes out clean, 15-18 minutes. Cool completely in pan on a wire rack.

3. Beat frosting ingredients until smooth; spread over cooled cake.

Per 1 piece: 257 cal., 5g fat (2g sat. fat), 10mg chol., 449mg sod., 51g carb. (30g sugars, 1g fiber), 3g pro.

BLACK BOTTOM
BRANDY BITES

Black Bottom Brandy Bites

The idea for these bite-size tarts started with little chocolate bottles of brandy. For an extra dash of fabulous, I place chocolate in the bottom of each pastry cup.

—ARLENE ERLBACH MORTON GROVE, IL

PREP: 30 MIN. • **BAKE:** 10 MIN. + COOLING • **MAKES:** 2 DOZEN

- 1 package (14.10 ounces) refrigerated pie pastry
- 1½ cups mascarpone cheese
- ¾ cup turbinado (washed raw) sugar or granulated sugar, divided
- ⅓ cup brandy
- ½ teaspoon ground ginger, divided
- ½ teaspoon vanilla extract
- ½ cup miniature semisweet chocolate chips, divided
- 1¼ teaspoons pumpkin pie spice

1. Preheat oven to 425°. Bring pie pastry sheets to room temperature.

2. Stir together mascarpone cheese and ½ cup sugar. Stir in brandy, ¼ teaspoon ginger and vanilla until well blended. Fold in ¼ cup chocolate chips; cover; refrigerate.

3. Combine pumpkin pie spice, remaining sugar and remaining ginger until well blended. On a lightly floured surface, unroll pastry sheets. Sprinkle sugar mixture evenly over sheets. Lightly roll pastry to help sugar mixture adhere. Cut into 24 circles with a 2½-in. biscuit or round cookie cutter; discard scraps. Lightly press circles, sugar side up, into 24 mini muffin cups coated with cooking spray. Pierce bottoms once with a fork.

4. Bake until golden brown, about 10 minutes; remove from oven. Immediately sprinkle ¼ teaspoon of chocolate chips into each pastry cup; spread to cover bottom. Cool in pan 15 minutes before removing to a wire rack.

5. When the pastry is completely cool, refrigerate until chocolate is set, about 20 minutes. Spoon brandy mixture into cups, or cut a small hole in the tip of a pastry bag or in a corner of a food-safe plastic bag, insert a star tip and pipe mixture into cups. Sprinkle with remaining chips and, if desired, additional pie spice. Chill until serving.

Per 1 tartlet: 244 cal., 18g fat (10g sat. fat), 38mg chol., 77mg sod., 17g carb. (9g sugars, 0 fiber), 3g pro.

BLUEBERRY PAN-CAKE WITH MAPLE FROSTING

Easy Coconut Cream Pie

This is my own recipe for a pie that I make often. It's been a family-favorite dessert since the '40s, when I made several of them at a time to serve a threshing crew of 21 men!

—VERA MOFFITT OSKALOOSA, KS

PREP: 20 MIN. + CHILLING • **MAKES:** 8 SERVINGS

- ¾ cup sugar
- 3 tablespoons all-purpose flour
- ⅛ teaspoon salt
- 3 cups whole milk
- 3 large eggs, beaten
- 1½ cups sweetened shredded coconut, toasted, divided
- 1 tablespoon butter
- 1½ teaspoons vanilla extract
- 1 pastry shell (9 inches), baked

1. In a medium saucepan, combine sugar, flour and salt. Add the milk; cook and stir over medium-high heat until thickened and bubbly. Reduce the heat; cook and stir 2 minutes longer.

2. Remove from the heat; gradually stir about 1 cup of hot mixture into beaten eggs. Return all to saucepan; cook and stir over medium heat until nearly boiling. Reduce heat; cook and stir about 2 minutes more (do not boil).

3. Remove from the heat; stir in 1 cup coconut, butter and vanilla. Pour into pie shell; sprinkle with the remaining coconut. Chill for several hours before serving.

Per 1 piece: 389 cal., 20g fat (12g sat. fat), 101mg chol., 266mg sod., 47g carb. (30g sugars, 1g fiber), 7g pro.

FLOURLESS
DARK CHOCOLATE CAKE

EASY COCONUT
CREAM PIE

EAT SMART Flourless Dark Chocolate Cake

Here's a simple cake that's rich, elegant and over-the-top chocolaty. For finishing touches, add powdered sugar, cocoa or liqueur-flavored whipped cream.

—MARIE PARKER MILWAUKEE, WI

PREP: 25 MIN. • **BAKE:** 30 MIN. + COOLING • **MAKES:** 12 SERVINGS

- 4 large eggs, separated
- 3 tablespoons butter
- 8 ounces dark baking chocolate, chopped
- ⅓ cup plus ¼ cup sugar, divided
- 1 container (2½ ounces) prune baby food
- 1½ teaspoons vanilla extract
  Confectioners' sugar

1. Place egg whites in a small bowl; let stand at room temperature 30 minutes. Preheat oven to 350°. Coat a 9-in. springform pan with cooking spray; place on a baking sheet.

2. In a small saucepan, melt butter and chocolate over low heat, stirring constantly. Remove from heat; cool slightly. In a large bowl, beat egg yolks on high speed 3 minutes or until slightly thickened. Gradually add ⅓ cup sugar, beating until thick and lemon-colored. Beat in baby food, vanilla and chocolate mixture.

3. With clean beaters, beat egg whites on medium until soft peaks form. Gradually add remaining sugar, 1 tablespoon at a time, beating on high after each addition until sugar is dissolved. Continue beating until stiff glossy peaks form. Fold a fourth of the whites into chocolate mixture, then fold in remaining whites.

4. Pour into prepared pan. Bake 30-35 minutes or until a toothpick inserted in center comes out with moist crumbs. Cool on a wire rack 20 minutes. Loosen sides from pan with a knife; remove rim from pan. Cool cake completely. Dust with confectioners' sugar before serving.

Per 1 slice: 188 cal., 11g fat (6g sat. fat), 78mg chol., 50mg sod., 22g carb. (18g sugars, 2g fiber), 4g pro.

**SUE GRONHOLZ'S
PECAN PUMPKIN CHEESECAKE**
PAGE 191

Just Desserts

Every fabulous meal deserves a **sweet and happy ending.** So why not **treat your family** and friends to a tempting cheesecake, creamy pudding, bubbly cobbler or freezer favorite tonight? **No one can resist** these lovely desserts.

ARTHA SELF'S D-TIME CUSTARD E CREAM *PAGE 194*

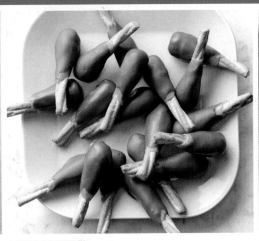

AMY LENTS' CHOCOLATE CARAMEL TURKEY LEGS *PAGE 192*

KATHRYN CONRAD'S STRAWBERRY SHAKES *PAGE 193*

WARM CHOCOLATE
MELTING CUPS

EAT SMART

Warm Chocolate Melting Cups

These creamy, chocolaty desserts are surprisingly rich and smooth. But what's even more surprising is that each one has fewer than 200 calories and only 6 grams of fat.

—**KISSA VAUGHN** TROY, TX

PREP: 20 MIN. • **BAKE:** 20 MIN. • **MAKES:** 10 SERVINGS

1¼ cups sugar, divided
½ cup baking cocoa
2 tablespoons all-purpose flour
⅛ teaspoon salt
¾ cup water
¾ cup plus 1 tablespoon semisweet chocolate chips
1 tablespoon brewed coffee
1 teaspoon vanilla extract
2 large eggs
1 large egg white
 Sliced fresh strawberries, optional

1. In a small saucepan, combine ¾ cup sugar, cocoa, flour and salt. Gradually stir in water. Bring to a boil; cook and stir for 2 minutes or until thickened. Remove from the heat; stir in the chocolate chips, coffee and vanilla until smooth. Transfer to a large bowl.
2. In another bowl, beat eggs and egg white until slightly thickened. Gradually add remaining sugar, beating until thick and lemon-colored. Fold into chocolate mixture.
3. Transfer to ten 4-oz. ramekins coated with cooking spray. Place ramekins in a baking pan; add 1 in. of boiling water to pan. Bake, uncovered, at 350° for 20-25 minutes or just until centers are set. Garnish with strawberries if desired. Serve immediately.
Per 1 dessert: 197 cal., 6g fat (3g sat. fat), 42mg chol., 51mg sod., 37g carb. (33g sugars, 2g fiber), 3g pro.

Patriotic Frozen Delight

My husband and I pick lots of fruit at berry farms in the area, then freeze our harvest to enjoy all year long. This frosty dessert showcases both blueberries and strawberries and has a refreshing lemon flavor.

—**BERNICE RUSS** BLADENBORO, NC

PREP: 10 MIN. + FREEZING • **MAKES:** 12 SERVINGS

1 can (14 ounces) sweetened condensed milk
⅓ cup lemon juice
2 teaspoons grated lemon peel
2 cups (16 ounces) plain yogurt
2 cups miniature marshmallows
½ cup chopped pecans
1 cup sliced fresh strawberries
1 cup fresh blueberries

In a bowl, combine the milk, lemon juice and peel. Stir in yogurt, marshmallows and pecans. Spread half into an ungreased 11x7-in. dish. Sprinkle with half of the strawberries and blueberries. Cover with the remaining yogurt mixture; top with the remaining berries. Cover and freeze. Remove from the freezer 15-20 minutes before serving.
Per 1 piece: 185 cal., 4g fat (0 sat. fat), 3mg chol., 71mg sod., 34g carb. (0 sugars, 0 fiber), 6g pro.
Diabetic Exchanges: 1 starch, 1 fruit, 1 fat.

PATRIOTIC
FROZEN DELIGHT

PATRIOTIC POPCORN
Follow Joan's directions below, but divide the popcorn; use both berry blue and fruit punch Jell-O.

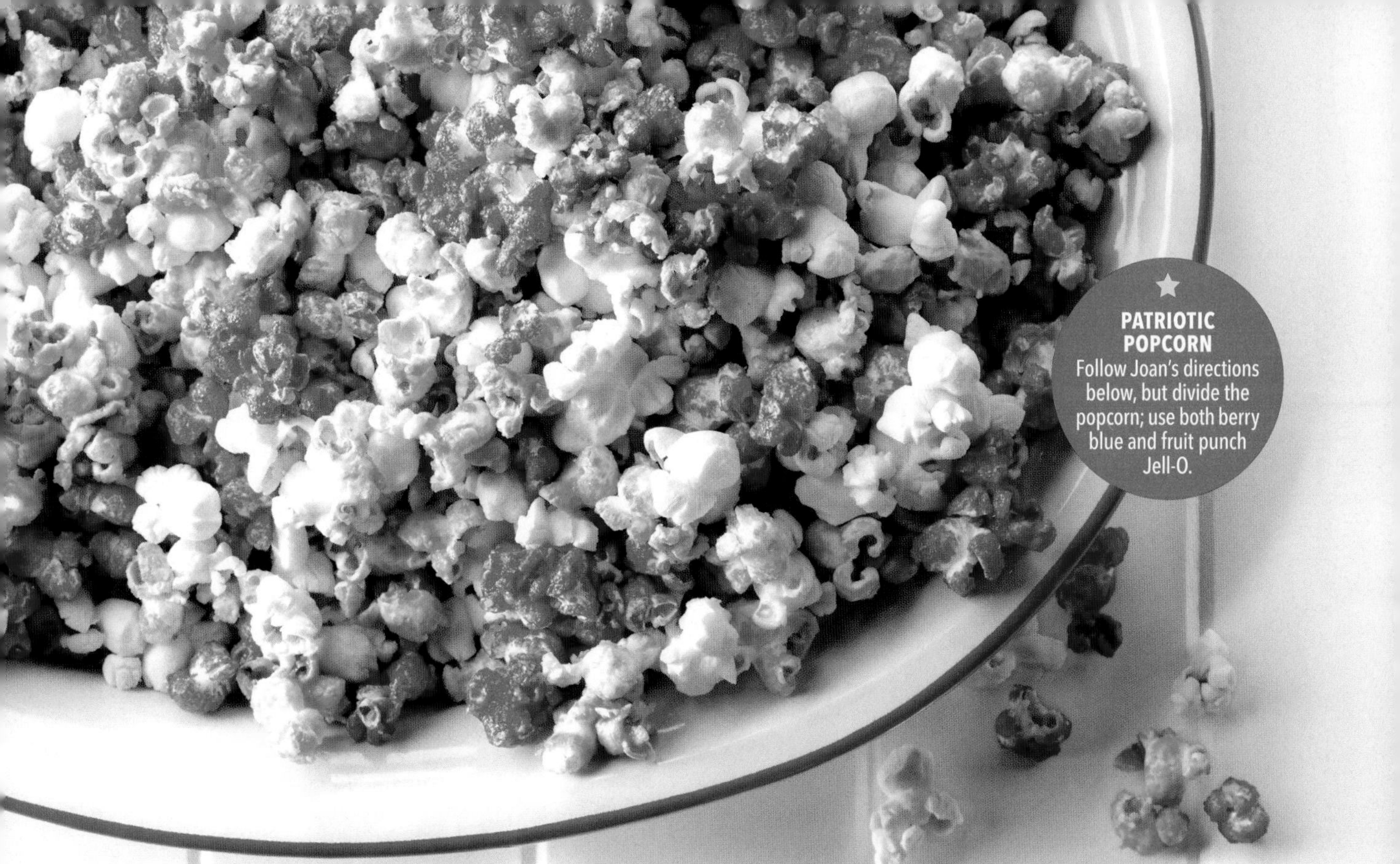

THE TASTY 10

HELLO, JELL-O

OUR FIELD EDITORS TAKE YOU OUT OF THE BOX WITH SUPER COOL SECRETS FOR THIS PANTRY STAPLE.

1 Movie time at our house finds us popping popcorn to yield about 8 cups, then adding about ¼ cup melted butter and one 4-oz. package of our favorite flavor of gelatin. Toss till all is mixed. My hubby loves grape, and I love peach or apricot.
—Joan Hallford, North Richland Hills, TX

2 Mix two 3-oz. packages of strawberry Jell-O, 6 cups of boiling water, 2 cups of sugar, 1 can of pineapple juice, frozen sliced strawberries, sliced lemons, 4 cups of orange juice, and 2 liters of Sprite for a fabulous punch!
—Lisa Allen, Joppa, AL

3 Add 1 cup each cottage cheese, prepared Jell-O (any flavor) and vanilla ice cream to a blender and mix well. This easy combination makes four high-protein mousselike desserts.
—Ann Marie Eberhart, Gig Harbor, WA

4 I stir 1-2 Tbsp. flavored gelatin powder into a container of Cool Whip for flavored frosting.
—Jennifer Patterson, Shoshone, ID

5 Dip large marshmallows in water and then roll in Jell-O. They crust over and make a sweet-sour snack perfect for a My Little Pony or rainbow-themed party.
—Angela Lively, Conroe, TX

6 My grandmother sprinkled strawberry-flavored gelatin over her award-winning pie filling before adding the top crust and baking. The added flavor always left everyone wondering what her secret ingredient was. I guess the secret is out!
—Anne Ormond, Dover, NH

7 A store-bought pound cake can be deliciously transformed by poking holes in it with a toothpick and then slowly pouring dissolved fruit gelatin over the top. Refrigerate until set; slice and serve with a dollop of whipped cream or Cool Whip.
—Ann Sheehy, Lawrence, MA

8 Add dissolved grape gelatin to blueberries and sweeten with honey. Pour into jars and voila! Shortcut blueberry jam.
—Raymonde Bourgeois, Swastika, ON

9 Prepare boxed angel food mix as directed, adding 2-3 Tbsp. Jell-O powder, whatever flavor you wish. Bake as directed.
—Ruth Hartunian-Alumbaugh, Willimantic, CT

10 For a quick salad, add dry orange or lime gelatin to cottage cheese. Stir in whipped topping and crushed pineapple.
—Sue Gronholz, Beaver Dam, WI

Skillet Caramel Apricot Grunt

Here's an old-fashioned pantry dessert made with ingredients you can easily keep on hand. Mix up a second batch of dry ingredients for the dumplings to save a few minutes next time you prepare it.

—**SHANNON ROUM** MILWAUKEE, WI

PREP: 20 MIN. + STANDING • **BAKE:** 20 MIN.
MAKES: 8 SERVINGS

- 2 cans (15¼ ounces each) apricot halves, undrained
- 2 teaspoons quick-cooking tapioca
- ⅓ cup packed brown sugar
- 1 tablespoon butter
- 1 tablespoon lemon juice

DUMPLINGS
- 1½ cups all-purpose flour
- ½ cup sugar
- 2 teaspoons baking powder
- 2 tablespoons cold butter
- ½ cup milk

TOPPING
- ¼ cup packed brown sugar
- 1 tablespoon water
  Half-and-half cream, optional

1. In a large saucepan, combine apricots and tapioca; let stand for 15 minutes. Add the brown sugar, butter and lemon juice. Cook and stir until mixture comes to a full boil. Reduce heat to low; keep warm.

2. For dumplings, in a large bowl, combine the flour, sugar and baking powder; cut in butter until crumbly. Add milk; mix just until combined. Pour warm fruit mixture into an ungreased 9- or 10-in. cast iron skillet. Drop the batter into six mounds onto fruit mixture.

3. Bake dessert, uncovered, at 425° for 15 minutes or until a toothpick inserted into a dumpling comes out clean. Stir together brown sugar and water; microwave 30 seconds or until sugar is dissolved, stirring frequently. Spoon over dumplings; bake 5 minutes longer. Serve with cream if desired.

Per 1 serving: 336 cal., 5g fat (3g sat. fat), 13mg chol., 170mg sod., 71g carb. (51g sugars, 2g fiber), 4g pro.

SKILLET CARAMEL
APRICOT GRUNT

Blueberry Cobbler

I was raised on a small farm in southeast Georgia, and tobacco was our main crop. Nowadays in our small town, we grow blueberries. This recipe was a recent winner at our blueberry festival.

—**EVELYN DUNLAP** NICOLLS, GA

PREP: 20 MIN. • **BAKE:** 40 MIN.
MAKES: 15 SERVINGS

- 6 cups fresh or frozen blueberries
- 1½ cups sugar
- ¼ cup water

CRUST
- ¾ cup butter, softened
- 1½ cups plus 2 tablespoons sugar, divided
- 3 large eggs
- 1 teaspoon vanilla extract
- 1½ cups all-purpose flour
- 1 teaspoon baking powder
- ½ teaspoon salt
- ¼ cup butter, melted
  Vanilla ice cream, optional

1. Place the blueberries in a greased 13x9-in. baking dish; set aside. In a small saucepan, bring sugar and water to a boil; cook and stir until sugar is dissolved. Pour over berries.

2. In a large bowl, cream butter and 1½ cups sugar until light and fluffy. Add eggs, one at a time, beating well after each addition. Beat in vanilla. Combine the flour, baking powder and salt; add to creamed mixture. Spread over berry mixture. Drizzle with melted butter; sprinkle with remaining sugar.

3. Bake at 350° for 40-45 minutes or until golden brown. Serve warm with ice cream if desired.

Per 1 serving: 362 cal., 13g fat (8g sat. fat), 74mg chol., 206mg sod., 60g carb. (48g sugars, 2g fiber), 3g pro.

✱
DID YOU KNOW?
Most vanilla comes from Madagascar and Reunion Island—formerly known as the Bourbon Islands—off the southeast coast of Africa. Bourbon vanilla is celebrated for its strong, clear vanilla flavor and creamy finish.

Pecan Pumpkin Cheesecake

I love to play with cheesecakes by mixing and matching flavors. This one with pumpkin and maple is the star of our Thanksgiving spread.

—SUE GRONHOLZ BEAVER DAM, WI

PREP: 30 MIN. • **BAKE:** 70 MIN. + CHILLING
MAKES: 16 SERVINGS

- 1 cup graham cracker crumbs
- 3 tablespoons granulated sugar
- 2 tablespoons butter, melted

FILLING
- 3 packages (8 ounces each) cream cheese, softened
- ½ cup packed brown sugar
- ⅓ cup granulated sugar
- ¼ cup maple syrup
- 3 large eggs, room temperature
- 1 can (15 ounces) solid-pack pumpkin
- 2 tablespoons cornstarch
- 3 teaspoons vanilla extract
- 1½ teaspoons pumpkin pie spice

TOPPING
- 1 cup heavy whipping cream
- ¾ cup maple syrup
- ½ cup chopped pecans, toasted

1. Preheat the oven to 325°. Wrap a double thickness of heavy-duty foil (about 18 in. square) around a greased 9-in. springform pan. Mix the cracker crumbs and the granulated sugar; stir in butter. Press onto bottom of prepared pan.

2. Beat cream cheese, sugars and maple syrup until smooth. Add eggs; beat on low just until blended. Whisk in pumpkin, cornstarch, vanilla and pie spice; pour over crust. Place the springform pan in a larger baking pan; add 1 in. of hot water to larger pan.

3. Bake until center is just set and top appears dull, 70-80 minutes. Remove springform pan from water bath. Cool cheesecake on a wire rack 10 minutes. Loosen sides from pan with a knife; remove the foil. Cool 1 hour longer. Refrigerate overnight, covering when completely cooled.

4. For topping, combine whipping cream and maple syrup in a small saucepan over medium heat; bring to a boil. Continue boiling it, stirring occasionally, until slightly thickened, 15-20 minutes. Stir in toasted pecans. Refrigerate until cold.

5. Remove rim from pan. Stir topping; spoon over chilled cheesecake.

Note: To toast nuts, bake in a shallow pan in a 350° oven for 5-10 minutes or cook in a skillet over low heat until they are lightly browned, stirring occasionally.

Per 1 slice: 393 cal., 26g fat (13g sat. fat), 106mg chol., 220mg sod., 38g carb. (30g sugars, 1g fiber), 5g pro.

MEMAW'S BANANA PUDDING

Memaw's Banana Pudding

Creamy and rich, this homemade banana pudding recipe is so easy. Layer it in a trifle bowl for a pretty presentation.

—RUTH KIZER SHIDLER, OK

PREP: 30 MIN. + CHILLING • **COOK:** 15 MIN.
MAKES: 12 SERVINGS

- 3 cups whole milk
- 2 cups half-and-half cream
- 6 large egg yolks
- 1½ cups sugar
- ½ cup cornstarch
- 1 teaspoon salt
- 3 tablespoons butter, softened
- 2 teaspoons vanilla extract
- 1 package (12 ounces) vanilla wafers
- 4 medium bananas, sliced
- 1 carton (12 ounces) frozen whipped topping, thawed

1. In a large heavy saucepan, bring milk and cream to a simmer. In a bowl, whisk together the egg yolks, sugar, cornstarch and salt. Whisk a small amount of hot milk mixture into egg yolk mixture; return all to the pan, whisking constantly.

2. Bring to a gentle boil; cook and stir 2 minutes. Remove from heat. Stir in butter and vanilla. Cool 15 minutes, stirring occasionally.

3. Line bottom of a 3-qt. trifle or other glass bowl with half of the vanilla wafers; top with half of the bananas and half of the pudding. Repeat layers. Press plastic wrap onto surface of pudding; refrigerate until cold. Just before serving, remove plastic and top with whipped topping.

Per 1 serving: 509 cal., 22g fat (12g sat. fat), 131mg chol., 380mg sod., 70g carb. (51g sugars, 2g fiber), 6g pro.

PECAN PUMPKIN CHEESECAKE

Apple Corn Bread Crisp

With its quick prep time, this warm apple crisp makes a smart dessert for any fall night. It reminds me of the recipe my grandmother would serve after our big family seafood dinners. It's absolutely wonderful topped with ice cream.

—JULIE PETERSON CROFTON, MD

PREP: 10 MIN. • **BAKE:** 30 MIN.
MAKES: 6 SERVINGS

- 4 cups peeled sliced tart apples (about 4-5 medium)
- ¾ cup packed brown sugar, divided
- 1 package (8½ ounces) corn bread/ muffin mix
- ½ cup quick-cooking oats
- 1 teaspoon ground cinnamon (or to taste)
- 5 tablespoons cold butter, cubed

1. Preheat oven to 350°. Stir together apples and ¼ cup brown sugar; set aside. Combine corn bread mix, oats, cinnamon and remaining brown sugar. Cut in butter until crumbly.
2. Add ½ cup corn bread mixture to apples. Transfer to a greased 8-in. square baking dish. Sprinkle the remaining corn bread mixture over top. Bake until filling is bubbly and topping golden brown, 30-35 minutes. Serve warm.
Per serving: 421 cal., 15g fat (7g sat. fat), 26mg chol., 413mg sod., 70g carb. (43g sugars, 5g fiber), 4g pro.

FUDGE POPS

APPLE CORN BREAD CRISP

(5)INGREDIENTS Fudge Pops

This chocolate frozen dessert makes the perfect summer treat! Invite your kids into the kitchen to help you stir the pudding.

—RUTH ANN STELFOX RAYMOND, AB

PREP: 10 MIN. + COOLING
COOK: 10 MIN. + FREEZING
MAKES: ABOUT 1 DOZEN

- 1 package (3.4 ounces) cook-and-serve chocolate pudding mix
- 3 cups whole milk
- ¼ cup sugar
- ½ cup heavy whipping cream, whipped
  Freezer pop molds or paper cups (3 ounces each) and wooden pop sticks

In a large saucepan over medium heat, combine pudding, milk and sugar; bring to a boil. Cook, stirring, for 2 minutes. Cool 30 minutes, stirring often. Fold in cream. Pour into plastic molds or 3-oz. paper cups; attach lids to molds or, if using cups, top with foil and insert pop sticks through foil. Freeze until firm, 3-4 hours.
Per 1 pop: 107 cal., 5g fat (3g sat. fat), 16mg chol., 58mg sod., 12g carb. (11g sugars, 0 fiber), 2g pro.

(5)INGREDIENTS FAST FIX
Chocolate Caramel Turkey Legs
(PICTURED ON P. 187)

Mention turkey legs made of pretzels and chocolate, and the kids come running. Let them help by unwrapping caramels for this easy no-bake treat.

—AMY LENTS GRAND FORKS, ND

START TO FINISH: 20 MIN.
MAKES: 20 SERVINGS

- 40 caramels
- 20 honey wheat braided pretzel twists
- 3 ounces milk chocolate, melted

Microwave the caramels on high until they're softened, 10-15 seconds. Mold two softened caramels around the lower half of each braided pretzel to resemble a turkey leg. Dip in melted chocolate; allow excess to drip off. Place on waxed paper; let stand until set. Store in an airtight container up to 1-2 weeks.
Per 1 piece: 112 cal., 3g fat (1g sat. fat), 2mg chol., 102mg sod., 21g carb. (16g sugars, 0 fiber), 1g pro.

Rhubarb Berry No-Bake Cheesecake

As soon as the strawberries and rhubarb come into season, I pull out this recipe so I'm ready to make it when the fruit is at its peak. The sweet-tart flavor simply can't be beat. This easy cheesecake truly tastes like springtime!

—**LEEANN MCCUE** CHARLOTTE, NC

PREP: 35 MIN. + CHILLING
MAKES: 8 SERVINGS

- 1 package (8 ounces) cream cheese, softened
- 1 can (14 ounces) sweetened condensed milk
- 6 tablespoons lemon juice
- 1 teaspoon grated lemon peel
- 1 teaspoon vanilla extract
  Dash salt
- 1 graham cracker crust (9 inches)

TOPPING

- 2 cups sliced fresh or frozen rhubarb
- ½ cup sugar
- ¼ cup water
- 1 pint fresh strawberries, hulled and halved lengthwise
- 2 teaspoons lemon juice

1. In a large bowl, beat cream cheese and milk until smooth. Beat in the lemon juice, lemon peel, vanilla and salt; pour into crust. Refrigerate the cheesecake, covered, 2 hours.

2. Meanwhile, in a large saucepan, bring rhubarb, sugar and water to a boil. Reduce the heat; simmer, uncovered, 6-8 minutes or until rhubarb is tender. Drain.

3. Stir in strawberries and lemon juice. Refrigerate until cold. Serve with cheesecake.

Per 1 piece: 435 cal., 20g fat (10g sat. fat), 48mg chol., 289mg sod., 59g carb. (53g sugars, 2g fiber), 8g pro.

---

⑤ INGREDIENTS FAST FIX ▶
Strawberry Shakes
(PICTURED ON P. 187)

Cool off with a thick and rich treat that will remind you of a malt shoppe!

—**KATHRYN CONRAD** MILWAUKEE, WI

START TO FINISH: 5 MIN.
MAKES: 2 SERVINGS

- ⅓ cup 2% milk
- 1½ cups vanilla ice cream
- ½ cup frozen unsweetened strawberries
- 1 tablespoon strawberry preserves

In a blender, combine all ingredients; cover and process until smooth. Pour into chilled glasses; serve immediately.

Per 1 cup: 257 cal., 12g fat (7g sat. fat), 47mg chol., 100mg sod., 35g carb. (28g sugars, 1g fiber), 5g pro.

GLAZED DOUGHNUT HOLES

⑤ INGREDIENTS
Glazed Doughnut Holes

The fruity tang and pretty pink hue of these easy treats make them irresistible. Surprise someone you love with a batch of these fancy doughnut holes.

—*TASTE OF HOME* TEST KITCHEN

PREP: 5 MIN. + STANDING
MAKES: 1 DOZEN

- 2 cups confectioners' sugar
- 3 to 5 tablespoons frozen grape, cherry-pomegranate or cranberry juice concentrate, thawed
- 12 doughnut holes

Whisk together sugar and enough juice concentrate to achieve a thick glaze. Dip doughnut holes in glaze; transfer to waxed paper.

Per 1 doughnut hole: 225 cal., 4g fat (2g sat. fat), 1mg chol., 69mg sod., 49g carb. (44g sugars, 0 fiber), 1g pro.

Lemon Glazed Doughnut Holes: Whisk confectioners' sugar and 5 tablespoons lemon juice until smooth. Dip doughnut holes; transfer to waxed paper.

RHUBARB BERRY NO-BAKE CHEESECAKE

Old-Time Custard Ice Cream

(PICTURED ON P. 187)

I think my most memorable summertime dessert for get-togethers has always been homemade ice cream. This recipe is so rich and creamy and the perfect splurge on a hot summer afternoon.

—**MARTHA SELF** MONTGOMERY, TX

PREP: 55 MIN. + CHILLING
PROCESS: 55 MIN./BATCH + FREEZING
MAKES: 2¾ QUARTS

- 1½ cups sugar
- ¼ cup all-purpose flour
- ½ teaspoon salt
- 4 cups whole milk
- 4 large eggs, lightly beaten
- 2 pints heavy whipping cream
- 3 tablespoons vanilla extract

1. In a large heavy saucepan, combine sugar, flour and salt. Gradually add milk until smooth. Cook and stir over medium heat until thickened and bubbly. Reduce heat to low; cook and stir 2 minutes longer. Remove from the heat.

2. In a small bowl, whisk a small amount of hot mixture into eggs; return all to pan, whisking constantly. Bring to a gentle boil; cook and stir 2 minutes. Remove from the heat immediately.

3. Quickly transfer to a large bowl; place bowl in a pan of ice water. Stir gently and occasionally for 2 minutes. Press plastic wrap onto surface of custard. Refrigerate for several hours or overnight.

4. Stir the cream and vanilla into the custard. Fill cylinder of the ice cream freezer two-thirds full; freeze it according to the manufacturer's directions. (Refrigerate remaining mixture until ready to freeze.) Transfer the ice cream to freezer containers, allowing headspace for expansion. Freeze 2-4 hours or until firm. Repeat with the remaining ice cream mixture.

Per ½ cup: 252 cal., 18g fat (11g sat. fat), 88mg chol., 98mg sod., 18g carb. (17g sugars, 0 fiber), 4g pro.

Mudslide Cheesecake

Change up cheesecakes with different liqueur flavorings. This mudslide version with coffee and Irish cream is my husband's favorite.

—**SUE GRONHOLZ** BEAVER DAM, WI

PREP: 30 MIN.
BAKE: 1 HOUR + COOLING
MAKES: 16 SERVINGS

- 1 cup chocolate wafer crumbs
- 3 tablespoons sugar
- 2 tablespoons butter, melted

FILLING

- 1 cup (6 ounces) semisweet chocolate chips
- 4 packages (8 ounces each) cream cheese, softened
- 1½ cups sugar
- 4 tablespoons all-purpose flour
- 4 large eggs, room temperature
- 2 teaspoons vanilla extract
- 2 tablespoons coffee liqueur
- ¾ cup Irish cream liqueur

GANACHE

- ½ cup (3 ounces) semisweet chocolate chips
- ¼ cup heavy whipping cream

1. Preheat the oven to 325°. Wrap a double thickness of heavy-duty foil (about 18 in. square) around a greased 9-in. springform pan. Mix the cookie crumbs and sugar; stir in butter. Press onto bottom of prepared pan.

2. To prepare filling, microwave chocolate chips on high until melted, about 1 minute. Beat cream cheese and sugar until smooth. Add flour; mix well. Add eggs and vanilla; beat on low just until blended. Measure out 2 cups batter, and stir in coffee liqueur; add melted chocolate chips and stir until blended. Pour over crust. Add Irish cream liqueur to remaining batter; spoon over chocolate layer. Place springform pan in a larger baking pan; add 1 in. of hot water to larger pan.

3. Bake until center is just set and top appears dull, 60-75 minutes. Remove springform pan from water bath. Cool cheesecake on a wire rack 10 minutes. Loosen sides from pan with a knife; remove the foil. Cool 1 hour longer. Refrigerate overnight, covering when completely cooled.

4. For ganache, microwave chocolate chips and whipping cream on high until chips melt; cool slightly. Remove rim from pan; spread ganache on chilled cheesecake.

Per 1 slice: 485 cal., 31g fat (16g sat. fat), 118mg chol., 280mg sod., 44g carb. (37g sugars, 1g fiber), 6g pro.

MUDSLIDE CHEESECAKE

BLACK FOREST PANETTONE PUDDING

Black Forest Panettone Pudding

My chocolate-cherry bread pudding uses panettone, the holiday bread people often receive but aren't sure how to use. I make a glorious sauce for it using ice cream.
—**DEVON DELANEY** WESTPORT, CT

PREP: 15 MIN. • **BAKE:** 40 MIN.
MAKES: 10 SERVINGS

- 3 large eggs
- 1½ cups half-and-half cream
- 1½ teaspoons almond extract
- 6 cups cubed panettone bread (2-inch cubes, about 12 ounces)
- 1 cup semisweet chocolate chips
- 1 cup sliced fresh or frozen pitted dark sweet cherries, thawed
- 1 cup sliced almonds, toasted

VANILLA BUTTER SAUCE
- ¼ cup unsalted butter
- ¼ cup packed light brown sugar
- 1 cup vanilla bean ice cream

1. Preheat the oven to 350°. Whisk together eggs, cream and extract. Add the panettone cubes; soak 3 minutes, turning to coat. Meanwhile, pulse the chocolate chips in a food processor until finely ground.

2. In a greased 9 in. deep-dish pie plate, layer half of each of the following: cubed panettone, ground chocolate, cherries and almonds. Repeat the layers. Bake until a knife inserted in the center comes out clean, 40-45 minutes.

3. Meanwhile, for sauce, melt butter over medium heat in a small saucepan. Whisk in brown sugar until sauce resembles caramel. Stir in ice cream; simmer over low heat until it coats a spoon, about 5 minutes. Transfer to a bowl to cool completely. The sauce will thicken as it cools. Serve with bread pudding.

Notes: Panettone can be found in stores mostly during the holiday season and online during the rest of the year. To toast the nuts, bake in a shallow pan in a 350° oven for 5-10 minutes or cook in a skillet over low heat until lightly browned, stirring occasionally.

Per 1 piece with 2 tablespoons sauce: 420 cal., 25g fat (12g sat. fat), 108mg chol., 106mg sod., 42g carb. (32g sugars, 3g fiber), 8g pro.

⑤INGREDIENTS Honey Caramel Apples

When apple season arrives, we roll these caramel-dipped treats in chopped honey-roasted peanuts. For a different crunch factor, use salted pecans and drizzle them with homemade fudge.
—**CORI COOPER** FLAGSTAFF, AZ

PREP: 5 MIN. • **COOK:** 35 MIN. + STANDING
MAKES: 6 SERVINGS

- 1 cup heavy whipping cream
- 1 cup honey
- 6 wooden pop sticks
- 6 medium green apples, chilled
  Chopped honey-roasted peanuts, optional

1. In a large saucepan, combine whipping cream and honey over medium heat. Bring to a boil; reduce heat and simmer until thermometer reads 260°, about 30 minutes. Remove the blend from heat; allow to thicken 5-7 minutes, stirring occasionally.

2. Meanwhile, insert a wooden pop stick into the core of each apple. Dip apples in caramel mixture, rolling to coat evenly. If desired, roll in honey-roasted peanuts. Place on waxed paper; refrigerate or store in a cool location until caramel is set, about 30 minutes.

Per 1 caramel apple: 386 cal., 15g fat (9g sat. fat), 55mg chol., 19mg sod., 68g carb. (63g sugars, 4g fiber), 1g pro.

HONEY CARAMEL APPLES

HONEY PEAR
CHEESECAKE

Honey Pear Cheesecake

We have two pear trees, so I'm always adding the fruit to new desserts. When I want some extra zing, I stir ¼ cup chopped crystallized ginger into the filling.

—**NANCY ZIMMERMAN** CAPE MAY COURT HOUSE, NJ

PREP: 25 MIN. • **BAKE:** 1½ HOURS + CHILLING • **MAKES:** 12 SERVINGS

- 1½ cups crushed gingersnap cookies (about 30)
- ¼ cup sugar
- 4 to 6 tablespoons butter, melted

FILLING

- 3 packages (8 ounces each) cream cheese, softened
- 1 cup honey, divided
- 1 tablespoon lemon juice
- 2 teaspoons minced fresh gingerroot
- 4 large eggs, lightly beaten
- 3 peeled and chopped medium pears (about 1½ cups), divided
- ⅓ cup golden raisins
- 1 tablespoon butter
- 1 cup chopped pecans, toasted

1. Preheat oven to 325°. Securely wrap a double thickness of heavy-duty foil (about 18 in. square) around and under a greased 9-in. springform pan. Combine the crushed gingersnaps and sugar; stir in 4 tablespoons butter, adding more as necessary. Press onto bottom and 1½ in. up sides of prepared pan.

2. Beat cream cheese until fluffy, gradually adding ⅔ cup honey, lemon juice and minced ginger. Add eggs; beat on low speed just until blended. Fold in 1 cup chopped pears and raisins. Pour into crust. Place springform pan in a larger baking pan; add 1 in. of hot water to larger pan. Bake until the center is just set and top appears dull, for about 1½ to 1¾ hours. Remove from oven; remove springform from water bath.

3. Cool cheesecake on a wire rack 10 minutes. Loosen sides from pan with a knife; remove foil. Cool 1 hour longer. Refrigerate overnight, covering when completely cooled. Remove rim from pan.

4. In a large skillet, melt butter over medium heat. Add remaining honey and pears; cook and stir until pears are tender. Stir in pecans. Top cake with pear-pecan mixture.

Note: To toast nuts, bake in a shallow pan in a 350° oven for 5-10 minutes or cook in a skillet over low heat until lightly browned, stirring occasionally.

Per 1 slice: 552 cal., 36g fat (17g sat. fat), 142mg chol., 374mg sod., 54g carb. (40g sugars, 3g fiber), 8g pro.

EAT SMART **5 INGREDIENTS** # Honeydew Granita

This is a very refreshing summer treat when melons are ripe and flavorful. It's also so easy to make. I like to garnish each serving with a sprig of mint or a small slice of honeydew.

—**BONNIE HAWKINS** ELKHORN, WI

PREP: 10 MIN. • **COOK:** 5 MIN. + FREEZING • **MAKES:** 5½ CUPS

- 1 cup sugar
- 1 cup water
- 6 cups cubed peeled honeydew
- 2 tablespoons sweet white wine

1. In a small saucepan, bring the sugar and water to a boil over medium-high heat. Cook and stir until sugar is dissolved. Cool.

2. Pulse honeydew, sugar syrup and wine in batches in a food processor until smooth, 1-2 minutes. Transfer to an 8-in. square dish. Freeze 1 hour. Stir with a fork. Freeze, stirring every 30 minutes, until frozen, 2-3 hours longer. Stir again with a fork just before serving.

Per ½ cup: 107 cal., 0 fat (0 sat. fat), 0 chol., 17mg sod., 27g carb. (26g sugars, 1g fiber), 1g pro.

Diabetic Exchanges: 1½ starch, ½ fruit.

Honeydew Sorbet: After processing honeydew mixture, pour into the cylinder of an ice cream freezer; freeze according to manufacturer's directions. Transfer to a freezer container; freeze for 4 hours or until firm.

HONEYDEW
GRANITA

RED VELVET CHEESECAKE

Red Velvet Cheesecake

This cheesecake will become a fixture on your holiday menu. The red velvet filling is spiked with cocoa, baked in a chocolate cookie crumb crust, and topped with fluffy cream cheese frosting.

—**KAREN DIVELY** CHAPIN, SC

PREP: 30 MIN. • **BAKE:** 1 HOUR + CHILLING • **MAKES:** 16 SERVINGS

- 17 chocolate cream-filled chocolate sandwich cookies, crushed
- ¼ cup butter, melted
- 1 tablespoon sugar

FILLING
- 3 packages (8 ounces each) cream cheese, softened
- 1½ cups sugar
- 1 cup (8 ounces) sour cream
- ½ cup buttermilk
- 3 tablespoons baking cocoa
- 2 teaspoons vanilla extract
- 4 large eggs, lightly beaten
- 1 bottle (1 ounce) red food coloring

FROSTING
- 1 package (3 ounces) cream cheese, softened
- ¼ cup butter, softened
- 2 cups confectioners' sugar
- 1 teaspoon vanilla extract

1. Place a greased 9-in. springform pan on a double thickness of heavy-duty foil (about 18 in. square). Securely wrap foil around pan.

2. In a small bowl, combine the cookie crumbs, butter and sugar. Press onto the bottom of prepared pan.

3. In a large bowl, beat cream cheese and sugar until smooth. Beat in the sour cream, buttermilk, cocoa and vanilla. Add eggs; beat on low speed just until combined. Stir in food coloring. Pour over crust. Place springform pan in a large baking pan; add 1 in. of hot water to larger pan.

4. Bake at 325° for 60-70 minutes or until center is just set and top appears dull. Remove springform pan from water bath. Cool on a wire rack for 10 minutes. Carefully run a knife around edge of pan to loosen; cool 1 hour longer. Refrigerate overnight. Remove sides of pan.

5. For frosting, in a small bowl, beat cream cheese and butter until fluffy. Beat in confectioners' sugar and vanilla until smooth. Frost top of cheesecake. Chill until serving.
Per 1 slice: 463 cal., 29g fat (17g sat. fat), 131mg chol., 276mg sod., 46g carb. (39g sugars, 1g fiber), 7g pro.

Cranberry Peach Cobbler

This cobbler is a little non-traditional, but it will soon be at the front of your recipe list because it's an easy and tasty dessert. Serve it warm with French vanilla ice cream.

—**GRACE SANDVIGEN** ROCHESTER, NY

PREP: 15 MIN. • **BAKE:** 45 MIN. • **MAKES:** 15 SERVINGS

- ½ cup butter, melted
- 2 cans (29 ounces each) sliced peaches
- 1 package (15.6 ounces) cranberry-orange quick bread mix
- 1 large egg
- 2 tablespoons grated orange peel, divided
- ⅓ cup dried cranberries
- ⅓ cup sugar

1. Preheat oven to 375°. Pour butter into a 13x9-in. baking dish. Drain peaches, reserving 1 cup juice. Pat peaches dry and set aside. In a large bowl, combine quick bread mix, egg, 1 tablespoon orange peel and reserved peach juice.

2. Drop batter by tablespoonfuls over butter, spreading slightly. Arrange the peaches over the top; sprinkle with cranberries. Combine sugar and remaining orange peel; sprinkle over peaches. Bake until golden brown, about 45-50 minutes. Serve warm.
Per serving: 271 cal., 10g fat (5g sat. fat), 33mg chol., 193mg sod., 44g carb. (32g sugars, 1g fiber), 1g pro.

CRANBERRY PEACH COBBLER

**MICHELLE BERAN'S
ZIPPY PORK CHILI**
PAGE 204

Potluck Pleasers

Dazzle the crowd at your next neighborhood gathering, church social or dinner party with the special **appetizers, main dishes, drinks, salads and snacks** you'll find here. Folks will line up for a helping—and go back for seconds.

**KELLY ALANIZ'S
SHRIMP & CUCUMBER ROUNDS**
PAGE 203

**ANNETTE GRAHL'S
MINI HOT BROWNS**
PAGE 207

**JEANNE HOLT'S
COOKIE SWIRL COBBLER**
PAGE 208

EAT SMART

Firehouse Chili

As one of the cooks at the firehouse, I used to prepare meals for 10 men. This chili was among their favorites.

—RICHARD CLEMENTS SAN DIMAS, CA

PREP: 20 MIN. • **COOK:** 1½ HOURS
MAKES: 12 SERVINGS (ABOUT 3 QUARTS)

- 2 tablespoons canola oil
- 4 pounds lean ground beef (90% lean)
- 2 medium onions, chopped
- 1 medium green pepper, chopped
- 4 cans (16 ounces each) kidney beans, rinsed and drained
- 3 cans (14½ ounces each) stewed tomatoes, cut up
- 1 can (14½ ounces) beef broth
- 3 tablespoons chili powder
- 2 tablespoons ground coriander
- 2 tablespoons ground cumin
- 4 garlic cloves, minced
- 1 teaspoon dried oregano

In a Dutch oven, heat canola oil over medium heat. Brown beef in batches, crumbling meat, until no longer pink; drain. Add onions and green pepper; cook until tender. Return meat to Dutch oven. Stir in remaining ingredients. Bring to a boil. Reduce heat; simmer, covered, until flavors are blended, about 1½ hours.

Per 1 cup: 444 cal., 16g fat (5g sat. fat), 94mg chol., 703mg sod., 36g carb. (9g sugars, 10g fiber), 41g pro.
Diabetic Exchanges: 5 lean meat, 2½ starch, ½ fat.

ORANGE-GLAZED
PORK LOIN

FIREHOUSE CHILI

EAT SMART

Orange-Glazed Pork Loin

This amazing pork loin sprinkled with thyme and ginger is one of the best pork recipes I've ever tried. I often serve it to dinner guests because it's both elegant and easy.

—LYNNETTE MIETE ALNA, ME

PREP: 10 MIN. • **BAKE:** 1 HOUR 20 MIN. + STANDING
MAKES: 16 SERVINGS

- 1 teaspoon salt
- 1 garlic clove, minced
- ¼ teaspoon dried thyme
- ¼ teaspoon ground ginger
- ¼ teaspoon pepper
- 1 boneless pork loin roast (5 pounds)

GLAZE

- 1 cup orange juice
- ¼ cup packed brown sugar
- 1 tablespoon Dijon mustard
- ⅓ cup cold water
- 1 tablespoon cornstarch

1. Preheat oven to 350°. Combine the first five ingredients; rub over roast. Place fat side up on a rack in a shallow roasting pan. Bake, uncovered, for 1 hour.

2. Meanwhile, in a saucepan over medium heat, combine orange juice, brown sugar and mustard. In a small bowl, mix water and cornstarch until smooth. Add to orange juice mixture. Bring to a boil; cook and stir 2 minutes. Reserve 1 cup glaze for serving; brush half of the remaining glaze over roast.

3. Bake until a thermometer reads 145°, 20-40 minutes longer, brushing occasionally with remaining glaze. Let stand 10 minutes before slicing. Reheat reserved glaze; serve with roast.

Per 4 ounces cooked pork: 199 cal., 7g fat (2g sat. fat), 71mg chol., 212mg sod., 6g carb. (5g sugars, 0 fiber), 28g pro.
Diabetic Exchanges: 4 lean meat, ½ starch.

Tuscan Truffles

For holiday potlucks, I make an appetizer truffle out of prosciutto, figs and toasted pine nuts. The creaminess comes from goat cheese and mascarpone.
—**ROXANNE CHAN** ALBANY, CA

PREP: 25 MIN. + CHILLING • **MAKES:** 3 DOZEN

- 2 logs (4 ounces each) fresh goat cheese
- 1 carton (8 ounces) mascarpone cheese
- 6 tablespoons grated Parmesan cheese
- 3 garlic cloves, minced
- 1½ teaspoons olive oil
- 1½ teaspoons white balsamic vinegar
- ¾ teaspoon grated lemon peel
- 6 tablespoons finely chopped prosciutto
- 6 tablespoons finely chopped dried figs
- 3 tablespoons minced fresh parsley
- ¼ teaspoon pepper
- 1 cup pine nuts, toasted and chopped

In a large bowl, combine the first 11 ingredients until well blended. Shape into 36 balls; roll in pine nuts. Refrigerate, covered, until chilled.

Note: To toast pine nuts, bake in a shallow pan in a 350° oven for 5-10 minutes or cook in a skillet over low heat until lightly browned, stirring occasionally.

Per 1 appetizer: 80 cal., 7g fat (3g sat. fat), 15mg chol., 90mg sod., 3g carb. (1g sugars, 0 fiber), 3g pro.

BAKED PUMPKIN
GOAT CHEESE
ALFREDO WITH BACON

Baked Pumpkin Goat Cheese Alfredo with Bacon

This is a unique and delicious pasta, perfect for fall. I made this for my girlfriends, and all of them asked for the recipe!
—**ASHLEY LECKER** GREEN BAY, WI

PREP: 35 MIN. • **BAKE:** 20 MIN. • **MAKES:** 10 SERVINGS

- 1 pound cellentani
- 4 tablespoons butter
- 1 tablespoon olive oil
- 3 garlic cloves, minced
- 2 shallots, minced
- 2 cups heavy whipping cream
- 1 cup whole milk
- 4 ounces crumbled goat cheese
- ½ cup grated Parmesan cheese
- ½ cup canned pumpkin
- ½ teaspoon white pepper
- 2 tablespoons chopped fresh sage

TOPPINGS
- 1 pound bacon strips, cooked and crumbled
- 2 ounces crumbled goat cheese
- ¼ cup grated Parmesan cheese

1. Preheat oven to 350°. Cook pasta according to package instructions.

2. Meanwhile, in a large saucepan, heat butter and olive oil over medium heat. Add garlic and shallots; cook and stir for 1-2 minutes. Add the next six ingredients. Reduce heat to low. Cook, stirring constantly, until reduced, 6-8 minutes. Add sage. Remove from heat.

3. Drain pasta; gently stir into cream sauce. Transfer to a greased 13x9-in. baking dish. Top with bacon, goat cheese and Parmesan. Bake, covered, about 15 minutes. Uncover; bake until the cheeses are melted, about 5 minutes longer.

Per 1 cup: 559 cal., 37g fat (20g sat. fat), 111mg chol., 535mg sod., 40g carb. (5g sugars, 3g fiber), 19g pro.

TUSCAN TRUFFLES
Roxanne Chan
Albany, CA

SPECIAL
MUSHROOM
LASAGNA

(5) INGREDIENTS
Epiphany Ham

I wanted to cook a ham but didn't have the ingredients for my usual glaze recipe, so I made substitutions. You can, too! Instead of black cherry, try another flavored soda, or use sweet-and-sour sauce in place of duck sauce.

—**EDITH GRIFFITH** HAVRE DE GRACE, MD

PREP: 10 MIN. • **BAKE:** 3 HOURS
MAKES: 12 SERVINGS

- 1 fully cooked bone-in ham (8 to 10 pounds; not spiral cut)
- 1 can (12 ounces) black cherry soda
- 2 teaspoons Chinese five-spice powder
- ⅔ cup duck sauce

1. Preheat oven to 350°. Place ham on a rack in a baking pan or dish; pour soda over ham. Sprinkle with five-spice powder. Cover with aluminum foil; bake 30 minutes.

2. Remove foil and discard. Baste with duck sauce; return to oven and bake, uncovered, until a thermometer reads 140°, about 2½ hours, basting again halfway through baking.

Per 6 ounces ham: 303 cal., 8g fat (3g sat. fat), 133mg chol., 1659mg sod., 13g carb. (9g sugars, 0 fiber), 45g pro.

EPIPHANY HAM

Special Mushroom Lasagna

This rich, cheesy recipe proves that casseroles can be both convenient and classy. If you want to take it even further, stir in fresh crabmeat.

—**AMANDA BLAIR** LEBANON, OR

PREP: 2 HOURS • **BAKE:** 55 MIN. + STANDING
MAKES: 12 SERVINGS

- 6 tablespoons butter, divided
- 3½ pounds sliced baby portobello mushrooms
- 1 large onion, thinly sliced
- 1 cup marsala wine
- 8 garlic cloves, minced, divided
- 2 tablespoons dried minced onion
- 12 uncooked lasagna noodles
- 5 tablespoons all-purpose flour
- 1 teaspoon onion powder
- ½ teaspoon white pepper
- ½ teaspoon ground nutmeg
- ¼ teaspoon cayenne pepper
- 3 cups whole milk
- 1 package (8 ounces) cream cheese, softened
- ½ cup minced chives
- 1 jar (2 ounces) diced pimientos, drained
- 1 tablespoon lemon juice
- ½ teaspoon grated lemon peel
- ½ teaspoon salt
- 2 cups grated Parmesan cheese
- 6 ounces fresh crabmeat, optional

CRUMB TOPPING
- 1 French bread demi-baguette (about 4 ounces)
- ½ cup grated Parmesan cheese
- 2 tablespoons butter, melted
- ½ cup minced chives

1. In a Dutch oven, melt 2 tablespoons butter over medium heat. Add sliced mushrooms and onion; saute until tender. Add wine, four minced garlic cloves and minced onion; bring to a boil. Cook until liquid is absorbed, about 30 minutes.

2. Meanwhile, cook lasagna noodles according to package directions. In a large saucepan over medium heat, melt remaining butter. Stir in next five ingredients and remaining garlic until blended; gradually add milk. Bring to a boil; cook and stir until thickened, 1-2 minutes. Stir in next six ingredients until blended. Remove from heat.

3. Preheat oven to 350°. Drain lasagna noodles. Spread 1 cup cream cheese sauce in a greased 13x9-in. baking pan. Layer with three noodles, 1 cup sauce, a third of the mushroom mixture and ⅔ cup Parmesan cheese. Repeat layers, adding crabmeat if desired, between mushrooms and Parmesan. Layer with three more noodles, 1 cup sauce, remaining mushroom mixture and remaining Parmesan cheese. Top with remaining noodles and sauce.

4. For crumb topping, pulse baguette, cheese and butter in a food processor until finely chopped. Stir in chives. Sprinkle over lasagna. Bake, covered, about 50 minutes. Uncover; bake until bubbly, 5-10 minutes longer. Let stand 10 minutes before cutting.

Per 1 piece without crabmeat: 423 cal., 22g fat (13g sat. fat), 60mg chol., 616mg sod., 41g carb. (9g sugars, 3g fiber), 17g pro.

Shrimp & Cucumber Rounds

(PICTURED ON P. 199)

I always make these appetizers for get-togethers. They're easy to prepare and a snappy addition to any party or potluck.
—**KELLY ALANIZ** EUREKA, CA

START TO FINISH: 25 MIN.
MAKES: 3 DOZEN

- ½ pound cooked shrimp, peeled, deveined and finely chopped
- ½ cup reduced-fat mayonnaise
- 2 green onions, thinly sliced
- 1 celery rib, finely chopped
- 1 teaspoon dill pickle relish
  Dash cayenne pepper
- 1 medium English cucumber, cut into ¼-inch slices

In a small bowl, combine the first six ingredients. Spoon onto cucumber slices. Serve immediately.
Per 1 appetizer: 20 cal., 1g fat (0 sat. fat), 11mg chol., 38mg sod., 1g carb. (0 sugars, 0 fiber), 1g pro.

Icy Holiday Punch

Pull out the punch bowl for this rosy thirst-quencher that dazzles at Christmas parties. It's easy to prepare, and the base can be made ahead.
—**MARGARET MATSON** METAMORA, IL

PREP: 10 MIN. + FREEZING
MAKES: 30 SERVINGS (ABOUT 5¾ QUARTS)

- 1 package (6 ounces) cherry gelatin
- ¾ cup sugar
- 2 cups boiling water
- 1 can (46 ounces) unsweetened pineapple juice
- 6 cups cold water
- 2 liters ginger ale, chilled

In a 4-qt. freezer-proof container, dissolve gelatin and sugar in boiling water. Stir in pineapple juice and cold water. Cover and freeze overnight. Remove 2 hours before serving. Place in a punch bowl; stir in ginger ale just before serving.
Per ¾ cup: 89 cal., 0 fat (0 sat. fat), 0 chol., 19mg sod., 22g carb. (21g sugars, 0 fiber), 1g pro.

BLACKBERRY SRIRACHA CHICKEN SLIDERS
Julie Peterson
Crofton, MD

Blackberry Sriracha Chicken Sliders

Dump everything in a slow cooker and watch these spicy-sweet sliders become an instant party classic.
—**JULIE PETERSON** CROFTON, MD

PREP: 20 MIN. • **COOK:** 5 HOURS
MAKES: 1 DOZEN

- 1 jar (10 ounces) seedless blackberry spreadable fruit
- ¼ cup ketchup
- ¼ cup balsamic vinegar
- ¼ cup Sriracha Asian hot chili sauce
- 2 tablespoons molasses
- 1 tablespoon Dijon mustard
- ¼ teaspoon salt
- 3½ pounds bone-in chicken thighs
- 1 large onion, thinly sliced
- 4 garlic cloves, minced
- 12 pretzel mini buns, split
  Additional Sriracha Asian hot chili sauce
  Leaf lettuce and tomato slices

1. In a 4- or 5-qt. slow cooker, stir together the first seven ingredients. Add chicken, onion and garlic. Toss to combine.
2. Cook, covered, on low until chicken is tender, 5-6 hours. Remove chicken. When cool enough to handle, remove bones and skin; discard. Shred meat with two forks. Reserve 3 cups cooking juices; discard remaining juices. Skim fat from reserved juices. Return the chicken and reserved juices to slow cooker; heat through. Using slotted spoon, serve on pretzel buns. Drizzle with additional Sriracha; top with lettuce and tomato.
Per 1 slider: 352 cal., 14g fat (3g sat. fat), 63mg chol., 413mg sod., 35g carb. (12g sugars, 1g fiber), 21g pro.

EAT SMART (5) INGREDIENTS FAST FIX ▶

Sliced Tomato Salad

This treasured recipe is from my grandmother. It's a perfect platter to serve with burgers or hot sandwiches.
—**KENDAL TANGEDAL** PLENTYWOOD, MT

START TO FINISH: 25 MIN. • **MAKES:** 12 SERVINGS

- 8 large tomatoes, cut into ¼-inch slices
- 2 large sweet onions, halved and thinly sliced
- ⅓ cup olive oil
- 2 tablespoons lemon juice
- 1 teaspoon dried oregano
- ¾ teaspoon salt
- ¼ teaspoon pepper
- 2 tablespoons minced fresh parsley

Arrange tomatoes and onions on a large rimmed serving platter. In a small bowl, whisk the oil, lemon juice, oregano, salt and pepper. Drizzle over top. Sprinkle with parsley.

Per serving: 94 cal., 6g fat (1g sat. fat), 0 chol., 159mg sod., 9g carb. (6g sugars, 2g fiber), 2g pro.
Diabetic Exchanges: 2 vegetable, 1 fat.

EAT SMART Zippy Pork Chili

(PICTURED ON P. 198)

In addition to eating this chili the traditional way (with a spoon), my family likes to scoop bites onto tortilla chips. The leftovers are delicious rolled in tortillas and warmed up. It's so comforting to have a pot simmering when cold Kansas winds are blowing.
—**MICHELLE BERAN** CLAFLIN, KS

PREP: 10 MIN. • **COOK:** 2¼ HOURS
MAKES: 10 SERVINGS (ABOUT 2½ QUARTS)

- 2 tablespoons canola oil
- 1 boneless pork loin roast (3 to 4 pounds), cut into 1-inch cubes
- 1 medium onion, chopped
- 1 garlic clove, minced
- 2 cans (16 ounces each) chili beans, undrained
- 2 cans (10 ounces each) diced tomatoes with mild green chilies, undrained
- 1 can (14½ ounces) diced tomatoes, undrained
- 1 cup water
- 1 teaspoon beef bouillon granules
  Chili powder, pepper and cayenne pepper to taste
  Sour cream, tortilla chips and shredded cheddar cheese, optional

1. In a Dutch oven, heat canola oil over medium heat. Brown pork in batches until no longer pink. Add onion; cook until tender. Add garlic; cook 1 minute longer.
2. Add beans, tomatoes, water, bouillon and seasonings to taste. Bring to a boil. Reduce heat; simmer, covered, until meat is tender, about 2 hours. If desired, serve with toppings.

Per 1 cup: 303 cal., 10g fat (3g sat. fat), 68mg chol., 638mg sod., 24g carb. (7g sugars, 7g fiber), 32g pro.
Diabetic Exchanges: 4 lean meat, 1½ starch, ½ fat.

NACHO TOTS

Nacho Tots

This is an easy, versatile party appetizer. If you can't find chorizo, ground beef or ground chicken are great, too. Top as you like!
—**CONNIE KRUPP** RACINE, WI

PREP: 15 MIN. • **BAKE:** 50 MIN. • **MAKES:** 12 SERVINGS

- 1 package (32 ounces) frozen Tater Tots
- 7 ounces fresh chorizo or bulk spicy pork sausage
- 1 can (14½ ounces) diced tomatoes with mild green chilies, undrained
- 12 ounces process cheese (Velveeta), cubed
- 1 can (15 ounces) black beans, rinsed and drained
- ½ cup pickled jalapeno slices
- ¼ cup minced fresh cilantro
- ⅓ cup thinly sliced green onions
- 1 medium ripe avocado, cubed
- 1 medium tomato, chopped
- ½ cup sour cream

1. Preheat oven to 425°. Place Tater Tots in an ungreased 13x9-in. baking dish. Bake, uncovered, 40 minutes.
2. Meanwhile, in a large skillet, cook chorizo over medium heat until no longer pink, breaking into crumbles; drain. Remove from pan and set aside. In same skillet, add diced tomatoes and cheese. Cook, uncovered, over medium heat until blended and cheese is melted, stirring occasionally. Pour over Tater Tots. Sprinkle with chorizo and black beans.
3. Bake, uncovered, 10 minutes. Sprinkle with jalapenos, cilantro and green onions. Top with avocado and tomato. Serve with sour cream.

Per 1 serving: 378 cal., 23g fat (9g sat. fat), 45mg chol., 1152mg sod., 29g carb. (5g sugars, 5g fiber), 13g pro.

HOT TO TOT

MAKE LIKE OUR STAFFERS AND MASH, TOP, DIP OR WRAP YOUR TATERS INTO UNEXPECTED DELIGHTS.

1 TOT POUTINE
For a variation on poutine, top cooked Tater Tots with beef gravy and deep-fried cheese curds.
—James Schend, Food Editor

2 BACON CHEESE TOTS
Top a pile of Tater Tots with crumbled bacon, lots of shredded Colby Jack and a cool drizzle of sour cream.
—Dana Meredith, Associate Editor

3 SRIRACHA BACON TOTS
Take a slice of precooked bacon and wrap it around a Tater Tot; repeat. Bake till crispy and dip into a mix of Sriracha and mayo.
—Holli Fletcher, Executive Assistant

4 BREAKFAST TOT-KABOBS
We make Tot-kabobs for an extra-fun breakfast. Prepare a plain omelet and cut into 1-in. squares. Cut cooked breakfast sausage links into thirds and thread onto skewers alternately with cooked Tater Tots and egg squares. Dip into maple syrup.
—Ellie Martin Cliffe, Senior Editor

5 EGGS BENEDIC-TOTS
My favorite! Top pan-fried Tater Tots with a couple of poached eggs and hollandaise sauce. To spice things up, I like to add chopped chipotle peppers to the hollandaise.
—Julie Blume Benedict, Content Director

6 PIZZA CRUST TOTS
Press thawed Tater Tots into a waffle iron and cook until crispy. Use cooked Tots as a pizza crust, top with your favorite pizza toppings—yep, a fried egg's one of mine—and bake.
—Nick Iverson, Lead Test Cook

7 CHIMICHURRI TOTS
When I'm feeling posh, I make chimichurri sauce to dip my Tater Tots in.
—Chris McLaughlin, Copy Editor

8 SLOPPY JOE TOTS
Top Tots with your favorite sloppy joe recipe, then sprinkle on shredded cheese and green onions.
—Sue Stetzel, Field Editor and Community Moderator

9 TOTS A LA BEEF BOURGUIGNON
Bake Tots until super crispy, then toss with salt, pepper and parsley. Load them onto a platter, and top with beef bourguignon, shaved Parmesan cheese and more parsley. Simply amazing!
—Kathryn Conrad, Lead Food Stylist

10 FRIT-TOT-TA
Cook 16 oz. Tater Tots in 2 tsp. olive oil until softened. Mash Tots into bottom of nonstick skillet to form a crust; cook until light golden on bottom. Whisk 8 eggs with ½ tsp. salt and pepper; stir in 1 lb. diced asparagus. Pour over crust. Cook, covered, over low heat until eggs are set.
—Emily Tyra, Editor

FAST FIX ▶ Sweet Potato Tartlets

My family can't resist sweet potatoes that are mashed, stuffed into phyllo shells and topped with marshmallows. The bite-sized tarts attract kids of all ages.

—MARLA CLARK MORIARTY, NM

START TO FINISH: 30 MIN. • **MAKES:** 15 TARTLETS

- 1 medium sweet potato, peeled and chopped
- 1 tablespoon butter
- 1 tablespoon maple syrup
- ⅛ teaspoon ground cinnamon
- ⅛ teaspoon ground nutmeg
- 1 package (1.9 ounces) frozen miniature phyllo tart shells
- 15 miniature marshmallows

1. Place sweet potato in a small saucepan; cover with water. Bring to a boil. Reduce heat; cover and simmer for 10-15 minutes or until tender. Drain.

2. In a small bowl, mash sweet potato with butter, syrup, cinnamon and nutmeg. Place 1 tablespoon potato mixture in each tart shell. Place on an ungreased baking sheet. Top with marshmallows. Bake at 350° for 8-12 minutes or until marshmallows are lightly browned.

Per 1 tartlet: 41 cal., 2g fat (0 sat. fat), 2mg chol., 16mg sod., 6g carb. (2g sugars, 0 fiber), 1g pro.
Diabetic Exchanges: ½ starch.

SPRINGTIME BEIGNETS

Springtime Beignets

I've always loved beignets, but never thought I could make them myself. Turns out they're easy! Sometimes I'll even make a quick berry whipped cream and pipe it inside for a fun surprise.

—KATHI HEMMER GRAND JUNCTION, CO

PREP: 25 MIN. + CHILLING • **COOK:** 25 MIN. • **MAKES:** 4 DOZEN

- ¼ cup butter, room temperature
- ¾ cup granulated sugar
- ½ teaspoon salt
- ½ teaspoon ground cinnamon
- ½ cup plus 2 tablespoons warm water (120° to 130°), divided
- ½ cup evaporated milk
- 1 package (¼ ounce) quick-rise yeast
- 1 large egg
- 3¼ to 3¾ cups all-purpose flour
   Oil for deep-fat frying
   Confectioners' sugar
   Berries and whipped topping, optional

1. Beat butter, sugar, salt and cinnamon until crumbly. Beat in ½ cup water and the evaporated milk. In another bowl, dissolve yeast in remaining water; add to milk mixture. Beat in egg until blended.

2. Add 2 cups flour; mix until well blended. Stir in enough remaining flour to form a soft dough (dough will be sticky). Place in a greased bowl, turning once to grease the top. Cover; refrigerate 4 hours or overnight.

3. Bring dough to room temperature. On a floured surface, roll dough into a 16x12-in. rectangle. Cut into 2-in. squares. In an electric skillet or deep fryer, heat oil to 375°. Drop beignets, a few at a time, into hot oil. Fry until golden brown, about 1 minute per side. Drain on paper towels. Dust with confectioners' sugar. If desired, serve with assorted berries and whipped topping.

Per 1 beignet: 74 cal., 3g fat (1g sat. fat), 7mg chol., 36mg sod., 10g carb. (3g sugars, trace fiber), 1g pro.

SWEET POTATO TARTLETS

Mini Hot Browns

Here's my take on the famous Hot Brown sandwich. Guests quickly line up for juicy turkey and crisp bacon, piled high on toasted rye bread and then topped with a rich cheese sauce.
—**ANNETTE GRAHL** MIDWAY, KY

START TO FINISH: 30 MIN. • **MAKES:** 1½ DOZEN

- 1 teaspoon chicken bouillon granules
- ¼ cup boiling water
- 3 tablespoons butter
- 2 tablespoons all-purpose flour
- ¾ cup half-and-half cream
- 1 cup shredded Swiss cheese
- 18 slices snack rye bread
- 6 ounces sliced deli turkey
- 1 small onion, thinly sliced and separated into rings
- 5 bacon strips, cooked and crumbled
- 2 tablespoons minced fresh parsley

1. Preheat the oven to 350°. Dissolve bouillon in water; set aside.

2. In a small saucepan, melt butter over medium heat. Stir in flour until smooth; add cream and bouillon mixture. Bring to a boil; cook and stir until thickened, 1-2 minutes. Stir in cheese until melted. Remove from heat.

3. Place bread on two baking sheets. Layer each slice with turkey, onion and cheese mixture. Bake until heated through, 10-12 minutes. (Or preheat broiler and broil until edges of bread are crisp and sauce is bubbly, 3-5 minutes.) Sprinkle with bacon and parsley.

Per 1 appetizer: 98 cal., 6g fat (3g sat. fat), 21mg chol., 246mg sod., 5g carb. (1g sugars, 1g fiber), 5g pro.

Try them as sliders: Double the amount of bread slices but only top half. After assembling, use the remaining bread slices to top your mini sandwiches.

SLOW COOKER CHEDDAR BACON ALE DIP

MINI HOT BROWNS

Slow Cooker Cheddar Bacon Ale Dip

My tangy, smoky dip won the top prize at our office party recipe contest. Other beers can work, but steer clear of dark varieties.
—**ASHLEY LECKER** GREEN BAY, WI

PREP: 15 MIN. • **COOK:** 3 HOURS • **MAKES:** 4½ CUPS

- 18 ounces cream cheese, softened
- ¼ cup sour cream
- 1½ tablespoons Dijon mustard
- 1 teaspoon garlic powder
- 1 cup amber beer or nonalcoholic beer
- 2 cups shredded cheddar cheese
- 1 pound bacon strips, cooked and crumbled, divided
- ¼ cup heavy whipping cream
- 1 green onion, thinly sliced
  Soft pretzel bites

1. In a greased 3-qt. slow cooker, combine cream cheese, sour cream, mustard and garlic powder until smooth. Stir in the beer, cheese and all but 2 tablespoons bacon. Cook, covered, on low, stirring occasionally, until heated through, 3-4 hours.

2. In last 30 minutes, stir in cream. Top finished dip with onion and remaining bacon. Serve with pretzel bun bites.

Per ¼ cup without pretzels: 213 cal., 19g fat (10g sat. fat), 60mg chol., 378mg sod., 2g carb. (1g sugars, 0 fiber), 8g pro.

Cookie Swirl Cobbler

(PICTURED ON P. 199)
An extra-rich chocolate chip cookie dough and crescent roll topping provide a tasty twist on cherry cobbler.
—**JEANNE HOLT** MENDOTA HEIGHTS, MN

PREP: 20 MIN. • **BAKE:** 25 MIN. + COOLING
MAKES: 12 SERVINGS

- 1 cup (about 8 ounces) refrigerated chocolate chip cookie dough, softened
- 2 tablespoons brown sugar
- ⅓ cup white baking chips
- ¼ cup plus 2 tablespoons toasted sliced almonds, divided
- 1 can (21 ounces) cherry pie filling
- ½ teaspoon almond extract, divided
- 2 cups fresh or frozen raspberries
- 1 tube (8 ounces) refrigerated crescent rolls
- ¾ cup confectioners' sugar
- 3 to 4 teaspoons 2% milk
  Vanilla ice cream, optional

1. Preheat oven to 350°. Combine cookie dough, brown sugar, baking chips and ¼ cup almonds. Set aside. In a large saucepan, heat cherry pie filling over medium heat until bubbly. Remove from heat; stir in ¼ teaspoon almond extract. Fold in raspberries. Transfer cherry mixture to a greased 13x9-in. baking dish.
2. Unroll crescent dough into one long rectangle; press perforations to seal. Drop small spoonfuls of cookie dough mixture over top; spread gently to cover. Roll up jelly-roll style, starting with a long side; pinch seam to seal. Cut crosswise into 12 slices; arrange cut side up on cherry mixture.
3. Bake until golden brown, 25-30 minutes. Cool 10 minutes. Meanwhile, combine the confectioners' sugar, remaining almond extract and enough milk to make a medium-thick glaze. Drizzle rolls with glaze; sprinkle with remaining toasted almonds. Serve warm with vanilla ice cream, if desired.
Note: To toast nuts, bake in a shallow pan in a 350° oven for 5-10 minutes or cook in a skillet over low heat until lightly browned, stirring occasionally.
Per serving: 308 cal., 11g fat (4g sat. fat), 2mg chol., 224mg sod., 49g carb. (22g sugars, 2g fiber), 3g pro.

CHUNKY
SOUTHWEST CHILI

Chunky Southwest Chili

What started out as a basic chili has evolved over the years to one with a punch! If you like your chili a little thicker, stir in some canned pumpkin. It adds fiber and nutrition without altering the taste.
—**SHAWN BARTO** WINTER GARDEN, FL

PREP: 30 MIN. + SOAKING
COOK: 1½ HOURS
MAKES: 10 SERVINGS (ABOUT 2½ QUARTS)

- 6 dried ancho or guajillo chilies or a mixture (about 3 ounces)
- 3 tablespoons olive oil, divided
- 3 pounds beef stew meat, trimmed and cut into 1-inch cubes
- 1 large onion, chopped
- 2 garlic cloves, minced
- 1½ teaspoons salt
- ½ teaspoon pepper
- ½ teaspoon ground cumin
- 2⅔ cups water, divided
- 1 bottle (46 ounces) V8 juice
- 1 can (14½ ounces) beef broth
  Sliced seeded jalapeno peppers, optional

1. In a stockpot over medium heat, toast chilies 2-3 minutes (do not burn).

Remove from heat; transfer to a small bowl. Add hot water to cover. Soak 30 minutes.
2. Meanwhile, in the same stockpot, heat 2 tablespoons olive oil over medium heat. Brown beef in batches. Remove with a slotted spoon. Add onion and remaining oil to stockpot; cook and stir until onion is tender, about 5 minutes. Add garlic; cook 1 minute more. Remove from heat.
3. Drain and split chilies, discarding stems and seeds. Pulse, covered, with salt, pepper, cumin and ⅔ cup water in a blender until pureed, adding water if needed (mixture should be a slightly runny paste).
4. Return beef to stockpot and stockpot to stovetop. Add V-8 juice, broth, chili mixture and remaining water. Bring to a boil. Reduce the heat; simmer, uncovered, stirring occasionally, until thickened and meat is tender, 1½-1¾ hours. If desired, top with jalapeno pepper slices.
Per 1 cup: 375 cal., 18g fat (5g sat. fat), 106mg chol., 1195mg sod., 16g carb. (6g sugars, 5g fiber), 36g pro.

FAST FIX ▸ Cuban Sliders

It's easy to make these delicious Cuban-style sliders by the panful, which is great because they go fast! Bake the pan until the rolls are lightly toasted and the cheese melts, then set them out and just watch them disappear.

—SERENE HERRERA DALLAS, TX

START TO FINISH: 30 MIN.
MAKES: 2 DOZEN

- 2 packages (12 ounces each) Hawaiian sweet rolls
- 1¼ pounds thinly sliced deli ham
- 9 slices Swiss cheese (about 6 ounces)
- 24 dill pickle slices

TOPPING

- ½ cup butter, cubed
- 2 tablespoons finely chopped onion
- 2 tablespoons Dijon mustard

1. Preheat oven to 350°. Without separating rolls, cut each package of rolls in half horizontally; arrange bottom halves in a greased 13x9-in. baking pan. Layer with ham, cheese and pickles; replace top halves of rolls.
2. In a microwave, melt butter; stir in onion and mustard. Drizzle over rolls. Bake, covered, 10 minutes. Uncover; bake until golden brown and heated through, 5-10 minutes longer.

Per 2 sliders: 382 cal., 19g fat (11g sat. fat), 84mg chol., 1065mg sod., 34g carb. (12g sugars, 2g fiber), 19g pro.

CUBAN SLIDERS

WHISKEY PINEAPPLE CHICKEN
Jodi Taffel
Altadena, CA

Whiskey Pineapple Chicken

Everyone in my family loves this recipe and its sweet marinade with ginger, pineapple and a splash of whiskey. Want even more intense flavor? Let the chicken marinate for two full days. Wow!

—JODI TAFFEL ALTADENA, CA

PREP: 20 MIN. + MARINATING
GRILL: 15 MIN.
MAKES: 10 SERVINGS

- 2 cups bourbon
- 2 cups unsweetened pineapple juice
- 1 cup hoisin sauce
- 2 tablespoons minced fresh gingerroot
- 2 tablespoons coarsely ground pepper, divided
- 4 teaspoons Worcestershire sauce
- 8 garlic cloves, minced
- 1 tablespoon kosher salt, divided
- 5 pounds boneless skinless chicken thighs
- 1 cup sliced sweet red pepper
- 1 cup sliced yellow onions
- 2 tablespoons olive oil

1. Whisk together bourbon, pineapple juice, hoisin sauce, ginger, 1 tablespoon pepper, Worcestershire sauce, garlic and 1 teaspoon salt until blended.
2. Place chicken in a shallow dish. Add half of marinade; turn to coat. Cover and refrigerate overnight, turning occasionally. Cover and refrigerate remaining marinade.
3. Drain chicken, discarding the marinade. Grill chicken, covered, on a greased grill rack over medium-high direct heat until a thermometer reads 170°, 5-6 minutes on each side.
4. Meanwhile, toss pepper and onion slices in oil and remaining salt and pepper. Grill, turning frequently, until soft, 5-7 minutes. In a small saucepan on the grill, cook reserved marinade over medium heat until slightly thickened, stirring occasionally, about 10 minutes. Chop grilled pepper and onion. Sprinkle over chicken; serve with sauce.

Note: It's important to use coarsely crushed pepper. Anything finer and the pepper flavor will be overpowering. If finely ground is all you have, reduce amount of pepper by about one-third.

Per serving: 439 cal., 20g fat (5g sat. fat), 152mg chol., 735mg sod., 13g carb. (8g sugars, 1g fiber), 43g pro.

**ELOISE NEELEY'S
SNOW PUNCH**
PAGE 233

Holiday & Seasonal Celebrations

Gather your friends and family for **holiday feasts,** summer festivities and **anytime fun.** Celebrate all year long with a special **Easter** brunch, three **summer** picnic menus, a Caribbean **getaway** and plenty of dazzling holiday **magic.**

BOBBIE MORGAN'S FAVORITE BARBECUED CHICKEN *PAGE 217*

MARY ANN LEE'S MARINATED MOZZARELLA & TOMATO APPETIZERS *PAGE 218*

JANET ZEGER'S HAM BALLS WITH BROWN SUGAR GLAZE *PAGE 230*

Easter Special

Spring is in the air and the ham (potpie!) is in the oven. Every year, this Seattle cook outdoes herself with an extraordinary Sunday spread.

RECIPES & STORY BY **ALLY PHILLIPS** MURRELLS INLET, SC

My wonderful grandmas, who both grew their own vegetables, taught me the love of cooking. All those delicious traditions live on in the Easter parties I host every year. I've cooked for both intimate soirees and big 50-person bashes with adult Easter egg hunts. Good thing eggs are plentiful at my house—my husband, Skip, and I raise ducks, seven chickens and a rooster, and they all come when I call. I also use their eggs to make deviled eggs, soaking them first in pickled beet juice overnight to make them pink, just because it's Easter!

Herb Dip with Spring Vegetables

When you're having a large party and focusing on the entrees, it's smart to have nibbles ready ahead of time. There's nothing simpler than making dip a day or two ahead and putting it out for guests. I'm a huge fan of ranch, so this is my pick.

PREP: 10 MIN. + CHILLING • **MAKES:** 2 CUPS

- 2 **cups (16 ounces) sour cream**
- ¼ **cup ranch salad dressing mix**
- 2 **tablespoons onion soup mix**
- ¼ **cup minced fresh parsley**
- 2 **tablespoons chopped fresh rosemary**
  Fresh rainbow baby carrots and watermelon (or plain) radishes

Stir together first five ingredients; refrigerate, covered, overnight. Sprinkle with additional parsley and rosemary before serving with rainbow carrots and assorted radishes.
Per 2 tablespoons dip: 76 cal., 6g fat (4g sat. fat), 7mg chol., 559mg sod., 5g carb. (1g sugars, trace fiber), 1g pro.

HERB DIP WITH SPRING VEGETABLES

Buttermilk Biscuit Ham Potpie

As part of my job as a caterer, I helped conceptualize a biscuit-themed food truck and spent months coming up with recipes, including this Easter spin on potpie.

PREP: 45 MIN. • **BAKE:** 25 MIN. + STANDING • **MAKES:** 8 SERVINGS

- 3 **celery ribs, diced**
- 2 **medium onions, diced**
- 2 **medium carrots, diced**
- ½ **fennel bulb, diced**
- 2 **tablespoons olive oil**
- ¼ **cup unsalted butter, cubed**
- ½ **cup all-purpose flour**
- 1 **carton (32 ounces) reduced-sodium chicken broth**
- 1 **teaspoon dried thyme**
- 2 **cups cubed fully cooked ham**
- 1 **tablespoon chopped fresh tarragon**
- ¼ **teaspoon salt**
- ¼ **teaspoon pepper**

BUTTERMILK BISCUITS

- 2 **cups all-purpose flour**
- 1 **tablespoon baking powder**
- ½ **teaspoon kosher salt**
- ½ **teaspoon baking soda**
- ⅔ **cup unsalted butter, cubed**
- ¾ **cup buttermilk**

1. Preheat oven to 425°. Toss celery, onions, carrots and fennel in oil to coat. Spread vegetables in a single layer over a 15x10x1-in. baking pan. Roast, stirring occasionally, until lightly browned, 20-25 minutes. Cool. Reduce heat to 350°.
2. Meanwhile, in a large saucepan, melt butter. Stir in flour until smooth. Gradually whisk in broth; add thyme. Bring to a boil, stirring constantly; reduce heat and simmer for 10 minutes. Add roasted vegetables, ham, tarragon, salt and pepper, cooking until heated through. Transfer to a greased 13x9-in. baking dish.
3. For biscuits, pulse flour, baking powder, salt and baking soda in a food processor until blended. Add cubed butter; pulse until butter is the size of peas. Transfer to a large bowl; stir in buttermilk until no flour is visible. Turn onto a

BUTTERMILK
BISCUIT HAM
POTPIE

floured surface; knead gently 8-10 times. Roll dough into a 13x9-in. rectangle; cut into shapes of your choice.

4. Arrange biscuit pieces, overlapping slightly, over the ham mixture. Bake until biscuit topping is golden brown, 25-30 minutes. Let stand 10 minutes before serving.
Per serving: 444 cal., 27g fat (14g sat. fat), 78mg chol., 1239mg sod., 37g carb. (4g sugars, 3g fiber), 15g pro.

Beet, Grapefruit & Onion Salad

My husband loves, *loves* pickled beets, so I paired them with a little citrus for an Eastery salad. The color combination really stands out!

PREP: 15 MIN. • **BAKE:** 50 MIN. + COOLING • **MAKES:** 8 SERVINGS

- 6 **medium fresh beets (about 2 pounds)**
- ¼ **cup extra virgin olive oil**
- 3 **tablespoons lemon juice**
- 2 **tablespoons cider vinegar**
- 2 **tablespoons honey**
- ¼ **teaspoon salt**
- ¼ **teaspoon pepper**
- 2 **large ruby red grapefruit, peeled and sectioned**
- 2 **small red onions, halved and thinly sliced**

1. Preheat oven to 425°. Scrub beets, trimming tops to 1 in. Wrap in foil; bake beets on a baking sheet until tender, 50-60 minutes. Remove foil; cool completely. Peel, halve and thinly slice beets. Place in a serving bowl.
2. Whisk together the next six ingredients. Pour over beets; add grapefruit and onions. Toss gently to coat.

Per ¾ cup: 161 cal., 7g fat (1g sat. fat), 0 chol., 162mg sod., 24g carb. (20g sugars, 4g fiber), 3g pro.
Diabetic Exchanges: 1½ fat, 1 starch, 1 vegetable.

BEET, GRAPEFRUIT
& ONION SALAD

Fun on the Farm

Open spaces and family recipes make a down-home celebration sweet.

(5)INGREDIENTS

Iced Raspberry Tea

Frozen raspberries lend fruity flavor and lovely color to this pretty iced tea that's good year-round. The recipe calls for just a few common ingredients and offers make-ahead convenience.
—**LOIS MCGRADY** HILLSVILLE, VA

PREP: 10 MIN. + CHILLING • **MAKES:** 16 SERVINGS (4 QUARTS)

- 1½ cups sugar
- 4 quarts water
- 1 package (12 ounces) frozen unsweetened raspberries
- 10 tea bags
- ¼ cup lemon juice
  Fresh raspberries and lemon slices, optional

1. In a Dutch oven over high heat, bring sugar and water to a boil. Remove from heat; stir until sugar is dissolved. Add raspberries, tea bags and lemon juice. Steep, covered, for 3 minutes. Strain; discard berries and tea bags.

2. Transfer tea to a large container or pitcher. Refrigerate until chilled. Serve over ice. If desired, serve with fresh raspberries and lemon slices.

Touch-of-Mint Iced Tea: Bring 2 quarts of water to a boil. Steep 5 individual tea bags for 5 minutes and discard; cool for 15 minutes. Add 1⅓ cups packed fresh mint and steep for 5 minutes. Strain tea and stir in 1 cup lemonade concentrate. Refrigerate until chilled. Serve over ice. Makes about 2 quarts.

Per 1 cup: 87 cal., 0 fat (0 sat. fat), 0 chol., 8mg sod., 22g carb. (20g sugars, 0 fiber), 0 pro.

★ ★ ★ ★ ★ **READER REVIEW**

"This tea is delicious. It can be made a day ahead of an event and kept in the fridge. I made ice cubes with the tea so as not to dilute it with regular ice. Served the tea in wine glasses with pink ice cubes and a thin slice of lemon on the rim for presentation. Will definitely make again!"

PARKSVILLE
TASTEOFHOME.COM

BACON PEA SALAD

ICED
RASPBERRY
TEA

JIGGLY
APPLESAUCE

GARDEN
VEGETABLE
CORN BREAD

FAVORITE
BARBECUED
CHICKEN

⑤ INGREDIENTS
Jiggly Applesauce

My cousin Dave brings this to our annual family cookout. If you can't find Red Hots, use cinnamon applesauce instead of plain.
—**JOSH HOPPERT** CUDAHY, WI

PREP: 10 MIN. + CHILLING
MAKES: 8 SERVINGS

- 2 **cups boiling water**
- ¼ **cup Red Hots, crushed**
- 2 **packages (3 ounces each) strawberry gelatin**
- 2 **cups cold unsweetened applesauce Finely chopped fresh strawberries, optional**

Add boiling water and crushed Red Hots to gelatin. Stir 2 minutes to completely dissolve gelatin and candy. Stir in cold applesauce. Pour into individual serving glasses or an 8-in. square dish. Refrigerate until firm, about 2 hours. If desired, serve with finely chopped strawberries.
Per ½ cup: 130 cal., 0 fat (0 sat. fat), 0 chol., 50mg sod., 32g carb. (29g sugars, 1g fiber), 2g pro.

GARDEN VEGETABLE CORN BREAD

JIGGLY APPLESAUCE

EAT SMART
Garden Vegetable Corn Bread

When I was a kid, my parents would make corn bread for my siblings and me. We would slather butter and maple syrup over the warm bread—it was delicious. Today, I experiment a lot with recipes, just like my grandma and mom did, and that's how my healthier version of their easy corn bread recipe was born!
—**KIM MOYES** KENOSHA, WI

PREP: 20 MIN. • **BAKE:** 20 MIN.
MAKES: 9 SERVINGS

- 1 **cup yellow cornmeal**
- ¾ **cup whole wheat flour**
- 2½ **teaspoons baking powder**
- 2 **teaspoons minced fresh chives**
- ¾ **teaspoon salt**
- 2 **large eggs**
- 1 **cup 2% milk**
- 2 **tablespoons honey**
- ¾ **cup shredded carrots (about 1½ carrots)**
- ¼ **cup finely chopped sweet red pepper**
- ¼ **cup finely chopped fresh poblano pepper, seeded**

1. Preheat oven to 400°. Whisk together the first five ingredients. In another bowl, whisk eggs, milk and honey until blended. Add to cornmeal mixture; stir just until moistened. Fold in carrots and peppers.
2. Transfer to a greased 8-in. square baking pan. Bake until a toothpick inserted in center comes out clean, 20-25 minutes. Serve warm.
Per 1 piece: 149 cal., 2g fat (1g sat. fat), 44mg chol., 367mg sod., 28g carb. (6g sugars, 2g fiber), 5g pro.
Diabetic Exchanges: 2 starch.

Favorite Barbecued Chicken

(PICTURED ON P. 215)

What better place to find a fantastic barbecue sauce than Texas, and that's where this one is from—it's my father-in-law's own recipe. We've served it at many family reunions and think it's the best!
—**BOBBIE MORGAN** WOODSTOCK, GA

PREP: 15 MIN. • **GRILL:** 35 MIN.
MAKES: 12 SERVINGS

- 2 broiler/fryer chickens (3 to 4 pounds each), cut into 8 pieces each
- Salt and pepper

BARBECUE SAUCE
- 2 tablespoons canola oil
- 2 small onions, finely chopped
- 2 cups ketchup
- ¼ cup lemon juice
- 2 tablespoons brown sugar
- 2 tablespoons water
- 1 teaspoon ground mustard
- ½ teaspoon garlic powder
- ¼ teaspoon pepper
- ⅛ teaspoon salt
- ⅛ teaspoon hot pepper sauce

1. Sprinkle chicken pieces with salt and pepper. Grill skin side down, uncovered, on a greased grill rack over medium heat for 20 minutes.

2. Meanwhile, in a small saucepan, make barbecue sauce by heating oil over medium heat. Add onion; saute until tender. Stir in remaining sauce ingredients and bring to a boil. Reduce the heat; simmer, uncovered, for 10 minutes.

3. Turn chicken; brush with barbecue sauce. Grill 15-25 minutes longer, brushing frequently with sauce, until a thermometer reads 165° when inserted in the breast and 170°-175° in the thigh.

Per serving: 370 cal., 19g fat (5g sat. fat), 104mg chol., 622mg sod., 15g carb. (14g sugars, 0 fiber), 33g pro.

BACON PEA SALAD
Angela Lively
Conroe, TX

(5) INGREDIENTS

Bacon Pea Salad

My husband absolutely loves peas. My middle son isn't the biggest fan, but he loves bacon. So I decided to combine the two, and it was perfect! This salad is an awesome dish for a barbecue.
—**ANGELA LIVELY** CONROE, TX

PREP: 10 MIN. + CHILLING
MAKES: 6 SERVINGS

- 4 cups frozen peas (about 16 ounces), thawed
- ½ cup shredded sharp cheddar cheese
- ½ cup ranch salad dressing
- ⅓ cup chopped red onion
- ¼ teaspoon salt
- ¼ teaspoon pepper
- 4 bacon strips, cooked and crumbled

Combine the first six ingredients; toss to coat. Refrigerate, covered, for at least 30 minutes. Stir in the bacon before serving.

Per ¾ cup: 218 cal., 14g fat (4g sat. fat), 17mg chol., 547mg sod., 14g carb. (6g sugars, 4g fiber), 9g pro.

Block Party

Everyone's invited to hang out on the patio with fun and family in tow.

Marinated Mozzarella & Tomato Appetizers

This party hit was inspired by a dish I ate at a restaurant. It's best served chilled and should marinate for a few days. My daughter puts the mozzarella on her antipasti platters.
—**MARY ANN LEE** CLIFTON PARK, NY

PREP: 15 MIN. + MARINATING • **BAKE:** 5 MIN. • **MAKES:** 16 SERVINGS

- ½ **cup Italian salad dressing**
- 2 **tablespoons minced fresh basil**
- 2 **tablespoons minced fresh chives**
- ½ **teaspoon coarsely ground pepper**
- 2 **cartons (8 ounces each) miniature fresh mozzarella cheese balls, drained**
- 2 **cups cherry tomatoes**
- 12 **slices French bread baguette (½ inch thick), cut into quarters**
- 2 **teaspoons olive oil**
- ⅛ **teaspoon salt**

1. Preheat oven to 450°. Combine salad dressing, basil, chives and pepper. Add cheese and tomatoes; toss to coat. Refrigerate, covered, at least 3 hours to let flavors blend. Meanwhile, toss baguette pieces with oil and salt; arrange on a baking sheet. Bake until toasted, 4-5 minutes. Cool completely. Just before serving, add toasted bread to cheese mixture; toss to combine. If desired, thread tomatoes, cheese and bread on skewers for serving.
Per ¼ cup: 119 cal., 8g fat (4g sat. fat), 22mg chol., 171mg sod., 5g carb. (2g sugars, 0 fiber), 6g pro.

SUN-DRIED TOMATO MAYONNAISE

EAT SMART
Mama's Warm German Potato Salad

My grandmother, Mama, made this potato salad for family gatherings at her home. Every relative would arrive with their specialties in hand. She never wrote the recipe down, so I had to re-create it from memory. Years later, it's just about right.
—**CHARLENE CHAMBERS** ORMOND BEACH, FL

PREP: 20 MIN. • **COOK:** 30 MIN. • **MAKES:** 12 SERVINGS

- 3 **pounds small red potatoes**
- ⅓ **cup canola oil**
- 2 **tablespoons champagne vinegar**
- 1 **teaspoon kosher salt**
- ½ **teaspoon coarsely ground pepper**
- ½ **English cucumber, very thinly sliced**
- 2 **celery ribs, thinly sliced**
- 1 **small onion, chopped**
- 6 **bacon strips, cooked and crumbled**
- 1 **tablespoon minced fresh parsley**

Place potatoes in a large saucepan; add water to cover. Bring to a boil. Reduce heat; cook, uncovered, until tender, 18-21 minutes. Drain; cool slightly. Peel and thinly slice. Whisk oil, vinegar, salt and pepper. Add potatoes; toss to coat. Add remaining ingredients; toss to combine. Serve warm.
Per ¾ cup: 163 cal., 8g fat (1g sat. fat), 4mg chol., 246mg sod., 20g carb. (2g sugars, 2g fiber), 4g pro.
Diabetic Exchanges: 1½ fat, 1 starch.

MAMA'S WARM GERMAN
POTATO SALAD

MARINATED MOZZARELLA &
TOMATO APPETIZERS

ALL-AMERICAN
HAMBURGERS

All-American Hamburgers

We do a lot of camping and outdoor cooking. Hamburgers are on our menu more than any other food.
—**DIANE HIXON** NICEVILLE, FL

START TO FINISH: 20 MIN. • **MAKES:** 4 SERVINGS

- 1 **pound ground beef**
- 2 **tablespoons finely chopped onion**
- 2 **tablespoons chili sauce**
- 2 **teaspoons Worcestershire sauce**
- 2 **teaspoons prepared mustard**
- 4 **slices process American cheese or cheddar cheese, halved diagonally**
- 2 **slices Swiss cheese, halved diagonally**
- 4 **hamburger buns, split and toasted**
  Lettuce, tomato, onion and bacon, optional

1. Combine first five ingredients, mixing lightly but thoroughly. Shape into four patties. Grill burgers, covered, on a greased rack over medium direct heat until a thermometer reads 160° and juices run clear, about 6 minutes on each side.

2. During the last minute of cooking, top each patty with two triangles of American cheese and one triangle of Swiss cheese. Serve on buns; if desired, top with lettuce, tomato, onion, bacon, ketchup or mustard.

Per 1 burger: 421 cal., 21g fat (11g sat. fat), 82mg chol., 760mg sod., 27g carb. (6g sugars, 1g fiber), 30g pro.

GOES GREAT WITH

Sun-Dried Tomato Mayonnaise

Stir together ½ cup mayonnaise and 2 Tbsp. sun-dried tomato pesto until well blended. —*Debbie Glasscock, Conway, AR*

BUTTER UP!

Start with softened butter, then stir in seasonings and slather onto cooked corn.

California-Style

1 stick butter + 2 tsp. minced fresh rosemary + 1 Tbsp. minced black olives

Southwest

1 stick butter + ½ tsp. ground chipotle pepper + zest of 1 lime + 1 tsp. minced cilantro

CORN IN THE U.S.A.

Here you have it—the secret to the perfect cob. And, aw shucks, butter always makes it better. These regionally inspired versions will have you smiling from ear to ear.

Heartland
1 stick butter
+ 2 Tbsp. crumbled
Maytag blue cheese

East Coast
1 stick butter + 2 tsp.
Old Bay Seasoning
+ zest of 1 lemon

Dairy State
1 stick butter + 2 Tbsp.
grated Parmesan cheese
+ 2 Tbsp. finely grated
cheddar cheese

⑤ INGREDIENTS FAST FIX ▶

Roast Corn on the Cob

Every summer, my family looks forward to corn on the cob. I make it extra special by roasting it all wrapped up on the grill.
—JOHNNIE MCLEOD BASTROP, LA

START TO FINISH: 30 MIN.
MAKES: 6 SERVINGS

- 6 **ears fresh sweet corn**
- 6 **tablespoons butter**
- 6 **ice cubes**
- **Salt and pepper to taste**
- **Additional butter, optional**

1. Remove husks and silk from corn. Place each ear on a double thickness of heavy-duty foil (about 18x12 in.). Add 1 tablespoon butter and 1 ice cube. Wrap securely, twisting ends of foil to make handles for turning.

2. Grill corn, covered, turning occasionally, over medium direct heat until tender, about 25 minutes. Open carefully to allow steam to escape. Sprinkle with salt and pepper; if desired, serve with additional butter.

Per 1 ear of corn with 1 tablespoon butter: 190 cal., 13g fat (8g sat. fat), 31mg chol., 107mg sod., 19g carb. (6g sugars, 2g fiber), 3g pro.

Beach Bash

Sand, sun and snacks are what make summer so delicious.

GARDEN PESTO PASTA SALAD

EAT SMART

Mojito-Style Yellow Tomato Salsa

With grilled tomatoes, crunchy peppers and a sprinkle of mint, this fresh salsa is good on just about everything. Try it in fish tacos, on tortilla chips or by the spoonful!

—PATTERSON WATKINS PHILADELPHIA, PA

PREP: 20 MIN. • **GRILL:** 10 MIN. + CHILLING • **MAKES:** 4 CUPS

- 2 **pounds large yellow tomatoes, halved**
- 1 **tablespoon olive oil**
- 2 **garlic cloves, minced**
- 1 **teaspoon chopped shallot**
- ¾ **teaspoon salt, divided**
- 3 **medium limes**
- 2 **teaspoons coarse sugar**
- 12 **fresh mint leaves**
- ¼ **cup chopped Cubanelle or banana peppers**

1. Grill tomatoes, uncovered, on an oiled rack over high heat (or broil 3-4 in. from the heat) until skin is slightly charred, 3-4 minutes per side. Cool to room temperature. Meanwhile, combine oil, garlic, shallot and ¼ teaspoon salt. When tomatoes are cool enough to handle, finely chop; stir in garlic mixture until well combined.

2. Finely grate peel of each lime; set aside. Peel and discard white membranes; section limes. In a food processor, pulse lime sections, sugar, mint and remaining salt until finely chopped. Combine with tomatoes; add peppers and lime peel. Mix well.

3. Refrigerate at least 1 hour. Serve with chips or grilled meats.

Per ¼ cup: 23 cal., 1g fat (0 sat. fat), 0 chol., 161mg sod., 4g carb. (1g sugars, 1g fiber), 1g pro.
Diabetic Exchanges: 1 vegetable.

CHIPOTLE
GUACAMOLE

MOJITO-STYLE YELLOW
TOMATO SALSA

ITALIAN HERO BRAID

Italian Hero Braid

(PICTURED ON P. 223)

My mother-in-law made these pastry pockets for my husband when he was growing up. After we got married, I changed her recipe a little to fit our family's tastes.

—AMANDA KOHLER REDMOND, WA

PREP: 20 MIN. • **BAKE:** 25 MIN.
MAKES: 8 SERVINGS

- ½ **pound bulk Italian sausage**
- 1 **package (¼ ounce) active dry yeast**
- 1 **cup warm water (110° to 115°)**
- 2¾ to 3¼ **cups all-purpose flour**
- 1 **tablespoon butter, melted**
- ⅓ **pound sliced provolone cheese**
- ⅓ **pound thinly sliced Genoa salami**
- 1 **cup shredded cheddar cheese**
- 1 **large egg white**

1. Preheat oven to 400°. In a large skillet over medium heat, cook and crumble Italian sausage until no longer pink, 4-6 minutes; drain.

2. Meanwhile, dissolve the yeast in warm water. In another bowl, combine 1½ cups flour and butter; add yeast mixture. Beat on medium speed until smooth. Stir in enough remaining flour to form a soft dough.

3. Turn onto a lightly floured surface; roll into a 13x10-in. rectangle. Transfer to a parchment paper-lined baking sheet. Layer cheese and salami slices down center of rectangle; top with crumbled sausage and shredded cheddar. On each long side, cut 1-in.-wide strips about 2 in. into the center. Starting at one end, fold alternating strips at an angle across filling. Pinch both ends to seal.

4. Whisk egg white; brush over pastry. Bake until golden brown, 25-30 minutes.

Per 1 piece: 436 cal., 23g fat (11g sat. fat), 64mg chol., 823mg sod., 35g carb. (0 sugars, 1g fiber), 21g pro.

GARDEN PESTO PASTA SALAD
Sarah Mathews
Ava, MO

EAT SMART

Garden Pesto Pasta Salad

My family and I live on a homestead in the Missouri Ozarks and produce much of our own food. In the summer, when the garden is bursting with fresh vegetables and it's too hot to cook, I like to use the seasonal veggies for pasta salads and other cool meals.

—SARAH MATHEWS AVA, MO

PREP: 15 MIN. + CHILLING
MAKES: 10 SERVINGS

- 3 **cups uncooked spiral pasta (about 9 ounces)**
- ½ **cup prepared pesto**
- 3 **tablespoons white wine vinegar**
- 1 **tablespoon lemon juice**
- ½ **teaspoon salt**
- ¼ **teaspoon pepper**
- ¼ **cup olive oil**
- 1 **medium zucchini, halved and sliced**
- 1 **medium sweet red pepper, chopped**
- 1 **medium tomato, seeded and chopped**
- 1 **small red onion, halved and thinly sliced**
- ½ **cup grated Parmesan cheese**

1. Cook pasta according to package directions; drain. Rinse with cold water and drain well.

2. Meanwhile, whisk together pesto, vinegar, lemon juice and seasonings. Gradually whisk in oil until blended.

3. Combine vegetables and pasta. Drizzle with pesto dressing; toss to coat. Refrigerate, covered, until cold, about 1 hour. Serve with Parmesan cheese.

Per serving: 217 cal., 11g fat (2g sat. fat), 3mg chol., 339mg sod., 23g carb. (3g sugars, 2g fiber), 6g pro.
Diabetic Exchanges: 2 fat, 1½ starch.

Chipotle Guacamole

My guacamole is so good because it has just a hint of smoke from the chipotle peppers. Stir them in or put a dollop in the center of the dip so people who aren't into peppers can scoop around them.
—**GAYLE SULLIVAN** SALEM, MA

PREP: 15 MIN. + CHILLING • **MAKES:** 3 CUPS

- 4 **medium ripe avocados, peeled and pitted**
- 1 **small tomato, seeded and chopped**
- ⅓ **cup finely chopped red onion**
- 3 **garlic cloves, minced**
- 2 **tablespoons lemon juice**
- 2 **tablespoons olive oil**
- ¼ **teaspoon salt**
- 1 **to 2 tablespoons minced fresh cilantro, optional**
- 1 **finely chopped chipotle pepper in adobo sauce plus 1 teaspoon adobo sauce**
  Tortilla chips

Mash avocados. Stir in next six ingredients and, if desired, cilantro. Dollop chipotle pepper and adobo sauce over center of guacamole. Refrigerate 1 hour. Serve with chips.
Per ¼ cup: 103 cal., 9g fat (1g sat. fat), 0 chol., 70mg sod., 5g carb. (1g sugars, 3g fiber), 1g pro.

PEACH CRUMB BARS

CHIPOTLE GUACAMOLE

Peach Crumb Bars

I had the most beautiful peaches and really wanted to bake with them. I started with my blueberry crumb bar recipe, and after a couple of tries, I am so happy with the results. My co-worker taste-testers are happy, too!
—**AMY BURNS** NEWMAN, IL

PREP: 30 MIN. • **BAKE:** 40 MIN. + COOLING
MAKES: 2 DOZEN

- 3 **cups all-purpose flour**
- 1½ **cups sugar, divided**
- 1 **teaspoon baking powder**
- ½ **teaspoon salt**
  Dash ground cinnamon
- 1 **cup shortening**
- 1 **large egg**
- 1 **teaspoon vanilla extract**
- 9 **medium peaches, peeled and chopped**
- 1 **teaspoon almond extract**
- 4 **teaspoons cornstarch**

1. Preheat oven to 375°. Whisk flour, 1 cup sugar, baking powder, salt and cinnamon; cut in shortening until crumbly. In another bowl, whisk egg and vanilla until blended; add to flour mixture, stirring with a fork until crumbly.

2. Reserve 2½ cups crumb mixture for topping. Press remaining mixture onto bottom of a greased 13x9-in. baking pan.

3. Toss peaches with almond extract. In another bowl, mix cornstarch and remaining sugar; add to peaches and toss to coat. Spread over crust; sprinkle with reserved topping.

4. Bake until lightly browned and filling is bubbly, 40-45 minutes. Cool completely in pan on a wire rack. Cut into bars.
Per 1 bar: 207 cal., 9g fat (2g sat. fat), 8mg chol., 73mg sod., 30g carb. (17g sugars, 1g fiber), 2g pro.

Jamaican Weekend

Jenn Hall's dad introduced her to the world dish by dish, making the dinner table the focal point of their family.

STORY BY **JENN HALL** | RECIPES BY **MATT SULLIVAN (AKA DAD)**

Dad loves the islands, and when the workweek ends, laid-back tunes are piped in 24/7 from Pirate Radio Key West. As kids, we groaned. Now, I get it.

The weekend also finds Dad deeply immersed in some culinary experiment. He boils. He bakes. He lights fires and scatters ingredients. Dad's epic menus are impressive feats of brining, mixing spices and making sausages from scratch. Most legendary among them is his jerk chicken, a two-day affair built on spice and magic.

This year for my birthday, I set up camp and cooked alongside him. The glorious thing is that all of these ingredients are easy to find—and nothing's difficult. You just need time. To get in the spirit, stream Caribbean radio, crack a frosty beverage and gather your favorite people. Then prepare to feast...this is a vacation in your own backyard.

EAT SMART

Island Mango Slaw

The cooling effect of mango and Greek yogurt meets jalapeno spice in this snappy take on coleslaw. To ensure ripeness, you may want to buy the mango a day or two in advance.

PREP: 25 MIN. + CHILLING • **MAKES:** 12 SERVINGS

- ½ **medium head Savoy cabbage, thinly sliced into 3-inch strips (about 8 cups)**
- ½ **small head red cabbage, thinly sliced into 3-inch strips (about 6 cups)**
- 2 **medium carrots, cut into thin 2-inch strips**
- 1 **small sweet yellow pepper, cut into thin 2-inch strips**
- 1 **small sweet red pepper, cut into thin 2-inch strips**
- 1 **small red onion, halved and thinly sliced**
- ½ **medium mango, peeled, cut into thin 2-inch strips**
- ½ **jalapeno pepper, seeded and finely chopped**

DRESSING
- ½ **cup plain Greek yogurt**
- ¼ **cup thawed orange juice concentrate**
- 4 **teaspoons lime juice**
- ½ **teaspoon olive oil**
- ½ **medium mango, peeled and coarsely chopped**
- 2 **teaspoons minced fresh gingerroot**
- 1 **teaspoon kosher salt**
- ½ **jalapeno pepper, seeded and coarsely chopped**
- ¼ **teaspoon pepper**

In a serving bowl, combine first eight ingredients. Process the dressing ingredients in a blender until smooth. Toss dressing with coleslaw at least 30 minutes before serving. Refrigerate.

Per ¾ cup: 66 cal., 1g fat (1g sat. fat), 3mg chol., 188mg sod., 13g carb. (9g sugars, 3g fiber), 2g pro.
Diabetic Exchanges: 1 vegetable, ½ fat.

ISLAND MANGO SLAW

CARIBBEAN COCONUT RUM CAKE

ISLAND MANGO SLAW

MATT'S JERK CHICKEN

MATT'S JERK CHICKEN

FREEZE IT

Matt's Jerk Chicken

Get ready for a trip to the islands! You may think jerk chicken is complicated, but really, all it takes is time. Throw on some tunes, grab an icy drink and prepare to be transported. Have a smoker? You can smoke the chicken first and then finish it on the grill.

PREP: 25 MIN. + MARINATING
GRILL: 50 MINUTES
MAKES: 16 SERVINGS

- 1 **large onion, chopped**
- 3 **green onions, chopped**
- ¾ **cup white vinegar**
- ½ **cup orange juice**
- ¼ **cup dark rum**
- ¼ **cup olive oil**
- ¼ **cup soy sauce**
- 2 **tablespoons lime juice**
- 1 **habanero or Scotch bonnet pepper, seeded and minced**
- 2 **tablespoons garlic powder**
- 1 **tablespoon sugar**
- 1 **tablespoon ground allspice**
- 1 **tablespoon dried thyme**
- 1½ **teaspoons cayenne pepper**
- 1½ **teaspoons rubbed sage**
- 1½ **teaspoons pepper**
- ¾ **teaspoon ground nutmeg**
- ¾ **teaspoon ground cinnamon**
- 8 **pounds bone-in chicken breast halves and thighs**
- ½ **cup whole allspice berries**
- 1 **cup applewood chips**
- ½ **cup ketchup**

1. Process first 18 ingredients, covered, in a blender until smooth. Divide the chicken into two large resealable plastic bags; pour half of onion mixture into each. Seal bags; turn to coat. Refrigerate overnight.
2. Soak allspice berries in water for 30 minutes. Drain chicken, reserving 1½ cups marinade. Preheat grill and prepare for indirect heat. On a piece of heavy-duty foil (12 in. square), place the soaked allspice berries; fold foil around berries to form a packet, crimping edges to seal. Using a small skewer, poke holes in packet. Repeat process for the applewood chips. Place packets over heat on grate of gas grill or in coals of charcoal grill.
3. Place chicken on greased grill rack, skin side down. Grill, covered, over indirect medium heat until a thermometer reads 165° when inserted into breasts and 170°-175° when inserted into thighs, 50-60 minutes.
4. Meanwhile, in a small saucepan over high heat, bring reserved marinade to a full rolling boil for at least 1 minute. Add ketchup; cook and stir until heated through. Remove from heat.
5. To serve Jamaican-style, remove meat from bones and chop with a cleaver. Toss chicken with sauce.

To freeze: Arrange grilled chicken pieces in a greased 13x9-in. baking dish; add sauce. Cool; cover and freeze. To use, partially thaw in refrigerator overnight. Remove from refrigerator 30 minutes before baking. Preheat oven to 350°. Reheat the chicken, covered, until a thermometer reads 165°, 40-50 minutes.

Per serving: 346 cal., 18g fat (5g sat. fat), 109mg chol., 419mg sod., 7g carb. (4g sugars, 1g fiber), 36g pro.

Get Real Jamaican Flavor Don't skip the applewood chips or allspice berries on the grill. It's as close to the flavor of Jamaican pimento wood as you can get.

Caribbean Coconut Rum Cake

My take on the boozy treats that weigh down suitcases returning from Jamaica, this moist cake packs a rum punch. You may wish to card your guests before serving. The longer the rum soaks in, the better. Overnight is best.

PREP: 25 MIN. • BAKE: 1 HOUR + STANDING
MAKES: 12 SERVINGS

- ½ cup unsalted butter, softened
- 1½ cups sugar
- 4 large eggs
- 1 teaspoon coconut extract
- ¾ cup amber rum
- ¾ cup whole milk
- 1¾ cups all-purpose flour
- 1 package (3.4 ounces) instant vanilla pudding mix
- ¼ cup cornstarch
- 4 teaspoons baking soda
- 1 teaspoon salt

SYRUP
- ½ cup unsalted butter
- ½ cup water
- ½ cup sugar
    Dash salt
- ½ cup amber rum
- 1 teaspoon coconut extract

1. Preheat oven to 325°. Cream butter and sugar until light and fluffy. Add eggs, one at a time, beating well after each addition. Beat in coconut extract. In a small bowl, combine rum and milk. In a large bowl, whisk the flour, pudding mix, cornstarch, baking soda and salt; add to the creamed mixture alternately with rum mixture, beating well after each addition.

2. Transfer to a greased and floured 10-in. fluted tube pan. Bake until a toothpick inserted in center comes out clean, about 1 hour. Cool for about 10 minutes. Remove from pan briefly to prevent sticking; replace in pan. Cool on wire rack.

3. Meanwhile, for the syrup, melt butter in a small saucepan over medium heat. Add water, sugar and salt; bring to a boil, stirring constantly. Remove from the heat; add rum and coconut extract.

4. Using a small skewer, poke holes in cake. Slowly pour syrup over cake until it's all absorbed. Cover and let stand overnight.

Per 1 slice: 461 cal., 18g fat (10g sat. fat), 104mg chol., 823mg sod., 58g carb. (41g sugars, 1g fiber), 5g pro.

CARIBBEAN COCONUT RUM CAKE

Merry Meatballs

We've rounded up some juicy, savory, sweet-and-spicy bites for your appetizer spread. Grab a toothpick and have a ball.

FESTIVE TURKEY MEATBALLS

HAM BALLS WITH BROWN SUGAR GLAZE

Festive Turkey Meatballs

A spicy-sweet sauce makes my turkey meatballs extra zesty. I put them in the holiday spirit with a sprinkle of green herbs and diced red pepper on top.

—**AUDREY THIBODEAU** GILBERT, AZ

PREP: 25 MIN. • **BAKE:** 30 MIN.
MAKES: ABOUT 3½ DOZEN

- 1 large egg, beaten
- ½ cup dry bread crumbs
- ¼ cup finely chopped onion
- ½ teaspoon curry powder
- ¼ teaspoon ground ginger
- ¼ teaspoon ground cinnamon
- ¼ teaspoon salt
- ¼ teaspoon pepper
- 1 pound ground turkey

SAUCE
- 1 cup honey
- ¼ cup Dijon mustard
- ½ teaspoon curry powder
- ½ teaspoon ground ginger

OPTIONAL ADDITIONS
- Fresh basil leaves
- Fresh cilantro leaves
- Fresh mint leaves
- Lime wedges

1. Preheat oven to 350°. Combine the first eight ingredients. Add turkey; mix well. Shape into 1-in. balls. Place meatballs on a greased rack in a 15x10-in. baking pan. Bake, uncovered, until cooked through and juices run clear, 20-25 minutes.

2. Meanwhile, combine sauce ingredients in a small saucepan; whisk over medium heat until heated through. Brush meatballs with ¼ cup sauce; return to oven for 10 minutes. Serve meatballs with remaining sauce for dipping and, if desired, fresh herbs and lime wedges.

Per 1 meatball: 46 cal., 1g fat (0 sat. fat), 11mg chol., 61mg sod., 7g carb. (6g sugars, 0 fiber), 2g pro.

Ham Balls with Brown Sugar Glaze

These smoky meatballs are a Pennsylvania Dutch specialty. I like setting them out when folks come to visit.

—**JANET ZEGER** MIDDLETOWN, PA

PREP: 30 MIN. • **BAKE:** 30 MIN. • **MAKES:** ABOUT 6 DOZEN

- 1 pound fully cooked ham, cubed
- 1 pound ground pork
- 1 cup milk
- 1 cup crushed cornflakes
- 1 large egg, lightly beaten
- ¼ cup packed brown sugar
- 1 tablespoon ground mustard
- ½ teaspoon salt

GLAZE
- 1 cup packed brown sugar
- ¼ cup vinegar
- 1 tablespoon ground mustard

1. Preheat oven to 350°. Pulse ham in batches in a food processor until finely ground. Combine with the next seven ingredients just until mixed. Shape into 1-in. balls; place in a single layer on greased 15x10-in. rimmed baking pans.

2. For glaze, cook and stir all ingredients in a small saucepan over medium heat until sugar is dissolved. Spoon over ham balls. Bake until ham balls are just beginning to brown, 30-35 minutes, rotating pans and carefully stirring halfway through. Gently toss in glaze. Serve warm.

Per 1 meatball: 52 cal., 2g fat (1g sat. fat), 11mg chol., 113mg sod., 5g carb. (4g sugars, 0 fiber), 3g pro.

EAT SMART

Classic Swedish Meatballs

I'm a *svenska flicka* (Swedish girl) from northwest Iowa, where many Swedes settled at the turn of the century. This recipe was given to me by a Swedish friend. It's obviously a 20th century version of a 19th century favorite, since back then they didn't have bouillon cubes or evaporated milk! I think you'll agree that these modern-day *kottbullar* are very tasty.

—**EMILY GOULD** HAWARDEN, IA

PREP: 20 MIN. + CHILLING • **COOK:** 20 MIN. • **MAKES:** 3½ DOZEN

- 1⅔ cups evaporated milk, divided
- ⅔ cup chopped onion
- ¼ cup fine dry bread crumbs
- ½ teaspoon salt
- ½ teaspoon allspice
  Dash pepper
- 1 pound lean ground beef (90% lean)
- 2 teaspoons butter
- 2 teaspoons beef bouillon granules
- 1 cup boiling water
- ½ cup cold water
- 2 tablespoons all-purpose flour
- 1 tablespoon lemon juice
  Canned lingonberries, optional

1. Combine ⅔ cup evaporated milk with the next five ingredients. Add beef; mix lightly. Refrigerate until chilled.
2. With wet hands, shape meat mixture into 1-in. balls. In a large skillet, heat butter over medium heat. Brown the meatballs in batches. Dissolve bouillon in boiling water. Pour over meatballs and bring to a boil. Cover; simmer 15 minutes.
3. Meanwhile, stir together cold water and flour. Remove meatballs from skillet; skim fat, reserving juices. Add flour mixture and remaining evaporated milk to pan juices; cook, uncovered, over low heat, stirring until sauce thickens.
4. Return meatballs to skillet. Stir in lemon juice. If desired, top with lingonberries.
Per 1 meatball: 36 cal., 2g fat (1g sat. fat), 10mg chol., 87mg sod., 2g carb. (1g sugars, 0 fiber), 3g pro.

Cranberry Appetizer Meatballs

Everyone needs a go-to party snack, and we like tangy meatballs flavored with cranberry and chili sauces. Make plenty; they vanish.

—**JIM ULBERG** ELK RAPIDS, MI

PREP: 30 MIN. • **BAKE:** 15 MIN. • **MAKES:** ABOUT 7 DOZEN

- 2 large eggs, lightly beaten
- 1 cup dry bread crumbs
- ⅓ cup minced fresh parsley
- ⅓ cup ketchup
- 2 tablespoons finely chopped onion
- 2 tablespoons soy sauce
- 2 garlic cloves, minced
- ½ teaspoon salt

CRANBERRY APPETIZER MEATBALLS

CLASSIC SWEDISH MEATBALLS

- ¼ teaspoon pepper
- 2 pounds ground beef

CRANBERRY SAUCE
- 1 can (14 ounces) whole-berry cranberry sauce
- 1 bottle (12 ounces) chili sauce
- 1 tablespoon brown sugar
- 1 tablespoon prepared mustard
- 1 tablespoon lemon juice
- 2 garlic cloves, minced

1. Preheat oven to 400°. Combine the first nine ingredients. Crumble ground beef over mixture and mix well. Shape into 1-in. balls.
2. Place meatballs on a rack in a shallow baking pan. Bake until no longer pink, about 15 minutes. Transfer to a 3-qt. slow cooker or chafing dish.
3. Meanwhile, in a large saucepan, combine all sauce ingredients; simmer 10 minutes, stirring occasionally. Pour over meatballs. Serve warm.
Per 1 meatball: 39 cal., 1g fat (1g sat. fat), 11mg chol., 124mg sod., 4g carb. (2g sugars, 0 fiber), 2g pro.

PLEASED AS PUNCH

LIFT A LADLE AND TOAST THE SEASON. READERS SHARE THE FRUITY AND FESTIVE RECIPES THAT MAKE THE PUNCH BOWL THE LIFE OF THE PARTY.

1. Holiday Eggnog Mix

In a food processor, combine 6⅔ cups nonfat dry milk powder, two 3.4-ounce packages instant vanilla pudding mix, 1 cup buttermilk blend powder and 1 tablespoon nutmeg; blend. Store in airtight containers in a cool dry place for up to 6 months. To serve, place ⅓ cup mix in a glass. Stir in ¾ cup cold whole milk.
Serves 18.
—Melissa Hansen
Milwaukee, WI

2. Candy Cane Punch

Melt 24 ounces strawberry jelly with 2 cups lemon-lime soda over low heat; chill. Place 6 cups peppermint ice cream in a punch bowl; stir in the jelly mixture. Add 6 cups chilled lemon-lime soda. Garnish with scoops of peppermint ice cream and bits of crushed candy canes.
Serves 14.
—Neva Schnauber
Fort Collins, CO

3. Brandy Slush

Combine 2 cups boiling water and 4 tea bags. Steep 5 minutes; discard tea bags. Transfer to a freezer container; add 2 cups brandy, 12 ounces each thawed lemonade and orange juice concentrates and 7 cups water. Freeze. To serve, scoop ¾ cup slush into a glass; top with ¼ cup lemon-lime soda.
Serves 20.
—Sarah Thompson
Greenfield, WI

4. Hot Spiced Berry Punch

In a slow cooker, combine 4 cups frozen unsweetened mixed berries, ¼ cup sugar, 2 cinnamon sticks, 6 whole star anise and 8 cups cranberry-raspberry juice. Cook, covered, on low for 2-3 hours; strain.
Serves 10.
—Judy Batson
Tampa, FL

5. White Christmas Sangria

In a punch bowl, combine 6 cups chilled white cranberry juice, ¾ cup thawed lemonade concentrate and three chilled 750 milliliter bottles of sparkling white grape juice.
Serves 20.
—Taste of Home
Test Kitchen

6. Bubbly Champagne Punch

Line a 4½-cup ring mold with orange slices. Combine 2½ cups pineapple juice and 1½ cups ginger ale. Pour over fruit; freeze. Unmold into punch bowl. Stir in two 750 milliliter bottles of champagne and one 375 milliliter bottle sweet white wine. Add 12 ounces lemonade concentrate. **Serves 16.**

—Anita Geoghagan
Woodstock, GA

7. Snow Punch

In a blender, combine 1 cup lemon juice, 5 medium ripe bananas and 1 cup sugar; blend until smooth. Add 2 cups half-and-half cream; blend. Chill mixture. Pour into a punch bowl and add 1 liter chilled lemon-lime soda. Top with scoops of lemon sherbet and, if desired, flaked coconut. **Serves 10.**

—Eloise Neeley
Norton, OH

8. Creamy Peppermint Punch

In a punch bowl, combine ½ gallon softened peppermint ice cream, 1 liter chilled club soda and 4 cups eggnog. **Serves 16.**

—Linda Foreman
Locust Grove, OK

9. Grinch Punch

Dissolve ⅓ cup sugar in 3 tablespoons water over medium heat; transfer to a bowl. Stir in ⅓ cup evaporated milk and ½ teaspoon almond extract. Chill. Transfer to a punch bowl. Stir in 12 drops neon green food coloring and 2 liters chilled lemon-lime soda. Top with scoops of vanilla ice cream. **Serves 16.**

—Janice Hodge
Custer, SD

10. Mulled Cider

Place 3 cinnamon sticks, 3 whole cloves, 2 whole allspice berries and 1 bay leaf in a spice bag. Combine 3 quarts apple cider, ¼ cup each orange and lemon juice, 2 tablespoons brown sugar, 1 tablespoon grated orange peel, dash salt and spice bag. Simmer 30 minutes. Discard spice bag; strain mixture. Add 1-1½ cups brandy if desired. **Serves 12.**

—Taste of Home
Test Kitchen

Merry Sweets

It'll begin to look a lot like Christmas when you whip up the season's best cookies, truffles, fudge and coffee cake. How sweet it is!

Striped Icebox Cookies

I've been making cookie dough with stripes since I was a little girl. It's easier than cutout cookies, and you can mix and match your favorite ingredients. I like mine with chocolate and cherries.
—**PATRICIA REESE** PEWAUKEE, WI

PREP: 30 MIN. + CHILLING • **BAKE:** 10 MIN./BATCH + COOLING
MAKES: 5 DOZEN

- 1 **cup butter, softened**
- 1½ **cups sugar**
- 1 **large egg**
- 2½ **cups all-purpose flour**
- 1½ **teaspoons baking powder**
- ¼ **teaspoon salt**
- ¼ **cup chopped maraschino cherries, drained**
- 2 **drops red food coloring**
- 2 **ounces semisweet chocolate, melted**
- 4 **teaspoons nonpareils**

1. Cream butter and sugar until light and fluffy. Beat in egg. In another bowl, whisk together flour, baking powder and salt; gradually beat into creamed mixture.

2. Divide into thirds. Add cherries and food coloring to one portion, chocolate to another portion and nonpareils to remaining portion.

3. Line a 9x5-in. loaf pan with waxed paper. Spread cherry dough over bottom. Cover with chocolate dough, then remaining dough. Refrigerate, covered, until firm, about 2 hours.

4. Preheat oven to 375°. Remove dough from pan; cut in half lengthwise. Cut each portion into ¼-in. slices. For easier handling, freeze until firm, 10-15 minutes. Bake 1 in. apart on lightly greased baking sheets until edges begin to brown, 10-12 minutes. Remove to wire racks to cool.

Per 1 cookie: 74 cal., 4g fat (2g sat. fat), 11mg chol., 46mg sod., 10g carb. (6g sugars, 0 fiber), 1g pro.

FROSTED CUTOUT SUGAR COOKIES

RASPBERRY LINZER COOKIES

SPARKLY MERINGUE SNOWMEN

GERMAN CHRISTMAS COOKIES

COOKIES & CREAM TRUFFLE BALLS

STRIPED ICEBOX COOKIES

CHOCOLATE-MINT DREAM SANDWICH COOKIES

German Christmas Cookies

This little spice cookie tastes very European and is similar to pfeffernuesse. We make ours with cozy spices, anise flavoring, almonds and candied citron.
—**CAROLE MUELLER** FLORISSANT, MO

PREP: 30 MIN. • **BAKE:** 10 MIN./BATCH
MAKES: 12 DOZEN

- 2 cups all-purpose flour
- 1 cup granulated sugar
- 1 teaspoon ground cinnamon
- ½ teaspoon baking soda
- ½ teaspoon ground cloves
- ¼ teaspoon ground nutmeg
- ¼ teaspoon ground allspice
- 2 large eggs
- ½ cup butter, melted
- ½ teaspoon grated lemon peel
- ½ teaspoon anise extract
- 1½ cups chopped almonds
- ½ cup chopped candied citron
  Confectioners' sugar

1. Preheat oven to 350°. Combine first seven ingredients. In another bowl, combine eggs, butter, lemon peel and extract. Stir into dry ingredients just until moistened. Fold in almonds and citron.
2. Shape into ½-in. balls and place 1 in. apart on greased baking sheets. Bake until set, 8-10 minutes. Roll warm cookies in confectioners' sugar; cool on wire racks. Store in an airtight container.
Per 1 cookie: 29 cal., 1g fat (0 sat. fat), 4mg chol., 13mg sod., 4g carb. (2g sugars, 0 fiber), 1g pro.

✳

DID YOU KNOW?
Citron is a funny-looking citrus fruit prized for its thick and flavorful peel, which often gets candied. The fruit looks like a giant lemon—each can grow up to 1 foot long—with a rough and bumpy appearance. Most of the United States is too cold to successfully grow citron, but it does grow in Puerto Rico and on other Caribbean, Pacific and Mediterranean islands. Candied citron is a popular ingredient in fruitcakes, cookies and sweet rolls.

CHOCOLATE-MINT DREAM SANDWICH COOKIES
Shannon Koene
Blacksburg, VA

Chocolate-Mint Dream Sandwich Cookies

For the family cookbook, my cousin submitted a cookie I've since tinkered with, and it's a showstopper. These dreamy cookies with chocolate and mint pretty much melt in your mouth.

—**SHANNON KOENE** BLACKSBURG, VA

PREP: 45 MIN. • **BAKE:** 10 MIN. + COOLING
MAKES: ABOUT 1½ DOZEN

- ¾ **cup butter, softened**
- ½ **cup confectioners' sugar**
- 2 **ounces unsweetened chocolate, melted and cooled**
- ¾ **teaspoon peppermint extract**
- 1½ **cups all-purpose flour**
- 1 **cup (6 ounces) miniature semisweet chocolate chips**

FILLING
- 1½ **cups confectioners' sugar**
- 3 **tablespoons butter, softened**
- 5 **to 6 teaspoons 2% milk**
- ¾ **teaspoon peppermint extract**

CHOCOLATE GLAZE
- 1½ **cups (9 ounces) dark chocolate chips**
- 2 **teaspoons shortening**
- ⅛ **teaspoon peppermint extract**
  Crushed candy canes

1. Preheat oven to 375°. Beat butter and confectioners' sugar until creamy. Beat in cooled chocolate and extract. Gradually beat in flour. Fold in chocolate chips.

2. Drop by tablespoonfuls 2 in. apart onto ungreased baking sheets. Flatten to ¼-in. thickness. Bake until set, 6-8 minutes. Cool on pans 2 minutes before removing cookies to wire racks to cool completely.

3. Meanwhile, mix filling ingredients. Cut a small hole in the tip of a pastry bag or in a corner of a food-safe plastic bag; insert a star tip. Transfer filling to bag; pipe onto bottom halves of cookies. Top with remaining cookies.

4. For glaze, microwave chocolate chips and shortening on high until melted, stirring every 30 seconds; add peppermint extract. Dip about two-thirds of each cookie into glaze, allowing excess to drip off; top with crushed candy canes. Place on waxed paper; refrigerate until set.

Per 1 sandwich cookie: 306 cal., 19g fat (12g sat. fat), 23mg chol., 77mg sod., 36g carb. (26g sugars, 2g fiber), 3g pro.

Raspberry Linzer Cookies

Raspberry-filled sandwich cookies take a little extra effort, but when I see the delight on everyone's faces, it's worth the prep and additional steps.

—**SCHELBY THOMPSON**

CAMDEN WYOMING, DE

PREP: 30 MIN. + CHILLING
BAKE: 10 MIN./BATCH + COOLING
MAKES: 2 DOZEN

- 1 **cup butter, softened**
- 1⅓ **cups granulated sugar, divided**
- 2 **large eggs, separated**
- 2½ **cups all-purpose flour**
- ¼ **teaspoon salt**
  Confectioners' sugar
- ½ **cup ground almonds**
- 1 **cup seedless raspberry preserves**

1. Cream butter, gradually adding ⅔ cup sugar; beat until light and fluffy. Add egg yolks, one at a time, beating well after each addition. Combine flour and salt; gradually add to creamed mixture and mix well. Shape dough into a ball; cover and refrigerate until firm, 30-45 minutes.

2. Preheat oven to 350°. On a surface dusted with confectioners' sugar, roll dough to ⅛-in. thickness; cut with a floured 2½-in. round cookie cutter. Using a floured 1-in. cookie cutter, cut out centers of half of the cookies.

3. Beat egg whites until frothy. Mix almonds and remaining sugar. Brush cookies with egg whites; sprinkle with almond mixture. Bake solid cookies and window cookies 1 in. apart on greased baking sheets until lightly browned, 6-8 minutes. Remove to wire racks to cool completely.

4. Spread 2 teaspoons raspberry preserves over the bottoms of solid cookies. Top with window cookies, almond side up.

Per 1 cookie: 209 cal., 9g fat (5g sat. fat), 36mg chol., 92mg sod., 30g carb. (19g sugars, 1g fiber), 2g pro.

✳

TEST KITCHEN TIP
For variety, substitute apricot, strawberry or whatever kind of preserves you prefer in place of raspberry.

RASPBERRY
LINZER COOKIES

EAT SMART

Sparkly Meringue Snowmen

For my son's first Christmas home from Iraq, I wanted everything to feel magical. He loves meringue cookies, so I made a big batch of minty snowflakes and snowmen.

—**PATRICIA LINDSAY** INDEPENDENCE, KS

PREP: 30 MIN. + STANDING • **BAKE:** 1 HOUR 20 MIN./BATCH
MAKES: ABOUT 1 DOZEN

> 2 **large egg whites**
> ⅛ **teaspoon cream of tartar**
> ½ **cup sugar**
> ½ **teaspoon mint or vanilla extract**
> **Black nonpareils**
> **Orange sprinkles**

1. Let egg whites stand at room temperature 30 minutes.
2. Preheat oven to 200°. Add cream of tartar to egg whites; beat on medium speed until foamy. Gradually add sugar, 1 tablespoon at a time, beating on high after each addition until sugar is dissolved. Continue beating until stiff glossy peaks form. Fold in extract.
3. Cut a small hole in the tip of a pastry bag or in a corner of a food-safe plastic bag; insert a #12 round tip. Transfer meringue to bag. Pipe snowmen about 4 in. tall, 2 in. apart, onto parchment paper-lined baking sheets. Decorate with black nonpareils and orange sprinkles. Bake until firm to the touch, 80-90 minutes.
4. Remove to wire racks to cool completely. Store in an airtight container.
Per 1 cookie: 31 cal., 0 fat (0 sat. fat), 0 chol., 8mg sod., 7g carb. (7g sugars, 0 fiber), 1g pro.
Diabetic Exchanges: ½ starch.

COOKIES & CREAM TRUFFLE BALLS

⑤INGREDIENTS

Cookies & Cream Truffle Balls

For easy truffles, I roll cookies and cream cheese into balls and dunk them in white chocolate. They're merry and bright in one irresistible bite!

—**CARLA GIORGIO** NEW YORK, NY

PREP: 30 MIN. + CHILLING
MAKES: ABOUT 3 DOZEN

> 1 **package (14.3 ounces) Oreo cookies**
> 1 **package (8 ounces) cream cheese, softened**
> 1 **package (10 to 12 ounces) white baking chips**
> **Sprinkles, optional**

1. Pulse cookies in a food processor until fine crumbs form. Add cream cheese; pulse just until blended. Refrigerate, covered, until easy to handle. Shape into 1-in. balls; freeze several hours or overnight.
2. Microwave baking chips on high until melted; stir until smooth. Dip balls in melted chips; allow excess to drip off. Place on waxed paper. Drizzle with remaining chocolate or, if desired, decorate with sprinkles. Let stand until set. Store in the refrigerator.
Per 1 ball without sprinkles: 106 cal., 6g fat (3g sat. fat), 7mg chol., 66mg sod., 12g carb. (9g sugars, 0 fiber), 1g pro.

SPARKLY MERINGUE SNOWMEN

FROSTED CUTOUT
SUGAR COOKIES

Frosted Cutout Sugar Cookies

When I was a girl, Mom and I made these simple cutout cookies. Iced and sprinkled with colored sugar, they remind me of our handiwork together.

—**SONJA STROMSWOLD** MOHALL, ND

PREP: 30 MIN. + CHILLING • **BAKE:** 10 MIN./BATCH + COOLING
MAKES: 5 DOZEN

- **3 cups all-purpose flour**
- **1 cup granulated sugar**
- **1 teaspoon baking soda**
- **¼ teaspoon salt**
- **½ cup shortening**
- **½ cup cold butter**
- **2 large eggs**
- **1 tablespoon whole milk**
- **1 teaspoon vanilla extract**

FROSTING

- **½ cup butter, softened**
- **4 cups confectioners' sugar**
- **1 teaspoon vanilla extract**
- **2 to 4 tablespoons half-and-half cream**

Food coloring, optional
Colored sugar, optional
Decorating candies, optional

1. Combine flour, granulated sugar, baking soda and salt. Cut in shortening and butter until crumbly. In another bowl, whisk eggs, milk and vanilla; add to flour mixture and mix well. Divide dough into three balls; cover and refrigerate until easy to handle, about 2 hours.
2. Preheat oven to 325°. Remove one portion of dough from the refrigerator at a time. On a lightly floured surface, roll dough to ¼-in. thickness. Cut with a floured 2-in. cookie cutter. Place 1 in. apart on ungreased baking sheets. Repeat with remaining dough.
3. Bake until edges are lightly browned, 8-10 minutes. Cool 1 minute before removing to wire racks to cool completely.
4. For frosting, cream butter, confectioners' sugar, vanilla and enough cream to achieve spreading consistency. If desired, tint with food coloring. Frost cookies. Decorate with colored sugar and candies if desired.

Per 1 cookie: 112 cal., 5g fat (2g sat. fat), 15mg chol., 58mg sod., 16g carb. (11g sugars, 0 fiber), 1g pro.

GINGERBREAD MEN COOKIES

BUTTER PECAN FUDGE

Gingerbread Men Cookies

No holiday cookie platter would be complete without gingerbread men! This is a tried-and-true recipe I love to share.

—**MITZI SENTIFF** ANNAPOLIS, MD

PREP: 40 MIN. + CHILLING
BAKE: 10 MIN./BATCH + COOLING
MAKES: ABOUT 2 DOZEN

- ½ cup butter, softened
- ¾ cup packed dark brown sugar
- ⅓ cup molasses
- 1 large egg
- 2 tablespoons water
- 2⅔ cups all-purpose flour
- 1 teaspoon baking soda
- ½ teaspoon salt
- 2 teaspoons ground ginger
- ½ teaspoon ground cinnamon
- ½ teaspoon ground nutmeg
- ½ teaspoon ground allspice
   Frosting of choice

1. Cream butter and brown sugar until light and fluffy. Beat in molasses, egg and water. In another bowl, whisk together remaining ingredients minus frosting; gradually beat into creamed mixture. Divide dough in half. Shape each into a disk; wrap each disk in plastic. Refrigerate until easy to handle, about 30 minutes.
2. Preheat oven to 350°. On a lightly floured surface, roll each portion of dough to ⅛-in. thickness. Cut with a floured 4-in. gingerbread man cookie cutter. Place 2 in. apart on greased baking sheets.
3. Bake until edges are firm, 8-10 minutes. Remove to wire racks to cool completely. Frost as desired.
Per 1 cookie without frosting: 118 cal., 4g fat (2g sat. fat), 17mg chol., 128mg sod., 19g carb. (9g sugars, 0 fiber), 2g pro.

★ ★ ★ ★ ★ **READER REVIEW**

"This is one keeper of a cookie. Wow! If you love soft, just-right-spiced gingerbread men, this is a must-try recipe. You won't be disappointed."

DAWN HURNING
TASTEOFHOME.COM

Butter Pecan Fudge

Toasted pecans add a nutty crunch to this creamy, buttery fudge. I give this candy, with its wonderful caramel flavor, as gifts at Christmastime, and people always rave about it!

—**PAM SMITH** ALTA LOMA, CA

PREP: 10 MIN. • **COOK:** 10 MIN. + COOLING
MAKES: ABOUT 1½ POUNDS (64 PIECES)

- 1 teaspoon plus ½ cup butter, cubed
- ½ cup granulated sugar
- ½ cup packed brown sugar
- ½ cup heavy whipping cream
- ⅛ teaspoon salt
- 1 teaspoon vanilla extract
- 2 cups sifted confectioners' sugar
- 1 cup coarsely chopped pecans, toasted

1. Line an 8x8-in. pan with foil; grease foil with 1 teaspoon butter.
2. In a large heavy saucepan, combine remaining butter, granulated and brown sugars, cream and salt. Bring to a rapid boil over medium heat, stirring constantly. Cook, without stirring, until a candy thermometer reads 234° (soft-ball stage). Remove from heat. Add vanilla to pan (do not stir).
3. Cool, without stirring, to 110°, about 30 minutes. Beat with a spoon until fudge just begins to thicken. Gradually stir in confectioners' sugar until smooth; add nuts and continue stirring until fudge becomes very thick and just begins to lose its sheen. Immediately spread into prepared pan. Cool.
4. Using foil, lift fudge out of pan. Remove foil; cut fudge into 1-in. squares. Store between layers of waxed paper in an airtight container.
Note: To toast nuts, bake in a shallow pan in a 350° oven for 5-10 minutes or cook in a skillet over low heat until lightly browned, stirring occasionally.
Per 1 piece: 59 cal., 3g fat (1g sat. fat), 7mg chol., 18mg sod., 7g carb. (7g sugars, 0 fiber), 0 pro.

Candy Cane Coffee Cakes

I make my festive-looking coffee cakes at Christmas and for breakfast company.
—**KELLEY WINSHIP** WEST RUTLAND, VT

PREP: 40 MIN. + RISING • **BAKE:** 15 MIN.
MAKES: 3 COFFEE CAKES (12 SLICES EACH)

- 2 **cups (16 ounces) sour cream**
- 2 **packages (¼ ounce each) active dry yeast**
- ½ **cup warm water (110° to 115°)**
- ¼ **cup butter, softened**
- ⅓ **cup sugar**
- 2 **teaspoons salt**
- 2 **large eggs, beaten**
- 5¼ **to 6 cups all-purpose flour**
- 1½ **cups (12 ounces) finely chopped dried apricots**
- 1½ **cups finely chopped well-drained maraschino cherries**
- 2 **tablespoons butter, melted**

ICING

- 2 **cups confectioners' sugar**
- 2 **to 3 tablespoons water**

1. In a small saucepan, heat the sour cream until lukewarm. Set aside. In a large bowl, dissolve yeast in warm water. Add sour cream, softened butter, sugar, salt, eggs and 2 cups flour. With an electric mixer, beat until smooth. Stir in just enough of remaining flour to form a soft dough.

2. Turn out onto a floured surface and knead until smooth and elastic. Place in a greased bowl, turning once to grease top. Cover and let rise in a warm place until doubled, about 1 hour.

3. Punch dough down; divide into three equal parts. On a lightly floured surface, roll each part into a 15x6-in. rectangle. Place on greased baking sheets. With scissors, make 2-in. cuts at ½-in. intervals on the long sides of each rectangle. Combine apricots and cherries; spread one-third of mixture down the center of each rectangle.

4. Crisscross strips over filling. Stretch dough to 22 in. long and curve to form cane. Let rise until doubled, about 45 minutes.

5. Preheat oven to 375°. Bake for 15-20 minutes. While warm, brush canes with melted butter. Combine icing ingredients and drizzle over tops.

Per 1 slice: 176 cal., 5g fat (3g sat. fat), 19mg chol., 161mg sod., 30g carb. (14g sugars, 1g fiber), 3g pro.

ERIN FRAKES'
PRETZEL JELL-O DESSERT
PAGE 251

Classic Comeback

Sample **the best of decades past** with these time-honored dishes. The chapter brings **contemporary twists** to **all-time favorites** such as shrimp cocktail, Chicken a la King and cheese fondue.

BETTY CLAYCOMB'S CROWN ROAST OF PORK WITH MUSHROOM DRESSING
PAGE 249

ANNIE HENDRICKS' PEACH WINE COOLERS
PAGE 244

JANICE THOMAS' RUMAKI
PAGE 251

Peach Wine Coolers

(PICTURED ON P. 243)

The fantastic flavors of honey, wine and brandy come through to make a special drink for your fiesta. It's like sunshine in a glass!
—**ANNIE HENDRICKS** BURBANK, CA

PREP: 15 MIN. + CHILLING • **MAKES:** 9 SERVINGS

2 cups frozen unsweetened sliced peaches, thawed
½ cup brandy
⅓ cup honey
½ lemon, very thinly sliced
1 bottle (750 milliliters) dry white wine
1½ cups carbonated water, chilled
    Ice cubes

1. In a 2-qt. pitcher, combine the peach slices, brandy, honey and lemon slices; stir in wine. Refrigerate for 2-4 hours or until chilled.
2. Just before serving, stir in the sparkling water. Serve over ice.
Per ¾ cup: 151 cal., 0 fat (0 sat. fat), 0 chol., 5mg sod., 16g carb. (14g sugars, 1g fiber), 0 pro.

Lemon Pudding Dessert

After a big meal, folks really go for this light, lemony treat. The crisp shortbread crust is the perfect base for the fluffy layers above. I've prepared this sunny dessert for church suppers for years and I always get recipe requests.
—**MURIEL DEWITT** MAYNARD, MA

PREP: 20 MIN. + CHILLING • **BAKE:** 20 MIN. • **MAKES:** 16 SERVINGS

1 cup cold butter, cubed
2 cups all-purpose flour
1 package (8 ounces) cream cheese, softened
1 cup confectioners' sugar
1 carton (8 ounces) frozen whipped topping, thawed, divided
3 cups cold whole milk
2 packages (3.4 ounces each) instant lemon pudding mix

1. Preheat oven to 350°. Cut butter into flour until crumbly. Press into an ungreased 13x9-in. baking dish. Bake until light brown, 18-22 minutes. Cool on a wire rack.
2. Meanwhile, beat cream cheese and sugar until smooth. Fold in 1 cup whipped topping. Spread over cooled crust.
3. Beat milk and pudding mix on low speed for 2 minutes. Carefully spread over cream cheese layer. Top with remaining whipped topping. Refrigerate at least 1 hour.
Per 1 piece: 348 cal., 20g fat (13g sat. fat), 49mg chol., 305mg sod., 35g carb. (22g sugars, 0 fiber), 4g pro.

VANILLA CREAM
FRUIT TART

Vanilla Cream Fruit Tart

It's well worth the effort to whip up this creamy tart bursting with juicy summer berries. A friend gave me the recipe, and it always receives rave reviews at gatherings.
—**SUSAN TERZAKIS** ANDOVER, MA

PREP: 25 MIN. • **BAKE:** 25 MIN. + CHILLING • **MAKES:** 12 SERVINGS

¾ cup butter, softened
½ cup confectioners' sugar
1½ cups all-purpose flour
1 package (10 to 12 ounces) white baking chips, melted and cooled
¼ cup heavy whipping cream
1 package (8 ounces) cream cheese, softened
½ cup pineapple juice
¼ cup granulated sugar
1 tablespoon cornstarch
½ teaspoon lemon juice
1½ to 2 cups fresh strawberries, sliced
1 cup fresh blueberries
1 cup fresh raspberries

1. Preheat oven to 300°. Cream butter and confectioners' sugar until light and fluffy. Beat in flour (mixture will be crumbly). Pat onto a greased 12-in. pizza pan. Bake until lightly browned, 25-28 minutes. Cool.
2. Beat melted chips and cream until smooth. Beat in cream cheese until smooth. Spread over crust. Refrigerate 30 minutes. Meanwhile, in a small saucepan, combine pineapple juice, granulated sugar, cornstarch and lemon juice. Bring to a boil over medium heat; cook and stir until thickened, about 2 minutes. Cool.
3. Arrange berries over cream cheese layer; brush with pineapple mixture. Refrigerate 1 hour before serving.
Per 1 piece: 433 cal., 28g fat (17g sat. fat), 60mg chol., 174mg sod., 43g carb. (28g sugars, 2g fiber), 5g pro.

Classic Cobb Salad

Making this salad is a lot like putting in a garden. I plant everything in nice, neat sections, just as I do with seedlings.
—**PATRICIA KILE** ELIZABETHTOWN, PA

START TO FINISH: 20 MIN. • **MAKES:** 4 SERVINGS

- 6 cups torn iceberg lettuce
- 2 medium tomatoes, chopped
- 1 medium ripe avocado, peeled and chopped
- ¾ cup diced fully cooked ham
- 2 hard-boiled large eggs, chopped
- ¾ cup diced cooked turkey
- 1¼ cups sliced fresh mushrooms
- ½ cup crumbled blue cheese
  Salad dressing of choice
  Sliced ripe olives and lemon wedges, optional

Place lettuce on a platter or in a large serving bowl. Arrange remaining ingredients in rows or sections as desired. Serve with dressing of choice; if desired, serve with sliced ripe olives and lemon wedges.

Per 1 serving: 260 cal., 15g fat (5g sat. fat), 148mg chol., 586mg sod., 10g carb. (5g sugars, 4g fiber), 23g pro.
Diabetic Exchanges: 3 lean meat, 2 vegetable, 2 fat.

BLACKENED TILAPIA WITH ZUCCHINI NOODLES

CLASSIC COBB SALAD

Blackened Tilapia with Zucchini Noodles

I love quick and bright meals like this one-skillet wonder. Homemade pico de gallo is easy to make the night before.
—**TAMMY BROWNLOW** DALLAS, TX

START TO FINISH: 30 MIN. • **MAKES:** 4 SERVINGS

- 2 large zucchini (about 1½ pounds)
- 1½ teaspoons ground cumin
- ¾ teaspoon salt, divided
- ½ teaspoon smoked paprika
- ½ teaspoon pepper
- ¼ tsp garlic powder
- 4 tilapia fillets (6 ounces each)
- 2 teaspoons olive oil
- 2 garlic cloves, minced
- 1 cup pico de gallo

1. Trim ends of zucchini. Using a spiralizer, cut zucchini into thin strands.
2. Mix cumin, ½ teaspoon salt, smoked paprika, pepper and garlic powder; sprinkle generously onto both sides of tilapia. In a large nonstick skillet, heat oil over medium-high heat. In batches, cook tilapia until fish just begins to flake easily with a fork, 2-3 minutes per side. Remove from pan; keep warm.
3. In same pan, cook zucchini with garlic over medium-high heat until slightly softened, 1-2 minutes, tossing constantly with tongs (do not overcook). Sprinkle with remaining salt. Serve with tilapia and pico de gallo.
Note: If a spiralizer is not available, zucchini may also be cut into ribbons using a vegetable peeler. Saute as directed, increasing time as necessary.

Per 1 serving: 203 cal., 4g fat (1g sat. fat), 83mg chol., 522mg sod., 8g carb. (5g sugars, 2g fiber), 34g pro.
Diabetic Exchanges: 5 lean meat, 1 vegetable, ½ fat.

FAST FIX ▶ Three-Cheese Fondue

I got this easy recipe from my daughter, who lives in France. It's become my go-to fondue, and I make it often for our family.
—**BETTY MANGAS** TOLEDO, OH

START TO FINISH: 30 MIN. • **MAKES:** 4 CUPS

- ½ pound each Emmenthaler, Gruyere and Jarlsberg cheeses, shredded
- 2 tablespoons cornstarch, divided
- 4 teaspoons cherry brandy
- 2 cups dry white wine
- ⅛ teaspoon ground nutmeg
- ⅛ teaspoon paprika
  Dash cayenne pepper
  Cubed French bread baguette, boiled red potatoes and/or tiny whole pickles

1. In a large bowl, combine cheeses and 1 tablespoon cornstarch. In a small bowl, combine remaining cornstarch and brandy; set aside. In a large saucepan, heat wine over medium heat until bubbles form around sides of pan.
2. Reduce heat to medium-low; add a handful of cheese mixture. Stir constantly, using a figure-eight motion, until cheese is almost completely melted. Continue adding cheese, one handful at a time, allowing cheese to almost completely melt between additions.
3. Stir the brandy mixture; gradually stir into cheese mixture. Add the spices; cook and stir until mixture is thickened and smooth.
4. Transfer to a fondue pot and keep warm. Serve with bread cubes, potatoes and/or pickles.
Per ¼ cup without dippers: 191 cal., 12g fat (7g sat. fat), 37mg chol., 151mg sod., 3g carb. (1g sugars, 0 fiber), 12g pro.

THREE-CHEESE FONDUE

CABBAGE ROLL CASSEROLE

Cabbage Roll Casserole

I layer cabbage with tomato sauce and beef to create a hearty casserole that tastes like cabbage rolls, but without all the work.
—**DOREEN MARTIN** KITIMAT, BC

PREP: 20 MIN. • **BAKE:** 55 MIN. + STANDING • **MAKES:** 12 SERVINGS

- 2 pounds ground beef
- 1 large onion, chopped
- 3 garlic cloves, minced
- 2 cans (15 ounces each) tomato sauce, divided
- 1 teaspoon dried thyme
- ½ teaspoon dill weed
- ½ teaspoon rubbed sage
- ¼ teaspoon salt
- ¼ teaspoon pepper
- ¼ teaspoon cayenne pepper
- 2 cups cooked rice
- 4 bacon strips, cooked and crumbled
- 1 medium head cabbage (2 pounds), shredded
- 1 cup shredded part-skim mozzarella cheese
  Coarsely ground pepper, optional

1. Preheat oven to 375°. In a large skillet, cook beef and onion over medium heat, crumbling beef, until meat is no longer pink. Add garlic; cook 1 minute longer. Drain. Stir in one can of tomato sauce and next six ingredients. Bring to a boil. Reduce heat; simmer, covered, 5 minutes. Stir in rice and bacon; remove from heat.
2. Place a third of the cabbage in a greased 13x9-in. baking dish. Top with half of meat mixture. Repeat layers; top with remaining cabbage. Pour remaining tomato sauce over top.
3. Cover and bake 45 minutes. Sprinkle with cheese. Bake, uncovered, until cheese is melted, about 10 minutes. Let stand 5 minutes before serving. If desired, sprinkle with coarsely ground pepper.
Per 1 piece: 256 cal., 13g fat (5g sat. fat), 56mg chol., 544mg sod., 17g carb. (4g sugars, 3g fiber), 20g pro.

Bacon Cheddar Potato Skins

Both crisp and hearty, this restaurant-quality snack is one that's often requested by my family.

—**TRISH PERRIN** KEIZER, OR

START TO FINISH: 30 MIN. • **MAKES:** 8 SERVINGS

- 4 large baking potatoes, baked
- 3 tablespoons canola oil
- 1 tablespoon grated Parmesan cheese
- ½ teaspoon salt
- ¼ teaspoon garlic powder
- ¼ teaspoon paprika
- ⅛ teaspoon pepper
- 8 bacon strips, cooked and crumbled
- 1½ cups shredded cheddar cheese
- ½ cup sour cream
- 4 green onions, sliced

1. Preheat oven to 475°. Cut potatoes in half lengthwise; scoop out pulp, leaving a ¼-in. shell (save pulp for another use). Place potato skins on a greased baking sheet.

2. Combine oil with next five ingredients; brush over both sides of skins.

3. Bake until crisp, about 7 minutes on each side. Sprinkle bacon and cheddar cheese inside skins. Bake until cheese is melted, about 2 minutes longer. Top with sour cream and onions. Serve immediately.

Per 1 potato skin: 350 cal., 19g fat (7g sat. fat), 33mg chol., 460mg sod., 34g carb. (2g sugars, 4g fiber), 12g pro.

BACON CHEDDAR
POTATO SKINS

HOT DOG ROLL-UPS

⑤ INGREDIENTS FAST FIX
Hot Dog Roll-Ups

Not only do my grandchildren love these cheese-and-bacon-filled hot dogs, but they enjoy helping put the meal together, too. It's the perfect solution to a last-minute lunch.

—**LYLETTA SEARLE** MORGAN, UT

START TO FINISH: 30 MIN. • **MAKES:** 8 SERVINGS

- 8 hot dogs
- 1 block (4 ounces) cheddar cheese, cut into 8 strips
- 2 bacon strips, cooked and crumbled
- 1 tube (8 ounces) refrigerated crescent rolls

Cut a lengthwise slit in each hot dog; fill with a strip of cheese and about ½ teaspoon bacon. Separate crescent dough into eight triangles. Place a hot dog on the wide end of each triangle; roll toward the point. Place cheese side up on an ungreased baking sheet. Bake at 375° for 12 minutes or until golden brown.

Per 1 roll-up: 325 cal., 25g fat (10g sat. fat), 41mg chol., 797mg sod., 12g carb. (3g sugars, 0 fiber), 11g pro.

TRADITIONAL LASAGNA
Lorri Foockle
Granville, IL

Traditional Lasagna

My family tasted this rich lasagna at a friend's home on Christmas Eve, and it became our holiday tradition. My sister's Italian in-laws request it often—and that's a big compliment.

—LORRI FOOCKLE GRANVILLE, IL

PREP: 30 MIN. + SIMMERING
BAKE: 70 MIN. + STANDING
MAKES: 12 SERVINGS

- 1 pound ground beef
- ¾ pound bulk pork sausage
- 3 cans (8 ounces each) tomato sauce
- 2 cans (6 ounces each) tomato paste
- 2 garlic cloves, minced
- 2 teaspoons sugar
- 1 teaspoon Italian seasoning
- ½ to 1 teaspoon salt
- ¼ to ½ teaspoon pepper
- 3 large eggs
- 3 tablespoons minced fresh parsley
- 3 cups (24 ounces) 4% small-curd cottage cheese
- 1 carton (8 ounces) ricotta cheese
- ½ cup grated Parmesan cheese
- 9 lasagna noodles, cooked and drained
- 6 slices provolone cheese (about 6 ounces)
- 3 cups shredded part-skim mozzarella cheese, divided

1. In a large skillet over medium heat, cook and crumble beef and sausage until no longer pink; drain. Add next seven ingredients. Bring to a boil. Reduce heat; simmer, uncovered, 1 hour, stirring occasionally. Adjust seasoning with additional salt and pepper, if desired.
2. Meanwhile, in a large bowl, lightly beat eggs. Add parsley; stir in cottage cheese, ricotta and Parmesan cheese.
3. Preheat oven to 375°. Spread 1 cup meat sauce in an ungreased 13x9-in. baking dish. Layer with three noodles, provolone cheese, 2 cups cottage cheese mixture, 1 cup mozzarella, three noodles, 2 cups meat sauce, remaining cottage cheese mixture and 1 cup mozzarella. Top with remaining noodles, meat sauce and mozzarella (dish will be full).
4. Cover; bake 50 minutes. Uncover; bake until heated through, 20 minutes. Let stand 15 minutes before cutting.
Per 1 piece: 503 cal., 27g fat (13g sat. fat), 136mg chol., 1208mg sod., 30g carb. (9g sugars, 2g fiber), 36g pro.

Double Chocolate Banana Muffins

Combining two favorite flavors like rich chocolate and soft banana makes these muffins doubly good.

—DONNA BROCKETT KINGFISHER, OK

PREP: 15 MIN. • **BAKE:** 20 MIN.
MAKES: ABOUT 1 DOZEN

- 1½ cups all-purpose flour
- 1 cup sugar
- ¼ cup baking cocoa
- 1 teaspoon baking soda
- ½ teaspoon salt
- ¼ teaspoon baking powder
- 1⅓ cups mashed ripe bananas (about 3 medium)
- ⅓ cup canola oil
- 1 large egg
- 1 cup (6 ounces) miniature semisweet chocolate chips

1. Preheat oven to 350°. Whisk together the first six ingredients. In a separate bowl, whisk bananas, oil and egg until blended. Add to the flour mixture; stir just until moistened. Fold in chocolate chips.
2. Fill greased or paper-lined muffin cups three-fourths full. Bake until a toothpick inserted in center comes out clean, 20-25 minutes. Cool 5 minutes before removing from pan to a wire rack. Serve warm.
Per 1 muffin without optional topping: 278 cal., 11g fat (3g sat. fat), 16mg chol., 220mg sod., 45g carb. (28g sugars, 2g fiber), 3g pro.
Optional streusel topping: Combine ½ cup sugar, ⅓ cup all-purpose flour and ½ teaspoon ground cinnamon; cut in ¼ cup cold butter until crumbly. Before baking, sprinkle over filled muffin cups; bake as directed.

DOUBLE CHOCOLATE BANANA MUFFINS

Crown Roast of Pork with Mushroom Dressing

(PICTURED ON P. 243)

I always thought pork crown roasts were fussy until I got up the courage to make one. My family loves the juicy pork and savory mushroom stuffing.

—**BETTY CLAYCOMB** ALVERTON, PA

PREP: 15 MIN. • **BAKE:** 2 HOURS
MAKES: 10 SERVINGS

- 1 pork loin crown roast
  (10-12 ribs, about 6-8 pounds)
- ½ teaspoon seasoned salt

MUSHROOM DRESSING

- ¼ cup butter, cubed
- 1 cup sliced fresh mushrooms
- ½ cup diced celery
- 3 cups cubed day-old bread
- ¼ teaspoon salt
- ¼ teaspoon pepper
- ⅓ cup apricot preserves
- 1 cup whole fresh cranberries,
  optional

1. Preheat oven to 350°. Place roast, rib ends up, in a shallow roasting pan; sprinkle with seasoned salt. Cover rib ends with foil. Bake, uncovered, for 1¼ hours.

2. Meanwhile, melt butter over medium-high heat. Add mushrooms and celery; saute until tender. Stir in bread cubes, salt and pepper. Spoon around roast. Brush sides of roast with preserves. Bake until thermometers inserted into meat between ribs reads 145°, 45-60 minutes. Remove foil; let meat stand 10 minutes before slicing.

3. If desired, thread cranberries on a 20-in. string or thread. Transfer roast to a serving platter. Loop cranberry string in and out of rib ends. Slice between ribs to serve.

Per 1 pork rib plus stuffing: 404 cal., 17g fat (7g sat. fat), 106mg chol., 314mg sod., 16g carb. (7g sugars, 1g fiber), 45g pro.

✳

TEST KITCHEN TIP
A classic adornment for crown roast is a little paper frill placed on each bone (they are also called chop frills or chop holders). Your butcher may be able to provide them when you order the roast, or you can find paper frills in kitchen-supply stores.

MAKEOVER BEEF STROGANOFF

EAT SMART **FAST FIX**
Makeover Beef Stroganoff

I trimmed the calories, fat and sodium from a classic beef Stroganoff, and my comfy, cozy version still tastes like a Russian masterpiece.

—**CANDACE CLARK** KELSO, WA

START TO FINISH: 30 MIN.
MAKES: 6 SERVINGS

- ½ cup plus 1 tablespoon all-purpose flour, divided
- ½ teaspoon pepper, divided
- 1 beef top round steak (1½ pounds), cut into thin strips
- 2 tablespoons canola oil
- 1 cup sliced fresh mushrooms
- 1 small onion, chopped
- 1 garlic clove, minced
- 1 can (14½ ounces) reduced-sodium beef broth
- ½ teaspoon salt
- 1 cup (8 ounces) reduced-fat sour cream
  Chopped fresh parsley, optional
  Coarsely ground pepper, optional
- 3 cups cooked yolk-free noodles

1. Combine ½ cup of the flour and ¼ teaspoon of the pepper in a large resealable plastic bag. Add the beef, a few pieces at a time, and shake to coat.

2. In a large nonstick skillet, heat oil over medium-high heat. Cook beef in batches until no longer pink. Remove and keep warm. In the same skillet, saute mushrooms and onion in drippings until tender. Add garlic; cook 1 minute longer.

3. Whisk remaining flour with broth until smooth; stir into skillet. Bring to a boil; cook and stir until thickened, about 2 minutes. Add beef, salt and remaining pepper. Stir in sour cream; heat through (do not boil). If desired, sprinkle with parsley and coarsely ground pepper. Serve with noodles.

Per 1 cup beef stroganoff with ½ cup noodles: 349 cal., 12g fat (4g sat. fat), 78mg chol., 393mg sod., 25g carb. (5g sugars, 2g fiber), 33g pro.
Diabetic Exchanges: 3 lean meat, 2 fat, 1½ starch.

Skillet Pineapple Upside-Down Cake

For a change of pace, you can substitute fresh or frozen peach slices for the pineapple in this old-fashioned recipe.

—**BERNARDINE MELTON** PAOLA, KS

PREP: 20 MIN. • **BAKE:** 30 MIN. + COOLING
MAKES: 10 SERVINGS

- ½ cup butter
- 1 cup packed brown sugar
- 1 can (20 ounces) sliced pineapple
- ½ cup chopped pecans
- 3 large eggs, separated
- 1 cup sugar
- 1 teaspoon vanilla extract
- 1 cup all-purpose flour
- 1 teaspoon baking powder
- ¼ teaspoon salt
  Maraschino cherries

1. Preheat oven to 375°. Melt butter in a 9- or 10-in. ovenproof skillet. Add brown sugar; mix until sugar is melted. Drain pineapple, reserving ⅓ cup juice. Arrange about eight pineapple slices in a single layer over sugar (refrigerate remaining slices for another use). Sprinkle pecans over pineapple; set aside.
2. In a large bowl, beat egg yolks until thick and lemon-colored. Gradually add sugar, beating well. Blend in vanilla and reserved pineapple juice. Combine the flour, baking powder and salt; gradually add to batter and mix well.
3. In a small bowl, beat egg whites on high speed until stiff peaks form; fold into batter. Spoon into skillet.
4. Bake until a toothpick inserted in the center comes out clean, 30-35 minutes (cover loosely with foil if cake browns too quickly). Let stand 10 minutes before inverting onto serving plate. Place cherries in center of pineapple slices.
Per 1 slice: 380 cal., 15g fat (7g sat. fat), 88mg chol., 224mg sod., 59g carb. (48g sugars, 1g fiber), 4g pro.

LAYERED SALAD FOR A CROWD

FAST FIX ▶

Layered Salad for a Crowd

This salad is a favorite of my three sons. I took it to a luncheon honoring our school district's food service manager and she asked for the recipe! I like to make the dressing the day before so the flavors blend together.

—**LINDA ASHLEY** LEESBURG, GA

START TO FINISH: 20 MIN. • **MAKES:** 20 SERVINGS

- 1 cup mayonnaise
- ¼ cup whole milk
- 2 teaspoons dill weed
- ½ teaspoon seasoning blend
- 1 bunch romaine, torn
- 2 medium carrots, grated
- 1 cup chopped red onion
- 1 medium cucumber, sliced
- 1 package (10 ounces) frozen peas, thawed
- 1½ cups shredded cheddar cheese
- 8 bacon strips, cooked and crumbled

1. For dressing, in a small bowl, whisk the mayonnaise, milk, dill and seasoning blend.
2. In a 4-qt. clear glass serving bowl, layer the romaine, carrots, onion and cucumber (do not toss). Pour dressing over the top; sprinkle with peas, cheese and bacon. Cover and refrigerate until serving.
Note: This recipe was tested with Nature's Seasons seasoning blend by Morton. Look for it in the spice aisle.
Per ⅔ cup: 151 cal., 13g fat (4g sat. fat), 16mg chol., 216mg sod., 5g carb. (2g sugars, 1g fiber), 4g pro.

SKILLET PINEAPPLE
UPSIDE-DOWN CAKE

Pretzel Jell-O Dessert

(PICTURED ON P. 242)

This is one of my mother's absolute favorite desserts. The salty pretzel crust is the perfect compliment to the sweet cream cheese filling.

—ERIN FRAKES MOLINE, IL

PREP: 30 MIN. + CHILLING • **MAKES:** 12 SERVINGS

- 2 cups crushed pretzels
- ¾ cup butter, melted
- 2 tablespoons sugar

FILLING

- 1 package (8 ounces) cream cheese, softened
- 1 cup sugar
- 1 carton (8 ounces) frozen whipped topping, thawed

TOPPING

- 2 packages (3 ounces each) strawberry gelatin
- 2 cups boiling water
- ½ cup cold water
  Fresh strawberries and additional whipped topping, optional

1. Preheat oven to 350°. Mix crushed pretzels, melted butter and sugar; press onto bottom of an ungreased 13x9-in. baking dish. Bake 10 minutes. Cool completely.

2. For filling, beat cream cheese and sugar until smooth. Stir in whipped topping; spread over crust. Refrigerate, covered, until cold.

3. In a small bowl, dissolve gelatin in boiling water. Stir in cold water; refrigerate until partially set. Pour carefully over filling. Refrigerate, covered, until firm, 4-6 hours.

4. Cut into squares. If desired, serve with strawberries and additional whipped topping.

Per 1 piece: 401 cal., 22g fat (14g sat. fat), 50mg chol., 401mg sod., 48g carb. (37g sugars, 1g fiber), 4g pro.

EAT SMART **SLOW COOKER**

Slow-Cooked Chicken a la King

When I know I'll be having a busy day with little time to prepare a meal, I use my slow cooker to make Chicken a la King. It smells so good while it's cooking.

—ELEANOR MIELKE SNOHOMISH, WA

PREP: 10 MIN. • **COOK:** 7½ HOURS • **MAKES:** 6 SERVINGS

- 1 can (10¾ ounces) reduced-fat reduced-sodium condensed cream of chicken soup, undiluted
- 3 tablespoons all-purpose flour
- ¼ teaspoon pepper
  Dash cayenne pepper
- 1 pound boneless skinless chicken breasts, cubed
- 1 celery rib, chopped
- ½ cup chopped green pepper
- ¼ cup chopped onion
- 1 package (10 ounces) frozen peas, thawed
- 2 tablespoons diced pimientos, drained
  Hot cooked rice

SLOW-COOKED CHICKEN
A LA KING

In a 3-qt. slow cooker, combine soup, flour, pepper and cayenne until smooth. Stir in chicken, celery, green pepper and onion. Cover and cook on low for 7-8 hours or until meat is no longer pink. Stir in peas and pimientos. Cook 30 minutes longer or until heated through. Serve with rice.

Per 1 cup without rice: 174 cal., 3g fat (1g sat. fat), 44mg chol., 268mg sod., 16g carb. (6g sugars, 3g fiber), 19g pro.

Diabetic Exchanges: 2 lean meat, 1 starch.

Rumaki

(PICTURED ON P. 243)

Sweet pineapple and crunchy water chestnuts wrapped in bacon and topped with barbecue sauce—yum! These Polynesian-inspired, can't-eat-just-one appetizers are great party food. The sauce is also amazing with smoked sausages, so you can set out a whole platter of mixed goodies.

—JANICE THOMAS MILFORD, NE

PREP: 30 MIN. • **BROIL:** 10 MIN. • **MAKES:** 14 APPETIZERS

- ½ cup packed brown sugar
- ¼ cup mayonnaise
- ¼ cup chili sauce
- 14 whole water chestnuts, drained
- 1 can (8 ounces) pineapple chunks, drained
- 7 bacon strips, halved

1. In a small saucepan, combine the brown sugar, mayonnaise and chili sauce. Cook and stir over medium heat until mixture comes to a boil; set aside.

2. Place a water chestnut and pineapple chunk on each piece of bacon; roll up bacon and secure with a toothpick. Place on a broiler pan. Broil 4-5 in. from the heat for 4-5 minutes on each side or until the bacon is crisp. Serve with sauce.

Per 1 appetizer: 92 cal., 4g fat (1g sat. fat), 4mg chol., 162mg sod., 12g carb. (11g sugars, 0 fiber), 2g pro.

SHRIMP COCKTAIL SPREAD

Cookie Jar Gingersnaps

My grandma kept two cookie jars, and one was always filled with these chewy gingersnaps. My daughter baked this recipe for a 4-H competition and won the blue ribbon.

—**DEB HANDY** POMONA, KS

PREP: 20 MIN. • **BAKE:** 15 MIN./BATCH
MAKES: 3 DOZEN

- ¾ cup shortening
- 1 cup plus 2 tablespoons sugar, divided
- 1 large egg
- ¼ cup molasses
- 2 cups all-purpose flour
- 2 teaspoons baking soda
- 1½ teaspoons ground ginger
- 1 teaspoon ground cinnamon
- ½ teaspoon salt

1. Preheat oven to 350°. Cream the shortening and 1 cup sugar until light and fluffy. Beat in egg and molasses. In another bowl, combine the next five ingredients; gradually add to creamed mixture and mix well.

2. Shape level tablespoonfuls of dough into balls. Dip one side into remaining sugar; place 2 in. apart, sugary side up, on greased baking sheets. Bake until lightly browned and crinkly, 12-15 minutes. Remove to wire racks to cool.

Per 1 cookie: 92 cal., 4g fat (1g sat. fat), 5mg chol., 106mg sod., 13g carb. (7g sugars, 0 fiber), 1g pro.

Shrimp Cocktail Spread

There's no secret to this creamy seafood appetizer...it's simply delicious! I first tasted it at a friend's house and liked it so much, I requested the recipe.

—**BRENDA BUHLER** ABBOTSFORD, BC

START TO FINISH: 20 MIN.
MAKES: 20 SERVINGS

- 1 package (8 ounces) cream cheese, softened
- ½ cup sour cream
- ¼ cup mayonnaise
- 1 cup seafood cocktail sauce
- 12 ounces frozen cooked salad shrimp, thawed
- 2 cups shredded mozzarella cheese
- 1 medium green pepper, chopped
- 1 small tomato, chopped
- 3 green onions with tops, sliced
  Assorted crackers

1. In a large bowl, beat the cream cheese, sour cream and mayonnaise until smooth.

2. Spread mixture on a round 12-in. serving platter. Top with seafood sauce. Sprinkle with the shrimp, mozzarella, green pepper, tomato and onions. Cover and refrigerate. Serve with crackers.

Per 2 tablespoons: 136 cal., 10g fat (5g sat. fat), 62mg chol., 372mg sod., 4g carb. (3g sugars, 1g fiber), 8g pro.

COOKIE JAR GINGERSNAPS

Cheeseburger Soup

A local restaurant enjoys a cult following thanks to its cheeseburger soup, a recipe the chef keeps top secret. I made my own version with beef, Velveeta and potatoes.
—JOANIE SHAWHAN MADISON, WI

PREP: 45 MIN. • **COOK:** 10 MIN.
MAKES: 8 SERVINGS (2¼ QUARTS)

- ½ pound ground beef
- 4 tablespoons butter, divided
- ¾ cup chopped onion
- ¾ cup shredded carrots
- ¾ cup diced celery
- 1 teaspoon dried basil
- 1 teaspoon dried parsley flakes
- 1¾ pounds (about 4 cups) cubed peeled potatoes
- 3 cups chicken broth
- ¼ cup all-purpose flour
- 1 package (16 ounces) Velveeta process cheese, cubed
- 1½ cups whole milk
- ¾ teaspoon salt
- ¼ to ½ teaspoon pepper
- ¼ cup sour cream

1. In a large saucepan over medium heat, cook and crumble beef until no longer pink; drain and set aside. In same saucepan, melt 1 tablespoon butter over medium heat. Saute onion, carrots, celery, basil and parsley until tender, about 10 minutes. Add the potatoes, beef and broth; bring to a boil. Reduce the heat; simmer, covered, until potatoes are tender, 10-12 minutes.
2. Meanwhile, in a small skillet, melt remaining butter. Add flour; cook and stir until bubbly, 3-5 minutes. Add to soup; bring to a boil. Cook and stir for 2 minutes. Reduce heat to low. Stir in cheese, milk, salt and pepper; cook until cheese melts. Remove from heat; blend in sour cream.
Per 1 cup: 450 cal., 27g fat (15g sat. fat), 100mg chol., 1421mg sod., 33g carb. (8g sugars, 3g fiber), 19g pro.

EAT SMART

Must-Have Tiramisu

Here's the perfect guilt-free version of a beloved classic dessert. My friends even say that they prefer my healthy recipe over other tiramisu.
—ALE GAMBINI BEVERLY HILLS, CA

PREP: 25 MIN. + CHILLING
MAKES: 9 SERVINGS

- ½ cup heavy whipping cream
- 2 cups (16 ounces) vanilla yogurt
- 1 cup fat-free milk
- ½ cup brewed espresso or strong coffee, cooled
- 24 crisp ladyfinger cookies
  Baking cocoa
  Fresh raspberries, optional

1. In a small bowl, beat cream until stiff peaks form; fold in yogurt. Spread ½ cup cream mixture onto bottom of an 8-in. square dish.
2. In a shallow dish, mix milk and espresso. Quickly dip 12 ladyfingers into coffee mixture, allowing excess to drip off. Arrange in the dish in a single layer, breaking to fit as needed. Top with half of the remaining cream mixture; dust it with cocoa. Repeat the layers.
3. Refrigerate, covered, for at least 2 hours before serving. If desired, serve with raspberries.
Per 1 piece without raspberries: 177 cal., 6g fat (4g sat. fat), 41mg chol., 80mg sod., 25g carb. (18g sugars, 0 fiber), 6g pro.
Diabetic Exchanges: 1 starch, ½ fat-free milk, 1 fat.

MUST-HAVE TIRAMISU

Special Occasion Beef Bourguignon

I've found many rich and satisfying variations for beef Bourguignon, including an intriguing peasant version that used beef cheeks for the meat and a rustic table wine. To make the stew gluten-free, use white rice flour instead of all-purpose.

—LEO COTNOIR JOHNSON CITY, NY

PREP: 50 MIN. • **BAKE:** 2 HOURS
MAKES: 8 SERVINGS

- 4 bacon strips, chopped
- 1 beef sirloin tip roast (2 pounds), cut into 1½-inch cubes and patted dry
- ¼ cup all-purpose flour
- ½ teaspoon salt
- ½ teaspoon pepper
- 1 tablespoon canola oil
- 2 medium onions, chopped
- 2 medium carrots, coarsely chopped
- ½ pound medium fresh mushrooms, quartered
- 4 garlic cloves, minced
- 1 tablespoon tomato paste
- 2 cups dry red wine
- 1 cup beef stock
- 2 bay leaves
- ½ teaspoon dried thyme
- 8 ounces uncooked egg noodles

1. Preheat oven to 325°. In a Dutch oven, cook and stir the bacon over medium-low heat until crisp. Remove with a slotted spoon, reserving drippings; drain on paper towels.

2. In batches, brown beef in drippings over medium-high heat; remove from pan. Toss with flour, salt and pepper.

3. In same pan, heat 1 tablespoon oil over medium heat; saute onions, carrots and mushrooms until onions are tender, 4-5 minutes. Add garlic and tomato paste; cook and stir 1 minute. Add wine and stock, stirring to loosen browned bits from pan. Add herbs, bacon and beef; bring to a boil.

4. Transfer to oven; bake, covered, until meat is tender, 2-2¼ hours. Remove bay leaves.

5. Cook noodles according to package directions; drain. Serve with stew.

To freeze: Freeze cooled stew in freezer containers. To use, partially thaw in the refrigerator overnight. Heat through in a saucepan, stirring occasionally and adding a little stock or broth if necessary.

Per ⅔ cup stew with ⅔ cup noodles: 422 cal., 14g fat (4g sat. fat), 105mg chol., 357mg sod., 31g carb. (4g sugars, 2g fiber), 31g pro.

Diabetic Exchanges: 4 lean meat, 2 fat, 1½ starch, 1 vegetable.

Slow Cooker Tuna Noodle Casserole

We tweaked this family-friendly classic to work for the slow cooker. It's easy, wholesome and totally homemade!

—TASTE OF HOME TEST KITCHEN

PREP: 25 MIN.
COOK: 4 HOURS + STANDING
MAKES: 10 SERVINGS

- ¼ cup butter, cubed
- ½ pound sliced fresh mushrooms
- 1 medium onion, chopped
- 1 medium sweet pepper, chopped
- 1 teaspoon salt, divided
- 1 teaspoon pepper, divided
- 2 garlic cloves, minced
- ¼ cup all-purpose flour
- 2 cups reduced-sodium chicken broth
- 2 cups half-and-half cream
- 4 cups uncooked egg noodles (about 6 ounces)
- 3 cans (5 ounces each) light tuna in water, drained
- 2 tablespoons lemon juice
- 2 cups shredded Monterey Jack cheese
- 2 cups frozen peas, thawed
- 2 cups crushed potato chips

1. In a large skillet, melt butter over medium-high heat. Add mushrooms, onion, sweet pepper, ½ teaspoon salt and ½ teaspoon pepper; cook and stir 6-8 minutes or until tender. Add garlic; cook 1 minute longer. Stir in flour until blended. Gradually whisk in broth. Bring to a boil, stirring constantly; cook and stir 1-2 minutes or until thickened.

2. Transfer to a 5-qt. slow cooker. Stir in cream and noodles. Cook, covered, on low 4-5 hours or until noodles are tender. Meanwhile, combine tuna and lemon juice with the remaining salt and pepper.

3. Remove insert from slow cooker. Stir cheese, tuna mixture and peas into noodle mixture. Let stand, uncovered, 20 minutes. Just before serving, sprinkle with potato chips.

Per 1 cup: 393 cal., 21g fat (12g sat. fat), 84mg chol., 752mg sod., 28g carb. (5g sugars, 3g fiber), 22g pro.

SLOW COOKER TUNA NOODLE CASSEROLE

Best Crescent Rolls

My daughter and I have cranked out dozens of homemade crescent rolls. It's a real team effort. I cut the dough into pie-shaped wedges; she rolls.

—**IRENE YEH** MEQUON, WI

PREP: 40 MIN. + CHILLING
BAKE: 10 MIN./BATCH • **MAKES:** 32 ROLLS

3¾ to 4¼ cups all-purpose flour
2 packages (¼ ounce each) active dry yeast
1 teaspoon salt
1 cup whole milk
½ cup butter, cubed
¼ cup honey
3 large egg yolks
2 tablespoons butter, melted

1. Combine 1½ cups flour, yeast and salt. In a small saucepan, heat milk, cubed butter and honey to 120°-130°. Add to the dry ingredients; beat on medium speed 2 minutes. Add egg yolks; beat on high 2 minutes. Stir in enough remaining flour to form a soft dough (dough will be sticky).

2. Turn dough onto a floured surface; knead until smooth and elastic, about 6-8 minutes. Place in a greased bowl, turning once to grease the top. Cover with plastic wrap and let rise in a warm place until doubled, about 45 minutes.

3. Punch down dough; place in a resealable plastic bag. Seal and refrigerate overnight.

4. To bake, turn dough onto a lightly floured surface; divide in half. Roll each portion into a 14-in. circle; cut each circle into 16 wedges. Lightly brush wedges with melted butter. Roll up from wide ends, pinching pointed ends to seal. Place rolls 2 in. apart on parchment paper-lined baking sheets, point side down. Cover with lightly greased plastic wrap; let rise in a warm place until doubled, about 45 minutes.

5. Preheat oven to 375°. Bake until golden brown, 9-11 minutes. Remove from pans to wire racks; serve warm.

To freeze: Immediately after shaping, freeze rolls on parchment paper-lined baking sheets until firm. Transfer to a resealable plastic bag; return to freezer. Freeze up to 4 weeks. To use, let rise and bake as directed, increasing rise time to 2½-3 hours.

Per 1 roll: 104 cal., 4g fat (3g sat. fat), 28mg chol., 107mg sod., 14g carb. (3g sugars, 1g fiber), 2g pro.

Note: To make filled crescent rolls, sprinkle dough with filling of choice immediately after brushing with butter; shape and bake as directed.

Chive Crescents: Divide ⅔ cup minced fresh chives between two circles of dough.

Orange-Pecan Crescents: Toss 1 cup finely chopped pecans with ⅓ cup sugar and 4 teaspoons grated orange peel; divide mixture between two circles.

Cranberry-Thyme Crescents: Toss 1 cup finely chopped dried cranberries with ⅔ cup finely chopped walnuts and 2 teaspoons minced fresh thyme leaves; divide mixture between two circles.

Olive-Stuffed Celery

My grandmother taught me and my mom this easy recipe. We always serve it at Christmas and Thanksgiving. The stuffing is so yummy, you'll love the end result.

—**STACY POWELL** SANTA FE, TX

START TO FINISH: 25 MIN.
MAKES: 2 DOZEN

1 dill pickle spear plus 1 teaspoon juice
3 sweet pickles plus 1 teaspoon juice
6 pitted ripe olives plus 1 teaspoon juice
6 pimiento-stuffed olives plus 1 teaspoon juice
1 package (8 ounces) cream cheese, softened
⅓ cup Miracle Whip
¼ teaspoon salt
¼ cup finely chopped pecans, toasted
6 celery ribs, cut into 2-inch pieces

1. Finely chop the pickles and olives; set aside. In a small bowl, beat the cream cheese, Miracle Whip, juices and salt until blended. Stir in the pickles, olives and pecans.

2. Spoon mixture into celery sticks. Or, transfer to a small food-safe plastic bag. Cut a small hole in the corner of the bag; pipe into celery sticks. Store in the refrigerator.

Per 1 piece: 61 cal., 5g fat (2g sat. fat), 12mg chol., 228mg sod., 2g carb. (1g sugars, 0 fiber), 1g pro.

BEST CRESCENT ROLLS

(5) INGREDIENTS SLOW COOKER

Buffet Meatballs

I need only five ingredients to fix these easy appetizers. Grape juice and apple jelly are the secrets behind the sweet yet tangy sauce that complements convenient packaged meatballs.

—JANET ANDERSON CARSON CITY, NV

PREP: 10 MIN. • **COOK:** 4 HOURS
MAKES: ABOUT 10½ DOZEN

- 1 cup grape juice
- 1 cup apple jelly
- 1 cup ketchup
- 1 can (8 ounces) tomato sauce
- 1 package (64 ounces) frozen fully cooked Italian meatballs

1. In a small saucepan, combine the juice, jelly, ketchup and tomato sauce. Cook and stir over medium heat until jelly is melted.

2. Place meatballs in a 5-qt. slow cooker. Pour sauce over the top and gently stir to coat. Cover and cook on low for 4-5 hours or until heated through.

Per 3 meatballs: 161 cal., 11g fat (5g sat. fat), 32mg chol., 398mg sod., 10g carb. (6g sugars, 1g fiber), 6g pro.

German Chocolate Cake

This cake is my husband's favorite! Every bite has a light crunch from the pecans, a sweet taste of coconut and a luscious drizzle of chocolate.

—JOYCE PLATFOOT WAPAKONETA, OH

PREP: 30 MIN. • **BAKE:** 30 MIN. + COOLING
MAKES: 12 SERVINGS

- 4 ounces German sweet chocolate, chopped
- ½ cup water
- 1 cup butter, softened
- 2 cups sugar
- 4 large eggs, separated
- 1 teaspoon vanilla extract
- 2½ cups cake flour
- 1 teaspoon baking soda
- ½ teaspoon salt
- 1 cup buttermilk

FROSTING
- 1½ cups sugar
- 1½ cups evaporated milk
- ¾ cup butter
- 5 large egg yolks, beaten
- 2 cups sweetened shredded coconut

GERMAN CHOCOLATE CAKE

- 1½ cups chopped pecans
- 1½ teaspoons vanilla extract

ICING
- 2 ounces semisweet chocolate
- 1 teaspoon shortening

1. Line three greased 9-in. round baking pans with waxed paper. Grease waxed paper and set aside. In small saucepan, melt chocolate with water over low heat; cool.

2. Preheat oven to 350°. In a large bowl, cream butter and sugar until light and fluffy. Beat in 4 egg yolks, one at a time, beating well after each addition. Blend in melted chocolate and vanilla. Combine flour, baking soda and salt; add to the creamed mixture alternately with buttermilk, beating well after each addition.

3. In a small bowl and with clean beaters, beat the 4 egg whites until stiff peaks form. Fold a fourth of the egg whites into creamed mixture; fold in remaining whites.

4. Pour batter into prepared pans. Bake for 24-28 minutes or until a toothpick inserted in center comes out clean. Cool 10 minutes; remove from pans to wire racks to cool completely.

5. For frosting, in a small saucepan, heat sugar, milk, butter and egg yolks over medium-low heat until mixture is thickened and golden brown, stirring constantly. Remove from heat. Stir in coconut, pecans and vanilla extract. Cool until thick enough to spread. Spread a third of the frosting over each cake layer and stack the layers.

6. In a microwave, melt chocolate and shortening. Stir until smooth; drizzle over cake.

Per 1 slice: 910 cal., 53g fat (28g sat. fat), 237mg chol., 511mg sod., 103g carb. (76g sugars, 4g fiber), 11g pro.

Brie in Puff Pastry

My husband was in the Air Force, so we've entertained guests in many parts of the world. I acquired this recipe while in California. It's one of my favorites.

—SANDRA TWAIT TAMPA, FL

PREP: 15 MIN. • **BAKE:** 20 MIN. + STANDING
MAKES: 10 SERVINGS

- 1 round (13.2 ounces) Brie cheese
- ½ cup crumbled blue cheese
- 1 sheet frozen puff pastry, thawed
- ¼ cup apricot jam
- ½ cup slivered almonds, toasted
- 1 large egg, lightly beaten
  Assorted crackers

1. Preheat oven to 400°. Cut Brie horizontally in half. Sprinkle bottom half with blue cheese; replace top.
2. On a lightly floured surface, roll pastry into a 14-in. square. Trim corners to make a circle. Spoon jam onto center of pastry; sprinkle with almonds. Top with Brie.
3. Lightly brush edges of pastry with beaten egg. Fold pastry over cheese, pinching edges to seal; trim excess pastry as desired.
4. Transfer to an ungreased baking sheet, seam side down. Brush pastry with beaten egg. Bake 20-25 minutes or until golden brown.
5. Immediately remove from pan to a serving plate; let stand 45 minutes before serving. Serve with crackers.

Per 1 wedge without crackers: 328 cal., 22g fat (10g sat. fat), 64mg chol., 424mg sod., 20g carb. (3g sugars, 2g fiber), 13g pro.

BEST EVER
MAC & CHEESE

BRIE IN PUFF PASTRY

Best Ever Mac & Cheese

To make the best mac, I prepare a sauce loaded with three different cheeses to toss with the noodles. When baked, it's ooey, gooey and cheesy good. And don't get me started on the crunchy topping!

—BETH JACOBSON MILWAUKEE, WI

PREP: 40 MIN. • **BAKE:** 10 MIN.
MAKES: 12 SERVINGS

- 1 package (16 ounces) uncooked elbow macaroni
- 4 slices hearty white bread (4 ounces), torn into large pieces
- 6 tablespoons butter, cubed and divided
- ½ cup grated Parmesan cheese
- 1 teaspoon salt, divided
- 1 teaspoon pepper, divided
- ¼ cup finely chopped onion
- 1 teaspoon ground mustard
- ¼ teaspoon cayenne pepper
- ¼ cup all-purpose flour
- 3 cups whole milk
- 2 cups half-and-half cream
- 1 cup (4 ounces) cubed process cheese (Velveeta)
- 1 block (8 ounces) sharp cheddar cheese, shredded
- 1 block (8 ounces) Monterey Jack cheese, shredded
- 1 teaspoon Worcestershire sauce

1. Preheat oven to 400°. In a Dutch oven, cook macaroni according to package directions for al dente; drain and return to pan. In a food processor, pulse the bread, 2 tablespoons of butter, Parmesan, ½ teaspoon salt and ½ teaspoon pepper until coarsely ground.
2. Meanwhile, in a large skillet over medium heat, melt remaining butter. Add onion and cook until tender, about 3 minutes. Stir in ground mustard and cayenne until blended. Stir in flour until smooth, about 3 minutes. Slowly whisk in milk and cream; bring to a boil. Reduce heat to medium-low; simmer, stirring constantly, until thickened, about 5 minutes. Remove from the heat; stir in Velveeta. Slowly add the remaining cheeses, a handful at a time, stirring until the cheese is melted. Add Worcestershire and remaining salt and pepper. Pour over macaroni; toss to coat.
3. Transfer to a greased 13x9-in. baking dish. Sprinkle bread crumbs over top of casserole. Bake until the topping is golden brown and the sauce is bubbly, 10-12 minutes.

Per 1 cup: 762 cal., 43g fat (25g sat. fat), 134mg chol., 1138mg sod., 61g carb. (10g sugars, 3g fiber), 32g pro.

✳

TEST KITCHEN TIP
Swap 2 cups coarsely crushed pork rinds, potato chips or Ritz crackers for the bread crumb topping.

**JULIE PETERSON'S
APPLE-PEANUT
BLONDIES** PAGE 266

Field Editor Favorites

Taste of Home Field Editors—**cooks like you** from around the country—**love to share** their signature dishes. Savor this chapter loaded with **seasonal** ingredients, Super Bowl **munchies,** dips, bars and recipes for the **best Thanksgiving ever.**

LYNNE GERMAN'S CREAMY RED PEPPER VEGGIE DIP *PAGE 265*

J. FLEMING'S CRAN-RASPBERRY HONEY SPREAD *PAGE 273*

RAWHIDE'S WHISKEY CAKE FROM CINDY WORTH *PAGE 277*

CINCINNATI
CHILI DOGS

BEER-BRAISED
PULLED HAM

Super Bowl Snacks

Field Editors know the game plan for slow-cooked eats that make guests flip their lids. Just cover, cook and share.

FREEZE IT **SLOW COOKER** 🍲

Beer-Braised Pulled Ham

To jazz up leftover ham, I slow-cooked it with a beer sauce. Buns loaded with ham, pickles and mustard are irresistible.
—**ANN SHEEHY** LAWRENCE, MA

PREP: 10 MIN. • **COOK:** 7 HOURS
MAKES: 16 SERVINGS

- 2 bottles (12 ounces each) beer
- ¾ cup German or Dijon mustard, divided
- ½ teaspoon coarsely ground pepper
- 1 fully cooked bone-in ham (about 4 pounds)

- 4 fresh rosemary sprigs
- 16 pretzel hamburger buns, split
  Dill pickle slices, optional

1. In a 5-qt. slow cooker, whisk together beer and ½ cup mustard. Stir in the pepper. Add ham and rosemary. Cook, covered, on low until tender, 7-9 hours.
2. Remove ham; cool slightly. Discard rosemary sprigs. Skim fat. When ham is cool enough to handle, shred meat with two forks. Discard bone. Return to slow cooker; heat through.

3. Using tongs, place shredded ham on pretzel buns; top with remaining mustard and, if desired, pickle slices.
To freeze: Freeze cooled ham mixture in freezer containers. To use, partially thaw in refrigerator overnight. Heat through in a covered saucepan, stirring gently and adding a little water if necessary.
Per 1 sandwich: 378 cal., 9g fat (1g sat. fat), 50mg chol., 1246mg sod., 50g carb. (4g sugars, 2g fiber), 25g pro.

SLOW COOKER 🍲

Cincinnati Chili Dogs

My in-laws are from Ohio, so we have Cincinnati chili at many family gatherings. I spiced up the classic with cinnamon and cocoa and ladled it over hot dogs.
—**JENNIFER GILBERT** BRIGHTON, MI

PREP: 20 MIN. • **COOK:** 4 HOURS
MAKES: 10 SERVINGS

- 1½ pounds ground beef
- 2 small yellow onions, chopped and divided
- 2 cans (15 ounces each) tomato sauce

1½ teaspoons baking cocoa
½ teaspoon ground cinnamon
¼ teaspoon chili powder
¼ teaspoon paprika
¼ teaspoon garlic powder
2 tablespoons Worcestershire sauce
1 tablespoon cider vinegar
10 hot dogs
10 hot dog buns, split
   Shredded cheddar cheese

1. In a large skillet over medium heat, cook and stir ground beef, crumbling meat, until no longer pink; drain.
2. In a 3-qt. slow cooker, combine beef with one chopped onion; add next eight ingredients. Cook, covered, on low about 2 hours; add hot dogs. Continue cooking, covered, on low until heated through, about 2 hours longer.
3. Serve on buns; top with shredded cheese and remaining chopped onion.

Per 1 chili dog: 419 cal., 24g fat (9g sat. fat), 67mg chol., 1135mg sod., 29g carb. (6g sugars, 3g fiber), 23g pro.

FREEZE IT SLOW COOKER
Butter Chicken Meatballs

My husband and I love meatballs, and we love butter chicken. Before an appetizer party, we had the idea to combine these two loves, and they got rave reviews! Pair with basmati rice for a great main dish.
—**SHANNON DOBOS** CALGARY, AB

PREP: 30 MIN. • **COOK:** 3 HOURS
MAKES: ABOUT 3 DOZEN

1½ pounds ground chicken or turkey
1 large egg, lightly beaten
½ cup soft bread crumbs
1 teaspoon garam masala
½ teaspoon tandoori masala seasoning
½ teaspoon salt
¼ teaspoon cayenne pepper
3 tablespoons minced fresh cilantro, divided
1 jar (14.1 ounces) butter chicken sauce

Combine the first seven ingredients plus 2 tablespoons cilantro; mix lightly but thoroughly. With wet hands, shape into 1-in. balls. Place meatballs in a 3-qt. slow cooker coated with cooking spray. Pour the butter sauce over the meatballs. Cook, covered, on low until meatballs are cooked through, 3-4 hours. Top with remaining cilantro.
To freeze: Omitting remaining cilantro, freeze cooled meatball mixture in freezer containers. To use, partially thaw in refrigerator overnight. Microwave, covered, on high in a microwave-safe dish until heated through, stirring gently and adding a little water if necessary. To serve, sprinkle with remaining cilantro.
Notes: Look for butter chicken sauce in the Indian foods section and garam masala in the spice aisle. To make soft bread crumbs, tear bread into pieces and place in a food processor or blender. Cover and pulse until crumbs form. One slice of bread yields ½-¾ cup crumbs.
Per 1 meatball: 40 cal., 2g fat (1g sat. fat), 18mg chol., 87mg sod., 1g carb. (1g sugars, 0 fiber), 3g pro.

BUTTER CHICKEN MEATBALLS
Shannon Dobos,
Calgary, AB

Pod Squad

From pasta to pesto to crisp salad,
spring is the time to give peas a chance.

SWEET PEA PESTO CROSTINI
Amber Massey
Argyle, TX

EAT SMART **FAST FIX**

Sweet Pea Pesto Crostini

I made a healthier spin on my favorite
celebrity chef's recipe by using vegetable
broth and going easy on the cheese. To
top crostini, use less broth for a paste-like
pesto. For use on pasta, add more broth
for a saucier consistency.

—AMBER MASSEY ARGYLE, TX

START TO FINISH: 25 MIN.
MAKES: ABOUT 1½ DOZEN

- 12 ounces fresh or frozen peas, thawed
- 4 garlic cloves, halved
- 1 teaspoon rice vinegar
- ½ teaspoon salt
- ⅛ teaspoon lemon-pepper seasoning
- 3 tablespoons olive oil
- ¼ cup shredded Parmesan cheese
- ⅓ cup vegetable broth
- 1 whole wheat French bread demi-baguette (about 6 ounces and 12 in. long)
- 2 cups cherry tomatoes (about 10 ounces), halved or quartered

1. Preheat broiler. In a food processor
or blender, pulse peas, garlic, vinegar,
salt and lemon pepper until well
blended. Continue processing while
gradually adding oil in a steady stream.
Add cheese; pulse just until blended.
Add broth; pulse until mixture reaches
desired consistency.

2. Cut baguette into 20 slices, ½ in.
thick. Place on ungreased baking
sheet. Broil 4-5 in. from heat until
golden brown, 45-60 seconds per side.
Remove to wire rack to cool.

3. To assemble crostini, spread each
slice with about 1 tablespoon pesto
mixture; top with tomato pieces.

Per 1 crostini: 77 cal., 2g fat (trace sat.
fat), 1mg chol., 190mg sod., 11g carb.
(2g sugars, 1g fiber), 3g pro.
Diabetic Exchanges: ½ starch, ½ fat.

Spring Pea & Radish Salad

Winters can be very long here in New Hampshire. I always look forward to the first veggies of spring and making some lighter dishes like this fresh salad.

—**JOLENE MARTINELLI** FREMONT, NH

START TO FINISH: 20 MIN.
MAKES: 6 SERVINGS

- ½ pound fresh wax or green beans
- ½ pound fresh sugar snap peas
- 2 cups water
- 6 large radishes, halved and thinly sliced
- 2 tablespoons honey
- 1 teaspoon dried tarragon
- ¼ teaspoon kosher salt
- ¼ teaspoon coarsely ground pepper

1. Snip ends off beans and sugar snap peas; remove strings from snap peas. In a large saucepan, bring water to a boil over high heat. Add beans, reduce heat; simmer, covered, 4-5 minutes. Add sugar snap peas; simmer, covered, until both beans and peas are crisp-tender, another 2-3 minutes. Drain.
2. Toss beans and peas with radishes. Stir together honey, tarragon, salt and pepper. Drizzle over vegetables.
Per ⅔ cup: 50 cal., 0 fat (0 sat. fat), 0 chol., 86mg sod., 11g carb. (8g sugars, 2g fiber), 2g pro.
Diabetic Exchanges: 1 vegetable, ½ starch.

SPRING PEA & RADISH SALAD

AUTHENTIC PASTA CARBONARA

Authentic Pasta Carbonara

I learned on my culinary internship in Tuscany that real Italian cuisine is simpler than you think! This carbonara is quick, simple and delicious, just the way they like it in Italy.

—**LAUREN BRIEN-WOOSTER** SOUTH LAKE TAHOE, CA

PREP: 20 MIN. • **COOK:** 15 MIN.
MAKES: 8 SERVINGS

- 1 package (1 pound) spaghetti or linguine
- 6 bacon strips, chopped
- 1 cup fresh or frozen peas
- 2 tablespoons lemon juice
- 1½ teaspoons grated lemon peel
- 2 large eggs, lightly beaten
- 2 tablespoons minced fresh parsley
- ½ cup grated Parmigiano-Reggiano cheese
- ¼ teaspoon salt
- ¼ teaspoon pepper
   Additional grated Parmigiano-Reggiano cheese, optional

1. In a large saucepan, cook pasta according to package directions for al dente. Drain pasta, reserving water; keep pasta warm. In same pot, cook bacon over medium heat until crisp, stirring occasionally. Add peas; cook until just heated through.
2. Add pasta to pot; toss to combine. Stir in remaining ingredients, adding enough reserved pasta water for sauce to reach the desired consistency. If desired, serve with additional cheese.
Note: The heat of the pasta cooks the eggs, but they may not reach 160°, the temperature at which they're considered safe to eat. To avoid the risk of food-borne illness, use pasteurized eggs.
Per 1 cup: 353 cal., 12g fat (4g sat. fat), 65mg chol., 326mg sod., 46g carb. (3g sugars, 3g fiber), 14g pro.

✱

TEST KITCHEN TIP
Pancetta is the ingredient of choice for true Italian carbonara. But it can be a little hard to find, which is why we called for bacon. If you can get pancetta, your carbonara will be all the better for it.

Take a Dip

Field Editors bring you the dunkable dips that keep their party people happy.

9-LAYER
GREEK DIP

FRESH CORN
& AVOCADO DIP

HONEY
HORSERADISH DIP

CREAMY
RED PEPPER
VEGGIE DIP

HOT
CHEESE
DIP

Hot Cheese Dip

When a colleague brought this cheesy dip to school for a teachers' potluck, I immediately gave it an A+. I had to have this irresistibly creamy recipe!

—**ARDYCE PIEHL** POYNETTE, WI

START TO FINISH: 30 MIN.
MAKES: 3 CUPS

- 2 cups shredded part-skim mozzarella cheese
- 2 cups shredded cheddar cheese
- 2 cups mayonnaise
- 1 medium onion, minced
- 1 can (4 to 4½ ounces) chopped green chilies, drained
- ½ cup sliced ripe olives
- 1½ ounces sliced pepperoni
  Assorted crackers and fresh vegetables

Preheat oven to 325°. Combine the first five ingredients; spread into a greased shallow baking dish or pie plate. Top with olives and pepperoni. Bake until bubbly, about 25 minutes. Serve with crackers and fresh vegetables.
Per 2 tablespoons: 201 cal., 19g fat (5g sat. fat), 18mg chol., 285mg sod., 2g carb. (0 sugars, 0 fiber), 5g pro.

Creamy Red Pepper Veggie Dip

I got this recipe from a college roommate. Thick and creamy with just a touch of sweetness, the colorful dip is a winner served with chunky veggies.

—**LYNNE GERMAN** WOODLAND HLLLS, CA

PREP: 15 MIN. • **COOK:** 5 MIN. + CHILLING
MAKES: 2½ CUPS

- 2 large eggs, slightly beaten
- 2 tablespoons sugar
- 2 tablespoons cider vinegar
- 1 tablespoon butter, softened
- 1 tablespoon all-purpose flour
- 1 package (8 ounces) cream cheese, softened
- 1 small sweet red pepper, chopped
- 4 green onions (both white and green portions), chopped
  Fresh baby carrots
  Fresh broccoli florets

In a small saucepan over low heat, whisk together the first five ingredients. Increase heat to medium; whisk until thickened, 4-5 minutes. Remove from heat. Stir in cream cheese, pepper and onions; mix well. Refrigerate 2 hours; serve with baby carrots and broccoli florets.
Per ¼ cup: 121 cal., 10g fat (6g sat. fat), 63mg chol., 96mg sod., 5g carb. (4g sugars, 0 fiber), 3g pro.

EAT SMART
Honey Horseradish Dip

We love having appetizers instead of a meal on Friday nights, and during the summer we enjoy eating cooler foods. This horseradish dip has just the right amount of zing. Try it instead of classic cocktail sauce with shrimp.

—**ANN MARIE EBERHART** GIG HARBOR, WA

PREP: 10 MIN. + CHILLING
MAKES: 1 CUP

- ½ cup fat-free plain Greek yogurt
- ¼ cup stone-ground mustard
- ¼ cup honey
- 2 tablespoons prepared horseradish
  Cold cooked shrimp and fresh sugar snap peas

Combine yogurt, mustard, honey and horseradish; refrigerate 1 hour. Serve with shrimp and snap peas.
Per 2 tablespoons: 54 cal., 1g fat (0 sat. fat), 0 chol., 177mg sod., 11g carb. (10g sugars, 0 fiber), 2g pro.
Diabetic Exchanges: 1 starch.

EAT SMART
9-Layer Greek Dip

Rather than the same taco dip at every family event and potluck, try this flavorful Mediterranean-inspired alternative. It looks and tastes healthy—because it is!

—**SHAWN BARTO** WINTER GARDEN, FL

PREP: 20 MIN. + CHILLING
MAKES: 5½ CUPS

- 1 carton (10 ounces) hummus
- 1 cup refrigerated tzatziki sauce
- ½ cup chopped green pepper
- ½ cup chopped sweet red pepper
- ½ cup chopped peeled cucumber
- ½ cup chopped water-packed artichoke hearts, drained
- ½ cup chopped pitted Greek olives, optional
- ¼ cup chopped pepperoncini
- 1 cup crumbled feta cheese
  Baked pita chips

In a 9-in. deep-dish pie plate, layer the first six ingredients; top with olives, if desired, and pepperoncini. Sprinkle with feta cheese. Refrigerate until serving. Serve with pita chips.
Do it yourself: For that fresh-from-the-kitchen taste, make your own tzatziki sauce by combining ½ cup peeled, seeded and finely chopped cucumber with ½ cup plain Greek yogurt, 4 teaspoons lemon juice, 1 tablespoon chopped dill, 1 minced garlic clove and salt and pepper to taste. Refrigerate.
Per ¼ cup without pita chips: 60 cal., 4g fat (1g sat. fat), 5mg chol., 210mg sod., 4g carb. (1g sugars, 1g fiber), 3g pro.
Diabetic Exchanges: ½ starch, ½ fat.

EAT SMART FAST FIX ▶
Fresh Corn & Avocado Dip

I alter my sister's dip recipe by adding finely chopped jalapeno for a little heat. The dip keeps well in the fridge, so you can make it ahead.

—**PAT ROBERTS** THORNTON, ON

START TO FINISH: 20 MIN.
MAKES: 4 CUPS

- 2 cups fresh or frozen corn, thawed
- 1 medium ripe avocado, peeled and diced
- 1 small peach, peeled and chopped
- 1 small sweet red pepper, chopped
- 1 small red onion, chopped
- 2 tablespoons olive oil
- 2 tablespoons white wine vinegar
- 1 tablespoon lime juice
- 1½ teaspoons ground cumin
- 1 teaspoon minced fresh oregano
- 1 garlic clove, crushed
  Salt and pepper to taste
- 1 minced and seeded jalapeno pepper, optional
  Baked tortilla chips

Combine first 11 ingredients; add salt and pepper and, if desired, jalapeno. Serve with tortilla chips.
Per ¼ cup without chips: 52 cal., 3g fat (0 sat. fat), 0 chol., 4mg sod., 6g carb. (2g sugars, 1g fiber), 1g pro.
Diabetic Exchanges: ½ starch, ½ fat.

Stadium Sweets

It's a parking-lot party and these bars are scoring all the brownie points. Make 'em and take 'em for a win even before the game.

Apple-Peanut Blondies

My family and I love apples any time of the year, but in the fall they are crisp, juicy and absolutely perfect! I found a blondie recipe similar to this and did a little bit of tweaking to make it our own.
—**JULIE PETERSON** CROFTON, MD

PREP: 15 MIN. • **BAKE:** 25 MIN. + COOLING
MAKES: 9 SERVINGS

- 1 cup packed brown sugar
- ½ cup butter, melted
- 1 large egg
- 1 teaspoon vanilla extract
- 1 cup all-purpose flour
- ½ teaspoon baking powder
- ¼ teaspoon baking soda
- ¼ teaspoon salt
- 2 small apples (about 9 ounces), peeled and sliced
- ½ cup chopped salted peanuts

1. Preheat oven to 350°. Beat brown sugar and butter until light and fluffy. Add egg and vanilla; beat until smooth. Whisk together flour, baking powder, baking soda and salt; gradually beat into brown sugar mixture just until combined (batter will be thick).

2. Spread all but ¼ cup batter into a greased and floured 8-in. square baking dish. Layer with apple slices; dot with remaining batter. Sprinkle with peanuts. Bake until golden brown and center is set, 22-28 minutes. Cool on a wire rack.
Per 1 blondie: 302 cal., 15g fat (7g sat. fat), 48mg chol., 256mg sod., 39g carb. (26g sugars, 1g fiber), 4g pro.

⑤ INGREDIENTS

Toffee Turtle Squares

Here's an easy way to make turtle candy for a big group. These bars are very rich, so a little square will do ya.
—**GLENNA TOOMAN** BOISE, ID

PREP: 15 MIN. • **BAKE:** 15 MIN. + COOLING
MAKES: 4 DOZEN

- 2 cups all-purpose flour
- 1½ cups packed brown sugar, divided
- 1 cup plus 3 tablespoons softened butter, divided
- 1½ cups coarsely chopped pecans
- 1½ cups semisweet chocolate chips

1. Preheat oven to 350°. Line a 13x9-in. baking pan with parchment paper, letting ends extend up sides.
2. Beat flour, 1 cup brown sugar and ½ cup butter until well blended (mixture will be dry and crumbly). Firmly press into prepared pan. Sprinkle pecans over flour mixture.
3. In a small saucepan, combine remaining butter and remaining brown sugar. Bring to a boil over medium heat. Stirring constantly, boil until sugar is dissolved, about 1 minute. Carefully pour mixture over pecans. Bake until bubbly and edges start to brown, 15-20 minutes.
4. Remove from oven. Immediately sprinkle with chocolate chips. Let stand until chocolate begins to melt; spread evenly. Cool completely in pan on a wire rack. Lift with parchment paper to remove from pan and cut.
Per 1 bar: 134 cal., 9g fat (4g sat. fat), 12mg chol., 39mg sod., 15g carb. (10g sugars, 1g fiber), 1g pro.

TOFFEE TURTLE SQUARES

Sweet Potato Cream Cheese Bars

If you're looking for something other than pumpkin, these sweet potato bars are a yummy alternative. Go ahead and make them in advance. They're even better after being refrigerated overnight.

—**DEBBIE GLASSCOCK** CONWAY, AR

PREP: 20 MIN. • **BAKE:** 45 MIN. + CHILLING
MAKES: 2 DOZEN

- 1 package white cake mix (regular size)
- 1 cup chopped pecans, toasted
- ½ cup cold butter, cubed
- 1 package (8 ounces) cream cheese, softened
- ½ cup sugar
- 3 large eggs, divided
- 1 can (14 ounces) sweetened condensed milk, divided
- 3 cups cooked and mashed sweet potatoes (about 3 medium)
- 2 teaspoons pumpkin pie spice

1. Preheat oven to 350°. Combine cake mix and pecans; cut in butter until crumbly. Press onto bottom of a greased 13x9-in. baking dish.
2. Beat cream cheese, sugar, 1 egg and 2 tablespoons sweetened condensed milk until smooth; set aside. Stir together sweet potatoes, remaining eggs, remaining milk and pie spice; pour over pecan mixture. Dollop cream cheese mixture over sweet potato mixture. Cut through cream cheese mixture with a knife to swirl into sweet potato mixture.
3. Bake until set and slightly golden on top, about 45 minutes. Cool completely; chill before cutting .
Note: To toast nuts, bake in a shallow pan in a 350° oven for 5-10 minutes or cook in a skillet over low heat until lightly browned, stirring occasionally.
Per 1 bar: 304 cal., 15g fat (7g sat. fat), 51mg chol., 240mg sod., 40g carb. (27g sugars, 1g fiber), 5g pro.

APPLE-PEANUT BLONDIES

SWEET POTATO CREAM CHEESE BARS

Thanksgiving Secrets

Our volunteer Field Editors dish on the simplest, juiciest, most surprising ways to amp up your table game this year, from the bird all the way to dessert. (Shh! There's cumin in the sweet potatoes!)

CREAM CHEESE
MASHED POTATOES

MAPLE-SAGE BRINED TURKEY

MAKE-AHEAD MAPLE & SAGE GRAVY

Cream Cheese Mashed Potatoes

When I serve this easy mash, the bowl is always scraped clean. Before holiday feasts, I make it early and keep it warm in a slow cooker so I can focus on all the last-minute details.

—JILL THOMAS WASHINGTON, IN

PREP: 20 MIN. • **COOK:** 15 MIN.
MAKES: 20 SERVINGS

- 8 pounds russet potatoes
- 1 package (8 ounces) cream cheese, softened
- ½ cup butter, melted
- 2 teaspoons salt
- ¾ teaspoon pepper
  Additional melted butter, optional
- ¼ cup finely chopped green onions

1. Peel and cube potatoes. Place in a large stockpot; add water to cover. Bring to a boil. Reduce the heat; cook, uncovered, until tender, 12-15 minutes. Drain.
2. With a mixer, beat cream cheese, ½ cup melted butter, salt and pepper until smooth. Add potatoes; beat until light and fluffy. If desired, top with additional melted butter. Sprinkle with green onions.

Per ¾ cup: 185 cal., 9g fat (5g sat. fat), 25mg chol., 318mg sod., 25g carb. (2g sugars, 2g fiber), 3g pro.

★ ★ ★ ★ ★ **READER REVIEW**

"This recipe is so good! I used 1 teaspoon salt, ½ teaspoon pepper, ¼ cup melted butter and 4 potatoes. I *did* use the full 8 ounces cream cheese, and I mixed ½ chopped small onion into the potatoes, sprinkled it with paprika and baked for 45 minutes in 1-qt. casserole dish at 350°.

DELOWENSTEIN
TASTEOFHOME.COM

MAPLE-SAGE
BRINED TURKEY

Maple-Sage Brined Turkey

When the leaves start turning color, it's turkey time at our house. We use this maple-sage brine to help brown the bird and make the meat incredibly juicy.

—**KIMBERLY FORNI** LACONIA, NH

PREP: 40 MIN. + BRINING
BAKE: 2½ HOURS + STANDING
MAKES: 20 SERVINGS

- 4 quarts water
- 1½ cups packed brown sugar
- 1 cup sea salt
- 1 cup maple syrup
- 1 cup cider vinegar
- 24 fresh sage leaves
- 6 bay leaves
- 2 tablespoons yellow mustard
- 2 tablespoons coarsely ground pepper
- 1 teaspoon ground cloves
- 4 quarts ice water
- 2 turkey-size oven roasting bags
- 1 turkey (14 to 16 pounds)
TURKEY
- 2 tablespoons olive oil
- ½ teaspoon pepper
- ½ teaspoon salt, optional

1. In a large stockpot, combine first 10 ingredients; bring to a boil. Cook and stir until sugar and salt are dissolved. Remove from heat. Add 4 quarts ice water to cool the brine to room temperature.

2. Put one turkey-sized oven roasting bag inside the other; place in a large stockpot. Place turkey inside inner bag; pour in cooled brine. Seal bags, pressing out as much air as possible. Refrigerate 18-24 hours.

3. Preheat oven to 350°. Remove turkey from brine; rinse and pat dry. Discard brine. Place turkey on a rack in a shallow roasting pan, breast side up. Tuck wings under turkey; tie drumsticks together. Rub oil over outside of turkey; sprinkle with pepper and, if desired, salt.

4. Roast turkey, uncovered, until a thermometer inserted in thickest part of thigh reads 170°-175°, 2½- 3 hours. (Cover loosely with foil if turkey browns too quickly.)

5. Remove turkey from oven; tent with foil. Let stand 20 minutes before carving.

Per 7 ounces cooked turkey with skin: 384 cal., 18g fat (5g sat. fat), 172mg chol., 168mg sod., 0 carb. (0 sugars, 0 fiber), 51g pro.

Make-Ahead Maple & Sage Gravy

Turkey or chicken wings make a richly flavored stock, the base of my pour-it-on-everything herbed gravy.

—**ANGELA LIVELY** CONROE, TX

PREP: 15 MIN. • **COOK:** 3 HOURS
MAKES: 3½ CUPS

- 2 turkey wings, halved, or 1½ pounds chicken wings
- 1 small onion, quartered
- ¼ cup fresh sage leaves plus 1 tablespoon minced fresh sage, divided
- 1 carton (32 ounces) reduced-sodium chicken broth
- 4 cups water
- ½ cup butter
- ½ cup all-purpose flour
- 2 tablespoons maple syrup

1. Preheat oven to 450°. In a 15x10-in. pan coated with cooking spray, bake wings, uncovered, until dark golden brown, about 1 hour.

2. Transfer wings to a stockpot; add onion, sage leaves, broth and water. Slowly bring to a boil over low heat; gently simmer, partially covered, 1½ hours.

3. Strain broth, discarding solids. Measure broth and simmer until reduced to 5 cups. If using broth immediately, skim fat. Or cool, then refrigerate 8 hours or overnight; remove fat before using.

4. In a Dutch oven, melt butter over medium-low heat. Add flour and cook, stirring frequently, until dark golden brown, 10-12 minutes. Carefully stir in 4 cups broth. Bring to a boil; reduce heat and simmer, stirring constantly, 10 minutes. Stir in maple syrup and minced sage; add enough remaining broth to achieve desired consistency.

Per ¼ cup: 89 cal., 7g fat (4g sat. fat), 17mg chol., 216mg sod., 6g carb. (2g sugars, 0 fiber), 1g pro.

**MAKE-AHEAD MAPLE
& SAGE GRAVY**
Angela Lively
Conroe, TX

Soft Buttermilk Dinner Rolls

Warm, buttery dinner rolls are absolutely irresistible. I save time and use a stand mixer to make my dough.

—JENNIFER PATTERSON SHOSHONE, ID

PREP: 40 MIN. + RISING
BAKE: 20 MIN. + COOLING
MAKES: 20 SERVINGS

- 1 package (¼ ounce) active dry yeast
- ¼ cup warm water (110° to 115°)
- 1 cup plus 2 tablespoons warm buttermilk (110° to 115°), divided
- ½ cup plus 1 teaspoon softened butter, divided
- 1 large egg
- ⅓ cup sugar
- 1 teaspoon salt
- 4 cups bread flour

1. Dissolve yeast in warm water until foamy. In a large bowl, combine 1 cup buttermilk, ½ cup butter, egg, sugar, salt and yeast mixture. Add 3 cups flour; beat on medium speed until smooth, about 1 minute. Add the remaining flour, ¼ cup at a time, to form a soft dough.
2. Turn dough onto a lightly floured surface; knead until smooth and elastic, 6-8 minutes. Place in a greased bowl, turning once to grease the top. Cover with plastic wrap and let rise in a warm place until doubled, about 1 hour.
3. Punch down dough. Turn onto a lightly floured surface; divide and shape into 20 balls. Place in a greased 13x9-in. pan. Cover with a kitchen towel; let rise in a warm place until almost doubled, about 45 minutes.
4. Preheat oven to 350°. Brush rolls lightly with remaining buttermilk and butter. Bake until golden brown, 20-25 minutes. Cool in pan 20 minutes. Remove to a wire rack; serve warm.
Per 1 roll: 165 cal., 6g fat (3g sat. fat), 23mg chol., 187mg sod., 24g carb. (4g sugars, 1g fiber), 4g pro.

Brown Sugar Pound Cake

This tender pound cake is the first one I mastered. You'll want to eat the browned butter icing by the spoonful. It tastes just like pralines.

—SHAWN BARTO WINTER GARDEN, FL

PREP: 20 MIN. • **BAKE:** 55 MIN. + COOLING
MAKES: 16 SERVINGS

- 1½ cups unsalted butter, softened
- 2¼ cups packed brown sugar
- 5 large eggs, room temperature
- 2 teaspoons vanilla extract
- 3 cups all-purpose flour
- 1 teaspoon baking powder
- ¼ teaspoon salt
- 1 cup sour cream

GLAZE
- 3 tablespoons unsalted butter
- ¼ cup chopped pecans
- 1 cup confectioners' sugar
- ¼ teaspoon vanilla extract
  Dash salt
- 2 to 3 tablespoons half-and-half cream

1. Preheat oven to 350°. Grease and flour a 10-in. fluted tube pan.
2. Cream butter and brown sugar until light and fluffy. Add eggs, one at a time, beating well after each addition. Beat in vanilla. In another bowl, whisk flour, baking powder and salt; add to creamed mixture alternately with sour cream, beating after each addition just until combined.
3. Transfer to prepared pan. Bake until a toothpick inserted in center comes out clean, 55-65 minutes. Cool in pan 10 minutes before removing to a wire rack to cool completely.
4. For glaze, combine butter and pecans in a small saucepan over medium heat, stirring constantly, until the butter is light golden brown, 4-5 minutes. Stir into confectioners' sugar. Add vanilla, salt and enough cream to reach a drizzling consistency. Drizzle glaze over cake, allowing some to drip down sides. Let stand until set.
Note: To remove cakes easily, use solid shortening to grease both plain and fluted tube pans.
Per 1 slice: 473 cal., 25g fat (15g sat. fat), 121mg chol., 193mg sod., 57g carb. (38g sugars, 1g fiber), 5g pro.

SOFT BUTTERMILK DINNER ROLLS

CRANBERRY-
RASPBERRY
HONEY JAM

**BROWN SUGAR
POUND CAKE**
Shawn Barto
Winter Garden, FL

Cran-Raspberry
Honey Spread

Honey gives this tangy spread its
sweetness. I came up with the recipe
way back when our family first took up
beekeeping and we had a big harvest.

—**J. FLEMING** ALMONTE, ON

PREP: 15 MIN.
COOK: 20 MIN. + PROCESSING
MAKES: 6 HALF-PINTS

2½ cups fresh or frozen sweetened
    raspberries, thawed
  2 cups fresh or frozen cranberries,
    thawed
  1 cup chopped peeled apple
2½ cups honey
1½ cups sugar
  1 pouch (3 ounces) liquid fruit pectin

1. Pulse raspberries, cranberries and
apple in batches in a food processor
until almost smooth. Transfer to a
Dutch oven.
2. Stir in honey and sugar. Bring to a
full rolling boil over high heat, stirring
constantly. Stir in pectin. Continue to
boil 1 minute, stirring constantly.
Remove from heat; skim off foam.
3. Ladle hot mixture into six hot
half-pint jars, leaving ¼-in.
headspace. Remove air bubbles and
adjust headspace, if necessary, by
adding hot mixture. Wipe rims. Center
lids on jars; screw on bands until
fingertip tight.
4. Place jars into canner with
simmering water, ensuring that they
are completely covered with water.
Bring to a boil; process for 10 minutes.
Remove jars and cool.
Note: The processing time listed is for
altitudes of 1,000 feet or less. Add
1 minute to the processing time for each
1,000 feet of additional altitude.
Per 2 tablespoons: 84 cal., 0 fat (0 sat.
fat), 0 chol., 1mg sod., 22g carb. (21g
sugars, 1g fiber), 0 pro.

ROASTED BALSAMIC
SWEET POTATOES

MOM'S APPLE
CORN BREAD
STUFFING

HONEY GARLIC GREEN BEANS

Mom's Apple Corn Bread Stuffing

This recipe is the be-all, end-all stuffing in our family. We never have leftovers.

—**MARIE FORTE** RARITAN, NJ

PREP: 15 MIN. • **BAKE:** 35 MIN.
MAKES: 16 SERVINGS

- 6 large Granny Smith apples, peeled and chopped
- 1 package (14 ounces) crushed corn bread stuffing
- ½ cup butter, melted
- 1 can (14½ ounces) chicken broth

1. Preheat oven to 350°. Combine apples, stuffing and melted butter. Add broth; mix well.
2. Transfer the stuffing to a greased 13x9-in. baking dish. Bake until golden brown, 35-40 minutes.
Per ¾ cup: 183 cal., 7g fat (4g sat. fat), 16mg chol., 434mg sod., 28g carb. (8g sugars, 2g fiber), 3g pro.
Diabetic Exchanges: 2 starch, 1½ fat.

Roasted Balsamic Sweet Potatoes

By the end of summer, I'm done with the usual potato salad. This warm, spicy side kicks off cozy season.

—**KAREN VANDE SLUNT** WATERTOWN, WI

PREP: 30 MIN. • **COOK:** 30 MIN.
MAKES: 12 SERVINGS

- 6 medium sweet potatoes, cubed
- 1 teaspoon olive oil
- ½ teaspoon salt
- ½ teaspoon pepper
- 1 pound bacon strips, chopped
- 4 celery ribs, chopped
- 1 medium onion, thinly sliced
- 3 garlic cloves, minced
- 1 cup beef stock
- ⅔ cup balsamic vinegar
- 4 teaspoons paprika
- ¾ teaspoon ground cumin, optional
- 6 green onions, chopped
  Minced fresh parsley, optional

1. Preheat oven to 375°. Place sweet potatoes in a 15x10-in. pan; drizzle with olive oil and sprinkle with salt and pepper. Turn to coat. Bake until tender, 30-35 minutes.
2. Meanwhile, in a large skillet, cook the bacon over medium-low heat until crisp; drain. Discard all but 4 teaspoons drippings.
3. Cook celery and onion in drippings over medium heat until tender, 6-8 minutes. Add garlic; cook 1 minute. Add beef stock and balsamic vinegar; simmer until liquid is reduced by half, 5-8 minutes. Add paprika and, if desired, cumin; cook 1 minute longer.
4. Pour balsamic mixture over sweet potatoes; add bacon. Toss to coat. Top with green onions and, if desired, minced parsley; serve immediately.
Per ½ cup: 287 cal., 16g fat (5g sat. fat), 25mg chol., 413mg sod., 30g carb. (15g sugars, 4g fiber), 7g pro.

Honey Garlic Green Beans

Green beans are great, but they can seem sort of ordinary on their own. Just a few extra ingredients give them sweet and salty attitude.

—**SHANNON DOBOS** CALGARY, AB

START TO FINISH: 20 MIN.
MAKES: 8 SERVINGS

- 4 tablespoons honey
- 2 tablespoons reduced-sodium soy sauce
- 4 garlic cloves, minced
- ¼ teaspoon salt
- ¼ teaspoon crushed red pepper flakes
- 2 pounds fresh green beans, trimmed

1. Whisk together the first five ingredients; set aside. In a 6-qt. stockpot, bring 10 cups water to a boil. Add green beans in batches; cook, uncovered, 2-3 minutes or just until crisp-tender. Remove; immediately drop into ice water. Drain and pat dry.
2. Coat stockpot with cooking spray. Add the green beans; cook, stirring constantly, over high heat until slightly blistered, 2-3 minutes. Add soy sauce mixture; cook and stir until beans are coated and sauce begins to evaporate slightly, 2-3 minutes. Remove from the heat.
Per ¾ cup: 72 cal., 0 fat (0 sat. fat), 0 chol., 225mg sod., 18g carb. (12g sugars, 4g fiber), 2g pro.
Diabetic Exchanges: 1 vegetable, ½ starch.

TROPICAL CANDY
CANE FREEZE

Holiday Cheers

The gifts are wrapped and the kids are fast asleep.
Celebrate a job well done with these spiked sweets.

⑤INGREDIENTS FAST FIX

Tropical Candy Cane Freeze

When the midwestern winter drags on and on, this frosty cold drink takes me away to a warm tropical beach! The recipe can easily be made family friendly by substituting water for the alcohol.

—**JENNIFER STOWELL** MONTEZUMA, IA

START TO FINISH: 10 MIN.
MAKES: 10 SERVINGS

- 1 can (10 ounces) frozen nonalcoholic pina colada mix
- 10 cups ice cubes, divided
- 1⅓ cups rum or 2 cups water, divided
- 1 can (10 ounces) frozen nonalcoholic strawberry daiquiri mix

In a covered blender, process pina colada mix, 5 cups ice and ⅔ cup rum or 1 cup water until blended. Repeat with strawberry daiquiri mix and remaining ingredients. Slowly pour prepared pina colada and prepared strawberry daiquiri by ¼ cupfuls into the center of 10 highball glasses, alternating layers. Serve immediately.

Per 1 cup: 195 cal., 2g fat (1g sat. fat), 0 chol., 10mg sod., 30g carb. (29g sugars, 0 fiber), 0 pro.

Godiva Liqueur Brownies

Santa's eyes twinkle when he finds this very adult brownie on the cookie tray. With chocolaty liqueur and other spirits, it's definitely a merrymaker for grown-ups.

—**TERI RASEY** CADILLAC, MI

PREP: 20 MIN. • **BAKE:** 25 MIN. + COOLING
MAKES: 2 DOZEN

- ¾ cup butter, softened
- 1 cup granulated sugar
- 1 cup packed brown sugar
- 4 large eggs
- ½ cup Godiva Chocolate Liqueur
- 2 tablespoons chocolate vodka
- 2 tablespoons clear creme de cacao
- 1⅓ cups all-purpose flour
- ¾ cup baking cocoa
- 1 teaspoon baking powder
- ½ cup semisweet chocolate chips

GLAZE
- 1 cup confectioners' sugar
- 4 teaspoons butter, melted
- 2 tablespoons Godiva Chocolate Liqueur
- 1 tablespoon chocolate vodka
- 1 tablespoon clear creme de cacao

1. Preheat oven to 350°. Beat together butter and sugars until light and fluffy. Add the eggs, one at a time, beating well after each addition. Beat in the liqueur, vodka and creme de cacao until blended.

2. In a separate bowl, whisk together flour, cocoa and baking powder until well mixed. Stir in the semisweet chocolate chips. Fold the chocolate chip mixture into the butter mixture just until combined.

RAWHIDE'S
WHISKEY CAKE

3. Transfer to a 13x9-in. baking dish coated with cooking spray; bake just until center is set, 24-28 minutes (do not overbake). Cool completely in pan on a wire rack.

4. For the glaze, mix all ingredients until smooth; spread over brownies. Cut into bars. Store brownies in an airtight container.

Per 1 brownie: 233 cal., 9g fat (5g sat. fat), 48mg chol., 86mg sod., 34g carb. (25g sugars, 1g fiber), 3g pro.

Rawhide's Whiskey Cake

For several years, our neighbor gave us a moist whiskey-flavored cake during the holiday season. I've tweaked the recipe over the years, and now my friends request this cake instead of homemade cookie platters.

—CINDY WORTH LAPWAI, ID

PREP: 15 MIN. + STANDING • **BAKE:** 1 HOUR
MAKES: 16 SLICES

- 1 package spice cake mix with pudding (regular size)
- 1 package (3.4 ounces) instant vanilla pudding mix
- ¾ cup 2% milk
- ¾ cup whiskey
- ½ cup canola oil
- 4 large eggs
- 1⅓ cups coarsely chopped walnuts, divided

GLAZE
- 1 cup sugar
- ½ cup butter, cubed
- ½ cup whiskey
- 1 teaspoon water

1. Preheat oven to 300°. Grease and flour a 10-in. tube pan.

2. Combine the first six ingredients; beat on low speed 30 seconds. Beat on medium speed 2 minutes; fold in 1 cup nuts. Pour batter into prepared pan; sprinkle with remaining nuts. Bake until a toothpick inserted in center comes out clean, about 60-65 minutes. Cool in pan.

3. For glaze, mix all ingredients in a small saucepan; bring to a boil over medium-high heat. Reduce heat; simmer 10 minutes. Cool 3 minutes. Pour one-third of glaze over top of cake, allowing some to flow over sides. Let stand 1 hour. Remove from pan to cool completely; cover.

4. The next day, reheat glaze; brush half over cake, cooling before covering. Repeat the following day, using the remaining glaze.

Per 1 slice: 400 cal., 23g fat (6g sat. fat), 63mg chol., 298mg sod., 43g carb. (30g sugars, 1g fiber), 5g pro.

✳
TEST KITCHEN TIP
This cake requires planning ahead. You'll need three days from mixing to *ta-da!* To make sure your cake pops out perfectly, use solid shortening to grease the cake pan. Also, be sure to splurge on a good whiskey. Buy a pint for the perfect amount.

**MATTHEW'S BEST
EVER MEAT LOAF FROM
MATTHEW HASS** *PAGE 287*

Kitchen Techniques

Make your time in the kitchen even easier with **helpful how-to's** and tips from the **cooking experts** at *Taste of Home*. This expanded chapter offers more great ways to **help you** master the basics and advanced techniques alike.

JAMES SCHEND'S LIGHT & FLUFFY WAFFLES *PAGE 283*

KERI WHITNEY'S CREME DE MENTHE CUPCAKES *PAGE 298*

TONYA BRANHAM'S HOMEMADE CANNED SPAGHETTI SAUCE *PAGE 291*

Perfect Quiche

Buttery pastry crust, creamy custard filling, melty cheese and little pops of bacon that stay crisp—when it comes to quiche, we want it all. Lucky for us, Mark Clark's recipe nails it.

BREAKFAST QUICHE

TEST KITCHEN TIPS

KEEP IT CREAMY
Too many eggs makes the custard rubbery; too few makes it watery. We used 4 eggs to 2 cups liquid, the standard 1-egg-to-½-cup-cream ratio that delivers the best results.

GOT MILK?
For the dairy, you can use anything with a higher fat content than skim milk or 2%. Think whole milk, half-and-half, heavy cream or a combo.

Breakfast Quiche

With two kinds of cheeses, lots of crispy bacon and a dash of cayenne, this airy quiche makes a big impression with brunch guests. It's the recipe my friends always ask for.

—MARK CLARK TWIN MOUNTAIN, NH

PREP: 15 MIN. • **BAKE:** 30 MIN.
MAKES: 6 SERVINGS

- 1¼ cups all-purpose flour
- ¼ teaspoon salt
- ½ cup cold butter
- 3 to 5 tablespoons ice water

FILLING

- 12 bacon strips, cooked and crumbled
- ½ cup shredded pepper jack or Monterey Jack cheese
- ½ cup shredded sharp cheddar cheese
- ⅓ cup finely chopped onion
- 4 large eggs
- 2 cups heavy whipping cream
- ¾ teaspoon salt
- ¼ teaspoon sugar
- ⅛ teaspoon cayenne pepper

1. Combine flour and salt; cut in butter until crumbly. Gradually add 3-5 tablespoons ice water, tossing with a fork until dough holds together when pressed. Wrap dough in plastic and refrigerate 1 hour.

2. Preheat oven to 450°. On a lightly floured surface, roll dough to a ⅛-in.-thick circle; transfer to a 9-in. pie plate. Trim pastry to ½ in. beyond rim of plate; flute edge. Line unpricked pastry shell with a double thickness of heavy-duty foil. Bake 5 minutes; remove foil. Bake 5 minutes longer; remove from oven and cool on a wire rack. Reduce heat to 375°.

3. Sprinkle bacon, cheeses and onion over crust. Beat remaining ingredients until blended; pour over top. Bake until a knife inserted in center comes out clean, 30-35 minutes. Let stand for 10 minutes before cutting.

Per 1 piece: 709 cal., 60g fat (35g sat. fat), 290mg chol., 980mg sod., 24g carb. (3g sugars, 1g fiber), 19g pro.

HERE'S HOW:

TO-DO'S AND TA-DA'S!

- Wrap and refrigerate the pie pastry before prebaking to solidify butterfat.
- To prebake, line pastry with foil; fill with dried beans or ceramic pie weights.
- There will be a little jiggle to the quiche when it comes out of the oven. The quiche is set if a knife comes out clean.

UNLEASH THE QUICHE

Master the original recipe, then make it your own with these flavor combos. Or get creative with your favorite ingredients!

- Steamed Spinach, Onions & Swiss Cheese
- Ham & Asparagus
- Smoked Salmon, Dill & Creme Fraiche
- Mushroom & Leek
- Bacon, Caramelized Onions & Gruyere Cheese

Homemade Waffles

For this best-loved family breakfast, call 'em to the kitchen while the iron's hot. Food Editor James Schend turns everyday ingredients into come-and-get-it gold.

LIGHT & FLUFFY WAFFLES
James Schend
Pleasant Prairie, WI

Light & Fluffy Waffles

These melt-in-your-mouth waffles are so tender, you can skip the butter and syrup. (But why would you want to?)

—**JAMES SCHEND** PLEASANT PRAIRIE, WI

PREP: 15 MIN. • **COOK:** 5 MIN./BATCH
MAKES: 12 WAFFLES

- 2 large eggs
- 1½ cups all-purpose flour
- ½ cup cornstarch
- 1 teaspoon baking powder
- ½ teaspoon baking soda
- ½ teaspoon salt
- ½ cup 2% milk
- 5 tablespoons canola oil
- 2 teaspoons vanilla extract
- 1 teaspoon white vinegar
- 2 tablespoons sugar
- ½ cup club soda, chilled
  Butter and maple syrup, optional

1. Separate eggs. Place egg whites in a clean, dry bowl; let stand at room temperature 30 minutes.
2. In another bowl, whisk together next five ingredients. In a small bowl, whisk egg yolks, milk, oil, vanilla and vinegar until blended. Beat egg whites until soft peaks form. Gradually add sugar; continue beating until stiff peaks form.
3. Preheat waffle maker. Stir together flour mixture, egg mixture and club soda just until combined. Fold egg whites into batter. Bake waffles according to manufacturer's directions until golden brown. Serve with butter and syrup if desired.
Per 2 waffles: 312 cal., 14g fat (2g sat. fat), 64mg chol., 421mg sod., 39g carb. (5g sugars, 1g fiber), 6g pro.

TEST KITCHEN TIPS

KEEP 'EM CRISPY
Replacing some of the flour with cornstarch guarantees a waffle that's crispy on the outside with a fluffy texture inside.

SPRING FOR SODA
Using club soda instead of water in waffle or crepe batter makes a finished food that's nice and fluffy. Try it in puff pancake recipes, too!

HERE'S HOW:

TO-DO'S AND TA-DA'S!

- Whisk dry ingredients, or use a flour sifter or mesh strainer, to distribute baking powder evenly throughout the mixture so the waffles rise evenly.
- Beating egg whites may seem like an extra step, but it's crucial to keep the waffles light and to give them some structure.
- Fold the egg whites into the batter as gently as possible so you don't deflate them. A few streaks of egg white in the batter is just fine.
- To feed a crowd, place cooked waffles in a single layer on a baking sheet in a 200° oven.

FREEZE IT
For a quick and easy breakfast later, lay leftover waffles on a cookie sheet and place in freezer. Once frozen, stack the waffles between sheets of waxed paper, place in a freezer bag and return to the freezer. To reheat just a few, putting them in a toaster for a minute or two does the trick. For feeding a crew, pop the waffles into a preheated 325° oven for 5 minutes.

Strawberry Shortcake

For all things homey and sweet, go straight to the authority: Grandma. Angela Lively shares her gran's recipe for family-treasure biscuits, strawberry sauce and hand-whipped cream.

GRANDMA'S OLD-FASHIONED STRAWBERRY SHORTCAKE

TEST KITCHEN TIPS

WHIP SMART

Make sure the cream is cold when you whip it—you'll get more volume. Start out on low speed and be patient. You can whip the cream up to 2 hours ahead, then gently stir when you're ready to serve it.

IN A PINCH

If you don't have buttermilk handy, put a tablespoon of white vinegar or lemon juice in a measuring cup and fill with regular milk to reach the 1-cup mark.

Grandma's Old-Fashioned Strawberry Shortcake

This is my grandma's shortcake recipe, although she always served it with vanilla ice cream—usually homemade!

—ANGELA LIVELY CONROE, TX

PREP: 30 MIN. + STANDING • **BAKE:** 20 MIN.
MAKES: 8 SERVINGS

- 6 cups sliced fresh strawberries
- ½ cup sugar
- 1 teaspoon vanilla extract

SHORTCAKE

- 3 cups all-purpose flour
- 5 tablespoons sugar, divided
- 3 teaspoons baking powder
- 1 teaspoon baking soda
- ½ teaspoon salt
- ¾ cup cold butter, cubed
- 1 cup buttermilk
- 2 tablespoons heavy whipping cream

TOPPING

- 1½ cups heavy whipping cream
- 2 tablespoons sugar
- ½ teaspoon vanilla extract

1. Combine strawberries with sugar and vanilla; mash slightly. Let stand at least 30 minutes, tossing occasionally.

2. Preheat oven to 400°. For the shortcake, whisk together flour, 4 tablespoons sugar, baking powder, baking soda and salt. Cut in butter until crumbly. Add buttermilk; stir just until combined (do not overmix). Drop batter by ⅓ cupfuls 2 in. apart onto an ungreased baking sheet. Brush with 2 tablespoons heavy cream; sprinkle with remaining 1 tablespoon sugar. Bake 18-20 minutes. Remove to wire racks to cool completely.

3. For topping, beat heavy whipping cream until it begins to thicken. Add sugar and vanilla; beat until soft peaks form. To serve, cut biscuits in half; top with strawberries and whipped cream.

Per 1 shortcake with ½ cup strawberries and ⅓ cup whipped cream: 635 cal., 36g fat (22g sat. fat), 102mg chol., 696mg sod., 72g carb. (33g sugars, 4g fiber), 8g pro.

HERE'S HOW:

TO-DO'S AND TA-DA'S!

- The longer the strawberries stand in the sugar syrup, the softer they'll get.
- Ensure the butter is cold, and cut it in until it's about pea-size; as it melts during baking, small air pockets are created, giving the biscuit its flakiness.
- Brushing the biscuit tops with cream helps the sugar stay in place.

LITTLE CAKE, BIG FLAVOR

Bump up the Biscuit
Stir grated lemon peel, orange peel or a bit of spice such as ground cardamom into the biscuit mixture. Add a pinch of cinnamon and nutmeg to the sugar on top.

Swap the Fruit
Add fresh herbs or a favorite liqueur to the strawberry mixture, or substitute sliced mangoes or peaches and blueberries for the strawberries.

Top It Off Right
Fold lemon curd or a spoonful of melted Nutella or caramel into the whipped cream. Top with toasted sliced almonds, toasted coconut or candied pecans.

MATTHEW'S BEST EVER MEAT LOAF
Matthew Hass
Franklin, WI

The Almighty Meat Loaf

Test Cook Matthew Hass takes the king of comfort food to a whole new level with loads of veggies and a tangy sauce that's over the top. There's only one rule: Save some for sandwiches.

Matthew's Best Ever Meat Loaf

This is comfort food at its best. Mushrooms, beef stock, tomato paste, Worcestershire and soy sauce help boost the meaty flavor of this classic diner staple.

—**MATTHEW HASS** FRANKLIN, WI

PREP: 30 MIN. • **BAKE:** 1¼ HOURS + STANDING
MAKES: 8 SERVINGS

- 3 slices white bread, torn into small pieces
- ½ cup beef stock
- 2 large portobello mushrooms (about 6 ounces), cut into chunks
- 1 medium onion, cut into wedges
- 1 medium carrot, cut into chunks
- 1 celery rib, cut into chunks
- 3 garlic cloves, halved
- 1 tablespoon olive oil
- 2 tablespoons tomato paste
- 2 large eggs, lightly beaten
- 1¼ pounds ground beef
- ¾ pound ground pork
- 1 tablespoon Worcestershire sauce
- 1 tablespoon reduced-sodium soy sauce
- 1¼ teaspoons salt
- ¾ teaspoon pepper

GLAZE
- ½ cup ketchup
- 2 tablespoons tomato paste
- 2 tablespoons brown sugar
- 1 teaspoon ground mustard

1. Preheat oven to 350°. Combine bread and stock; let stand until liquid is absorbed.
2. Meanwhile, pulse mushrooms, onion, carrot, celery and garlic in a food processor until finely chopped. In a large skillet, heat oil over medium heat. Add mushroom mixture; cook and stir until tender and liquid is evaporated, 5-6 minutes. Stir in tomato paste; cook 1 minute longer. Cool slightly.
3. Add next seven ingredients and cooked vegetables to the bread mixture; mix thoroughly. Place a 12x7-in. piece of foil on a rack in a foil-lined rimmed baking pan. Transfer meat mixture to the foil and shape into a 10x6-in. loaf.
4. Bake 1 hour. Mix together the glaze ingredients; spread over loaf. Bake until a thermometer reads 160°, about 15-25 minutes longer. Let stand 10 minutes before slicing into eight pieces.
Per 1 piece: 341 cal., 18g fat (6g sat. fat), 119mg chol., 832mg sod., 19g carb. (11g sugars, 2g fiber), 25g pro.

HERE'S HOW:

TO-DO'S AND TA-DA'S!

- Soaking the bread crumbs first helps keep the loaf moist.
- Speed up prep time by pulsing veggies in a food processor. The finer the veggies are chopped, the better they'll be distributed throughout the loaf, making for a smoother texture.
- An all-beef loaf can have a coarse texture. Go for a beef-pork mixture to get a finer consistency.
- Before cooking, place a cooling rack in a foil-lined baking pan; top the rack with a piece of foil slightly larger than the formed meat loaf. Set the loaf on the foil. This keeps the loaf from sinking into the rack and allows the grease to drip down into the pan.

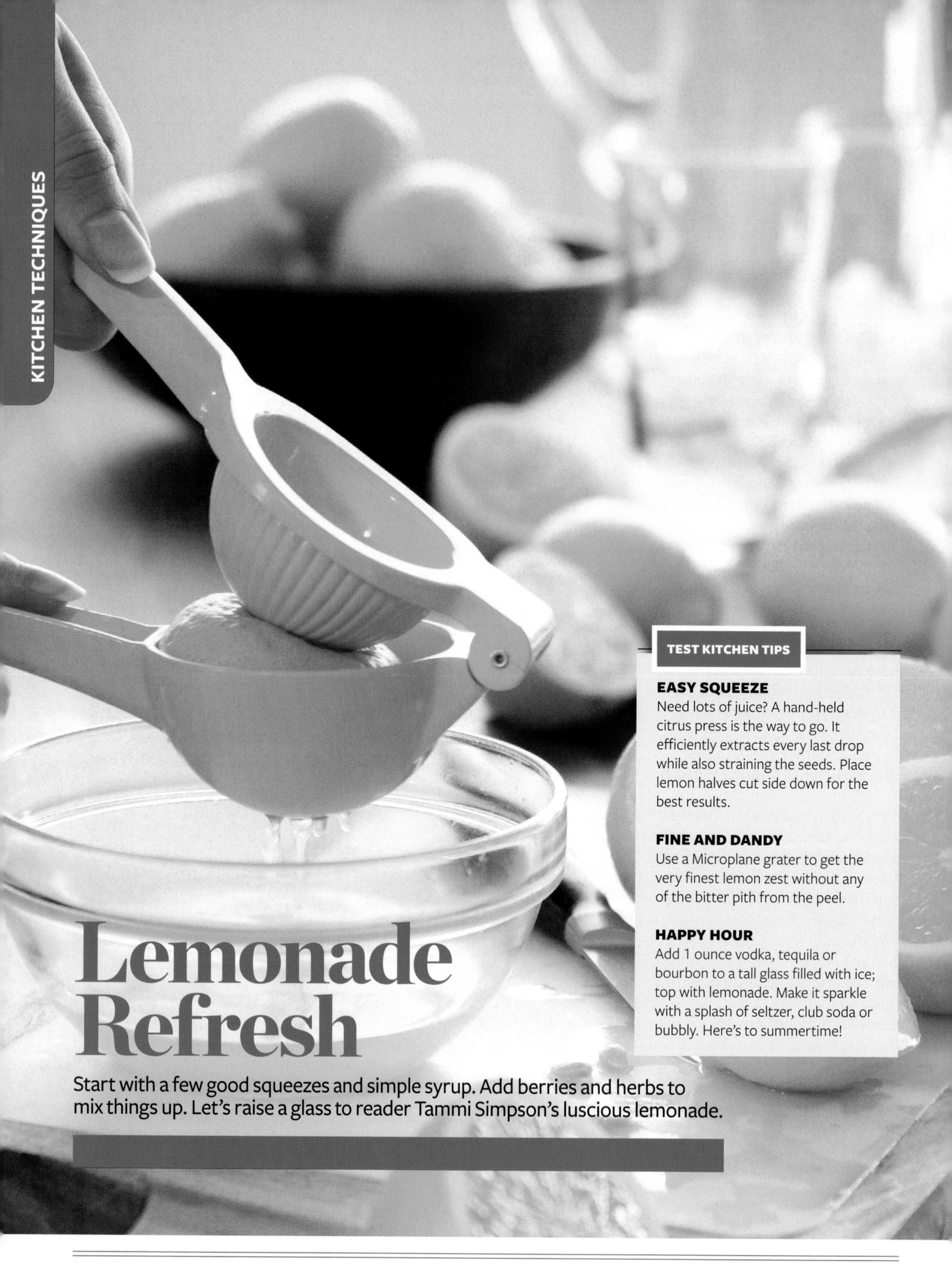

Lemonade Refresh

Start with a few good squeezes and simple syrup. Add berries and herbs to mix things up. Let's raise a glass to reader Tammi Simpson's luscious lemonade.

TEST KITCHEN TIPS

EASY SQUEEZE
Need lots of juice? A hand-held citrus press is the way to go. It efficiently extracts every last drop while also straining the seeds. Place lemon halves cut side down for the best results.

FINE AND DANDY
Use a Microplane grater to get the very finest lemon zest without any of the bitter pith from the peel.

HAPPY HOUR
Add 1 ounce vodka, tequila or bourbon to a tall glass filled with ice; top with lemonade. Make it sparkle with a splash of seltzer, club soda or bubbly. Here's to summertime!

OLD-FASHIONED
LEMONADE

⑤ INGREDIENTS
Old-Fashioned Lemonade

This sweet-tart lemonade is a traditional part of my Memorial Day and Fourth of July menus. Folks can't get enough of the classic fresh-squeezed flavor.

—**TAMMI SIMPSON** GREENSBURG, KY

PREP: 10 MIN. • **COOK:** 5 MIN. + CHILLING
MAKES: 7 SERVINGS

- 1⅓ cups sugar
- 5 cups water, divided
- 1 tablespoon grated lemon peel
- 1¾ cups lemon juice (about 10 large lemons)

In a large saucepan, combine sugar, 1 cup water and lemon peel. Cook and stir over medium heat until sugar is dissolved, about 4 minutes. Remove from heat. Stir in lemon juice and remaining water; refrigerate until cold. Serve over ice.

Per 1 cup: 142 cal., 0 fat (0 sat. fat), 0 chol., 1mg sod., 37g carb. (35g sugars, 0 fiber), 0 pro.

TO-DO'S AND TA-DA'S!

- To get the most juice from the lemons, first roll them with the palm of your hand firmly over the counter, or heat in the microwave on high for 10–20 seconds.
- Making a simple syrup allows the sugar to dissolve and disperse completely instead of sinking to the bottom.

SUNSHINE IN A GLASS

Tweak the basic lemonade recipe for a refreshing flavor twist.

Old-Time Limeade
Substitute lime peel for lemon peel and limes for lemons.

Ginger-Mint Lemonade
Add 1 tablespoon fresh grated ginger and ¼ cup fresh mint leaves with the lemon peel when making the syrup. Strain after cooling.

Herb Lemonade
Add 2 tablespoons chopped fresh basil, rosemary or lavender with the lemon peel when making the syrup. Strain after cooling.

Berry Lemonade
Substitute 1 cup pureed, strained fresh strawberries or raspberries for 1 cup water when making the lemonade.

Get Saucy

Grab your biggest pot. Home cooks are turning tomato bounty into summery goodness that will be a welcome treat when leaves start to fall.

SPICY CHUNKY SALSA

HERE'S HOW:

TO-DO'S AND TA-DA'S!

- To quickly peel tomatoes, wash them, then remove the cores with a paring knife.
- Cut a shallow "X" on the bottom of each tomato.
- Using a slotted spoon, place tomatoes, a few at a time, in boiling water for 30-60 seconds or just until skin at the "X" begins to loosen. Remove tomatoes and immediately drop into ice water.
- Pull off skins with the tip of a knife; discard skins.

TOMATO KNOW-HOW

Ripe, soft tomatoes require less boiling than firm ones.

Stubborn skin? Plop the tomato into the boiling water for a few more seconds and repeat.

HOMEMADE CANNED SPAGHETTI SAUCE

Homemade Canned Spaghetti Sauce

This DIY pasta sauce is a tomato-grower's dream come true! Use up your garden bounty and enjoy it later in the year.

—TONYA BRANHAM MOUNT OLIVE, AL

PREP: 1½ HOURS + SIMMERING
PROCESS: 40 MIN. • **MAKES:** 9 QUARTS

- 25 pounds tomatoes
- 4 large green peppers, seeded
- 4 large onions, cut into wedges
- 2 cans (12 ounces each) tomato paste
- 1 cup canola oil
- ⅔ cup sugar
- ¼ cup salt
- 8 garlic cloves, minced
- 4 teaspoons dried oregano
- 2 teaspoons dried parsley flakes
- 2 teaspoons dried basil
- 2 teaspoons crushed red pepper flakes
- 2 teaspoons Worcestershire sauce
- 2 bay leaves
- 1 cup plus 2 tablespoons bottled lemon juice

1. In a Dutch oven, bring 2 quarts water to a boil. Using a slotted spoon, place tomatoes, a few at a time, in boiling water for 30-60 seconds. Remove each tomato and immediately plunge into ice water. Peel and quarter tomatoes; place in a stockpot.
2. Pulse green peppers and onions in batches in a food processor until finely chopped; transfer to stockpot. Stir in next 11 ingredients. Add water to cover; bring to a boil. Reduce heat; simmer, uncovered, 4-5 hours, stirring occasionally.

3. Discard the bay leaves. Add 2 tablespoons lemon juice to each of nine hot 1-qt. jars. Ladle hot mixture into jars, leaving ½-in. headspace. Remove air bubbles and adjust headspace, if necessary, by adding hot mixture. Wipe rims. Center lids on jars; screw on bands until they are fingertip tight.
4. Place jars into canner with simmering water, ensuring that they are completely covered with water. Bring to a boil; process for 40 minutes. Remove jars and cool.
Per ¾ cup: 118 cal., 5g fat (0 sat. fat), 0 chol., 614mg sod., 17g carb. (11g sugars, 4g fiber), 3g pro.
Diabetic Exchanges: 1 starch, 1 fat.

Spicy Chunky Salsa

Vinegar adds a refreshing tang to this sweet tomato salsa. It's wonderful as is, but for more heat, leave in some hot pepper seeds.

—DONNA GOUTERMONT SEQUIM, WA

PREP: 1½ HOURS • **PROCESS:** 15 MIN.
MAKES: 8 PINTS

- 6 pounds tomatoes
- 3 large green peppers, chopped
- 3 large onions, chopped
- 2 cups white vinegar
- 1 large sweet red pepper, chopped
- 1 can (12 ounces) tomato paste
- 4 jalapeno peppers, seeded and chopped
- 2 serrano peppers, seeded and chopped
- ½ cup sugar
- ½ cup minced fresh cilantro
- ½ cup bottled lemon juice
- 3 garlic cloves, minced
- 4 teaspoons ground cumin
- 1 tablespoon salt
- 2 teaspoons dried oregano
- 1 teaspoon hot pepper sauce

1. In a Dutch oven, bring 2 quarts water to a boil. Using a slotted spoon, place tomatoes, a few at a time, in boiling water for 30-60 seconds. Remove each tomato and immediately plunge into ice water. Drain and pat dry. Peel and finely chop tomatoes to measure 9 cups; place in a stockpot.
2. Stir in remaining ingredients. Add water to cover; bring to a boil. Reduce heat; simmer, uncovered, until slightly thickened, about 30 minutes.
3. Ladle hot mixture into hot 1-pint jars, leaving ½-in. headspace. Remove air bubbles and adjust headspace, if necessary, by adding hot mixture. Wipe rims. Center lids on jars; screw on bands until fingertip tight.
4. Place jars into canner with simmering water, ensuring that they are completely covered with water. Bring to a boil; process for 15 minutes. Remove jars and cool.
Note: When cutting hot peppers, disposable gloves are recommended. Avoid touching your face.
Per ¼ cup: 25 cal., 0 fat (0 sat. fat), 0 chol., 117mg sod., 6g carb. (4g sugars, 1g fiber), 1g pro.
Diabetic Exchanges: ½ starch.

TEST KITCHEN TIPS

FOR EASY CLEANUP, use a canning funnel when filling jars. To get the tightest seal, wipe each rim with a clean cloth before putting on the lid.

HIGH-ALTITUDE PROCESSING
The processing times above are for altitudes of 1,000 feet or less.
- For altitudes up to 3,000 feet, add 5 minutes
- 6,000 feet, add 10 minutes
- 8,000 feet, add 15 minutes
- 10,000 feet, add 20 minutes

Party Potatoes

After 16 batches, our Culinary Team Assistant Aria Thornton has perfected the potatoes we all want. Here's her method...with a little crunch on top.

THE BEST CHEESY SCALLOPED POTATOES
Aria Thornton
Milwaukee, WI

The Best Cheesy Scalloped Potatoes

Here's my tried-and-true version of scalloped potatoes. I slice them extra thin and toss them in a rich, creamy cheese sauce. Then, to make them the best ever, I sprinkle the top with homemade bread crumbs that get nice and crispy in the oven. Make room for this dish at all of your family get-togethers.

—ARIA THORNTON MILWAUKEE, WI

PREP: 40 MIN.
BAKE: 1¼ HOURS + STANDING
MAKES: 10 SERVINGS

- 4 tablespoons butter
- ½ cup chopped onion
- 1 teaspoon ground mustard
- 1 teaspoon salt
- ½ teaspoon coarsely ground pepper
- 2 garlic cloves, minced
- ¼ cup all-purpose flour
- 2 cups whole milk
- 12 ounces sharp cheddar cheese (in block form), shredded and divided
- 4 ounces Monterey Jack cheese (in block form), shredded
- 3 pounds russet potatoes, peeled and thinly sliced
- ¾ cup dry bread crumbs
  Minced chives, optional

1. Preheat oven to 350°. In a Dutch oven, melt butter over medium heat. Add onion, mustard, salt and pepper; cook until the onion is tender, about 6-8 minutes. Add garlic; cook until fragrant. Whisk in flour; continue whisking 3-5 minutes.
2. Whisk in milk; bring to a boil. Reduce heat; simmer, uncovered, until thickened slightly, 8-10 minutes. Gradually stir in 2 cups shredded cheddar cheese; stir in Monterey Jack cheese. Add potatoes and toss to coat. Simmer 10 minutes, stirring frequently.
3. Transfer potato mixture to a greased 13x9-in. baking dish. Top with remaining cheddar cheese. Bake, uncovered, for 1 hour. Top with bread crumbs; return oven until potatoes are tender, 10-15 minutes. Let stand 15 minutes before serving. If desired, sprinkle with chives.
Per ¾ cup: 378 cal., 22g fat (13g sat. fat), 61mg chol., 646mg sod., 31g carb. (5g sugars, 2g fiber), 15g pro.

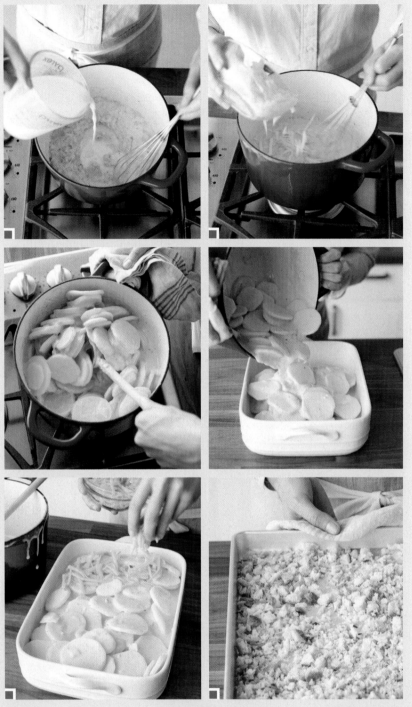

TO-DO'S AND TA-DA'S!

- Low and slow is key. Too much heat will cause the sauce to break. As soon as the sauce comes to a boil, turn down the heat.
- For a smoother sauce, use full-fat ingredients. Now's not the time to go reduced-fat!
- Shred cheese off the block (instead of using pre-shredded) for a creamier texture and noticeably bolder flavor.
- To get the crunchiest crumbs, choose bread with a crispy crust and chewy interior. French baguette, ciabatta and sourdough are all good choices here.

Spaghetti & Meatballs

Take pasta night over the top with super easy meatballs and saucy goodness. Pass the Parmesan and start twirling Mary Lou Koskella's entree!

BEST SPAGHETTI
& MEATBALLS

PRIMO PASTA
Cook the spaghetti in an ample amount of salted water—no need to add oil—stirring frequently, just until al dente (firm to the bite). For hot dishes, drain thoroughly but don't rinse. Rinsing washes away starches that help the sauce stick. If the pasta clumps, run it under hot water briefly, or mix in a spoonful of sauce.

MEATBALL MIXOLOGY
Your hands are the best tool for making the meat mixture—don't be squeamish! Gently combine all the ingredients just until blended. Avoid squeezing the meat, since this can result in a tough, dense meatball. To change up the flavor, make the meatballs with half ground pork and half ground beef.

Best Spaghetti & Meatballs

One evening, we had unexpected company. Since I had some of these meatballs left over in the freezer, I warmed them up as appetizers. Everyone raved! This classic recipe makes a big batch and is perfect for entertaining.
—**MARY LOU KOSKELLA** PRESCOTT, AZ

PREP: 30 MIN. • **COOK:** 2 HOURS
MAKES: 16 SERVINGS

- 2 tablespoons olive oil
- 1½ cups chopped onions
- 3 garlic cloves, minced
- 2 cans (12 ounces each) tomato paste
- 3 cups water
- 1 can (29 ounces) tomato sauce
- ⅓ cup minced fresh parsley
- 1 tablespoon dried basil
- 2 teaspoons salt
- ½ teaspoon pepper

MEATBALLS
- 4 large eggs, lightly beaten
- 2 cups soft bread cubes (cut into ¼-inch pieces)
- 1½ cups whole milk
- 1 cup grated Parmesan cheese
- 3 garlic cloves, minced
- 2 teaspoons salt
- ½ teaspoon pepper
- 3 pounds ground beef
- 2 tablespoons canola oil
- 2 pounds spaghetti, cooked

1. In a Dutch oven, heat olive oil over medium heat. Add onions; saute until softened. Add garlic; cook 1 minute longer. Stir in the tomato paste; cook 3-5 minutes. Add next six ingredients. Bring to a boil. Reduce heat; simmer, covered, for 50 minutes.
2. Combine the first seven meatball ingredients. Add beef; mix lightly but thoroughly. Shape into 1½-in. balls.
3. In a large skillet, heat canola oil over medium heat. Add meatballs; brown in batches until no longer pink. Drain. Add to sauce; bring to a boil. Reduce heat; simmer, covered, until flavors are blended, about 1 hour, stirring occasionally. Serve with hot cooked spaghetti.
Per serving: 519 cal., 18g fat (6g sat. fat), 106mg chol., 1043mg sod., 59g carb. (8g sugars, 4g fiber), 30g pro.

HERE'S HOW:

TO-DO'S AND TA-DA'S!

- Before adding the remaining sauce ingredients, cook the tomato paste a few minutes to caramelize the sugars in the paste, boosting the bright tomato flavor of the sauce.
- Wet your hands before rolling the meatballs so the meat doesn't stick to your fingers. Re-wet after two or three meatballs.
- As an alternative to the skillet, grab a sheet pan. The meatballs may be placed on a baking sheet and roasted in a 375° oven for about 20 minutes.

FREEZE IT
For a convenient freezer option, simmer the meatballs and sauce as directed, then place in freezer containers. Make sure the meatballs are covered with sauce so they don't dry out. Freeze. To reheat, place meatballs and sauce in a Dutch oven over medium heat or in a slow cooker on low until heated through.

CHRISTMAS STAR
TWISTED BREAD

Joy to the Swirl

Visions of rolled, marbled and twirly-topped sweets dance through our
holiday baking guide. Find smart tips and cool tricks sprinkled inside.

Christmas Star Twisted Bread

This gorgeous sweet bread swirled with jam may look tricky, but it's not. The best part is opening the oven to find this star-shaped beauty in all its glory.

—DARLENE BRENDEN SALEM, OR

PREP: 45 MIN. + RISING
BAKE: 20 MIN. + COOLING
MAKES: 16 SERVINGS

- 1 package (¼ ounce) active dry yeast
- ¼ cup warm water (110° to 115°)
- ¾ cup warm whole milk (110° to 115°)
- 1 large egg
- ¼ cup butter, softened
- ¼ cup granulated sugar
- 1 teaspoon salt
- 3¼ to 3¾ cups all-purpose flour
- ¾ cup seedless raspberry jam
- 2 tablespoons butter, melted
  Confectioners' sugar

1. Dissolve yeast in warm water until foamy. In another bowl, combine milk, egg, butter, sugar and salt; add yeast mixture and 3 cups flour. Beat on medium speed until smooth, about 1 minute. Stir in enough remaining flour to form a soft dough.

2. Turn onto a floured surface; knead until smooth and elastic, 6-8 minutes. Place in a greased bowl, turning once to grease top. Cover with plastic wrap; let rise in a warm place until doubled, about 1 hour.

3. Punch down dough. Turn onto a lightly floured surface; divide into four portions. Roll one portion into a 12-in. circle. Place on a greased 14-in. pizza pan. Spread with one-third of the jam to within ½ in. from edge. Repeat twice, layering dough and jam, and ending with final portion of dough.

4. Place a 2½-in. round cutter on top of the dough in center of circle (do not press down). With a sharp knife, make 16 evenly spaced cuts from round cutter to edge of dough, forming a starburst. Remove cutter; grasp two strips and rotate twice outward. Pinch the ends together. Repeat with the remaining strips.

5. Cover with plastic wrap; let rise until almost doubled, about 30 minutes. Preheat oven to 375°. Bake until golden brown, 18-22 minutes.

(Watch during final 5 minutes for any dripping.) Remove from oven; brush with melted butter, avoiding areas where jam is visible. Cool bread completely on a wire rack. Dust with the confectioners' sugar.

Per 1 piece: 193 cal., 5g fat (3g sat. fat), 24mg chol., 192mg sod., 33g carb. (13g sugars, 1g fiber), 4g pro.

Kickstart the flavor: Substitute blueberry jam and 1 teaspoon grated lemon peel for raspberry jam, or use blackberry jam and ½ teaspoon of ground cardamom.

HERE'S HOW:

RUGELACH WITH A TWIST

Rugelach with a Twist

Once I read about making rugelach with ice cream, there was no stopping me! My family loved these flaky cookies so much, I had to bake more right away.

—DIANE FUQUA BALTIMORE, MD

PREP: 25 MIN. + CHILLING
BAKE: 20 MIN./BATCH • **MAKES:** 32 COOKIES

- 1 cup butter, softened
- 2¾ cups all-purpose flour
- 1 cup vanilla ice cream, melted
- ¾ cup finely chopped pecans
- ¾ cup miniature semisweet chocolate chips
- ¼ cup granulated sugar
- ¼ cup firmly packed brown sugar
- 2 teaspoons ground cinnamon
- 1 large egg
- 1 tablespoon water

1. Beat butter and flour until blended. Beat in ice cream. Divide dough into four portions; shape each into a disk. Wrap in plastic; refrigerate 1 hour.

2. Preheat oven to 350°. Mix pecans and chocolate chips. In another bowl, mix sugars and cinnamon. Roll each portion of dough into a 10-in. circle; sprinkle each with 2 tablespoons of the sugar mixture and about ⅓ cup of the pecan mixture. Gently press pecan mixture into the dough. Cut each circle into eight wedges; roll up from the wide ends. Place 1 in. apart on parchment paper-lined baking sheets, point side down. Whisk together egg and water; brush over pastries.

3. Bake 18-22 minutes or until golden brown. Remove from pans to wire racks to cool.

Per 1 cookie: 151 cal., 10g fat (5g sat. fat), 23mg chol., 52mg sod., 16g carb. (6g sugars, 1g fiber), 2g pro.

Budapest Roll

If you're a fan of Yule logs, try my Swedish specialty made from hazelnut meringue. People are in awe every time I serve it.

—CATHERINE WALBRIDGE BOISE, ID

PREP: 25 MIN. + STANDING
BAKE: 20 MIN. + COOLING
MAKES: 12 SERVINGS

- 6 large egg whites
- ⅔ cup finely ground hazelnuts
- 6 tablespoons instant vanilla pudding mix
- 1⅓ cups sugar

FILLING
- 1⅓ cups heavy whipping cream
- 1 tablespoon sugar
- ½ teaspoon vanilla extract
- 1 can (11 ounces) mandarin oranges, drained
- 1 ounce bittersweet chocolate, chopped

1. Let egg whites stand at room temperature 30 minutes. Meanwhile, combine nuts and pudding mix. Line a 15x10-in. baking pan with parchment paper.

2. Preheat oven to 350°. Beat egg whites on medium speed until foamy. Gradually add the sugar, 1 tablespoon at a time, beating on high after each addition until sugar is dissolved. Continue beating until stiff glossy peaks form. Fold in nut mixture.

3. Pipe meringue in long strips or spread over prepared pan until entire pan is covered. Bake until set and dry, about 20 minutes. Cool completely. Cover meringue with parchment paper; place another baking pan on top. Flip the pans. Remove top pan; carefully peel parchment paper from meringue.

4. Beat cream until it begins to thicken. Add sugar and vanilla; beat until stiff peaks form. Spread cream over meringue and top with oranges; roll up jelly-roll style, starting with a long side and peeling paper away while rolling.

5. Microwave chocolate on high until melted, stirring occasionally. Drizzle melted chocolate over meringue roll.
Per 1 slice: 256 cal., 13g fat (7g sat. fat), 37mg chol., 68mg sod., 33g carb. (31g sugars, 1g fiber), 3g pro.

Change it up: Make this recipe your own by mixing and matching up to 1 cup total of mandarin oranges, chocolate chips, maraschino cherries and toasted nuts.

Creme de Menthe Cupcakes

We use creme de menthe to add a cool touch to these impressive mascarpone-frosted cupcakes.

—KERI WHITNEY CASTRO VALLEY, CA

PREP: 30 MIN. • **BAKE:** 15 MIN. + COOLING
MAKES: ABOUT 1 DOZEN

- ¾ cup butter, softened
- 1 cup granulated sugar
- 2 large eggs, room temperature
- ½ teaspoon mint extract
- 1½ cups cake flour
- 1½ teaspoons baking powder
- ¼ teaspoon salt
- ⅔ cup 2% milk
- 2 tablespoons white (clear) creme de menthe
  Green paste food coloring

FROSTING
- 1 carton (8 ounces) mascarpone cheese
- ⅓ cup heavy whipping cream
- ¼ cup confectioners' sugar
- 4 teaspoons white (clear) creme de menthe
  Green paste food coloring

1. Preheat oven to 350°. Cream butter and granulated sugar until light and fluffy. Add the eggs, one at a time, beating well after each addition. Add mint extract. In another bowl, whisk flour, baking powder and salt; add to creamed mixture alternately with milk and creme de menthe, beating well after each addition. Transfer two cups batter to a separate bowl. Mix food coloring paste into remaining batter.

2. Cut a small hole in the tip of a pastry bag or in a corner of a food-safe plastic bag; insert a #12 round tip. Spoon the batters alternately into bag. Pipe batter into 12 paper-lined muffin cups until three-fourths full. Bake until a toothpick comes out clean, about 15-20 minutes. Cool 10 minutes; remove from pan to a wire rack to cool completely.

3. For frosting, stir the mascarpone and whipping cream together until smooth. Add the confectioners' sugar and creme de menthe; stir until blended. Transfer half of the frosting to a separate bowl and mix green food coloring paste into remaining frosting. Stir each portion vigorously until stiff peaks form (do not overmix).

4. Cut a small hole in the tip of a pastry bag or in a corner of a food-safe plastic bag; insert a #12 round tip. Spoon the frostings alternately into the bag. Pipe onto cupcakes. Refrigerate leftovers.
Per 1 cupcake: 372 cal., 24g fat (14g sat. fat), 95mg chol., 222mg sod., 35g carb. (21g sugars, 0 fiber), 5g pro.
Note: For extra-thick frosting like that in the photo, double all ingredients.

HERE'S HOW:

BUDAPEST ROLL

CREME DE MENTHE CUPCAKES
Keri Whitney
Castro Valley, CA

(5) INGREDIENTS
Puff Pastry Christmas Palmiers

Palmiers (pronounced palm-YAY) come from France. They're usually sweet, but to make them savory, I swirl in pesto, feta and sun-dried tomatoes.

—DARLENE BRENDEN SALEM, OR

PREP: 15 MIN. + CHILLING • **BAKE:** 15 MIN.
MAKES: 2 DOZEN

- 1 package (17.3 ounces) frozen puff pastry, thawed
- 1 large egg
- 1 tablespoon water
- ¼ cup prepared pesto
- ½ cup feta or goat cheese, crumbled
- ¼ cup oil-packed sun-dried tomatoes, patted dry and finely chopped

1. Preheat oven to 400°. Unfold one sheet of puff pastry. Whisk egg and water; brush over pastry. Spread with half of the pesto. Sprinkle with half of the feta and half of the sun-dried tomatoes.

2. Roll up the left and right sides toward the center, jelly-roll style, until rolls meet in the middle. Repeat with the remaining puff pastry sheet and ingredients. Freeze until firm, about 30 minutes.

3. Cut each roll crosswise into 12 slices. On baking sheets lined with parchment paper, bake palmiers until golden and crisp, about 15 minutes.

Per 1 palmier: 121 cal., 7g fat (2g sat. fat), 9mg chol., 126mg sod., 12g carb. (0 sugars, 2g fiber), 2g pro.

RED & GREEN PINWHEELS

Red & Green Pinwheels

For the holidays, my mom would make red and green cookie dough, then roll them together for a twirly effect. Seeing these cookies brings back lots of happy memories.

—JILL HEATWOLE PITTSVILLE, MD

PREP: 30 MIN. + CHILLING
BAKE: 7 MIN./BATCH
MAKES: 6 DOZEN

- 10 tablespoons butter, softened
- ½ cup packed brown sugar
- ¼ cup granulated sugar
- 1 large egg
- ½ teaspoon peppermint extract
- 2 cups all-purpose flour
- ½ teaspoon baking powder
- ½ teaspoon salt
- ⅛ teaspoon baking soda
- ½ teaspoon red gel food coloring
- ¼ teaspoon green gel food coloring

1. Preheat oven to 375°. Cream butter and sugars until light and fluffy; beat in egg and extract. In another bowl, whisk together flour, baking powder, salt and baking soda; gradually add to creamed mixture, blending well.

2. Divide dough in half. Tint one portion red and the other green. Divide portions in half, for four altogether. Roll out each portion between sheets of waxed paper into a 9x6-in. rectangle. Refrigerate for 15 minutes.

3. Remove waxed paper. Place one green rectangle on a red rectangle. Roll up tightly jelly-roll style, starting with a long side; wrap in plastic. Repeat. Refrigerate until firm, about 1 hour. Unwrap and cut crosswise into ¼-in. slices. Place 1 in. apart on ungreased baking sheets. Bake until set, 7-9 minutes. Remove to wire racks to cool.

Per 1 cookie: 36 cal., 2g fat (1g sat. fat), 7mg chol., 36mg sod., 5g carb. (2g sugars, 0 fiber), 0 pro.

PUFF PASTRY CHRISTMAS PALMIERS

Giant Cinnamon Roll

This must-try cinnamon roll is all about the pillowy texture, the sweet spices and the homemade caramel drizzle.

—**LEAH REKAU** MILWAUKEE, WI

PREP: 30 MIN. + RISING • **BAKE:** 30 MIN.
MAKES: 12 SERVINGS

- 1 package (¼ ounce) active dry yeast
- ½ cup warm water (110° to 115°)
- ½ cup heavy whipping cream, warmed (110° to 115°)
- ½ cup sugar
- ½ teaspoon sea salt
- 3 to 4 cups all-purpose flour
- 1 large egg, beaten
- 3 tablespoons butter, melted

FILLING
- ¼ cup butter, softened
- ¼ cup sugar
- 1 tablespoon ground cinnamon

TOPPING
- 1 cup sugar
- 2 tablespoons water
- 6 tablespoons butter
- ½ cup heavy whipping cream
- 1 teaspoon sea salt

GIANT CINNAMON ROLL

1. Dissolve yeast in warm water and whipping cream until foamy. In another bowl, combine sugar and salt; add 3 cups flour, yeast mixture, egg and melted butter. Stir until moistened. Add enough remaining flour to form a soft dough.

2. Turn onto a lightly floured surface; knead dough until smooth and elastic, 3-4 minutes. Place in a greased bowl, turning once to grease top. Cover with plastic wrap; let rise in a warm place until doubled, about 30 minutes.

3. Punch down dough. Turn onto a lightly floured surface; roll into a 15x12-in. rectangle. Spread softened butter over dough. Sprinkle with sugar and cinnamon. Using a pizza cutter, cut into 2-in.-wide strips. Roll up one strip and place in the center of a greased 9-in. deep-dish pie plate; wrap remaining strips around center to form one giant roll. Cover with greased plastic wrap; let rise until doubled, about 1 hour.

4. Preheat oven to 350°. Bake roll until golden brown, 30-40 minutes. If it starts browning too quickly, cover lightly with foil. Cool on a wire rack.

5. To prepare topping, combine sugar and water in a small saucepan; cook over medium heat until it turns light amber. Add butter, stirring vigorously. Remove from heat; add cream while continuing to stir vigorously. Cool slightly. Pour ¾ cup sauce over warm roll; sprinkle with salt. Serve with remaining sauce.

Note: If you're feeling intimidated by this beauty, know that it's much easier to make than you think! The homespun look is our fave, so don't sweat it if your roll doesn't look perfect. It's perfectly imperfect.

Per 1 piece: 416 cal., 21g fat (13g sat. fat), 76mg chol., 354mg sod., 55g carb. (30g sugars, 1g fiber), 5g pro.

HERE'S HOW:

✻
TEST KITCHEN TIP
Reduce proofing (rising) times by giving the yeast a toasty place to hang out. If your kitchen is cold, microwave a bit of water to create a sauna, then add the bowl of dough to the microwave and close the door. Happy yeast, happy roll!

Substitutions & Equivalents

EQUIVALENT MEASURES

3 teaspoons	=	1 tablespoon	16 tablespoons	=	1 cup
4 tablespoons	=	1/4 cup	2 cups	=	1 pint
5-1/3 tablespoons	=	1/3 cup	4 cups	=	1 quart
8 tablespoons	=	1/2 cup	4 quarts	=	1 gallon

FOOD EQUIVALENTS

GRAINS

Macaroni	1 cup (3-1/2 ounces) uncooked	=	2-1/2 cups cooked
Noodles, Medium	3 cups (4 ounces) uncooked	=	4 cups cooked
Popcorn	1/3 to 1/2 cup unpopped	=	8 cups popped
Rice, Long Grain	1 cup uncooked	=	3 cups cooked
Rice, Quick-Cooking	1 cup uncooked	=	2 cups cooked
Spaghetti	8 ounces uncooked	=	4 cups cooked

CRUMBS

Bread	1 slice	=	3/4 cup soft crumbs, 1/4 cup fine dry crumbs
Graham Crackers	7 squares	=	1/2 cup finely crushed
Buttery Round Crackers	12 crackers	=	1/2 cup finely crushed
Saltine Crackers	14 crackers	=	1/2 cup finely crushed

FRUITS

Bananas	1 medium	=	1/3 cup mashed
Lemons	1 medium	=	3 tablespoons juice, 2 teaspoons grated peel
Limes	1 medium	=	2 tablespoons juice, 1-1/2 teaspoons grated peel
Oranges	1 medium	=	1/4 to 1/3 cup juice, 4 teaspoons grated peel

VEGETABLES

Cabbage	1 head	=	5 cups shredded	Green Pepper	1 large	=	1 cup chopped
Carrots	1 pound	=	3 cups shredded	Mushrooms	1/2 pound	=	3 cups sliced
Celery	1 rib	=	1/2 cup chopped	Onions	1 medium	=	1/2 cup chopped
Corn	1 ear fresh	=	2/3 cup kernels	Potatoes	3 medium	=	2 cups cubed

NUTS

Almonds	1 pound	=	3 cups chopped	Pecan Halves	1 pound	=	4-1/2 cups chopped
Ground Nuts	3-3/4 ounces	=	1 cup	Walnuts	1 pound	=	3-3/4 cups chopped

EASY SUBSTITUTIONS

When you need...		Use...
Baking Powder	1 teaspoon	1/2 teaspoon cream of tartar + 1/4 teaspoon baking soda
Buttermilk	1 cup	1 tablespoon lemon juice or vinegar + enough milk to measure 1 cup (let stand 5 minutes before using)
Cornstarch	1 tablespoon	2 tablespoons all-purpose flour
Honey	1 cup	1-1/4 cups sugar + 1/4 cup water
Half-and-Half Cream	1 cup	1 tablespoon melted butter + enough whole milk to measure 1 cup
Onion	1 small, chopped (1/3 cup)	1 teaspoon onion powder or 1 tablespoon dried minced onion
Tomato Juice	1 cup	1/2 cup tomato sauce + 1/2 cup water
Tomato Sauce	2 cups	3/4 cup tomato paste + 1 cup water
Unsweetened Chocolate	1 square (1 ounce)	3 tablespoons baking cocoa + 1 tablespoon shortening or oil
Whole Milk	1 cup	1/2 cup evaporated milk + 1/2 cup water

Cooking Terms

Here's a quick reference for some of the cooking terms used in *Taste of Home* recipes:

BASTE To moisten food with melted butter, pan drippings, marinades or other liquid to add more flavor and juiciness.

BEAT To combine ingredients with a rapid movement using a fork, spoon, wire whisk or electric mixer.

BLEND To combine ingredients until *just* mixed.

BOIL To heat liquids until bubbles form that cannot be "stirred down." In the case of water, the temperature will reach 212°.

BONE To remove all meat from the bone before cooking.

CREAM To beat ingredients together to a smooth consistency, usually in the case of butter and sugar for baking.

DASH A small amount of seasoning, less than 1/8 teaspoon. If using a shaker, a dash would comprise a quick flip of the container.

DREDGE To coat foods with flour or other dry ingredients. Most often done with pot roasts and stew meat before browning.

FOLD To incorporate several ingredients by careful and gentle turning with a spatula. Used generally with beaten egg whites or whipped cream when mixing into the rest of the ingredients to keep the batter light.

JULIENNE To cut foods into long thin strips much like matchsticks. Used most often for salads and stir-fry dishes.

MARINATE To tenderize and/or flavor foods, usually meat or raw vegetables, by placing in a liquid mixture of oil, vinegar, wine, lime or lemon juice, herbs and spices.

MINCE To cut into very fine pieces. Used often for garlic or fresh herbs.

PARBOIL To cook partially, usually used in the case of chicken, sausages and vegetables.

PARTIALLY SET Describes the consistency of gelatin after it has been chilled for a short amount of time. Mixture should resemble the consistency of egg whites.

PUREE To process foods to a smooth mixture. Can be prepared in an electric blender, food processor, food mill or sieve.

SAUTE To fry quickly in a small amount of fat, stirring almost constantly. Most often done with onions, mushrooms and other chopped vegetables.

SCORE To cut slits partway through the outer surface of foods. Often used with ham or flank steak.

STIR-FRY To cook meats and/or vegetables with a constant stirring motion in a small amount of oil in a wok or skillet over high heat.

General Index

This handy index lists every recipe by food category, major ingredient and/or cooking method, so you can easily locate recipes that suit your needs.

✓ Indicates an **EAT SMART** *recipe*

Alphabetical Index

This convenient index lists every recipe in alphabetical order, so you can easily find your favorite dishes.
✓Indicates an EAT SMART recipe